British Subjects

An Anthropology of Britain

Edited by
Nigel Rapport

Oxford • New York

First published in 2002 by
Berg
Editorial offices:
150 Cowley Road, Oxford, OX4 1JJ, UK
838 Broadway, Third Floor, New York, NY 10003-4812, USA

Berg is an imprint of Oxford International Publishers Ltd.

Library of Congress Cataloging-in-Publication Data
British subjects : an anthropology of Britain / edited by Nigel Rapport.
p. cm.
Includes bibliographical references and index.
ISBN 1-85973-551-7 (cloth) -- ISBN 1-85973-546-0 (pbk.)
1. Anthropology--Great Britain--History.   2. National characteristics,
British.   3. Great Britain--Social life and customs.   I. Rapport, Nigel,
1956-
GN17.3.G7 B75 2002
301'.0941--dc21   2001006901

British Library Cataloguing-in-Publication Data
A catalogue record for this book is available from the British Library.

ISBN 1 85973 551 7 (Cloth)
        1 85973 546 0 (Paper)

Typeset by JS Typesetting, Wellingborough, Northants.
Printed in the United Kingdom by Antony Rowe Ltd, Chippenham, Wiltshire.

British Subjects

Contents

List of Contributors   ix

Part I: Introduction

'Best of British!': An Introduction to the Anthropology of Britain
Nigel Rapport   3

Part II: Nationalism, Contestation and the Performance of Tradition

Introduction to Part II
Nigel Rapport   27

1   Subject Positions and 'Real Royalists': Monarchy and Vernacular Civil Religion in Great Britain
     Anne Rowbottom   31

2   National Day: Achieving Collective Identity on the Isle of Man
     Susan Lewis   49

3   Aesthetics at the Ballet: Looking at 'National' Style, Body and Clothing in the London Dance World
     Helena Wulff   67

Part III: Strategies of Modernity: Heritage, Leisure, Dissociation

Introduction to Part III
Nigel Rapport   87

4   On 'Old Things': The Fetishization of Past Everyday Life
     Sharon Macdonald   89

5   Leisure and Change in a Post-Mining Mining Town
     Andrew Dawson   107

6   Dissociation, Social Technology and the Spiritual Domain
     Tanya Luhrmann   121

Contents

Part IV: The Appropriation of Discourse

Introduction to Part IV
Nigel Rapport   141

7   The English Child: Toward a Cultural Politics of Childhood
     Identities
     Allison James   143

8   Bits and Bytes of Information
     Jeanette Edwards   163

9   Culture in a Network: Dykes, Webs and Women in London
     and Manchester
     Sarah Green   181

Part V: Methodologies and Ethnomethodologies

Introduction to Part V
Nigel Rapport   205

10   Interviews as Ethnography? Disembodied Social Interaction
     in Britain
     Jenny Hockey   209

11   Entering Secure Psychiatric Settings
     Christine Brown   223

12   Cultural Values and Social Organization in Wales: Is Ethnicity
     the Locus of Culture?
     Carol Trosset and *Douglas Caulkins*   239

**Part VI: The Making (and Unmaking) of Community: Ethnicity,
Religiosity, Locality**

Introduction to Part VI
Nigel Rapport   259

13   Armenian and Other Diasporas: Trying to Reconcile the
     Irreconcilable
     Vered Amit   263

Contents

14 Both Independent and Interconnected Voices: Bakhtin among the Quakers
Peter Collins   281

15 The Body of the Village Community: Between Reverend Parkington in Wanet and Mr Beebe in *A Room with a View*
Nigel Rapport   299

Part VII: Epilogue

The 'Best of British' – with More to Come . . .
Anthony P. Cohen   323

Index   331

List of Contributors

Vered Amit is an Associate Professor in the Department of Sociology and Anthropology at Concordia University, Montreal. She has conducted fieldwork in London (UK), Quebec and Grand Cayman; currently she is undertaking research on transnational consultancy. Among her previous publications are *Armenians in London: The management of social boundaries* (Manchester University Press 1989) and (editor) *Constructing the Field* (Routledge 2000). She is currently editing a *Biographical Dictionary of Anthropology* as well as a volume on *Realizing Community* (both for Routledge); and she is collaborating on a project with Nigel Rapport entitled *The Trouble with Community* (Pluto).

Christine Brown is Robert Baxter NHS Resarch Fellow at the University of Exeter, Department of Mental Health; she is also a practising psychiatrist and a PhD student in social anthropology at the University of St Andrews. Her current work is supported by the National Programme for Forensic Mental Health Research and Development, and focuses on personality disorders, and the relationship between psychiatric services and the criminal justice system in Britain.

D. Douglas Caulkins is Earl D. Strong Professor in Social Studies at Grinnell College, Iowa, where he has taught anthropology since 1970 (having obtained his PhD from Cornell University). His current research is on social capital in Norway, and on regional and national identity in the UK, particularly among hi-tech entrepreneurs. Among his recent publications are 'Consensus, Clines, and Edges in Celtic Cultures', *Cross-Cultural Research* 35(2), 2001, and (with Elaine S. Weiner) 'Enterprise and Resistance in the Celtic Fringe: High Growth, Low Growth and No Growth Firms', in R. Byron and J. Hutson (eds) *Local Enterprise on the North Atlantic Margin* (Ashgate 1999).

Anthony Cohen is Professor of Social Anthropology at the University of Edinburgh, and Provost of the Faculty Group of Law and Social Sciences. He conducted British fieldwork among the islanders of Whalsay, Shetland, over a seventeen-year period; currently he is involved in a project exploring forms of Scottish nationalism in urban working environments. Among his publications are *Self Consciousness: An Alternative Anthropology of Identity* (Routledge 1994), *Questions of Consciousness* (co-edited with N. Rapport) (Routledge 1995), and *Signifying Identities:*

Anthropological Perspectives on Boundaries and Contested Values (edited) (Routledge 2000).

Peter Collins is Lecturer in Anthropology at the University of Durham, having acquired his PhD from Manchester. His doctoral research was on British Quakers; he has since examined the case of the American Shakers, and lay and medical understandings of 'stress'; he is particularly interested in anthropological applications of 'narrative'. He has published widely in journals such as *Auto/Biography, Worship, Architecture and Design* and *Journal of Contemporary Religion*, and contributed to edited volumes on the topics of celibacy, fieldwork methods, and identity.

Andrew Dawson is Lecturer in Social Anthropology at the University of Hull. He has conducted extensive fieldwork in Britain, Ireland, Bosnia and Australia, and has worked principally on the issues of ageing, refugee experiences, post-modernism and post-industrialism. For his work on the latter he was selected in 1995 as the European Association of Rural Sociologists' 'Young Scientist'. His publications include the books *After Writing Culture* (co-edited with Allison James and Jenny Hockey) (Routledge 1997), and *Migrants of Identity* (co-edited with Nigel Rapport) (Berg 1998).

Jeanette Edwards is Senior Lecturer in Social Anthropology at the University of Manchester. She has carried out extensive fieldwork in the north-west of England and has recently held fellowships in the 'Public Understanding of Science' from the ESRC and the Wellcome Trust. Her research interests include kinship and new reproductive and genetic technologies, and the meaning of parenthood in contemporary British society. She is the author of *Born and Bred: Idioms of Kinship and New Reproductive Technologies in England* (Oxford University Press 2000) and co-author of *Technologies of Procreation: Kinship in the Age of Assisted Conception* (2nd edn Cambridge University Press 1999).

Sarah Green is Senior Lecturer in Social Anthropology at the University of Manchester; she has conducted ethnographic fieldwork in London and Manchester, also in Argolid (southern Greece) and on the Greek–Albanian border (Epirus). Her key theoretical concerns are with concepts of the person as they manifest themselves in notions of gender, sexuality, embodiment, place, landscape and environment, tourism and development, and new information and communication technologies. Among her publications is *Urban Amazons: Lesbian Feminism and Beyond in the Gender, Sexuality and Identity Battles of London* (Macmillan 1997).

Jenny Hockey is Senior Lecturer in the School of Comparative and Applied Social Science at the University of Hull. Her current research concerns theories of the life-course, spatialized approaches to ageing, and the material culture of death and dying. Recent publications include *Beyond the Body: Death and Social Identity* (co-authored with E. Hallam and G. Howarth) (Routledge 1999); *Ideal Homes: Social Change and Domestic Life* (co-edited with T. Chapman) (Routledge 1999); and *Grief, Mourning and Death Ritual* (co-edited with J. Katz and N. Small) (Open University Press 2001).

Allison James is Reader in Applied Anthropology at the University of Hull. Her research interests are in childhood, identity and the life-course; she is currently exploring the ways in which conceptualizations of childhood are enacted for children through law and social policy. Recent publications include *Childhood Identities* (Edinburgh University Press (1993), *Theorising Childhood* (co-authored with C. Jenks and A. Prout) (Polity 1997), *Research with Children* (co-authored with P. Christensen) (Falmer 2000), and *Social Identities Across the Life Course* (co-authored with J. Hockey) (MacMillan 2001).

Susan Lewis is a PhD student in social anthropology at the University of St Andrews, having spent many years as a training consultant in the computer industry and as an accountant; she also holds degrees in Art History and in Anthropology from the Universities of East Anglia and Kent. She has conducted recent fieldwork on the Isle of Man; her theoretical interests include identity and the individual, and the anthropology of the body.

Tanya Luhrmann is Professor of Anthropology on The Committee on Human Development at the University of Chicago; she has conducted fieldwork among white witches and 'new-agers' in London, and in American psychiatric clinics. Her publications include *Persuasions of the Witch's Craft* (Harvard University Press 1989), *The Good Parsi* (Harvard University Press 1996), and *Of Two Minds* (Knopf 2000).

Sharon Macdonald is Senior Lecturer in the Department of Sociological Studies, University of Sheffield. She has carried out ethnographic fieldwork in the Scottish Hebrides, the Science Museum (London), and in Franconia, Germany. Her recent publications include *Reimagining Culture* (Berg 1997), (editor) *The Politics of Display* (Routledge 1999), and (editor) *Approaches to European Historical Consciousness* (Koerber 2000).

Nigel Rapport is Professor of Anthropological and Philosophical Studies at the University of St Andrews. He has conducted ethnographic fieldwork in the English village of Wanet in the Cumbrian Dales, also in the Canadian city of St. John's, Newfoundland, and the suburb of Kilbride, and in the Israeli development town of Mitzpe Ramon; currently he is undertaking research in a Scottish hospital setting. His main theoretic concern is with individual consciousness and identity, and with the complexity of sociocultural milieux. Among his recent publications are *Transcendent Individual* (Routledge 1997), *Migrants of Identity* (co-edited with A. Dawson) (Berg 1998), and *Social and Cultural Anthropology: The Key Concepts* (co-authored with J. Overing) (Routledge 2000).

Anne Rowbottom is Senior Lecturer at the Centre for Human Communication at Manchester Metropolitan University. She researches into popular royalism in the United Kingdom. With Paul Henley (of the Granada Centre for Visual Anthropology, University of Manchester), she made 'Royal Watchers', a television documentary broadcast by BBC Television in 1997. Her current research interests include secular ritual and visual communication.

Carol Trosset is a lecturer in anthropology and Director of Institutional Research at Grinnell College, Iowa, having acquired her PhD from the University of Texas at Austin. She is the author of *Welshness Performed: Welsh Concepts of Person and Society* (University of Arizona Press 1993). Her current research in applied anthropology deals with student and faculty cultures in higher education, and among her recent publications is 'Obstacles to Open Discussion and Critical Thinking', *Change* September–October 1998.

Helena Wulff is Senior Lecturer in Social Anthropology at Stockholm University, from where she also received her PhD. She has carried out her British fieldwork on youth, ethnicity, technology, and ballet and the arts in London; she is also engaged in research on Irish contemporary dance. Among her publications are *Twenty Girls* (Almqvist and Wiksell 1988), *Ballet across Borders* (Berg 1998), and *Youth Cultures* (co-edited with V. Amit) (Routledge 1995).

Part I
Introduction

'Best of British!': an Introduction to the Anthropology of Britain

Nigel Rapport

[T]he human condition actually is more or less a constant: always in face of the same mysteries, the same dilemmas, the same temptation to despair, and always armed unexpectedly with the same energy.

John Berger *A Telling Eye*

Three Tenets

The anthropological study of modern-day Britain was, with the partial exception of the Mass Observation project between the two World Wars (and since), originally the province of geographers (Alwyn Rees, *Life in a Welsh Countryside* (1951); Bill Williams, *The Sociology of an English Village: Gosforth* (1956) and *A West Country Village: Ashworthy* (1963)) and sociologists (Michael Young and Peter Wilmott, *Family and Kinship in East London* (1957); Norman Dennis *et al.*, *Coal is our Life* (1956)). I will not rehearse here the reasons for this tardiness of disciplinary appreciation, but suffice it to say that this volume attends to a sea-change: the anthropological study of Britain can now call on a host of names, senior and junior in the profession, to swell its list of studies.

By an anthropology of 'Britain' I mean Great Britain, not the United Kingdom. That is, I include Wales, England and Scotland but I leave out Northern Ireland, for Northern Ireland (the island of Ireland per se) seems to have been accorded a sociocultural specificity by the armed struggle which has largely characterized the twentieth century's British–Irish relations both before the partition of 1921 into Northern Ireland and the Irish Free State and since. While an 'anthropology of Britain' engenders a certain broad sociocultural accounting, the inclusion of Ireland significantly alters the focus of this writing (narrows it, paradoxically) by seeming to demand that the yet-to-be-resolved 'troubles' over the status of Ulster be accorded an 'imperative status' and take centre stage (cf. Jenkins *et al.* 1986, Donnan and McFarlane 1997). Ireland, in short, warrants its own writing.

An Irish specificity is also seen reflected in its anthropology – the subject, until recently, of far more work than Britain (cf. Peace 1989). The first modern-day anthropological studies of Ireland tended to be conducted by Americans

(Conrad Arensberg, *The Irish Countryman* (1937), and he and Solon Kimball, *Family and Community in Ireland* (1940)). This early North American interest, moreover, has shown little sign of waning, with Ireland retaining its distinctive 'tropical' character in that continent's public imagination (John Messenger, *Inis Beag* (1969); Elliot Leyton, *The One Blood* (1975); Nancy Scheper-Hughes, *Saints, Scholars and Schizophrenics: Mental Illness in Rural Ireland* (1979)). This, in turn, stimulated an early and continuing institutional focus in Ireland on anthropology 'at home', exemplified best by work based at the island's largest anthropology department, Queen's University of Belfast (and now its Centre for Irish Studies).

North American interest in Britain has been more scant, and home-grown institutionalized foci likewise. Erving Goffman spent time in exile from America sojourning in the Scottish highlands and islands, other visitors to British-Celtic borderlands have followed (N. Dorian, D. Forsythe, K. Armstrong, C. Davies, J. Nadel-Klein), and latterly there have been strong ethnographic accounts published by North American scholars of such areas (Reg Byron, *Sea Change* 1985; Susan Parman, *Scottish Crofters* (1990); Carol Trosset, *Welshness Performed* 1993; Gwen Neville, *The Mother Town: Civic Ritual, Symbol and Experience in the Borders of Scotland* (1994)). By and large, however, and with the honourable exception of Michael Banton (*The Coloured Quarter: Negro Immigrants in an English City* (1955) and *The Policeman in the Community* (1964), of Ronald Frankenberg (*Communities in Britain* (1956) and *Village on the Border: A social study of religion, politics and football in a North Wales community* (1957)), and of Sheila Cunnison (*Wages and Work Allocation* (1966)), the anthropological study of Britain tended to be undertaken by British anthropologists who had turned their attention to their 'home' environments only after they had fulfilled their desires, at least in part, for apprehending more distant climes. And while the latter studies by 'returnees' gave rise to some extremely incisive contributions,[1] this remained, notwithstanding, anthropology in Britain conducted in the shadow of a more proper anthropology elsewhere.[2]

The whys and wherefores of this disciplinary history were comprehensively reviewed by Anthony Cohen in 1983, as part of an initiative to encourage the then Social Science Research Council (UK) to develop a properly anthropological – as distinct from sociological – British expertise (Cohen 1983). Suffice it to say, however, that an uncertainty concerning the legitimacy (even the possibility) of undertaking anthropology in Britain has continued to dog the British institutional scene almost up to the present day. Some outspoken critics (Maurice Bloch, for instance, 1988) have continued to claim that since other disciplines cover British sociocultural milieux in a variety of their aspects (historical, sociological, philosophical, literary, psychological), it should be anthropology's duty to fill in the gaps of study elsewhere – Madagascar and suchlike. At the least, individuals with an anthropological interest in Britain have had still to prove their mettle – had to blood themselves on exotica – before they could hope to acquire permissions, leaves, grants and audiences for work 'up the M1' (Okely 1987). The present volume, again, embodies a sea-change: all of its contributors can call Britain – at least western Europe – their first focus of professional anthropological study, and many have continued to centre their attention upon it. This is a book which makes Britain primary in anthropological terms and does not see the need always to legitimize itself by drawing comparisons between Britain and 'other cultures'; nor does it feel that its lack of formal 'exoticism' requires special pleading.

There were no doubt many moments in the past when the tide could be seen to be turning in this direction. Based in anthropology departments such as Manchester, Edinburgh, Cambridge, UCL, Durham, Oxford and Swansea (latterly, Hull, Keele, Brunel, SOAS, Sussex, Lampeter and St Andrews), there has been, especially since the 1970s, a steady growth in studies which began with participant-observation in a British locale (urban and rural, factory and farm, single- and multi-sited, 'ethnic' and 'white') and culminated in a monograph on an aspect of British sociocultural life. These have accompanied a number of changes in wider social-scientific and institutional milieux, including the growth of interest in analytical models of 'Western' society and culture, in particular of 'Europe' (Godard, Llobera and Shore 1994); the growing difficulty of gaining access to traditional, non-Western sites, and the political and moral questionableness of so doing; critique of a merely quantitative sociological appraisal of the West, also of the dichotomization between so-called 'pure' and 'applied' research in this regard; and a burgeoning appreciation of sophisticated studies being undertaken of their own societies and cultures by anthropologists in North America, Scandinavia, and also France (cf. Cohen 1980, 1988).[3]

A moment which cannot be overlooked, however, in the tide turning to flood (and one also pertaining to Frankenberg's and Cunnison's old departmental home, Manchester) concerns the efforts of Anthony Cohen from the early 1970s onwards. Cohen began fieldwork on the island of Whalsay (in Shetland) in 1973 and has maintained a research connection there ever since. His anthropological exegeses began appearing in academic papers in the later 1970s (e.g. 1978a, 1978b), and gave on to two magisterial edited collections in the 1980s. Reviewing the first of these (*Belonging* 1982) for the journal *Man*, as it then was (now *JRAI*), Brendan Quayle suggested he was witnessing a 'coming-of-age' of British ethnography (1984: 682); the second volume, meanwhile (*Symbolising Boundaries* 1986), reflected the growing number of aspiring anthropologists of Britain who could be called upon as contributors, and the increasing breadth of their foci: from 'rural cultures' to urban, industrial and migrant. Under Cohen's stewardship, Manchester University Press also instituted a book series on The Anthropology of Britain, and Cohen's own magnum opus on Shetland appeared under its rubric in 1987 (*Whalsay*). Anthony Cohen has since left Manchester for a Chair in Edinburgh, but he provides the epilogue to this volume in the form of a critical review: a reflection upon the progress of this regional anthropological accounting.

The present volume is not, then, the first compendium of studies of British anthropology (and besides Cohen's early edited volumes should also be mentioned Frankenberg's festschrift to his Manchester supervisor, Max Gluckman, *Custom and Conflict in British Society* (1982)), nor is it likely to be the last; a number of more recent collaborations have viewed Britain through the prisms of specific defining problematics such as ethnicity (Werbner and Anwar 1991) or new reproductive technologies (Edwards *et al.* 1993). I have, however, wanted to imbue this collection with a particular distinctive ethos. As mentioned, all the contributors have elected anthropology in Britain as their primary area of long-term field research and major study. They are, if you will, the descendants of those who first practised this kind of primacy (Banton, Cunnison, Cohen *et al.*), and those (Max Gluckman, Jimmy Littlejohn, Raymond Firth, Rosemary Harris, Joe Loudon) who first advocated participant-observation fieldwork being carried out in Britain in the same way as in areas of (British) anthropology's more traditional concern (Africa, New Guinea, South America), and advocated doctorates and jobs in British university departments being accorded these researchers as a result of their work. In inviting people to contribute, furthermore, I have asked that they consider instil-ling into their accounts three tenets in particular:

1. 'that anthropology in Britain is central to disciplinary concerns';
2. 'that anthropology in Britain might include and entail anything that concerns the discipline of anthropology: all human potentiality is there';
3. 'that anthropology in Britain, conducted by those whose mother-tongue is English (or Gallic, or Hindi, etc., where appropriate) or who are at least thoroughly bilingual, sets standards of excellence in terms of subtle ethnography and complex analysis that others might seek to match. Far from an anomaly, an anthropology "at home" in Britain might be seen to be paradigmatic'.

An anthropology 'at home' has come to be advocated on grounds of both ethics and expediency (cf. Jackson 1986). When Audrey Richards began taking students from Cambridge to 'practise' their fieldwork skills (before they undertook the pukka thing abroad) in the Essex village of Elmdon where she kept a holiday cottage (cf. Richards and Robin 1975; Strathern 1981), it was for similar reasons that many experienced fieldworkers turned to British settings later in their career: to hone their skills and interests by way of a milieu which was considered compassable, comparatively cheap, seemingly easy to access – simply 'there'. Latterly, the moral questions which have accompanied anthropology's literary turn and reflexive mood (concerning the proprieties of imposing one's study on others in order to draw conclusions, enunciate narratives and gain esteem of one's own (cf. Rapport 1994)) have led to calls possibly to study 'one's own' alone. Only in a home milieu can one be assured that hegemonic discourses have at least an equal chance of being suffered and commanded alike.

In this book, I have wanted to give an anthropology ('at home') in Britain a rather different grounding: in meritoriousness and significance.[4] Anthropology in Britain has the potential, I contend, of providing some of the best that the discipline can offer because an anthropologist thoroughly at home in linguistic denotation, and familiar with behavioural form, is more able to appreciate the connotative: to pick up on those niceties of interaction and ambivalences and ambiguities of exchange, where the most intricate (and interesting) aspects of sociocultural worlds are constructed, negotiated, contested and disseminated. '*Si bis faciunt idem non est idem* (if two people do the same thing it is not the same thing)' is a Classical appreciation of the kind of paradox that can still be claimed fundamental to human experience (as cited by Devereux 1978:125). By way of linguistic expertise (verbal and non-verbal) and extra-linguistic adroitness, the fieldworker at home in the milieu being studied is well placed to identify those vital differences and diversities (between ideals and practices, between appearances and actualities, between sayings and doings, between the sayings and doings of different individuals or of the same individual at different times) which provide the dynamo of cultural practice and social process. In the subtle apprehensions of such an anthropology, particularity and precision have more chance of holding out against generality and abstraction.[5]

It used to be said that an anthropology in a milieu in which one felt linguistically and behaviourally at home was hardly credible because of the trenchant difficulties of taking too much for granted; one simply could not gain a vantage-point upon those habituated 'common background expectancies' (Schuetz 1962) by which everyday life was mostly lived, and where 'culture' most deeply resided (Bloch 1998). This seems to be precisely wrong. Culture is not a secret, it is something experienced – the formal medium of an experience – and its study is not an esoteric pursuit so much as an exercise in concentration and will; anthropology as a frame of mind, and as a fieldwork practice, is not so much a perversion of an everyday mindset as an exaggeration of one. People are all and always anthropologists in and of their lives, to a variable degree pondering their selves, their worlds and others. People are all and always engaged in ethnomethodology: in the creation of relatively stable sociocultural forms and meanings out of the fragments and randomnesses of their experience. As Victor Turner concluded, memorably:

> [T]here were never any innocent, unconscious savages, living in a time of unreflective and instinctive harmony. We human beings are all and always sophisticated, conscious, capable of laughter at our own institutions. (cited in Ashley 1990:xix)

Or, more recently, Paul Rabinow:

> This is the ground of anthropology: . . . we can pretend that . . . the people we are studying are living amid various unconscious systems of determining forces of which they have no clue and to which only we have the key. But it is only pretence. (1977: 151–2)

What characterizes the professional anthropologist, in short, is not something counter-intuitive so much as super-intuitive; an anthropologist at home in Britain has the potential to make quite excellent science out of his or her everyday commonsensical habits of querying, interpreting, empathizing with and ironizing sociocultural milieux.

If anthropology in Britain is paradigmatic of the discipline's essential project in this way, then it is also instantiatory of the discipline's breadth and diversity. For nothing might be found in human experience that could not be found in Britain. By this I mean that what is central to anthropological discovery is the human psyche and this is a universal. Formal behaviours may statistically vary; there may be more 'bed-and-breakfast', rugby football, and discrimination on the basis of accent and skin colour in Britain, and, contrastively, there may be more female purdah, communitarian touting of the common good, and worship of supernatural artefacts, ancestors and spaces elsewhere – in sociocultural milieux in Africa, the Middle East, Asia or wherever. These, however, are surface phenomena, I would contend, and do not go to the heart of what the science of anthropology endeavours to elucidate: the psychic unity of humankind and the individual differentiation. In Arthur Schopenhauer's prescient phrasing:

> [T]he truly depicted life of the individual in a narrow sphere shows the conduct of men with all its nuances and forms . . . It is quite immaterial whether the objects on which the historical action hinges are, relatively speaking, farmhouses or kingdoms. For all these things are without significance in themselves. (1969: 247)

Certainly, I am less keen to hear about the variety of formal practices per se than about their particular, individual implementation. What feeds my anthropological interest is the account of the situational experiencing of these diverse forms: what people are saying through them, what meanings are being construed by them in the context of particular individual lives in particular groups and communities. The superficial forms of behaviour are not determinate; they are accidents of history, epiphenomena, and people are able to say and mean most anything by them. Hence, it is possible for the same thoughts and feelings to be humanly experienced, and the same motivations and gratifications willed, anywhere.

Psyches in Process

It might be the core of an anthropological science, I would suggest, to give a comparative account of individuals' meaningful experiences: the experiences situationally accrued and the meanings ongoingly construed by particular individuals in one moment or milieu (and the consequences of these experiences and meanings for the course of individuals' lives) as against those accrued and construed in others. Here is a study of the human psyche in (and as) process.

In studying 'the core, the content and the implications' of the human psyche, George Devereux distinguished between two complementary approaches: one could either study intensively a single psyche, or study extensively any number of others. Both approaches, Devereux argued, might lead to an elucidation of the same natural psychic phenomena (cited in Hook 1979: 4). A 'psychically intensive' discipline such as psychology and a more 'psychically extensive' discipline such as anthropology could thus be seen as closely related branches of the same human science.

The implication, as more lyrically phrased by Olive Schreiner (1986: 198), is that '[a]ll things are in all men'; or by Grahame Greene: '[y]ou don't see more of life . . . in one place than another. One man in a desert is enough life if you are trained to observe or have a bent for observation' (1985: 149). The anthropological study of Britain, for instance, might be expected to throw up as diverse an array of experiences and meanings as might be found anywhere. All of human life is here, inasmuch as social milieux in Britain could be said to contain all the potential of individual human creativity; in its capacities and its dispositions, the human psyche is a constant.

It is for this reason that I would refer to the forms of social or cultural life as 'surface phenomena'. As manifestations of contemporary negotiation and compromise, forms might represent a challenge to individual psychical practice but not (ordinarily) a constraint, and never a determinant; in its capacities and dispositions, the psyche can be said to exist independently of them. While there will be a dialectical relationship between psychical practice and sociocultural form, I would nevertheless contend that the psyche can be properly regarded as distinct from the sociocultural milieux in which it passes its life – through which its life is spent in passing – and that individual identity and vision can be taken to be in vital respects psychical in origin and nature. An anthropological science might embody an appreciation of the human psyche as individual, separate, self-energized, responsible for constructing life-worlds and life-courses which take their character from the playing out of individual world-views. It is in this way that I would understand Simmel's formula that '[a]ny history or description of a social situation is an exercise of psychological knowledge' (1971: 32).

To spell out, briefly, the further implications of the above contentions would be to see a shift in contemporary explanatory emphasis towards a 'post-cultural' anthropology. I mean by this an eschewing of determinism as seen to derive from such notions as society or culture (class or gender, nationality or ethnicity, discourse or habitus) and recognizing the dangers of their reification: 'society [*et al.*] is neither a substance nor a power nor an acting being' (von Mises, cited in Ions 1977: 154).

Positing the determination of hypostatized forms would, however, appear to be a practice which some branches of social science are loth to eschew. It can seem as if no sooner does one edifice of determination become discredited than another is raised. The history of social science might almost be read off from the series of hypostatizations which have been authorized: from a social structure of functioning institutions to one of relations of production, to one of symbolic texts, to one of unconscious signs. If these have seemed credible and have been authoritative versions in their time, then, as Ions puts it (1977: ix), it is because each schema has possessed its own teleology – as does astrology, say, or other metaphysical pursuits.

The conclusion of the quotation from von Mises, above, is that '[o]nly individuals act'; to which Ions is careful to add: and only individuals are consciously inactive too (1977: 124). Both action and the overt refraining from action (in favour of rest, contemplation, inscrutability, and so on) remain the provenance of individuals. It is individuals who remain, in Augé's words (1995: 20), 'the anthropological concrete'. There is a way out of metaphysical hypostatization, in other words, and the positing of impersonal schemas of determination, and that is to begin with the empirical fact of universal individuality. Universally there are individual actors accruing the experience of individual lives and it is an obfuscation (at best) to tie these experiences back to, and view them by way of, a causal metaphysic of generalization and impersonalization.[6] An 'existential' anthropology (in contradistinction to a cultural one) might then seek to elucidate the individual bases in whose terms experience is constructed, the foundations in individual bodies and minds on which worlds and selves are variously built, and the ways in which a coming together of these individuals' experiences give onto social structures (cf. Douglas and Johnson 1977).

The significant tensions in this anthropological reorientation are between individual and other, between individual action and inaction (or outer and inner, or public and private), and between the forms in which life is conducted in socio-cultural milieux and the meanings of those forms (the way they are experienced) for the individual participants. An important emphasis here is on maintaining the distance between individual experience and sociocultural context and insisting that there is no necessary, uniform or clear-cut relationship between the two (and certainly no relations of direct causation). The forms of sociocultural life are means by which individual lives formally overlap – means by which multiplicity can be superficially 'synthesised' (Simmel 1971:27), by which the diversity of individuality can be 'organized' (Wallace 1964) – and they have a historical and an accidental quality which often places them beyond individual control. By the same token, however, the individual lives publicly expressed in terms of these forms are not controlled by them or the effects of them. For, while the forms of sociocultural life often precede and outlive individual users, they possess no life or agency of their own, no logic, consequence or impact beyond their implementation by particular individuals in particular situations and outside these individual usages and interpretations. The forms of sociocultural life are matters of creation, negotiation and contestation by (any number of) individuals who come together by way of them. Precisely how and what is interpreted in them is an individual matter, and, at least initially, a private one. It is in this sense that individual experience can be described as having an individual origin. For there is no escaping the concreteness of separate and distinct bodies and minds and the discrete sensory worlds to which these amount; if interpretation is understood widely enough to include emotional, affective and sensual capacities as well as intellectual and cognitive ones, then it would be true to say that 'individuals interpret – themselves and their worlds – and therefore they are'. Nor is it appropriate to describe a form as in any meaningful sense hegemonic, for this is to overlook the work of interpretation which is ever necessary for forms to mean something and hence to have an effect – a process neither limitable nor predictable.

As a form of engagement, individual interpretation can be said to begin before birth and to continue throughout life. It is a recursive or dialectical process which individuals undertake with both what is 'within' themselves and what is 'without'. As a result, their identities and those of the worlds they inhabit take shape, achieve significance and become themselves *at the same time*; here are "'organism[s] plus environment[s]'", as Bateson put it, coming into being and maintaining themselves *as one living thing*: an 'organism-in-its-environment' (1972: 423, 426).

What is crucial to remember, however, is that the 'energy source' (Bateson 1972: 126) for this mutual becoming is the individual and his or her metabolism. Admittedly everything that the individual body physically comprises was once part of the surrounding material world, and will be again, but so long as individuals remain alive – distinct biological organisms – they will possess a distinctiveness, indeed a uniqueness, in physiological constituency, and a separateness in embod- iment, which have unique consequences. For they make the world what it is – or, better, make worlds what they are. Fired by their metabolism, a form of non-conscious energy, individuals move, explore, become conscious and make sense. In the same way that they come to inhabit their bodies in distinct ways – uniquely forming neuronal pathways in the brain, for instance, in order to move their limbs (cf. Edelman 1992) – so they come to inhabit their bodily surroundings. Or, to be more ontologically accurate, the 'they' that they are and the worlds that they inhabit become 'themselves' by way of the self-same process of movement and exploration.

Part of what individuals discover around them, part of the world they shape in their engagement with it, will be social in nature: other people, language, custom, institution and artefact. It is important to recognize, however, the personal nature of this meeting. As with the rest of the environment which individuals come to call their own, call part of themselves, sociocultural milieux are personalized as they are apprehended; in terms of their significance and identity, they are recreated in individuals' images. The language of the milieu becomes their language, the people and artefacts their people and artefacts, to the extent that they interpret these as existing and having a relevance for them. Not only the energy but also the vision behind this process originate within the individual rather than without; individuals decide what the language, the people, the artefacts will mean for them, how they will engage with them (if at all), how they will make them part of the furnishings of their becoming.

Indeed, it cannot be other; for individuals cannot discover how these 'others' are in or for themselves even should they wish to. The meaning of other people to themselves, the meaning of their words to themselves, of their artefacts – these are all closed off because individuals can only and ever approach them via their own processes of interpretation, their own bodily engagement. And since there are no out-of-body experiences there is no possibility for an individual to inhabit anyone's body but his or her own. When individuals try to learn other people's language, therefore, when they try to conform to customs they are instructed in, when they try to master an artefactual technique, just as when they first came to inhabit their bodies, they do so inevitably in an individual way, a personal way.

Knowledge of the world as experienced might be said to be inexorably individual and personal. This is both a freedom and a restriction. Human beings are, as Sartre put it (1997 [1948]), 'condemned to be free'. Even should others wish to force it to be otherwise – or individuals seek to force such on themselves – the conditions of individuals' experience of the world are entailed within the ongoing personal history (the story or narrative) of their meaningful engagement with the world. Individuals can but make sense in their own way, and the sense they make conditions the actions they take and the ongoing interpretation they make of those actions' consequences: a circuit with its own biography which only ends at death. In Hirsch's summing up (1988: 258):

> [T]he distance between one historical period [one cultural perspective] and another is a very small step in comparison to the huge metaphysical gap we must leap to understand the perspective of another person in any time and place.

In their engagement with language, people, artefacts, as in their physical engagements with their bodies and bodily surrounds, individuals personalize and create identities and make sense according to their own energies, visions, purposes and interests; it is this personal interpretation which shapes the course their lives take.

This is the case, I would argue, insofar as the social context is not characterized by such 'nihilistic violence' (Rapport 2000) that the sense which individuals would make of their lives is rendered irrelevant, is obviated, by their consociates being not so much intent on interaction and ongoing social relations as an obliteration; however they might interpret, the individuals are, for instance, put to death.[7] In most cases, however, social milieux can be said to offer a reciprocality of space within which aggregations of individuals make a diversity of meanings and act purposively on the basis of these. Symbolic forms are ambiguous enough and the behaviour of consociates sufficiently expectable and routine for individuals to continue to live their lives in their own terms. Ordinarily one can see in sociocultural milieux the simultaneous expression of a diversity of individual projects and life-worlds, in a variety of alignments one with another, all in the process of becoming.

To suggest that the human psyche becomes central to the post-cultural anthropological project and that 'all of human life' can be understood as potentially instantiated in one place, such as Britain, is to say that, ordinarily, what 'happens' to human beings is not a matter of events as such, as things-in-themselves, but of their being interpreted. It is to differentiate sharply between event and experience, and also to emphasize the human nature of the gap between the two: the human character, power, practice and need of interpretation. What distinguishes human beings as animals is the extent to which the relationship between event and experience (as of behavioural form and meaning) is one of their own ongoing making, their own will: a particular relationship whose character is not necessary, or necessarily linear or constant or logical, or knowable in advance. The relationship between event and human experience is a matter of the poetics of imagination, not the necessities and definitudes of either natural cause and effect or logical abstraction.[8] Human beings, Bateson concluded (1972: 429–30), live in worlds of maps not in territories of things-in-themselves; the phenomena which they experience are 'appearances' not noumena. And while a physical determinism of forces and impacts might well characterize the noumenal universe, the worlds of human beings (and of biological organisms more broadly) Bateson depicted as matters of 'mind', where effects are brought about by a perception of difference, by attribution.

The scientific aim, nonetheless, and the human need, Bateson foresaw (1980), was ultimately to connect up mind and 'nature'. This is feasible because while the phenomenology of human life is unpredictable and cannot be explained in terms of a reduction to a series of physical events, still there is a certain constancy to the (biological) nature of the human imagination, the world-views to which it gives rise and the life-worlds it gives onto. As the epigraph to this Introduction quoting John Berger warrants, human nature is characterized by the same energy, the same perspectivity, the same diversity, the same individuality; it is this which provides an existential anthropology with its subject-matter as a human science (cf. Rapport forthcoming). This also assures it of a particular problematic and necessitates a distinctive methodology, for approaching this individual human nature from the outside, from the position of otherness, is always to be faced with the same mystery. The project of an existential anthropology may be said to be an attempted exploration of the individual experiences inside the sociocultural forms in which they are expressed, the biographical conditions of their coming into being, their habitude and their spontaneity, and the diversity of the individual experiences which may abut against one another in the same sociocultural milieu.

Such a project might be described as a science of the particular, a meeting somewhere between literature or history on the one hand and psychology or biology on the other. The substantive details of individual lives are examined as manifestations of universal capacities and dispositions. An existential anthropology would thus provide evidence for a general understanding of the workings of human consciousness and the environing worlds to which it gives rise, worlds whose substance might be expected to remain particular and individual.

Themes and Issues

When Marc Augé describes the individual as 'the anthropological concrete', it might be emphasized that such individuality pertains not only to the ethnomethodology of how those whom the anthropologist meets conduct their lives but also to the anthropologist's own methodology. An existential anthropology recognizes itself to be written *by* individuals as well as *of* individuals, and in situations of concrete, individual specificity; it attempts to attain insight into individual life-worlds from positions of equally personal contextualization.

Nietzsche claimed that deliberations on human philosophy were to a large extent understandable as personal confession, a point reiterated a century later by Galen Strawson (1997: 3–4): '[People's] fundamental conceptions of human nature are almost always grounded in their inner experience of themselves'. Since the literary turn, anthropology has admitted this of itself too. 'I have always taken the line that, in ethnographic writing, cultural differences, though sometimes convenient, are temporary fictions', Edmund Leach 'confessed' (1989: 137); what every anthropological observer will see in the field and in their data will be something no one else recognizes, 'a kind of harmonic projection of the observer's own personality' (Leach 1984: 22).

The task for new anthropology in Britain (as elsewhere) might be to work through the implications of cultures as 'temporary fictions', as 'false beliefs' (Gellner 1995:6), to see beyond the seeming determinism of such hypostatizations to a study of the coming into being of individuals-in-environments. Recognizing our ('cultural' *et al.*) understandings of the world as confessional, as harmonic projections, might be a way to accede to a science of experience: a comparison of the meanings construed by particular individuals (anthropologists and their informants), and the recursive consequences of those meanings being acted upon, in particular moments and milieux.

The tenets and ethos in whose terms I introduce this volume (and characterize a form of anthropological science) remain arguable, nonetheless. I ground them in my own experiences of conducting fieldwork, endeavouring to make sense of interactions in the English village of Wanet, in the Canadian city of St. John's, in the Israeli development town of Mitzpe Ramon, and in the Scottish city of Easterneuk. In asking the contributors to this volume also to ground their pieces in their variegated fieldwork experiences, I do not expect them to have reached similar conclusions or ask them to write as if they had. The point of conceiving of a post-cultural anthropology as a 'confessional science' must surely be to anticipate and celebrate a 'methodological eclecticism' (Rapport and Overing 2000). A tension surrounding anthropological tenets and ethos imbues this volume.

While writing out of their own specific researches, however, contributors have also been asked to consider their work as engagements with issues and themes of broad disciplinary concern. Indeed, I asked each contributor to write his or her chapter under a specific thematic rubric, to wit: Power (*Anne Rowbottom*), Nationalism (*Susan Lewis*), History (*Sharon Macdonald*), Ethnicity (*Vered Amit*), Religion (*Peter Collins*), Rationality (*Tanya Luhrmann*), Science (*Jeanette Edwards*), Methodology (*Jenny Hockey*), Cultural Values (*Carol Trosset and Douglas Caulkins*), Work and Leisure (*Andrew Dawson*), Medicine and Health (*Christine Brown*), Childhood (*Allison James*), Sexuality (*Sarah Green*), Aesthetics (*Helena Wulff*), Literature and Writing (*Nigel Rapport*). I did not mean for each chapter to provide a review or overview of this specific area of anthropological debate but that, while grounded in individual research undertaken by a particular anthropologist, each chapter might be seen to be at the same time extensive with (and extending of) certain current and established anthropological discourses. Contributors were invited to consider their chapters in this way in the spirit of demonstrating anthropology in Britain to be potentially paradigmatic of the discipline's possibilities, skills and significance.

Areas of disciplinary concern reflect, of course, the lived concerns of the subjects of anthropological research. 'Rationality', 'Medicine and Health', 'Work and Leisure' and 'Nationalism' are labels for discourses in everyday use by which people symbolically assert, affirm and deny identity and belonging. These are among the gross markers of inclusion and exclusion in whose terms social worlds are classified and life practised. Each, in Barth's terms (1969: 17), represents a different 'imperative status', a different way in which people in Britain favour the construal and practising of the social game of 'self' and 'other' – on the basis of 'who is rational (like me) and who is not', 'who is healthy and who is not', 'who is in work or a particular kind of work and who is not', 'who shares my nationality and who does not', and so on. Bringing different languages ('language-games') to the fore, each chapter treats different forms and kinds of social expression and assertion (essential and situational, encompassing and partial) employed by individuals and groups in their ongoing construction of ordered social space.

It has been argued (Bernstein 1964; Marsh, Rosser and Harre 1978) that the everyday use of different public languages of identity in large-scale sociocultural milieux evidences the existence of 'microsocieties' or 'subcultures' between which communication might be expected to be restricted and oblique. A further feature of the chapters in this book, however, is the substantive overlaps and connections that also exist between the concerns that seem to be enunciated in the different languages people speak. Whether they speak a language of ethnicity, or age or aesthetics, for instance, issues surrounding the essential nature of social labels and categories might similarly arise, or questions concerning the relationship between social belonging and physical bodies, or between belonging and global movement. It had been my intention at one stage to arrange the chapters in the book by their written rubric; the Table of Contents would offer a list of thematic and specific chapter titles. On receiving and reviewing the essays, however, what became more apparent than their titular differences were their substantive samenesses. Issues surrounding the fragmentary nature of social life, for instance, or its enchantments and magic, or its ceremoniousness, issues to do with technologies and change, with the construing of community and with the fluidities and historical contingencies of identity, these kinds of overlap and connection struck me forcefully as true and significant. I have therefore ordered the contents of the book to reflect some of the underlying samenesses-in-diversity.

Five main book sections follow this introductory one, each containing three related chapters: 'Nationalism, Contestation and the Performance of Tradition'; 'Strategies of Modernity: Heritage, Leisure, Dissociation'; 'The Appropriation of Discourse'; 'Methodologies and Ethnomethodologies'; 'The Making (and Unmaking) of Community: Ethnicity, Religiosity, Locality'. I have written a short introduction to accompany each section, prefacing for the reader the chapters and their underlying commonalities. Finally, there is an 'Epilogue' in which Anthony Cohen appraises the volume's contributions in the light of a reading of anthropologies of Britain which have preceded them.

I want my ordering of chapters and sections to be seen as only one of many possible arrangements and drawings out of thematic connection; the note I aim to strike is of opening onto an anthropological terrain rather than of closing an area off. (I remember liking how David Lodge once introduced a volume of literary theory by offering two Tables of Contents, 'Historic' and 'Thematic', each offering a differing arrangement of chapters.)

More broadly, while I would see diversity and connectivity as key terms for this volume, 'comprehensiveness' and 'systematization' are not intended. This

'Anthropology in Britain' does not claim to compass social life in Britain as a whole, nor is that its aspiration: the diversity does not pretend to inclusivity. Indeed, I have contended above that 'Britain' – what it is, who belongs and how – cannot be essentialized or absolutely defined: anthropologically speaking, there is no 'representative Britain'. Likewise, there is no necessary 'whole' to British life to which all behavioural manifestations and interpretive constructions amount, in which some things or people must be included and some omitted. As has become a disciplinary truism in recent years, 'the locus of study is not the object of study' (Geertz 1975: 22), and to study in a place is not to make that place a thing-in-itself.

Not only are 'Britain' and 'British' not presumed as givens, but as has also been explained, this book does not take as its defining problematic any single 'imperative status' by which life in Britain might be classified and known as British – class, say, or race or locality or autochthony; no single logic or language-game of inclusion and exclusion is privileged. The range of such essentializing discourses with which the chapters below do engage – concerning 'Armenians', 'lesbians', 'royalists', 'Quakers', 'Manx', 'the mad', and so on – and the contingency and fluidity of their usage, show up the political rather than scientific nature of these discourses, and that of the claims arising from them. Rather than an identity politics which would treat social labels and collective categories as necessary or inescapable givens, this volume intends an appreciation of particular psyches in interpretive process through such categories and labels. A collection of case-studies is offered by anthropologists 'at home in British sociocultural milieux', the studies aiming to show, with subtlety, detail and depth, the particularity and diversity of individual lives, and the sense they make, together and apart, in and of 'Britain'.

Acknowledgements

I am very grateful to Anthony Cohen, Allison James, Helena Wulff, Jeanette Edwards, Ade Peace, John Gray, Emanuel Marx, Joanna Overing, Tristan Platt, Helle Johannessen and Francine Lorimer for commentaries they made as I was formulating this piece. The anonymous readers for Berg Publishers contributed some very useful suggestions for the volume, while Kathryn Earle has been an exceptionally supportive and active editor throughout, and George Pitcher a punctilious copy-editor.

Notes

1. Beginning with Raymond Firth (1956), one can think of important contributions continuing to the present day from the likes of Joe Loudon (1961), Jimmy

Littlejohn (1963), Clement Harris (a.k.a. William Lancaster) (1974), Marilyn Strathern (1981; 1992), Sandra Wallman (1982), Shirley Ardener (1984), Ruth Finnegan (1989), Pnina Werbner (1990), Ursula Sharma (1991), Simon Charsley (1992), Abner Cohen (1993), Sue Wright (1994), Gerd Baumann (1996), Danny Miller (1998), Jean La Fontaine (1998), Bob Simpson (1998), and John Gray (2000).

2. Even Tom Harrison, one of the founders of Mass Observation, turned to the recording of information on British folk life in the 1930s only after his rite of passage in the New Hebrides (Vanuatu); while Ronald Frankenberg turned his attention to Wales after an abortive attempt to undertake fieldwork in the West Indies.

3. Marc Augé's recent pronouncement that at the same time as enunciating a differentiation between 'the lineage-based world and the industrial world' it should be possible (and seen to be necessary) to conduct anthropology at home in the same fashion as away (1998: 111) – as if this were a novel or radical suggestion – is all the stranger, then, given the strong tradition of anthropology 'at home' in France. It is indicative, seemingly, of the continuing institutional distance and non-communication between these branches of the discipline even there.

4. I want to make it clear that I regard the same arguments for 'an anthropology (at home) in Britain' as applying to an anthropology at home in Israel (Marx 1980), say, or in India (Narayan 1989).

5. This is not to essentialize either 'Britain' or 'home'. No absolute criteria – birth, longevity, status – can define one who is 'at home' in Britain and who is not. (Contributors to this volume include a Scandinavian and several North Americans, as well as contributors from different regions of the British Isles, who might also be given different sociological profiles according to their 'ethnicity', 'gender', 'class', and so on.) Nor would I wish to delimit what is 'Britain' and what is not. Rather, what I am calling attention to here is a fluency in the forms of interaction in use in those British sociocultural milieux which are the focus of the research. Such fluency or competency in the general symbolic and behavioural forms which social life takes provides a felicitous grounding for an appreciation of the subtleties, depths and diversities of the particular lives lived within them.

6. Anthony Cohen (1989) has described generalization as an intellectually barren mode of discourse; whereas the metier of anthropology might be the substantive complexity, differentiation, particularity, diversity, irregularity and contradiction of sociocultural milieux: 'societies, cultures, as barely generalizable aggregations of difference rather than as fictive matrices of uniformity' (1989: 10).

7. There are occasions where the course of individual lives does not correspond with the meanings individuals construe and on which they would base their

action, but these are limiting cases: situations where mutual negotiation between actors and the effecting of reciprocal spaces wherein each might live out his or her life is replaced by a gratuitous terminating of the interaction – such as one party being exterminated by the other. In such nihilistically violent situations individuals' life-courses turn into 'catastrophes' that bear 'no more relation to their characters, motives or actions than an earthquake' (Dwight Macdonald, cited in Wheatcroft 2000: 10). Macdonald's words come from his description of the Holocaust: something he finds more like a natural 'horror' than a human 'tragedy', something characterized by a 'violence beyond logic' (Levi 1996). It is precisely because human lives can ordinarily be described as expressive of a certain logic and as distanced from a 'natural' world of brutishness and chance that such 'catastrophic' occasions are limiting cases. Nihilistic violence does not characterize most human lives lived in situations of ongoing social relations; in most cases, individuals' life-courses are conditioned by their interpretations, imagination and will, and their individual histories of these.

8. In Leach's words: 'The imaginative operations of the human mind are "poetic" and are not trammelled by fixed, easily specified rules of Aristotelian and mathematical logic' (1976: 5).

References

Ardener, S. (1984) *The Incorporated Wife*, London: Croom Helm.

Arensberg, C. (1937) *The Irish Countryman*, London: Macmillan.

—— and Kimball, S. (1940) *Family and Community in Ireland*, Cambridge MA: Harvard University Press.

Ashley, K. (1990) 'Introduction', in K. Ashley (ed.) *Victor Turner and the Construction of Cultural Criticism*, Bloomington: Indiana University Press.

Augé, M. (1995) *Non-places*, London: Verso.

—— (1998) *A Sense for the Other*, Stanford: Stanford University Press.

Banton, M. (1955) *The Coloured Quarter: Negro Immigrants in an English City*, London: Cape.

—— (1964) *The Policeman in the Community*, London: Tavistock.

Barth, F. (ed.) (1969) *Ethnic Groups and Boundaries*, Boston: Little, Brown.

Bateson, G. (1972) *Steps to an Ecology of Mind*, London: Paladin.

—— (1980) *Mind and Nature: A Necessary Unity*, Glasgow: Fonata.

Baumann, G. (1996) *Contesting Culture: Discourses of Identity in Multi-Ethnic London*, Cambridge: Cambridge University Press.

Berger, J. (1994) *A Telling Eye: The Work of John Berger*, BBC 2, 30 July.

Bernstein, B. (1964) 'Aspects of Language and Learning in the Genesis of the Social Process', in D. Hymes (ed.) *Language in Culture and Society*, New York: Harper and Row.

Bloch, M. (1988) 'In Interview with Gustaaf Houtman', *Anthropology Today* 4(1): 18–21.

—— (1998) *How We Think They Think*, Boulder: Westview.

Byron, R. (1985) *Sea Change*, St. John's, Nfld: Institute of Social and Economic Research Press.

Charsley, S. (1992) *Wedding Cakes and Cultural History*, London: Routledge.

Cohen, Abner (1993) *Masquerade Politics*, Oxford: Berg.

Cohen, Anthony P. (1978a) '"The same – but different!": The Allocation of Identity in Whalsay, Shetland', *Sociological Review* 26(3): 449–69.

—— (1978b) 'Ethnographic Method in the Real Community', *Sociologia Ruralis* XVIII(1): 1–21.

—— (1980) 'The Case for an Anthropology of Britain', paper presented at the SSRC conference, 'Anthropological Research in Scotland', University of Edinburgh.

—— (ed.) (1982) *Belonging: Identity and Social Organisation in British Rural Cultures*, Manchester: Manchester University Press.

—— (1983) 'Anthropological Studies of Rural Britain 1968–1983: A position paper', SSRC Report HG 6/27.

—— (ed.) (1986) *Symbolising Boundaries: Identity and Diversity in British Cultures*, Manchester: Manchester University Press.

—— (1987) *Whalsay: Symbol, Segment and Boundary in a Shetland Island Community*, Manchester: Manchester University Press.

—— (1988) 'La Tradition Britannique, et la Question de l'Autre', in M. Segalen (ed.) *Regards sur l'Ethnologie du Domaine Français*, Paris: CNRS.

—— (1989) 'Opposing the Motion that "Social Anthropology is a Generalizing Science or it is Nothing"', *Group for Debates in Anthropological Theory*, Dept of Social Anthropology, University of Manchester.

Cunnison, S. (1966) *Wages and Work Allocation*, London: Tavistock.

Dennis, N., Henriques, F. and Slaughter, C. (1956) *Coal is our Life*, London: Eyre & Spottiswoode.

Devereux, G. (1978) *Ethnopsychoanalysis*, Berkeley: University of California Press.

Donnan, H. and McFarlane, G. (1997) *Culture and Policy in Northern Ireland: Anthropology in the Public Arena*, Belfast: Institute of Irish Studies.

Douglas, J. and Johnson, J. (eds) (1977) *Existential Sociology*, Cambridge: Cambridge University Press.

Edelman, G. (1992) *Bright Air, Brilliant Fire: On the Matter of the Mind*, Harmondsworth: Penguin.

Edwards, J., Franklin, S., Hirsch, E., and Strathern, M. (1993) *Technologies of Procreation: Kinship in the Age of Assisted Conception*, Manchester: Manchester University Press.

Finnegan, R. (1989) *The Hidden Musicians: Music-making in an English Town*, Cambridge: Cambridge University Press.

Firth, R. (1956) *Two Studies of Kinship in London*, London: Athlone.

Frankenberg, R. (1956) *Communities in Britain*, Harmondsworth: Penguin.

—— (1957) *Village on the Border: A social study of religion, politics and football in a North Wales community*, London: Cohen & West.

—— (ed.) (1982) *Custom and Conflict in British Society*, Manchester: Manchester University Press.

Geertz, C. (1975) *The Interpretation of Cultures*, London: Hutchinson.

Gellner, E. (1995) 'Anything Goes: The Carnival of Cheap Relativism which Threatens to Swamp the Coming *fin de millenaire*', *Times Literary Supplement* 4811: 6–8.

Godard, V., Llobera, J., Shore, C. (eds) (1994) *The Anthropology of Europe: Identities and Boundaries in Conflict*, Oxford: Berg.

Gray, J. (2000) *At Home in the Hills*, Oxford: Berghahn.

Greene, G. (1985) *The Tenth Man*, London: Bodley Head.

Harris, C. (1974) *Hennage: A social system in miniature*, New York: Holt, Rinehart and Winston.

Hirsch, E.D. (1988), 'Faulty Perspectives', in D. Lodge (ed.) *Modern Criticism and Theory*, London: Longman.

Hook, R. (1979) 'Introduction', in R. Hook (ed.) *Fantasy and Symbol*, London: Academic.

Ions, E. (1977) *Against Behaviourism*, Oxford: Blackwell.

Jackson, A. (ed.) (1986) *Anthropology at Home*, London: Routledge.

Jenkins, R., Donnan, H. and McFarlane, G. (1986) 'The Sectarian Divide in Northern Ireland Today', *Royal Anthropological Institute* Occasional Paper no. 41.

La Fontaine, J. (1998) *Speak of the Devil*, Cambridge: Cambridge University Press.

Leach, E. (1976) *Culture and Communication*, Cambridge: Cambridge University Press.

—— (1984) 'Glimpses of the Unmentionable in the History of British Social Anthropology', *Annual Review of Anthropology* 13: 1–23.

—— (1989) 'Writing Anthropology: A Review of Clifford Geertz's *Works and Lives*', *American Ethnologist* 16(1): 137–41.

Levi, P. (1996) *The Drowned and The Saved*, London: Abacus.

Leyton, E. (1975) *The One Blood*, St. John's, Nfld: Institute of Social and Economic Research Press.

Littlejohn, J. (1963) *Westrigg: The Sociology of a Cheviot Parish*, London: Routledge & Kegan Paul.

Loudon, J. (1961) 'Kinship and Crisis in South Wales', *British Journal of Sociology* 12: 333–350.

Marsh, P., Rosser, E. and Harre, R. (1978) *The Rules of Disorder*, London: Routledge & Kegan Paul.

Marx, E. (ed.) (1980) *A Composite Portrait of Israel*, London: Academic.

Messenger, J. (1969) *Inis Beag*, New York: Holt, Rinehart and Winston.

Miller, D. (1998) *A Theory of Shopping*, Cambridge: Polity.

Narayan, K. (1989) *Storytellers, Saints and Scoundrels*, Philadelphia: University of Pennsylvania Press.

Neville, G. (1994) *The Mother Town: Civic Ritual, Symbol and Experience in the Borders of Scotland*, New York: Oxford University Press.

Okely, J. (1987) 'Fieldwork up the M1: Policy and Political Aspects', in A. Jackson (ed.) *Anthropology at Home*, London: Routledge.

Parman, S. (1990) *Scottish Crofters*, Fort Worth: Holt, Rinehart and Winston.

Peace, A. (1989) 'From Arcadia to Anomie: Critical Notes on the Constitution of Irish Society as an Anthropological Object', *Critique of Anthropology* IX(1): 89–111.

Quayle, B. (1984) 'Review of *Belonging*, edited by A.P. Cohen', *Man* 19(4): 682–4.

Rabinow, P. (1977) *Reflections on Fieldwork in Morocco*, Berkeley: University of California Press.

Rapport, N. (1994) *The Prose and the Passion: Anthropology, Literature and the Writing of E.M. Forster*, Manchester: Manchester University Press.

—— (2000) '"Criminals by Instinct": On the "Tragedy" of Social Structure and the "Violence" of Individual Creativity', in G. Aijmer and J. Abbink (eds) *Meanings of Violence: Symbolism and Structure in Violent Practice*, Oxford: Berg.

—— (forthcoming) 'The Humanistic Implications of Understanding Human Nature as Individual Nature', *Anthropological Theory* (special issue edited by Tim Ingold).

—— and Overing, J. (2000) *Social and Cultural Anthropology: Key Concepts*, London: Routledge.

Rees, A. (1951) *Life in a Welsh Countryside*, Cardiff: University of Wales Press.

Richards, A. and Robin, J. (1975) *Some Elmdon Families*, Saffron Walden: Audrey Richards.

Sartre, J.-P. (1997[1948]) *Existentialism and Humanism*, London: Methuen.

Scheper-Hughes, N. (1979) *Saints, Scholars and Schizophrenics: Mental Illness in Rural Ireland*, Berkeley: University of California Press.

Schopenhauer, A. (1969) *The World as Will and Representation* (volume I), New York: Dover.

Schreiner, O. (1986) *The Story of an African Farm*, Harmondsworth: Penguin.

Schuetz, A. (1962) 'Common Sense and Scientific Interpretation of Human Action', in M. Natanson (ed.) *Collected Papers I: The Problem of Social Reality*, Nijhoff: The Hague.

Sharma, U. (1991) *Complementary Medicine Today*, London: Routledge.

Simmel, G. (1971) *On Individuality and Social Forms* (ed. D. Levine), Chicago: University of Chicago Press.

Simpson, B. (1998) *Changing Families*, Oxford: Berg.

Strathern, M. (1981) *Kinship at the Core*, Cambridge: Cambridge University Press.

—— (1992) *After Nature: English Kinship in the Late Twentieth Century*, Cambridge: Cambridge University Press.

Strawson, G. (1997) 'In Deepest Sympathy: Towards a Natural History of Virtue', *Times Literary Supplement* 4887: 3–4.

Trosset, C. (1993) *Welshness Performed*, Tuscon: University of Arizona Press.

Wallace, A. (1964) *Culture and Personality*, New York: Random House.

Wallman, S. (1982) *Living in South London*, London: Gower.

Werbner, P. (1990) *The Migration Process*, Oxford: Berg.

—— and Anwar, M. (eds) (1991) *Black and Ethnic Leaderships in Britain*, London: Routledge.

Wheatcroft, G. (2000) 'Horrors Beyond Tragedy', *Times Literary Supplement* 5071: 9–10.

Williams, W. (1956) *The Sociology of an English Village: Gosforth*, London: Routledge & Kegan Paul.

—— (1963) *A West Country Village: Ashworthy*, London: Routledge & Kegan Paul.

Wright, S. (ed.) (1994) *The Anthropology of Organizations*, London: Routledge.

Young, M. and Wilmott, P. (1957) *Family and Kinship in East London*, London: Routledge & Kegan Paul.

Part II
Nationalism, Contestation and the
Performance of Tradition

Introduction to Part II
Nigel Rapport

The chapters in this section explore the links between nationalism and various kinds of ritual or ceremonial performance. The latter is seen to provide a stage on which nationalism can be both celebrated and contested, reconstituted or replaced by regional identities both intra-national and trans-national. At the same time nationalism is itself a discourse through which other aspects of identity are construed and negotiated: the hierarchical, the civil-religious, the autobiographical. Nationalism becomes a way of talking about altruism, home, cultural capital, pilgrimage and sacrifice, history and myth. A dialectic thus exists between nationalism as a subject of ceremonial and of everyday exchange and as a symbolic form under whose aegis individual identities and everyday relations and rituals are themselves validated in practice.

In Chapter One, 'Subject Positions: Royalty, Royalists and Vernacular Ceremonials in British Culture', Anne Rowbottom studies the way in which ritual and ceremony highlight sociocultural boundaries and dramatize who people are taken to be. More specifically, rituals surrounding the British Royal Family highlight a paradox in British socio-political culture: many people seem to like being 'subjects' in this democracy.

As Head of State, Supreme Governor of the Church of England and the living symbol of national unity, the British monarch embodies the political and religious institutions of the United Kingdom. Furthermore, the ceremonies and events involving the monarch and the royal family constitute a central part of a civil religion of the British nation-state, of which the public mourning and outpouring of grief surrounding the death of Diana Princess of Wales (in 1997) provided an extraordinary instance. The folk religiosity surrounding Diana's death, the pilgrimages and domestic shrines vividly demonstrate the magic, for some people, of the monarchy in contemporary life.

The primary focus of this chapter is a more mundane but far more sustained example of public interactions with the monarchy: a network of self-styled ardent royalists who regularly travel the country to present flowers and other gifts and tributes to the royal family as they carry out their public duties. Their practice, it is suggested, constructs a vernacular version of the official civil religion.

In particular, the chapter is concerned with the ways in which these royalists negotiate their socially inferior positioning; they switch between the competing discourses of democratic egalitarianism on the one hand and hereditary privilege on the other so as to construct a positive view of the monarchy and the nation and themselves. The royalists ultimately achieve a form of transcendency, Rowbottom contends, through alternating, in their interpretations, between frames of difference and unity concerning relations between monarchy and them.

It remains an open question how this discourse of Monarchy-as-Britain will fare in the context of increasing European unification and of British devolution.

In Chapter Two, 'National Day: Achieving Collective Identity on the Isle of Man', Susan Lewis gives an account of The Tynwald Ceremony on the Isle of Man. She portrays it as a key to understanding the complexities and contradictions involved in an island society continuing to undergo significant social change while at the same time seeking to manufacture a sense of national identity which is inclusive and encompassing of a range of discrete interests.

The sociocultural character of the Isle of Man, Lewis argues, is influenced largely by the island's anomalous position: geographically central among 'The British Isles' while politically and economically peripheral to mainland life. In particular, the Tynwald Ceremony – the Isle of Man's National Day – demonstrates the ambiguities of independence and colonialism in Manx life. The Ceremony is a stable ritual form which bespeaks continuity, amid a plethora of symbolic interpretation which provides commentaries on present demands, past glories and views of the future; Tynwald Day is constant, flexible, multivalent and accommodating. In Lewis's ethnography we find displayed a ceremony performed by, before and for all of those who might wish to belong: nationalists, incomers, stay-at-homes, returnees, representatives of local government or of offshore banking and Big Business.

In Chapter Three, 'Aesthetics at the Ballet: Looking at "National" Style, Body and Clothing in the London Dance World', Helena Wulff asks how ballet considered as a 'visual feast' might interweave with a sense of the dance form as an expression of nationalism. The tension between an art form as international, movable and – to an extent at least – timeless, and that art form as an instantiation of a particular local ethos is that which imbues her discussion: a tension which her informants themselves draw on and choreograph in their lives and performances as international artists.

The study of the making and remaking of Western art forms reveals central issues of identity and imagination in Western societies, Wulff suggests. In particular, nationalism is negotiated through the arts, music and dance; hence a study of changing notions of aesthetics in classical and contemporary ballet in late twentieth-century Britain tells a story of 'national character' and 'ethos' at once stereotypical, official and contested, since a discourse of a discrete national ballet style in Britain paradoxically bespeaks its opposite: transnational bodies and costume; a lessening sense of British national power; ethnically diverse dancers learning and practising the habitus of a variety of different national styles.

1

Subject Positions and 'Real Royalists': Monarchy and Vernacular Civil Religion in Great Britain

Anne Rowbottom

One warm summer evening I stood squashed among a mass of people, contained behind crush barriers, outside a cinema in London's West End. This crowd had not gathered to see a film, they were there to see the Duchess of York attend a charity performance. The Duchess, resplendent in evening gown and diamond tiara, arrived in a gleaming chauffeur-driven car to be met by bows and curtseys from her official reception party. As she swept past my section of the cheering crowd I overheard an American onlooker complain to his companion, 'Now I really feel like a peasant!' From the tone of self-disgust in his voice it was evident that his use of the term 'peasant' was not being used to denote an identity as a farmer, but carried the connotation of being a person of very low social standing.

Like all public appearances by members of the British royal family, this one by the Duchess was surrounded by ceremonial. Ceremonial, as Douglas (1966) reminds us, serves to highlight social and cultural boundaries and in doing so it dramatises identity (Buckley and Kenney 1995). For my unknown American this was an event in which the boundaries of social superiority and inferiority between royalty and the crowd were being highlighted and, in the dramatization of the high status of the Duchess, he read a corresponding statement of his own social inferiority. However, although a similar response was potentially open to everyone else present, the rest of the cheering and excited crowd gave no indication that they shared his interpretation. On the contrary, everyone else appeared to be experiencing the event in a positive rather than negative way.

This fieldwork anecdote represents, in microcosm, a paradox at the heart of British socio-political culture. Edgar Wilson (1989) provides a particularly vivid statement of this paradox when he marvels at the way monarchy is 'incompatible with democracy in principle, yet in practice, amidst widespread and caste based inequality, injustice and real deprivation, the ancient symbol and instrument of hereditary privilege remains unchallenged' (1989: 1). Wilson writes as a member of Republic, an organization that describes itself as an association of democrats

Figure 1.1 Holding National Flags while awaiting the Queen. Photograph: Anne Rowbottom

who regard the ideas of hereditary office and privilege as both socially divisive and morally repugnant. Wilson's critical stance demonstrates that negative interpretations of the institution of monarchy are not confined to Americans. Criticisms can be and indeed are made by Britons (see also Haseler, 1993; Hitchens 1990; Nairn 1988; Hamilton 1975; Birnbaum 1955). What Wilson regrets in his critique is that criticism of the institution of monarchy remains a quiet voice in British culture. Criticisms of members of the royal family, however, have been a different matter throughout the 1990s.

1992 was a year the Queen referred to as her 'annus horribilis'. The representation of an ideal stable family was severely damaged by the divorce of Princess Anne from her husband, followed by the marital separation of the Duke and Duchess of York, then that of the Prince and Princess of Wales. In both the latter cases marital breakdown was accompanied by media reports of unhappy relationships and sexual infidelity. The public reputation of the royal family suffered further from the revelation (Hall 1992) that the arrangements that legally exempted the monarch from taxation were not, as the public had been led to believe, a time-hallowed tradition, but an arrangement of relatively recent innovation. Press and public reaction was such that the Queen agreed to start paying taxes on income. Public indignation flared again when, following a fire at Windsor Castle, the government initially stated that the taxpayer would pay for the repairs. In the face of press and public anger the Queen volunteered to fund the repairs, raising revenue by opening Buckingham Palace to the fee-paying public for the first time. Some commentators began to fear that the behaviour of the royal family was threatening the future of the monarchy (see for example Wilson 1993), while others hoped it would lead to the establishment of a republic (Haseler 1993).

In 1997, the death of Diana Princess of Wales, brought to an end the conflict that had been a very public feature of the relationship between her and her ex-husband. Public mourning for Diana took place on a massive scale. Her death led 'to a most extensive and dramatic public response, with acts of tribute and memorial throughout the following week' (Davies 1999). During this week the royal family came under criticism for failing to mourn in the way expected by much of the press and public. Once again some media commentators began to fear, or in a few cases to hope, that the abolition of the monarchy would be put on the political agenda.

However, as Dorothy Thompson (1998) comments, 'the attitudes to the monarchy which were demonstrated in the course of the popular response never appear to have involved hostility to the crown as such. Had the crowd been republican it would surely have cared very little for the behaviour of a group of people who were due for removal anyway' (1998: 36). What people wanted from the royal family at this time, Thompson suggests, was 'good kingship'. In this case good kingship was popularly equated with leading, or at least being seen to share in the public mourning. As soon as the royal family finally complied with these expectations they began to be rehabilitated by the media (Walter 1999). It should also be noted that even when widespread dissatisfaction with the behaviour of the royal family was being expressed, the young princes, William and Harry, were always the objects of sympathy. Three years later (at the time of this volume's preparation), Thompson's analysis had proved accurate. The criticisms of the 1990s had not put the abolition of the monarchy onto the mainstream political agenda and the paradox of heredity and democracy remained embodied in the British constitution. It is this paradox which the 'real royalists' would have to negotiate.

The Real Royalists

So far I have been using the terms 'public' and 'people', but in a large-scale society this is an undifferentiated and ultimately nebulous term. As it does not provide a population that can be studied ethnographically, my focus of interest in this chapter is with a group of men and women who make a particularly enthusiastic engagement with the monarchy. I first became aware of the existence of these 'real royalists', as they style themselves, in the autumn of 1988. During 1989 and 1990 I carried out ethnographic fieldwork with them, as research for a PhD thesis in social anthropology (Rowbottom 1994) and for an accompanying film (Henley and Rowbottom 1993). A second period of intensive fieldwork followed in 1996/1997 for the making of a television documentary about one of the royalists (Henley and Rowbottom 1997), and I worked with the royalists again during the mourning for and funeral of Diana Princess of Wales (Rowbottom 1999). In between these periods of intensive fieldwork I have maintained contact with key informants. Ethnographic data drawn from this ten-year engagement informs this chapter.

The core of the group with whom I most frequently travelled consisted of fourteen people: nine women and five men. Three of the women were over sixty, one was a teenager, and the remaining five were middle-aged. Of the five men, one was a teenager and another was in his late twenties; the other three were middle-aged. Both the men and the women were almost exclusively drawn from an upper-working-class or lower-middle-class background. Without the practices they had developed none would normally expect to have close encounters with royalty.

All the royalists in this group collect pictures, books, ceramics and other memorabilia of the royal family. Some of these collections are quite small, but others have grown large enough to fill a whole room in their homes. Many of these items are commercially produced commemoratives of coronations, royal weddings, births, anniversaries and other events in the life cycle of the Queen and her family. Other items, such as scrapbooks and photograph albums, the royalists fashion for themselves. Among their most highly prized images are the photographs they take when attending royal visits.

The term 'royal visit' refers to the official visits made by members of the royal family to hundreds of civic, commercial and charitable organizations throughout Britain. During the course of any one year members of the royal family may enact two or three hundred such visits. At some point in the course of these events, usually just before departure, the royal personage walks over to the crowd to exchange greetings and brief pleasantries with some of the onlookers. This stage of the proceedings, which has become known as the 'walkabout', is central to the royalists' activities as it provides the chance of a face-to-face meeting with the royal family. In pursuit of this goal they regularly undertake long journeys, then stand for hours, in all weathers, finally drawing the royal visitor towards them through the offering of a gift. These gifts usually take the form of flowers or a photograph of the intended recipient taken at a previous meeting. Although the walkabout is part of the official proceedings, the royalists' presence and presentations have no official status, they are entirely self-motivated and self-organized. Indeed, it is the willingness, *regularly and voluntarily*, to undertake the discomforts of travelling and standing for hours in the vagaries of the British climate that constitutes their definition of a 'real royalist'.

The total number of people sharing the royalists' practices is difficult to calculate with any certainty. As they are not part of any formal organization there is no register of interested people. Consequently, their association with each other is based on the friendship networks that develop out of encounters with like-minded people at royal visits. Attendance at these events necessitates travelling to another part of the country, resulting in links being established between people who live at a distance from one another. Friendships are developed and maintained through letters and telephone calls in which information is exchanged and arrangements made to meet together at future events. Through involvement with the network of my key informant, 'Dan', a single man in his late forties, I met around sixty royalists who regularly travelled the country. In addition there were others that I encountered only once, as well as people I never met, but heard about in the royalists' stories, or who featured in media reports. It is, therefore, likely that there are other networks in existence, as well as other individuals who do not wish to be part of any grouping, however informally constituted.

Although only a small group in relation to the total population of Britain and even as a proportion of the crowds at royal events, the real royalists are representative of more widespread sentiments. They often remark that 'many people feel like we do' and this is evident, not only among the crowds at royal visits, but in descriptions of public responses to large-scale ceremonials such as the Coronation (Shils and Young 1953), the Investiture of Prince Charles as Prince of Wales (Blumler et al. 1971) and the Queen's Silver Jubilee (Ziegler 1977). The most recent example of large-scale public involvement in royal ceremonial is provided by the public mourning for Diana Princess of Wales (Walter 1999).

The main tributes offered to the Princess in death, such as flowers and her own image, mirrored the kind of objects the royalists offered to her in life and, indeed, continue to offer to members of the royal family. In discussing the objects used by the public to express mourning, folklorists have recognized the expression of a vernacular religiosity. This is especially apparent in the use of flowers, images and candles to construct shrines to the dead Princess (Bowman 1999; Chandler 1999). Chandler also draws attention to 'an obvious parallel between the journey to Kensington Palace Gates [the home of the Princess] and the purposive journey to some sacred place which is the core of most pilgrimage' (Chandler 1999: 150). In addition to Kensington Palace other sites of pilgrimage in central London included St James's Palace, where the body of the Princess lay in state, Westminster Abbey, where her funeral was held, and Buckingham Palace, the site most closely associated with royalty. The point I wish to draw from this is that the vernacular religiosity apparent in the mourning for Diana is paralleled in the practices of the real royalists. They also abandon their daily routine to undertake pilgrimages to sites temporarily made sacred by the presence of royalty, to make offerings of flowers and other small gifts. Like the images taken home by traditional pilgrims, the royalists' photographs 'are a way of bringing home something of the charisma of a special location' (Coleman and Elsner 1995: 220) or of a special person. In displaying these pictures in their homes often alongside other royal memorabilia, the royalists construct domestic shrines that, like traditional pilgrimage images and tokens, not only provide proof that the experience took place, but also 'help to reconstruct the sacred journey in the imagination' (Coleman and Elsner 1995: 6). Dan often told me how, when sitting at home looking at his pictures, he relived his meetings with the royals. He was also fully aware that in displaying these items he was making a strong statement of identity. It was his proud declaration that 'anyone who comes through my front door can see right away that I am a royalist'.

Standing among the crowds at royal visits, however, this identity is not so clearly stated. In common with religious pilgrims, the individuals and groups who make

Figure 1.2 'Photographs as Pilgrimage Tokens'. Photograph: Anne Rowbottom

up the crowd may interpret the reasons for their participation in varied ways. The issue for the royalists as members of the crowd is to establish their identity as 'real royalists'. As Eade and Sallnow note of pilgrimage, what is taking place here needs to be understood 'not merely as a field of social relations, but also as a realm of competing discourses' (Eade and Sallnow 1991: 5). In this realm one of the strategies employed by Dan and his friends is to take albums of their photographs with them on royal visits. Looking through these albums not only allows the reliving of shared experiences with their friends, but in attracting the attention of those around them proclaims the presence of 'real royalists'. In this way the albums act as 'portable shrines', supporting their narrative of a special devotion to and familiar relationship with royalty.

Religiosity is not restricted to objects, but is also apparent in the royalists' accounts of a transcendent experience. They refer to the feeling of belonging to something greater than their own individuality when they are in the presence of royalty. Dan, who had met the Queen on many occasions, described it in these words, 'Unless you have experienced it you can't understand it. Whenever I stand in front of the Queen, or any member of the royal family I am always filled with such feelings of loyalty and pride in being British.' Jennifer, who had also met the Queen on numerous occasions told me, 'I go to see the royals because I admire the royal family and the institution of monarchy and because the royal family represent Britain. When I speak to a royal I feel happy, exhilarated. It is a very emotional experience and I am often on the verge of tears.' The experience of belonging to something greater than themselves was supported by the others. When Dan described his feelings, as often happened, other royalists present would confirm that they too had this experience.

In describing the meaning their activities held for them, the royalists invariably make an association with 'Britain', or with 'being British', the most common kind of statements being, 'The monarchy means Britain', or 'Basically, its about being British'. To date, devolution has not weakened the royalist's identification with Britain as a United Kingdom. In elaborating on what being British meant to him, Dan told me 'I always realize how lucky we are to live in a country like this with a monarchy, with such traditions, heritage and customs which a lot of British people take for granted. People from abroad love to see the royal family and experience the pomp and pageantry of Britain. I wouldn't live anywhere else.' Pride in Britain, idealized as a green and pleasant land with worthy institutions, heritage and traditions, is common among the royalists. A strong belief in the royal family as the symbol and guarantee of this ideal is evident in a statement made by Marjorie, a married woman in her sixties: 'The monarchy is part of this country, its part of the history and part of today and it will be part of the future, I hope. Over the last twenty to thirty years we have lost our colonies, our industries and our British passports have been replaced by European ones, we have lost almost everything.

If we lose the royal family what is there? We are just an island with some people on it with nothing to say we are British.' The equation of the monarchy with the nation is not an idiosyncratic one. Michael Billig, in an analysis of conversations about the royal family recorded in sixty-three English households, also found expressions of belief in the monarchy as the guarantee of national identity (Billig 1992). As Billig notes, 'In the equation of the monarchy and nation, there is a claim to a deeper level – everyday life might continue, but, at another level, England/Britain would no longer be itself' (1992: 33). The equation is not culturally insignificant. What the royalists express as a personal experience echoes the official ideology of the civil religion of the British nation state.

Civil Religion

Civil religion is a sociological concept which has been defined as 'any set of beliefs and rituals, related to the past, present, and/or future of a people ('nation') which are understood in some transcendental fashion' (Hammond 1976: 171). The concept describes practices intended to generate loyalty to a particular nation state (Bocock 1985) in ways which transcend the boundaries of difference within a nation. Transcendence, integration and loyalty are said to be generated through public ceremonies designed to promote national unity and social cohesion (Bellah 1967). Civil religion is religious, therefore, in the Durkheimian sense of putting people in touch with the transcendent, through an engagement with symbols and ceremonies. It is also religious in the sense of providing 'a plausible myth of the ordering of existence' (Clark and Hoover 1997:17). In heterogeneous and highly differentiated societies, the concept of civil religion proposes a religious form through which national unity can be given expression. It also 'proposes a basis for the relationship of the individual to the larger modern society' (McGuire 1992: 184). In the United Kingdom, where the sovereign is constitutionally the Head of State, Supreme Governor of the Church of England and the living symbol of national unity (COI 1983: 10; Morrah 1958: 41), the monarchy retains its traditional role as the constitutional, religious and symbolic centre of the nation. Public appearances of members of the royal family, which are surrounded by ceremonial, form a central component in the official civil religion of the British nation state (Bocock 1985; cf. Thompson 1986; Blumler et al. 1971).

The extent to which any religion, civil or orthodox, can provide a 'sacred canopy' (Berger 1967) able to integrate all the complex elements of a modern society is 'not wholly convincing' (Turner 1991: 58). In a contemporary pluralist society it would be surprising if everyone interpreted and experienced a complex social phenomenon such as the monarchy in the same way. As Eade and Sallnow (1991) show with regard to pilgrimage, rather than marginalizing or suppressing hetero-geneity it is more productive to develop a new agenda which recognizes religion as an arena of competing discourses. Therefore, rather than making exaggerated claims for the integrative function of civil religion, I view it as a particular *discourse* on national unity. As this is put into the public domain through the agencies of the state, it constitutes an *official* discourse in which the monarch acts as the symbol and the guarantee of British identity. That this is a dominant discourse is evident in the way a competing discourse, such as republicanism, is characterized as one of opposition to an established norm. This position is explicitly acknowledged by the publishers of Hitchens' (1990) republican pamphlet, 'The Monarchy', where the contents are stated as expressing the voice of dissent and challenging the dominant values of our time. More recently an implicit acknowledgement of this can be seen in Merck (1998) where sceptical commentaries on the death of Diana Princess of Wales are subtitled 'Irreverent Elegies'. As with Hitchins, deliberate irreverence in refusing to respect the norm may offer a challenge, but at the same time carries an acknowledgement of its weaker position. At the end of the 1990s the discourse of republicanism remained, as it did at the start of the decade, a voice of dissent against the continuing legitimacy of the monarchy.

Competing discourses are also to be found within the civil religion. The Queen may provide 'the living symbol of national unity' (COI 1983: 10), but as her position at the apex of society is premised on hierarchy, the monarchy also provides a means of categorizing people into the socially superior and the socially inferior (Hayden 1987: 5). The monarchy may symbolize unity, but at the same time it emphasizes difference. Unity and difference are the contradiction at the heart of the constitutional monarchy and provide the major categories of the discourse on the monarchy. They do not, of course, exhaust the discursive complexity that surrounds the institution, discussion of which is beyond the scope and the intent of the present chapter. What I want to focus on here is how the royalists neutralize the conflict of these major categories by switching between them and how, in doing so, affirm and reaffirm their 'special' relationship with the royal family.

Framing Events

Acknowledgement of difference provides the royalists with the knowledge that guides their actions as royalists, setting limitations on what is and what is not possible. Difference provides them with their primary interpretive framework (Goffman 1974). Within this framing it is axiomatic that the royal family represent the nation by virtue of their traditional status at the apex of the social hierarchy. Acknowledgement of difference is evident in the royalists' description of the Queen and the royal family as being worthy of 'respect and admiration' because they are 'very special people'. In contrast they describe themselves as 'ordinary people' who are privileged to be able to speak with and give gifts to the royal family. The complexity of the relationship between difference and unity can be seen in the

observation by Newby (1975) that deference, when based on affective identification, may be perceived by the socially inferior as part of a partnership in a
cooperative enterprise. This perception can be seen in the way the royalists, in
elaborating on the meaning of their own activities, switch from the frame of
difference to the frame of unity. Marjorie, for example, maintained that 'by going
on royal visits, being interested in royalty and talking about them I believe I am
helping to actually keep the monarchy in the country'. The perception of partnership is also evident in the way the royalists view their activities. They describe
themselves as providing 'a familiar face in the crowd', with whom the royals can
'hold a friendly conversation', or 'share a laugh and a joke' about previous
encounters. In this way the royalists see themselves as lightening the burden of
greeting hundreds of strangers who are often 'overawed and tongue-tied' in
the unfamiliar presence of royalty. Through these and similar statements Marjorie
and her friends rhetorically frame themselves as engaged in a joint enterprise with
the royal family to maintain the monarchy and so secure the 'special' identity of
Britain.

As with all rhetorical framing, the royalists' understanding of their relationship
to the monarchy and the nation is heavily dependent upon the cooperation of others,
in this instance the royal family. In securing their cooperation the royalists utilize
the conventions of gift-giving in which offering a gift invokes a cultural obligation
to receive (Mauss 1990 [1950]). For the royalist donors a gracious acceptance
reaffirms their view of the royal recipient as being worthy of respect and admiration.
It also confirms that, as their presence is welcome, they are making a contribution
to the maintenance of the monarchy and the nation. The situation is not without
its dangers as, conversely, the rejection of a gift would threaten their beliefs and
the value invested in their practices. Cooperation by the royal family is therefore
essential to the maintenance of the royalists' beliefs and practices. Although
this is usually forthcoming there are exceptions. The following section describes
how one royalist transformed a potentially meaning-threatening experience by
constructing an account in which she switches between the frames of unity and
difference.

A Transformative Account

One cold winter afternoon I stood with five royalists around the midpoint of a
walkabout by Diana Princess of Wales. Three of the royalists, two middle-aged
women and one young man, had brought flowers, the other two, a young woman
and an older man, had each brought framed photographs of the Princess which
they had taken at a previous meeting. The young woman, 'Beth', was a little worried
that, because her photograph was very slightly out of focus, it might not be of
sufficiently good quality to offer to the Princess. The others, after admiring the

gilt frame in which the photograph had been placed, assured Beth that the Princess would like it. The walkabout began and proceeded according to everyone's expectations with the Princess shaking hands with as many people as possible and accepting gifts in her usual friendly way. However, when she reached Beth the following exchange took place:

Princess: Is that for me?
Beth: I'm afraid so.
Princess: Afraid so? Why don't you . . . Will you keep that? I've got plenty of pictures.
Beth: Are you sure?
Princess: Yes. You keep that.
Beth: Is it that bad?
Princess: It isn't that bad. No. I can look in the mirror if I want pictures. You keep that.
Beth: Whatever you say Ma'am.
Princess: You keep that.

The Princess then moved on, accepting gifts from others in the same way as before. Because the Princess was always held to be a warm, friendly and caring person, her response to Beth appeared as unusual as it was unexpected. Consequently, the royalists were presented with a meaning-threatening experience that required an explanation that would restore their fundamental assumptions. Immediately after the Princess had left, 'Patricia', one of the middle-aged women, began to develop her explanation of what had taken place.

Patricia began by stating in a puzzled and somewhat shocked tone: 'The Princess didn't take Beth's photograph did she? Poor Beth, she must be very upset. I don't understand why it wasn't accepted, do you? Perhaps she didn't take it because it was in a frame and she thought it was too expensive for her to accept from a member of the public.' In explaining the difficulty that might arise over an expensive gift, Patricia stressed the necessity of remembering that, however friendly the Princess might be, she was a member of the royal family. As royalty do not usually accept gifts from ordinary members of the public, it was a privilege to be able to offer them things and, therefore, in order to keep this privilege it was important not to seem presumptuous. Inexpensive items, such as flowers, or unframed photographs were appropriate, but more expensive items were not, as these might seem to presume too close a relationship. Patricia's worry was that if some royalists were perceived as being overly familiar with the royal family, then they might stop accepting gifts from the public altogether. On reflection, however, Patricia realized that as the Princess had accepted a framed photograph from another royalist, her explanation required modification.

Patricia then tried to construct an explanation around Beth's physical appearance, noting that, as Beth was not very tall and of slight build, people regularly thought her to be much younger than her nineteen years. Therefore, she reasoned, it was perfectly possible that the Princess had also assumed Beth to be much younger than her actual age. If so, perhaps the Princess thought that, unlike the adults around her, Beth could not afford to give a photograph in a frame and this was why she asked Beth to keep it. It was also possible, Patricia continued, that if the Princess had thought of Beth as a child, she may have thought she was merely being shown something that a young girl valued and had not realized it was being offered as a gift. Perhaps Beth had held it out in too hesitant a manner, suggesting to the Princess that it was being shown, rather than offered to her. In support of this, Patricia reasoned that the Princess could have understood Beth's 'I'm afraid so' in response to her own question 'Is that for me?' to mean that the photograph was something with which Beth was reluctant to part, rather than intended as an apology for offering a slightly blurred picture.

That the refusal had been kindly meant was evident, Patricia thought, by the pleasant and friendly manner of the Princess towards Beth. The photograph may not have been accepted, but there had been nothing nasty in the way it was refused. It was as if the Princess, knowing that Beth valued the picture, had wanted her to keep it for herself. Consequently, Patricia reasoned, Beth should not be embarrassed or distressed by what had taken place. Finally she went on to suggest that the photograph had now acquired something extra special as, in saying to Beth 'you keep that', it was as if the photograph had become a gift from the Princess to Beth herself.

Discussion

In constructing her interpretation Patricia transformed a potentially meaning-threatening encounter into something that restored her understanding of the character of the Princess and her relationship with the royalists. Goffman, describes this as 'remedial work', an activity motivated by the possibility that there has been a deliberate intention to cause offence. That is to say, in constructing her account Patricia understood the possibility of 'interpretations of the act that maximise either its offensiveness to others or its defaming implications for the actor himself [*sic*]' (Goffman 1972: 138–9). The task that Patricia had undertaken was to prevent a possible or, in Goffman's terminology, a *virtual* offence becoming an *actual* one. The problem she faced is that the potential offensiveness in the action of the Princess lay in the way it turned the logic of the gift against the royalists. In refusing the photograph the Princess could be seen as denying the relationship assumed by Beth and possibly, by association, all those who shared her practices. This possibility is apparent in an interpretation given by Woodhead (1991), a television producer who saw video footage of the encounter between the Princess and Beth. Writing in a travel magazine, Woodhead described the refusal of Beth's photograph as a rare occasion when the Princess bent under the strain of the royalists' attentions which at times, he suggests, 'must be more than the royals can bear' (Woodhead 1991: 15). Woodhead's interpretation illustrates some of the discursive complexity that surrounds the monarchy and which facilitates competing interpretations of the same events. In common with the royalists he invokes unity by identifying with the Princess and lays claim to understand what motivated her action. He uses the discourse of difference to position the royalists as being extraordinary not only in the level of their attentions, but also in their inability to see, as Woodhead claims the Princess did, that their presence was a nuisance rather than a support. From the royalists' perspective this is the worst possible interpretation of what had taken place. It threatens to undermine the basis on which the identity of the 'real royalists' rests and it is precisely this threat that Patricia's remedial work sought to avoid confirming.

According to Goffman, motive and intent are significant factors in determining whether an offence has actually taken place, but only the potential or virtual offender has direct knowledge of these. Usually, clarification can be sought from or is volunteered by the virtual offender (Goffman 1972). In this case, however, the social difference between the protagonists is such that the Princess could not be asked to justify her behaviour. Instead Patricia had to interpret what took place and render it safe, within her existing interpretive frameworks. She proceeded by initially confirming that Beth's gift was the only one to be refused. This established that an offence *might* have taken place, but effectively located the problem within the parameters of a specific interaction, rather than as a response to the group as a whole. The rest of her explanation could then concentrate on the circumstances peculiar to this one encounter between the Princess and Beth.

Within these parameters Patricia's remedial work began in the interpretive framework of difference. The inequalities of relative social status were highlighted in the suggestion that, by offering an apparently expensive gift, Beth was claiming too close a relationship. In Patricia's account this transgression of the status boundaries not only weakened the obligation to receive (Mauss 1990 [1950]), but also meant that the Princess displayed the right relationship to the rules of the social order governing interactions between royalty and commoners. This achieved one aim of remedial work in respect of the Princess, insofar as it minimised the defaming implications for her moral character (Goffman 1972). It was not fully successful, however, as it retained the suggestion that there was a deliberate intent on the part of the Princess to assert her superior status and to remind everyone else of his or her relative inferiority. In avoiding the danger of confirming this negative possibility, Patricia's developing explanation then switched to the framework of unity.

In underestimating the age of Beth and seeing her as not much more than a young girl, Patricia constructed the Princess as being just like everyone else. Her behaviour was now to be understood in terms of what anyone would think and do.

In this framing, unity takes the form of royalty being just 'ourselves writ large' (Williamson 1986: 76) and their actions can be understood through the knowledge acquired in ordinary, everyday living (Billig 1992). Patricia's attribution of the actions of the Princess to an understandable and common mistake offered a mitigating claim common to remedial work, namely, that 'the circumstances were such as to make the act radically different from what it appears to have been' (Goffman 1972: 140). That is to say, having wrongly identified Beth as a young girl, the Princess behaved in a protective way, refusing to deprive her of an apparently treasured possession. In this way her actions were radically transformed. Rather than an assertion of social superiority, the action of the Princess becomes one that any responsible and sympathetic adult would adopt towards a young person. In this way Patricia could acknowledge the refusal of the gift as the act of a social superior but, by applying the norms of everyday life, the basis of the superior and inferior relationship was changed. Rather than royal and commoner, the relationship became that of adult and child in which the intent of the Princess was not a potentially disturbing assertion of social superiority, but a highly acceptable expression of protectiveness and concern towards a young person.

Finally, in effecting a closure of her account, Patricia returned to the frame of difference, constructing the Princess as an extraordinary person. Through contact with the Princess the photograph was invested with some of her charisma, and her graciousness in returning the picture to Beth re-established the worthiness of the Princess as an object of respect and admiration. The link between royalists, royalty, the monarchy and, ultimately, the nation was reconnected.

Concluding Remarks

Patricia's interpretation was constructed in a very different way from that of the American who provided the starting point for this chapter. Like the negative interpretations of constitutional monarchy made by the British republicans (Wilson 1989; Hitchens 1990; Hamilton 1975; Birnbaum 1955), the response of the American was constructed solely within the interpretive framework of difference. In contrast, Patricia negotiated the possibility of making a negative interpretation of monarchy by switching her explanation from the framework of difference to that of unity, and then back to difference again. Switching in this way allowed her to construct an account in which a potentially demeaning experience could be transformed into a reaffirmation of the relationship between the royalists, the monarchy and the nation. In much the same way, traditional religion and ritual – by switching from the ordinary to the extraordinary – effect a reaffirmation of relations between humans and between humans and gods. In this case by using difference and unity as alternative and relatively discrete frames of interpretation Patricia was able to negotiate the central paradox of constitutional monarchy and of the civil religion. In her remedial work Patricia was following the method widely used by the royalists when explaining the meaning their encounters with royalty hold for them. By using difference and unity as alternative interpretive frames the royalists avoid having to confront the contradictions between democracy and hierarchy inherent in the central symbol of the civil religion.

This process of negotiation is not without political significance given that the centrality of the royal family as the guarantee of national identity is fundamental to the discourse of the civil religion. The importance of understanding the way the larger population of Britain negotiates this official discourse is likely to increase as the British political structure undergoes a substantial change. The present political situation includes a movement not only towards greater European unity, but also to an internal devolving of government to the constituent nations of Great Britain. The outcome of these changes remains uncertain. One possibility is that the break-up of Britain as a unified nation state has begun, another is that a movement towards federalism will take place. Whatever the outcome, a crisis of national identity seems likely which promises to be especially acute in England, where 'British' and 'English' are often treated as synonymous. In this developing situation the existing form of civil religion, centring on the monarchy, will also be subject to change. It could provide the official symbol of a pan-British identity, or it could become a focus for the development of a separate English nationalism. Alternatively, of course, the monarchy could fail to provide an adequate symbol of a new national identity and be replaced by something different. In the context of Britain and its constitutional monarchy, the way these changes are working out provides a relevant topic for research. What I have tried to demonstrate in this paper is that in understanding the development of these processes the vernacular religiosity that surrounds the official discourse of the civil religion provides fertile ground for further exploration and theorizing.

References

Bellah, R. (1967) 'Civil Religion in America', *Daedalus* 96: 1–21.

Berger, P. (1967) *The Sacred Canopy: Elements of a Sociological Theory of Religion*, Garden City, N.Y.: Doubleday.

Billig, M. (1992) *Talking of the Royal Family*, London and New York: Routledge.

Birnbaum, N. (1955) 'Monarchs and Sociologists: A Reply to Professor Shils and Michael Young', *Sociological Review,* (ns) 3: 5–23.

Blumer, H. (1986 [1969]) *Symbolic Interactionism,* California and London: University of California Press.

Blumler, J.G., Brown, J.R., Ewbank, A.J., and Nossiter, T.J. (1971) 'Attitudes to the Monarchy: Their Structure and Development during a Ceremonial Occasion', *Political Studies,* 19: 149–71.

Bocock, R. (1985) 'Religion in Modern Britain', in R. Bocock and K. Thompson (eds) *Religion and Ideology*, Manchester: Manchester University Press.

Bowman, M. (1999) 'A Provincial City Shows Respect: Shopping and Mourning in Bath', in T. Walter (ed.) *The Mourning for Diana*, Oxford: Berg.

Buckley, A.D. and Kenney, M.C. (1995) *Negotiating Identity: Rhetoric, Metaphor, and Social Drama in Northern Ireland*, Washington and London: Smithsonian Institution Press.

Central Office of Information (COI). (1983) *The Monarchy in Britain,* London: HMSO. Reference Number 102/RP/83.

Chandler, J. (1999) 'Pilgrims and Shrines', in T. Walter (ed.) *The Mourning for Diana*, Oxford: Berg.

Clark, L.S. and Hoover, S.M. (1997) 'At the Intersection of Media, Culture, and Religion: A Bibliographic Essay', in S.M. Hoover and K. Lundby (eds) *Rethinking Media, Religion, and Culture,* Thousand Oaks, London and New Delhi: Sage.

Coleman, S. and Elsner, J. (1995) *Pilgrimage*: *Past and Present in the World Religions*, London: British Museum Press.

Douglas, M. (1966) *Purity and Danger*, London: Routledge & Kegan Paul.

Eade, J. and Sallnow, M. (1991) *Contesting The Sacred: The Anthropology of Christian Pilgrimage,* London: Routledge.

Goffman, E. (1972) *Relations in Public*, Harmondsworth: Penguin.

—— (1974) *Frame Analysis,* Harmondsworth: Penguin.

Hall, P. (1992) *Royal Fortune: Tax, Money and the Monarchy*, London: Bloomsbury.

Hamilton, W. (1975) *My Queen and I*, London: Quartet.

Hammond, P.E. (1976) 'The Sociology of American Civil Religion: A Bibliographical Essay', *Sociological Analysis* 37(2):169–82.

Haseler, S. (1993) *The End Of The House Of Windsor: Birth of a British Republic,* London and New York: I.B. Tauris.

Hayden, I. (1987) *Symbol and Privilege: The Ritual Context of British Royalty,* Tucson: University of Arizona Press.

Henley, P. and Rowbottom, A. (1993) *Faces In the Crowd,* Granada Centre for Visual Anthropology, University of Manchester.

—— (1997) *Royal Watchers,* Mosaic Productions for BBC Television, London.

Hitchens, C. (1990) *The Monarchy*, London: Chatto & Windus.

McGuire, M.B. (1992) *Religion: The Social Context,* California: Wadsworth.

Mauss, M. (1990 [1950]) *The Gift: The Form and Reason for Exchange in Archaic Societies*, translated by W.D. Halls, London: Routledge.

Merck, M. (ed.) (1998) *After Diana: Irreverent Elegies*, London: Verso.

Morrah, D. (1958) *The Work of the Queen,* London: William Kimber.

Nairn, T. (1988) *The Enchanted Glass: Britain and its Monarchy*, London: Radius and Century Hutchinson.

Newby, H. (1975) 'The Deferential Dialectic', *Comparative Studies in Society and History* 17: 139–64.

Rowbottom, A. (1994) *Royal Symbolism and Social Integration*, Unpublished PhD Thesis, University of Manchester.

—— (1998) '"The Real Royalists": Folk Performance and Civil Religion at Royal Visits', *Folklore,* vol. 109: 77–88.

—— (1999) 'A Bridge of Flowers', in T. Walter (ed.) *The Mourning for Diana*, Oxford: Berg.

Schwartz, B. (1967) 'The Social Psychology of the Gift,' *American Journal of Sociology* 73,1: 1–11.

Shils, E. and Young, M. (1953) 'The Meaning of the Coronation', *Sociological Review* (n.s.) 1: 63–81.

Thompson, D. (1998) 'Mourning for a Better Monarchy', in M. Merck (ed.) *After Diana: Irreverent Elegies*, London: Verso.

Thompson, K. (1986) *Beliefs and Ideology,* London and New York: Tavistock Publications.

Turner, B.S. (1991) *Religion and Social Theory*, 2nd edn, London: Sage.

Walter, T. (ed.) (1999) *The Mourning for Diana*, Oxford: Berg.

Williamson, J. (1986) *Consuming Passions,* London: Boyer.

Wilson, A.N. (1993) *The Rise and Fall Of The House Of Windsor*, London: Sinclair-Stevenson.

Wilson, E. (1989) *The Myth of the Monarchy,* London: Journeyman Press, and Republic.

Woodhead, L. (1991) 'What Sacred Bushes, Naked Men, and Royalty Have In Common', *European Travel and Life* September, 14–15.

Ziegler, P. (1977) *Crown and People*, London: Collins.

National Day: Achieving Collective Identity on the Isle of Man

Susan Lewis

The fifth of July – Tynwald Day[1] – and the weather looked more than promising. It was still only 9.30 in the morning, and the sun was already warming the air. A few early arrivals were chatting and laughing as they walked up the road toward the centre of the village of St John's, and as they crested the small rise the focus of the day's forthcoming activities came into view. Framed by a backdrop of green hills, and the dense trees of the National Arboretum, the Tynwald Hill, site of the annual open-air sitting of the Manx parliament, stood adorned with a white canopy. The top of this circular, tiered and grassy mound also boasted a great chair, awaiting the Lieutenant-Governor. Flagpoles lining the processional pathway to the facing church proudly flew the bright red Manx national flags with their three-legged emblem, and Manannan's rushes already lay on the path. Behind, the temporary grandstand gleamed in the sunshine, and on the Front Field members of one of the traditional dance groups were preparing for their performance, the women in their distinctive jackets of bright red and the men in traditional grey-brown loghtan wool. The scene was set for another Tynwald Day.

On Old Midsummer's Day each year, the people of the Isle of Man gather – as it is said they have for over a thousand years – to hear the Island's new laws read aloud in both English and the Island's Gaelic language. It is a day of pageantry, a day for meeting friends, a day of historical importance and cultural significance, but also a day of contested meanings. The long and unbroken history of the gathering is mixed with the relatively recent presence of the British Crown, and its ceremony carries widely differing significance for all those – Manx-born, '*stayover*', '*comeover*', Crown representative – who have a connection to the Island. This chapter aims to elaborate and understand this diversity of interpretation. It draws on the sights and sounds of the day, and the dialectic between the two. It also draws on the divergent views of those present and not present. As such, it demonstrates the complexities and contradictions of contemporary Manx society, and aims to explore how a society which has undergone a period of recent and significant social change might begin to 'manufacture' an inclusive nationalism which satisfies all 'interests' (Cohen 2000).

Susan Lewis

Historical Introduction

The Isle of Man is situated midway between England and Ireland, in the centre of the Irish Sea. It is some 32 miles long by 13 miles wide, and covers an area of some 227 square miles. It has a landscape of amazing contrasts for an island of such relatively small size – low-lying, willow-edged fields in the north, a backbone of high moorland slopes, wooded river glens, rolling hills, and rugged cliffs at its southernmost tip. Four main towns all but mark the cardinal points; Douglas in the east serves as the modern capital, with Ramsey to the north. The ancient Norse capital of Peel guards the west coast, and its one-time successor Castletown, with its fine medieval castle, dominates the south. St John's, site of the National Day, lies at the heart of the Island, and other villages and hamlets pepper its valleys, a reminder of the Island's now diminished farming industry. The fishing fleets, too, have all but disappeared and tourism, which once provided healthy revenues, succumbed to the pressures of package holidays to sunnier climes in the 1950s. Faced with economic crisis, since the 1960s the Island's governments have created the fiscal conditions for the development of an offshore – now 'international' – finance industry. The population has grown, and today a third of the Island's current population of more than seventy thousand residents live in and around Douglas, the focus of that new and economically successful venture.[2]

Of Mann's earliest social history, tales are told of how Manannan, son of the Irish god Lír, made his home on the Island and gave it his name. He would hide the Island from potential invaders by bringing down a mist to obscure it from view, and ruled over the Manx until, in the fifth century, the Christian monks of St Patrick arrived to convert the pagan Celts. Today, it is 'Manannan' who guides visitors around the many heritage sites, and thus through the remainder of the Island's story: of how Mann came under the suzerainty of the Norse kings in the latter part of the eighth century, and of how the great king Godred Crovan took the Island in 1079; of its great hero Illiam Dhone, who surrendered the Island to Cromwell's Parliamentary forces in 1651, in return for retention of the Island's 'laws and liberties' (Kniveton 1997: 26); of its period of prosperity when the millworkers of Lancashire came as tourists, and of the dedicated men and women who worked to save the Gaelic language and folklore for future generations.

The rule of Godred Crovan was a golden age in Manx history, as the Island became the centre of an empire of 'Mann and the Isles': the Island's current political and legal structures are largely based on the Norse systems of this time.[3] The Crovan dynasty ruled until defeated by the Scots in 1266, and between 1290 and 1405 the Manx people suffered the consequences of the ongoing battle between Scotland and the English Crown. Henry IV finally granted the Island to Sir John Stanley, for payment to each succeeding British monarch of *'two falcons on the days of their coronations'*. The Stanley family, and later the Dukes of Atholl, ruled as Kings or Lords of Man until the 1765 *Act of Revestment* returned the Island to the British Crown. This move, which perhaps signals the beginning of 'colonial rule', was a response to customs revenues lost to the British exchequer due to the success of the enterprising Manx 'running trade'.

Although much of its political autonomy was lost after 1765, this has been won back through careful negotiation over the last 150 years.[4] Tynwald now has full responsibility for internal and taxation affairs, and the Island retains its own legal system. Since 1990, the Lieutenant-Governor no longer presides over the Tynwald Court,[5] but because it is a British Crown Dependency, the Island's foreign affairs and 'good government' remain the ultimate responsibility of the UK government. The Island is not part of the United Kingdom, and has no elected representation at Westminster. It also remains outside the European Union, but 'inside' the Community for trade and customs purposes.[6] Its anomalous situation, being at the same time at the geographic heart of the British Isles while 'outside' the political and economic body, is perhaps the major contributory factor to the Island's social and cultural predicament and potential.

The Tynwald Ceremony stands as a symbol both of continuity and of change; of colonial rule but also of retained independence. The extracts that follow are drawn from the three Tynwald ceremonies of 1998 to 2000, and the accompanying analyses will focus on both official representations and unofficial, or personal, reflections on the meaning of the Isle of Man's National Day.

The Tynwald Ceremony

As the starting time for the Ceremony approached, the grandstand started to fill, and the seated audience looked down on the green expanse of the Front Field with its gathering crowds. The ladies of the Manx Folk Dance Society weaved in and out of a complex jig. Hundreds of people jostled for position along the retaining wall of the processional pathway, keen to gain a good view. Further back, others wandered at leisure around the field, or in and out of the Homecomer's Tent, or played with children, or sat on the grass having an early snack, paying little attention to the 'goings on' near the grandstand. Perhaps they seen it all before, or were here for the atmosphere, to meet friends, or for the 'family day out'?

A commentary began. The military band took over from the fiddles and whistles, and a clear Manx-accented voice began with a 'history' of the Tynwald Day and its ceremony.[7]

If you are here this morning because you've been coming to the Tynwald Ceremony each year for as long as you can remember, you'll have a pretty good idea, probably without being told, of what's going to happen, and of course, we can't rewrite the history books.

The fact that so many people feel the need to come to the Tynwald Ceremony each year is a measure of the importance people attach to it. In the days when travel was less easy than it is now people used to meet friends here that they didn't see from one Tynwald Day to the next. They maybe still do.

So, why is it so important to Manx people? Well, it's the annual open-air sitting of the Isle of Man Parliament, the Tynwald Court, over one thousand years old and said to be the oldest parliamentary assembly in the world. The Vikings started it, as they did in many other places as well, but Tynwald is the only one that survives in the form that it was established. Basically, what we are to see here today is what separates the Isle of Man from the United Kingdom.

The commentator continued, sketching for his listeners the story of the British Crown's involvement, explaining the presence of a Lieutenant-Governor, or links to other parliaments elsewhere.[8] Then, as scheduled, and with the precision demanded by the 'meticulous planning' of state ritual (Cannadine 1992: 134), at 10.38 a.m. the Lieutenant-Governor arrived, alighting from his car to a fanfare. Dressed in a black uniform and a hat with impressive white plumes, he worked his way along a line of hand-shaking. The planned flypast by four RAF Hawk jets then entertained the assembled crowd, to the accompaniment of their laughter on learning from the commentator that the pilots were students, and that on previous years not all the expected aircraft had *"actually arrived"*. After the playing of the British National Anthem, the Lieutenant-Governor inspected the assembled military guard of British troops, and laid a wreath at the foot of the Island's War Memorial. As he then withdrew to the robing room, the commentary continued:

> The annual assembly was a place to proclaim the law and to punish those who broke it. Today, over 1,000 years later, the legislative part of this still remains, and we shall be hearing all the new laws passed by Tynwald in the last twelve months summarized in Manx as well as English. The whole ceremony is now quite unique in the world.

> For something as old as the Tynwald ceremony it's not surprising that all sorts of traditional customs have become associated with it. Like the Isle of Man and its people they're a mixture of Celtic and Norse, Christian and Pagan. One such Pagan tradition is the laying of the green rushes on the pathway leading to Tynwald Hill. In early times they would have been laid on Midsummer Eve, as a tribute to the great sea-god Manannan. One of the more obvious Christian traditions is that a church would always be built at the place of assembly, wherever that was.

Following the ecumenical service in the Chapel of St. Johns, the dignitaries processed along the connecting pathway to the Tynwald Hill, behind the Manx Sword of State. The Lieutenant-Governor led the celebrants, and took his place at the top of the hill, as representative of the 'Lord of Man'.[9] Resplendent in blue and gold robes and white wig, the President of Tynwald followed, and seated himself beside the Lieutenant-Governor. The members of the Legislative Council, the 'upper house', took their allocated spaces at the rear of the top tier, and the popularly elected Members of the Keys theirs on the tier below. Other officers of the Tynwald Court[10] followed. On the lowest tier, similarly attired in morning dress, were seated the Captains of the Parishes, with guests and visitors forming an audience around the base of the mound.

The Ceremony got under way. Officials 'fenced the court', declaring it a place of safety for the period the court is in session (Kinvig 1975 [1944]: 76). The Lieutenant-Governor pronounced the proceedings open, and the bewigged Deemsters, or legal officers, prepared to read the laws in both English and Manx Gaelic. All Acts of Tynwald must be promulgated on Tynwald Hill within eighteen months of enactment – pronounced for all to hear – or else they cease to have effect. These laws were at one time read from Tynwald Hill in full detail but for speed now are summarized; once the Deemsters had finished, the petitioners for future legislative changes were granted their traditional entrance to the Processional Way, and duly presented their '*Petitions for Redress of Grievance*' at the foot of the Hill. The Manx National Anthem was sung (with perhaps more enthusiasm than that of the United Kingdom?) and, once the Bishop had given his blessing,

Figure 2.1 The Tynwald Ceremony. Officials and guests of the Tynwald Court are seated on the Hill, while the people observe from the grandstand and the front Field. Photograph: Sue Lewis

Figure 2.2 The traditional dance group *Perree Bane* (Manx Gaelic for 'white jackets', referring to the men's costume) performing in the Fair Field after the Ceremony. Photograph: Sue Lewis

the Ceremony came to an end. The official attendees filed off the tiered Hill, and returned along the rush-strewn pathway. And as the members of the Court entered the church to participate in a sitting of Tynwald,[11] the audience also filed down from their seats on the shining grandstand, ready to enjoy whatever entertainments the rest of the day had to offer.

A wealth of opportunities beckoned. Behind the grandstand, the Fair Field was packed with stalls. The colours of the candy-striped awnings, the different aromas, the buzz of voices, all mingled with the sights and sounds of folk dancers whirling around to the sounds of traditional music. The police dog-handlers prepared to give their display. There were exhibition tents to visit, homemade teas to consume, raffles to enter, an evening concert and ceilidh to anticipate – and all-day access to the public houses to exploit. And, above all, there was the opportunity for friends to catch up on the *skeet* – the gossip.

Perspectives

The Tourist

For the tourist, Tynwald Day is surely a quaint and curious custom. As they sit in the grandstand – 'that's for the tourists', I'd been told – they have a commanding view of the whole scene. 'So where's this hill, then?' from one. Laughter as her friends pointed to the tiered mound to their right. 'Those poor soldiers, in this heat', sympathized another. They comment on the weather, on the regimental bands, on the outfits of those who pass by in the parade. They jostle for the best view of the dignitaries, and stumble through the hymns. They listen to the history of this long-standing custom, and enjoy the sheer pageantry of it. And, after the Ceremony, they eat lunch and wander around the stalls of the accompanying Fair. For them, then, a day of colourful experiences and curios.

A Day off Work

For centuries people have attended Tynwald Day not just to witness the parliamentary proceedings but also to meet with friends they may not have seen since the previous year. It is an important day, socially as well as symbolically; perhaps therefore surprisingly it is not officially a National Holiday. However, many companies do treat it as such. That said, the vast majority of the Island's residents are not interested in attending or participating in the event, and for them the 'National Day' simply offers an extra day away from work. This response is as likely to be found among the Manx-born as among incomers. One young man from an old Manx farming family told me he had never been to Tynwald, and had no interest in going. He would rather spend the day at the beach or in the mountains, with friends and away from the crowds. He added that although he would not wish Manx traditions to disappear, he felt it was good that people were becoming '. . . more the same. Many non-Manx have made a home here now, and it has to be their Island too'.

Colonialist Overtones

A woman of Manx birth explained that she had not been to Tynwald since returning to the Island after years of working away. Its colonialist overtones, she said, made her feel uncomfortable. She added that of course she was aware that the Ceremony was based on that which dated back over a thousand years, but for her it had been 'taken over' and 'colonialised' in a way she found both upsetting and distasteful. She referred to the playing of the two national anthems, arguing that the British anthem was played more often than the Manx. Whether or not this is actually the case, her example is merely a focus for her feelings that the dominant power here is that of the Crown and Westminster. By staying away she made her own silent protest, at the cost of missing that which remained of the very Manx tradition of using this day to share stories of the past year.

Nationalist Feelings

When asked his feelings about the 'National Day', a member of the Island's nationalist party, Mec Vannin, responded thus: 'The Tynwald ceremony is, perhaps, the most concise expression of the schizophrenic, colonially subverted mentality that pervades Manx society and most particularly, government . . . From Victorian times until the 1950s, the Hill was topped by a huge Union flag, despite the fact that Mannin has never been part of the United Kingdom. This stamp of colonial subjugation made a total mockery of the notion of independent government . . . The Ceremony has, since Norse times, been presided over by the ruler of Mannin or their deputy, which increasingly meant it was presided over by a governor . . . the Island was acquired by the British Crown in 1765, and since then the Tynwald Ceremony was always presided over by the Crown's Lieutenant-Governor on behalf of the absentee landlord . . . How important is Tynwald Day to the Manx nation? From a nationalist point of view, it is very important as a public assertion of independence, but to the vast majority of people here, it's simply a day off. It's not even an official public holiday!'

A Sales Opportunity

Among the charity stalls and food stands in the Fair Field were mingled tents that sheltered be-suited businessmen plying their corporate trade. Some days prior to Tynwald, a broadcaster on the Island's radio station had asked the Head of the Tynwald Committee if three-legged races were quite the order for today's Tynwalds. Surely Tynwald Day was THE day on which to showcase the Island? Rather, shouldn't they be encouraging the big firms now present on the Island to provide displays – so the Island could present itself to itself – rather than just being a 'good day out'? The Committee member had politely rejected the suggestion. Tynwald Day would retain its role as a meeting place, and not become a market place.

"I've No Objection"

The subject of who should preside at the Tynwald Ceremony has been the subject of some debate over recent years, particularly since many of the Lieutenant-Governor's executive powers have been transferred to the Manx legislature, and calls for greater or even complete independence have increased. When asked her opinion about whether or not the Queen's representative should preside at Tynwald, one Manx-born woman replied, 'I've no objection. After all, she is Lord of Man, and I'm happy to accept that'.

The Captain's View

Each of the 'parishes' in the Isle of Man has a 'Captain', whose duties today are mainly ceremonial. In 1999, much of the responsibility for the success of the day's 'added extras' fell to the Captain of the parish in which St John's falls: organizing the parish ladies to prepare and serve the endless cups of tea and plates of cakes, mustering the collectors of litter at the end of the day, finding lights for the ceilidh when darkness fell and the dancers could no longer see one another. From greeting the Lieutenant-Governor in his frock coat and top hat in the morning to passing the time of day with friends of long standing in the afternoon, he had been aware of both the foregrounded pageantry and background organization. This, too, had been the first Tynwald in many a year which aimed to offer more and extended entertainments to the crowd, encouraging people to stay for the whole afternoon and evening and enjoy the festivities. The Captain summed up his feelings, as he stood in the tent that evening, watching the dancers: 'this was a **real** Fair Day'.

"We Can't Rewrite the History Books"

'. . . and, of course, we can't rewrite the history books', the commentator had said. E. H. Carr in his famous lecture *'What is History?'* questioned that very point, concluding that history was 'an unending dialogue between the present and the past' (Carr 1964: 30). The ceremony's commentary had gone on to inform those assembled that Tynwald Day has survived, little changed, for more than a thousand years. What dialogue, therefore, was being presented here? If not an invention of 'tradition', à la Hobsbawm (1992: 1*ff*) – for the open-air sitting of the Manx parliament is clearly not a product of the last two hundred years – might it be the acting out of a 'custom' of unchanging, unchallengeable right to self-government? A subtle reminder to those gathered – Manx-born, more recently arrived residents, visitors and, most particularly perhaps, the representatives of the United Kingdom government – that this legislature had been in place long before the arrival of the colonial administrators, and would be here long after they had left? Played out in the calm assuredness of punctual pageantry, was there perhaps an element of defiance in the continuance of this ceremony? After all, Iceland had abandoned its open-air sitting of its parliament, the Althing, as far back as 1800. What, therefore, is its continued purpose, beyond being simply a 'good day out'?

Certainly a brief look at the subtle changes to the Ceremony that have evolved over the last few decades of the twentieth century might give evidence to some overarching message. Until the 1950s, the Union Flag would fly atop the Hill's canopy. That has now been replaced by the Manx flag. The Manx National Anthem now has the same prominence in the Ceremony as the United Kingdom National Anthem, and there are suggestions that in the future the President of Tynwald may preside, in place of the Lieutenant-Governor. All of which might be seen to complement consecutive Manx governments' stated objective to 'promote and continue the evolution of the constitutional relationship between the Isle of Man and the United Kingdom towards 'more complete self-government' in accordance with the declared and accepted policy of the United Kingdom for the self-determination of the peoples of dependent territories' (Solly 1994: 99).

For those who find it difficult to attend the Ceremony, the colonial trappings – the Lieutenant-Governor presiding, the playing of the United Kingdom National Anthem, the presence of the grey British battleship in Douglas harbour during Tynwald week, the British troops – all serve to make the Ceremony a reaffirmation of colonial power, rather than a stand against it. An overlying, then, of 'invented tradition' on existing custom? As Hobsbawm confirms, tracing 'where such traditions are partly invented, partly evolved' (op. cit.: 4) is a difficult task. Comparison of today's Ceremony with illustrations from Tynwald Days of previous centuries leaves a clear impression of an increase in both pageantry and formality; a change that might indeed be linked to the nineteenth-century 'colonial' period of increased control by Westminster. The precision of the ritual, the mode of formal dress, the uniforms, would certainly all fit with Hobsbawms's description of symbolic trappings (op.cit.: 4), or with an analysis of 'events-of-presentation' that 'display social order quite as their creators understand this – as determinate images that mirror collective or elite perceptions of what the mind-sets and the feeling states of participants ought to be' (Handelman 1990: 79). Yet the accompanying Fair and numerous entertainments, the subtle but significant changes in the ceremonial, along with overt statements present in the commentary, do speak of a 'resistance' to such social ordering. How then, does this Ceremony and its associated entertainments work as a symbol of the Island's uniqueness, and can they now absorb the changes of recent years to become a symbol of a new collective identity?

A Symbol that Separates?

The commentator asked us to ponder on why this day was so important to Manx people: 'what we see here today is what separates the Isle of Man from the United Kingdom'. The nationalist, whose perspective on the Ceremony is outlined above, demonstrates clearly the internal contradictions. For him, it both makes a 'mockery of independent government' and acts as a 'public assertion of independence'. His statement serves also as a reference to the contradictions in the wider social, cultural and political environment. The Island is not politically 'independent', yet control over its own affairs continues to increase. That said, the finance industry, with its global outlook, must be constantly courted if it is to remain on the Island.

For many people, however, such economic success has been achieved at a cultural and social cost. An old lady had complained to me of the 'dilution' of the Manx and their way of life. The influx of new ideas, the influx of new people, had all contributed to a loss of 'Manx-ness'. This was a loss that seemed to blur not only the social and cultural boundaries between the Island and 'the adjacent island', but more importantly for that lady and others like her, boundaries within the Island itself. Concerns have been expressed in terms of loss of the local accent, of the importation of 'foreign' customs such as Hallowe'en, which has all but supplanted the Manx *Hop-tu-naa*, and in a lack of knowledge of or interest in Manx history and culture on the part of those who have moved to the Island.

The fear, then, is of a disappearing culture. More positively, however, I would argue that here we are witnessing elements of what Paine terms 'cultural compression' (Paine 1992: 190ff). Rather than disappearing under the weight of an imported 'English' alternative, aspects of Manx culture are being maintained, and are in a process of creative reselection from a range of cultural resources that seeks to reassert the Island's cultural distinctiveness. It is a reselection that has the possibility to work both ways, allowing Manx-born and incomer alike to begin to identify with a 'new' set of symbols. That said, the process is not without its problems. The Island has always absorbed incomers, but there has been an intensity of concern about the changes of the last few decades of the twentieth century which has resulted not only in a 'cultural intensification' (Paine op.cit.: 199) and concomitant increase in the 'performance' of 'traditional Manx' culture, but also in more extreme forms of culturally motivated protest.

'For Sale'

In June 1988, a 'For Sale' sign was erected on the Tynwald Hill. This was a tangible sign of popular discontent at the Manx government's handling of the social changes and shifts in values which were seen as a direct result of the Island's recent economic success. For the previous two decades, the government had actively and successfully pursued its goal of creating a buoyant offshore finance centre. This had not only increased the Island's population and resulted in seemingly uncontrolled development of new housing and other amenities, but the finance sector itself was apparently poorly regulated[12] and open to potentially 'immoral' trading. Further, the new industry seemed to offer little employment opportunity to local Manx people. In the eyes of the protesters, the Manx government had abdicated its authority to the finance sector and to the new 'incomers'.

A campaign of direct action continued. Letters to the Manx national newspapers demonstrated wide support, if not for the actions, at least for the sentiments that drove them. Developments during the decade following the action, such as the 'Quality of Life' Survey of 1989 in which the government sought public opinion on social and cultural matters, moves to increase the teaching of the Manx language in schools, and growing financial support for cultural events and heritage, might seem to indicate a reactive shift in governmental priorities. Verbal opposition to government policies still continues, however, particularly in regard to planning, immigration controls, and the risk of further 'marginalization' of the Manx-born population and of 'Manx culture'.

Letters about the Island's future and identity are testament also to the public discourse that has been created, as is the growing local and external academic interest in a wide range of Island-based issues. Yet there are also implicit perform-ances at work. Manx social customs such as the *Oie'll Verrey*[13] and eisteddfods, which had never wholly ceased but had vastly reduced in number, underwent something of a renaissance from the mid-1980s onwards. If people are asked to explain this, the response is one of uncertainty, and so they suggest that 'it's better than staying at home in front of the television'. Taking turns to step up on stage to offer a song, a poem or a tune played on anything from a fiddle to a saw, they are at once performers and audience. People are using these events to perform a 'Manxness' to themselves, and for others who might wish to join in this performance of belonging.

For incomers are also using these sites of cultural performance to get to know, or participate in, their newly chosen 'home'. Those that do are often introduced as newcomers, but they are encouraged to overcome their reticence and become part of the event. The internal boundary between Islander and incomer is present, but is not clearly drawn or impermeable. It is open to a level of negotiation similar to that process of cultural resource selection described by Ingold in his analysis of Skolt and Finn interaction (Ingold 1976: 248). A new identity is available to those '*stayovers*' who believe their 'interests' may be satisfied by what a new 'Manxness' has to offer, and Island-born residents can partake of the opportunities offered by a buoyant economy, while retaining the sense of the 'uniqueness' of identity which is so clearly demonstrated on Tynwald Day.

Yet the current and prevailing image is still one of a community of two parts. An inclusive society, a member of the elected House of Keys observed, will require 'two different strands . . . forming one picture, so that the traditional purists can be catered for, but also . . . the new Island residents who feel very supportive towards the local community' (personal communication). The statement is a telling one. Public discourse has abstracted the debate into one of two sets of 'interests': 'the Manx' (those who are Island-born, or who have a familial connection with the Island) as opposed to the Finance Sector and its incomer employees. The statement obscures the reality that some of the 'purists' are themselves 'incomers', and some who are Island-born have no interest in saving 'traditional culture'.

What it does, however, is lead us to consider the role of the individual in this process, and points perhaps to an opportunity to create a new 'identity' via what

Cohen would refer to as people's construction of nation 'through the medium of their own experience' (Cohen 2000: 146). Devereux too, stresses that social 'movements and processes' do not result from the actions of identically motivated individuals, but rather because the 'movement or process' provides an 'ego-syntonic outlet' for diverse subjective motivations (Devereux 1978: 126). We have seen above how cultural performance might provide such an outlet. The same must surely apply to the 'performance' of the Tynwald Day Ceremony and its associated 'carnivalesque' entertainments.

Discussion

If the Tynwald Ceremony is a site of contestation, must it become a site of synthesis if collective identity, the M.H.K.'s 'one picture', is to be achieved? I would argue not. The change that the Isle of Man underwent in the last few decades of the twentieth century was certainly not unique in its history. It was dramatic and had a variety of consequences, but it remains the case that the Manx have always accepted incomers. 'The Manx' are not, and perhaps have never been, a clearly defined ethnic group. Rather 'Manx-ness' is an idea, a set of values, a way of relating to place and to each other. Defined thus, 'Manx identity' can be, and has been, shared with incomers; that is, is accessible to those 'diverse subjective motivations' suggested by Devereux.

Turner writes: '[w]hen a social group, whether it be family, clan, village, nation, congregation, or church, celebrates a particular event or occasion, such as a birth, harvest or national independence, it also "celebrates itself"' (Turner 1982: 16). That this kind of celebration occurs on Tynwald Day is clear. But, say Comaroff and Comaroff, Turner would also have us believe that the symbols used in such celebration relate to a finite and ahistorial set of referents. In contrast, their analysis concludes that 'rituals' are '[i]ntricately situated performances with complex historical potential', and vehicles for interpersonal communication (Comaroff and Comaroff 1993: xxi). The Manx National Day both contains a wealth of elements that lend themselves to an infinite number of interpretations and identifications, and is intrinsically linked to its historical context. The longevity and stability of its central form refers back to a continuous past, while the subtle changes demonstrate a flexibility that supports present demands and those of a developing future. It holds meaning for those individuals who attend and those who choose not to. Its commentary works to include those Islanders who identify with the set of values and relationships that are Manx culture, and exclude those who do not (wish to) belong. It also informs and guides those who wish for inclusion. And last, but not exhaustively least, it is a community performance – before themselves and for themselves.

Before themselves and for themselves, because the Day also serves as a focus for interaction, and in the sharing of ideas about the society that is being performed. Rapport observes that 'in gossip a community can be seen to paint a self-portrait . . . what characterises this portrait is its continuousness, its democratic completeness and, above all, its range' (Rapport 1994: 116). The very coming together – as it is believed they have for more than a thousand years – is as important, if not more so, than the main Ceremony itself. This meeting is the culmination of smaller meetings throughout the year, and of the daily *skeet* through which information about the community is shared. Even today, old friends will meet at Tynwald and spend the day sharing stories in the inn, or in the parish hall drinking tea, all but oblivious of the formalities on the Hill. This, and the added importance of the 'physicality' (Rapport op. cit.: 117) of meeting makes the withdrawal of some from the event all the more potent, and the choice of those who do not attend but share the day with others more meaningful. It is to these personal interactions that the Captain was referring when he said 'this was a real Fair Day'.

And we cannot ignore the importance of the 'popular celebration' that is the Fair. In his description of the Notting Hill carnival, Abner Cohen presents a picture of an 'interplay between cultural forms and political relations' (Cohen 1980: 67). In Tynwald Day, I would suggest we see something similar. The shared enjoyment of the 'fun of the Fair' and its recent revival speak of an accessible, flexible cultural form that acts as a commentary on the political manoeuvrings present in the central Ceremony. Not, then, a celebration focused on a limited set of cultural resources and divorced from historical context, but a locus for the symbolizing of adaptations and responses to political relationships over time. Added to which, the various personal perspectives expressed above provide an insight into the diversity of relationships individuals can and do have with this national 'performance'.

In considering the various elements that go to make up Tynwald Day, and the various perceptions of it, one is thus reminded more of what Handelman describes as an event of *re*-presentation, which offers a 'flexible format and permeable boundaries' (Handelman 1990: 54). The surface pageantry and formality of the Tynwald Ceremony itself are undoubtedly reminiscent of other state rituals,[14] but the renaissance and growing importance of the accompanying Fair and entertainments demonstrate a 'resistance' to the state of which this nation is not a part. It is not a 'ritual of rebellion' (cf. Gluckman 1963), but rather a constant, multivalent, flexible and accommodating performance 'by themselves to themselves'. The Tynwald Ceremony has absorbed the various political and cultural changes throughout its history and today demonstrates the contradictions present in contemporary Manx society, including, for some, the desire for a collective identity which preserves the Island's 'uniqueness' and accommodates its new diversities.

Close

And finally, as the sun set, those who were still at the dancing, or the inn, or simply out enjoying the warm night air, gathered again around the Hill to hear a band of pipes and drums play traditional tunes. Quietly and without direction, people began to hum along, and then to sing the words. Across on the grandstand, a group of tourists watched as the band and the impromptu choir together brought the day to a close with *Ellan Vannin*.[15]

Notes

1. The word 'Tynwald' comes from the Norse; from *thing*, or assembly, and *völlr*, meaning place (Kinvig 1944[1975]: 72). The annual open-air sitting of the Manx parliament – the Tynwald Court – takes place on Old Midsummer's Day, or 5 July, each year.
2. The figures are based on the 1991 census. The growth in population over the last four decades is linked to the in-migration of workers to the recently established finance industry. Although work permits are required, there is currently no restriction on residency for those not subject to British immigration controls, and many of the finance sector workers have settled on the Island. Others, however, take up only temporary residence. For a comparative study of offshore finance centres, see Amit-Talai (1998).
3. Although some have argued that the Tynwald gathering has its roots further back into Celtic political and social systems, the history of the Tynwald Court is dated from this time. Tynwald celebrated its millennium in 1979.
4. In 1866, '[r]epeated demands by the Keys for further financial control and by the inhabitants of the Isle of Man for a popularly elected House of Keys eventually bore fruit . . .' (Kermode 1979: 31). Kermode points out that 'home rule' initially was something of a myth, but greater control over Island affairs has gradually increased, and continues to be a stated objective of the Manx government.
5. The Lieutenant-Governor presided over the Tynwald Court, and retained executive authority in his capacity as the Queen's representative until 1990. Tynwald now appoints a 'President of Tynwald' from among its own number, and the Lieutenant-Governor's duties have been reduced to more of a ceremonial role.
6. Under Protocol 3 of the 1972 European Act of Accession.
7. The following extracts (given in italics, here and below) are taken from the commentary which accompanied the Tynwald Day ceremony on 9 July 1999, and which I recorded on tape.

8. Iceland's parliament, the 'Althing', has similar roots to those of Tynwald, and there is evidence from remaining place-names of similar meeting-places elsewhere (for example, Dingwall, north of Inverness in Scotland, and Tingwall in the Orkney Islands).

9. The reigning sovereign of the United Kingdom is also head of state of the Isle of Man, under the title 'Lord of Man'.

10. The Tynwald Court is the inclusive term used to denote the full legislature: that is, the popularly elected House of Keys, the Legislative Council, the President of Tynwald, and the sovereign or her (or his) representative.

11. The Ceremony is concluded with an official sitting of the full Tynwald Court, but contentious issues are no longer debated, the occasion being limited to the 'captioning' of the Acts that have just been promulgated (Solly 1994: 247).

12. Indeed, the SIB scandal of the mid-1980s brought many of the regulatory failings to light. Today, the Island's finance industry is closely regulated.

13. The *Oie'll Verrey*, or Mary's Eve, was a community gathering which would once have taken place on Christmas Eve. They now take place anytime from autumn to spring, in small chapels, where people gather to entertain one another with hymns, songs, music and poetry.

14. For comparative analyses of state rituals, see D. Cannadine (1992), and B. Cohn (1992, same volume), and Handelman's description of Israeli State ceremonies (1990). Pictorial, photographic and textual evidence relating to the Tynwald Ceremony would suggest that a more formal and structured style was adopted as the nineteenth century progressed, and as 'colonial' rule strengthened its hold. For examples, see the illustrations in Kinvig's *The Isle of Man*, pp. 128 and 169 facing.

15. *Ellan Vannin* means 'Isle of Mannin' in Manx Gaelic, and is the name of a favourite and well-known song, which could perhaps be termed the unofficial national anthem of the Island. First published in 1854, its words – *My own dear Ellan Vannin, With its green hills by the sea* – made it popular both with Islanders and with those who had emigrated (Bazin 1997: 124). While this 'unofficial' anthem tugs at the heart strings, the official anthem speaks of freedom and home rule.

References

Amit-Talai, V. (1998) 'Risky Hiatuses and the Limits of Social Imagination: Expatriacy in the Cayman Islands', in N. Rapport and A. Dawson (eds) *Migrants of Identity: Perceptions of Home in a World of Movement*, Oxford and New York: Berg.

Bazin, F. C. (1997) *Much Inclin'd to Music: The Manx and their Music before 1918*, Douglas: Manx Heritage Foundation.

Cannadine, D. (1992 [1983]) 'The Context, Performance and Meaning of Ritual: The British Monarchy and the Invention of Tradition, *c.*1820–1977', in E. Hobsbawm and T. Ranger (eds) *The Invention of Tradition*, Cambridge: Cambridge University Press.

Carr, E.H. (1964 [1961]) *What is History?* Harmondsworth: Pelican Books.

Cohen, Abner (1980) 'Drama and Politics in the Development of a London Carnival', *Man* 15, 65–87.

Cohen, Anthony (2000) 'Peripheral Vision: Nationalism, National Identity and the Objective Correlation in Scotland', in A. Cohen (ed.) *Signifying Identities: Anthropological Perspectives on Boundaries and Contested Values*, London and New York: Routledge.

Cohn, B (1992[1983]) 'Representing Authority in Victorian India', in E. Hobsbawm and T. Ranger (eds) *The Invention of Tradition*, Cambridge: Cambridge University Press.

Comaroff, J. and Comaroff, J. (eds) (1993) *Modernity and Its Malcontents: Ritual and Power in Postcolonial Africa*, Chicago: University of Chicago Press.

Devereux, G. (1978) *Ethnopsychoanalysis: Psychoanalysis and Anthropology as Complementary Frames of Reference*, Berkeley: University of California Press.

Gluckman, M. (1963[1952]) 'Rituals of Rebellion in South East Africa', in M. Gluckman *Order and Rebellion in Tribal Africa*, London: Cohen and West.

Handelman, D. (1990) *Models and Mirrors: Towards an Anthropology of Public Events*, New York, Oxford: Berghahn Books.

Hobsbawm, E. (1992[1983]) 'Introduction: Inventing Tradition', in E. Hobsbawm and T. Ranger (eds) *The Invention of Tradition*, Cambridge: Cambridge University Press.

Ingold, T. (1976) *The Skolt Lapps Today*, Cambridge: Cambridge University Press.

Kermode, D.G. (1979) *Devolution at Work: A Case Study of the Isle of Man*, Farnborough, England: Saxon House.

Kinvig, R.H. (1975 [1944]) *The Isle of Man: A Social, Cultural and Political History*, Liverpool: Liverpool University Press.

Kniveton, G.N. (1997) *An Illustrated Encyclopaedia of the Isle of Man*, Douglas: The Manx Experience.

Paine, R. (1992) 'The Marabar Caves, 1920–2020', in S. Wallman (ed.) *Contemporary Futures: Perspectives from Social Anthropology*, London and New York: Routledge.

Rapport, N. (1994) *The Prose and the Passion: Anthropology, Literature and the Writing of E.M. Forster*, Manchester: Manchester University Press.

Solly, M. (1994) *Government and Law in the Isle of Man*, Castletown, Isle of Man: Parallel Books.

Turner, V. (ed.) (1982) *Celebration: Studies in Festivity and Ritual*, Washington: Smithsonian Institution Press.

−3−

Aesthetics at the Ballet: Looking at 'National' Style, Body and Clothing in the London Dance World

Helena Wulff

Historical and political circumstances such as nationalism are often negotiated, both in terms of identification and repudiation, through the arts, music and dance. In the ballet world, which has a tradition of transnationality with ballet people moving to other countries or between different countries on longer or shorter stays, the idea of national ballet styles is still prominent, especially in transnational contexts. There is a constant awareness of the style and standard of dancing elsewhere in the ballet world, in particular in the centres: Paris, St Petersburg, Copenhagen, New York and London.

The Royal Ballet in Britain started out as a ballet school in the 1920s and was acclaimed transnationally after the Second World War. The establishment of the Royal Ballet as a national ballet company[1] thus corresponded with the weakening of Great Britain as a world power. This seems to have produced a combination of anxiety and guilt among the British, sometimes expressed in terms of an intensified nationalism, which also came across in the ballet world. This was especially obvious in connection with tours in the ex-colonies and/or the Commonwealth. Ex-members of the Royal Ballet recollect how they had been instructed by the ballet management that they were 'ambassadors of Britain' and therefore should dress and behave appropriately, i.e. modestly.

An atmosphere of threatened global British sovereignty thus forms the backdrop to the following exploration of aesthetics at the Royal Ballet in the mid-1990s. By aesthetics I mean *affecting presence* which was introduced as a concept by Robert Plant Armstrong (1971) for affecting things and events. I find it useful here because it emphasizes feeling and experience without restrictions to function or beauty. Armstrong belongs to the number of those who are uncomfortable with the concept of 'art', some of whom prefer the designation 'aesthetic anthropology' in order to facilitate a cross-cultural perspective. A combination of the study of arts and aesthetics into one research approach may be the most productive strategy, however.

Affecting presence seems to be what Howard Morphy (1996: 258) has in mind when he suggests that 'aesthetics is concerned with the qualitative effect of stimuli on the senses'. Such effects may be incited by manifest objects and events, as well as ideas. Here I would like to focus on *the visual* among the senses, and how the affecting presence of 'national' ballet style and transnational bodies and clothing occurs through visualization.[2]

This chapter engages with the anthropology of Britain on two levels: it starts out with a methodological reconstruction of the circumstances around my field study at the Royal Ballet raising questions about definitions of 'home' and 'foreignness', which are called for by the exclusive nature of British society in general and the ballet world at Covent Garden in particular. This leads over to the main topic of the chapter: the aesthetics of the national English ballet style, bodies and clothing at the Royal Ballet. The aim of the Royal Ballet and its school has been to groom, or rather to discipline, an 'English dancer' (the concept is used interchangeably by ballet people with that of a 'British dancer'), which presupposes British nationality and upbringing. For there was, and still is, a belief in the ballet world that national character or 'national personalities' as they are called, come through in how people dance.[3] This obviously raises analytical objections about stereotypicality and essentialism. But I will start from the beginning, with a Swedish anthropologist going to London to do a field study at Covent Garden.

At Home at the Ballet, Abroad in Britain

It was in the autumn of 1994 that I went to London to do what was in fact my second field study there. The first one, my rite-de-passage into anthropology, took place during altogether fifteen months in the early 1980s when I was studying a group of black and white teenage girls in an inner city area of South London for my PhD thesis (Wulff 1988, 1995).[4] This time I was heading for the other end of the British class and race system: as a part of a two-year study on ballet as a transnational career I was going to spend three months with the Royal Ballet (Wulff 1998a, b, 2000a).[5] Apart from the Royal Ballet, this study included one year with the Royal Swedish Ballet in Stockholm, three months with American Ballet Theatre in New York and three months with the contemporary ballet company, Ballett Frankfurt in Frankfurt-am-Main.[6]

Many times during both my field studies I thought of London as my second home city, a place I liked, where I could settle. In retrospect, this may just have been an aspect of the 'going native' phase of fieldwork, or sadness and anxiety over exiting the field (cf. Wulff 2000a). Early on I realized, however, that a foreigner is never accepted as British by the British, not even those who move to Britain, and spend most of their lives there. But then the British discriminate among themselves like no other people: accents and geographical place of origin maintain social inequalities. Not even Nigel Rapport (1993: x, 69–70) who came from Wales and whose Jewish family had lived for three generations in Britain, felt entirely

British as a young adult. When he was going to do fieldwork in a village in Cumbria he thought of himself as a 'neophyte Englishman' on a kind of pilgrimage to Britain, hoping not only to become an anthropologist in the process, but also – 'more completely British'.

Anthropology of Europe, and Britain, is often assumed to be native anthropology or anthropology at home, as well as autobiographical, but neither need be the case. In fact, it is probably more common that anthropology of Britain is not native, or at least not *entirely* native. When I did my field study with the Royal Ballet, the ballet world was familiar to me because I used to dance ballet for many years, and had just spent a year with the Royal Swedish Ballet. The ballet world is mostly homogeneous in a transnational perspective when it comes to work practices. National ballet worlds are also heterogeneous, however, since for one thing they are structured by national employment laws and funding systems.

I felt deeply at home in the ballet world. Fieldworking there was like a homecoming after twenty years away. Ballet and ballet culture are still inscribed in my body, and they came back to me through the senses:[7] there was the dry smell of rosin,[8] the austere but rhythmical sound of piano music accompanying training in run-down studios, the sight of constant practice, pain from injuries, old-fashioned discipline, low self-esteem, competition, but also camaraderie, the wonder of progress, and the pleasure and power of reaching into those trans-cendental states of flow (Csikszentmihalyi 1990) when the technique is forgotten and a zone of ballet art suddenly springs up. This can happen in the studio during rehearsal, as well as in performance on stage. But it cannot be planned, and it occurs very rarely. Such transcendental states usually include the audience, habitual ballet-goers as well as occasional visitors – but not necessarily. The audience, or parts of the audience, may be moved into aesthetic experiences, even during performances which the dancers are not pleased with.

At first mistaken for a critic, and thus a threat, or someone who was there to engage dancers for other companies, it did not take long before I found myself acting as a supporter of the dancers; women as well as men, famous as well as unknown dancers who were at an early stage of, in the middle of or toward the end of their career. I became especially close to some of the dancers, a confidante. The dancers trusted me because I grew up in the ballet world. By returning to the ballet world, I was not only coming home to the ballet world, which I had neglected for a long time, but simultaneously finding my 'home' in anthropology: dance, performance, the arts and aesthetics, and later dance and technology. Unexpectedly, things fell into place, and I sensed that I had reached a completeness. The ballet world and the university world represented two sides of my personality, an artistic inclination and an intellectual one, heart and mind, that used to be in conflict. After having stopped dancing, I just had not been able to figure out a productive way to make use of both these sides, and hence suppressed the artistic one. Now I knew better.

Analytically, 'home' is a concept with shifting references (cf. Hastrup 1993), which needs to include 'physical and cognitive movement within and between homes, and the relation between the two' (Rapport and Dawson 1998: 4). 'Home' can be demarcated by place as well as culture, and can incorporate biculturality and transnational communities such as the ballet world. I was on the whole at home at the Royal Ballet, but abroad in Britain, although I did not consider London a foreign city because of my previous fieldwork there. Besides, I was hardly the only foreigner at the Royal Ballet. This is in line with Kirin Narayan's (1993) suggestion that it is time to leave the dichotomy between 'native' and 'non-native' anthropology aside, and to accept the changing multiplex identities of fieldworkers: nativeness is often partial and processual, and so consequently is foreignness (Wulff 1998b, 2000a).

Class and Race at the Ballet

Princess Margaret is the president of the Royal Ballet and represents the very apex of British society in the ballet world, as do board members and sponsors from the aristocracy. I should point out, however, that there is a broad class-span in the ballet world, especially among those who work backstage. Although there is a certain change taking place, ballet audiences still tend to consist of middle- to upper-class people with relatively more cultural capital, while the majority of the dancers were brought up as somewhere between upper-working-class and middle-middle-class and usually lack much cultural capital. The paradox is thus that dancers create cultural capital for the audience without possessing much of it themselves. There is, however, an informal tradition in the ballet world of educating ballet students and young dancers in taste and good manners. Coaches take their favourite dancers to plays and art galleries in order to teach them how to appreciate these art forms. Dancers still do not have very much formal schooling, although a growing number complete secondary education. In contrast to the working-class black and white teenage girls in South London whom I was studying more than a decade earlier (Wulff 1988, 1995), the dancers at the Royal Ballet had heard of universities, and most of them even knew where Sweden is located. The ballet world may be closed in relation to its own country, but it is certainly cosmopolitan through extensive travel and mixture of ethnic and national identities of dancers and other people working in the theatres.

Of the eighty-eight dancers at the Royal Ballet in 1994–95 about 20 per cent were non-English. Almost half of the principals who are the most visible and known, and who represent the company at social functions both at home and abroad, were of foreign origin. Coming out of Renaissance European court milieux and formed by Romanticist ideals, there is still a reluctance to feature ethnic and racial mixture on stage in the ballet world, even though this is slowly changing, partly because of the increasing ethnic mixture in Euro-American society, partly because ethnic mixture has been used to create aesthetic effects by contemporary choreographers such as William Forsythe, for quite some time. Admittingly, this effect would not have been as forceful if ethnic mixture in society at large had actually removed the visibility and the implications of ethnic differentiation. Although the Royal Ballet has been slower than the American Ballet Theatre in New York or the Royal Swedish Ballet in Stockholm to accept black and non-white dancers, a male Japanese dancer was put at each side of a white English woman dancer in a ballet during my field study, which emphasized their 'foreign' looks. Another Royal Ballet dancer who had a black father concealed his dark skin with light make-up on stage. Since then the Royal Ballet has in fact started hiring a few black dancers who do not hide their skin or hair when they perform. Still, as English critic Nadine Meisner (1998: 74) laments, they are all men: 'So where are the black ballerinas?'

The 'Reservedness' of the English Ballet Style

In the essay 'Notes on the English Character', E.M. Forster (1996[1926]: 13) reflects on the incompleteness of national characters, especially the English character:

> But the English character is incomplete in a way that is particularly annoying to the foreign observer. It has a bad surface – self-complacent, unsympathetic, and reserved.

Perhaps the English need foreigners to release them. This seems at least to have been one explanation to the legendary partnership between Russian Rudolf Nureyev and English Margot Fonteyn. Their extraordinary rapport on stage created expressive yet exquisite dancing, which would in fact not have come about unless there had been a personal *and* a professional exchange going on. Neither of them ever danced with anyone else in the way that they danced with each other. Still, the national contrast of their dancing was important aesthetically.

This ties in with the notion of national ballet styles. According to this view the English dancers are unanimously distinguished for dancing 'magnificently, but slightly reserved' by non-English ballet people in Stockholm, New York and Frankfurt, the other places in this multi-locale study. English choreographer Ashley Page described the English ballet style as 'more reserved' than the 'powerful' Russian style, while the Russian dancer Irek Mukhamedov who worked with the Royal Ballet during my field study, found the English style 'all clean, completely closed, like squeezed orange juice'!

Darcey Bussell, prima ballerina at the Royal Ballet, told me that in comparison with the American speed and especially the 'quick footwork', the English style was characterized by 'a more contained feeling, but I think we're getting stronger and more confident'. Other Royal Ballet dancers talked about their style as 'very precise and controlled' but also 'refined' and 'more fragile, more detailed' (than the Russian). A Finnish dancer who had a Russian training but was in the process of learning the English style, since she had recently been accepted into the Royal Ballet, was thinking about ballet styles and said:

> It comes out in the culture and the history. The Russian style is more over the top, the English more conservative. If you can imagine English people compared to Russian: the English are very simple, reserved but very aristocratic. You have to look like you're very calm. The Russian style is more temperamental, more free in a way.

So 'reserved' comes back frequently both in Forster's rendering of the English character and in the discourse (and practice, if I may add that from my observations) about national ballet styles in the transnational ballet world, also by English dancers about themselves. Most of the time, however, the 'reserved' epithet, or something similar, is combined with a respectful reference to a perceived *grandeur* of the English style such as 'magnificent' or 'aristocratic'. The renowned New York critic Edwin Denby (1986: 467), for instance, described the Royal Ballet in the 1950s as 'discreetly majestic'. But Judith Mackrell (1997: 56), dance critic and correspondent during the 1990s in London, has a somewhat different emphasis when she talks about the English style. Although she too relates to 'the native temperament of the dancers' she sees the English style as 'detailed, lyrical and neat', not reserved or grand. Mackrell attributes the tendency of English dancers to move in a small way to the fact that – the English live on an island! She does add, however, that the English style was first worked out on small stages in the 1920 and 1930s, which is a less entertaining but probably more credible explanation for the comparatively small movements of English dancers.

I have not said yet that the basic steps in classical ballet are the same everywhere, and that they have French names. There are, however, only five national ballet styles, but obviously many more nations, which means that the national styles spread from centres to peripheries often within political domains such as the Commonwealth. Apart from the British and the Russian styles, there are the French, the Danish and the American national styles. (There is also an Italian style which is not connected to the idea of nationalism, possibly because Italy never really has been a nation.) The national styles are on the whole identified unanimously and are complementary from different vantage points in the ballet world. The national ballet styles have all evolved out of the work of prominent choreographers and ballet entrepreneurs who have had resources to build ballet schools. Since the ballet world has always been transnational, there are influences between the ballet styles such as a Russian line in the British style, which the *New York Times* critic

Anna Kisselgoff (1983) brings up in an article where she objects to the connection between ballet styles and national personalities, defining them all as stereotypes. Kisselgoff suggests that ballet styles have mostly been fashioned by individual choreographers who tend to relate to the national setting they happen to work in, whether they are natives or not. In an interview, Kisselgoff talked about the preference of the British audience for story-telling ballets rather than abstract ballets which, on the other hand, work very well in America. In the article Kisselgoff (ibid.) writes about another Russian heritage of the Royal Ballet, the one originating in Sergei Diaghilev's modern company, the Ballets Russes. One of the dancers of that company was Ninette de Valois who went on to set up the Royal Ballet. It is interesting to note in this context that Ninette de Valois (who died in 2001) was not English. The founder and Grande Dame of the Royal Ballet, this company which thrives on an exclusive and sometimes arrogant Englishness, was in fact Irish! Or Anglo-Irish, to be precise. She was born Edris Stannus, the first dance she learnt was an Irish jig, and she kept her fondness of Ireland (de Valois 1959). It is common that ballet people change their names, either to an Anglicized form when they move to England or the United States, usually from Russia. But also many English dancers who work in England take on what is considered a more marketable or prestigious name in the ballet world.

Not only the form of ballet, the quality of the execution, is thought of in national terms; so also are the contents, the stories. There are national themes in many ballets, especially in modern and contemporary productions, often drawing on mythology, folk legends or literary work from the country of the company and/or the choreographer. These productions are especially important on transnational tours, as signature pieces, in order to acquire or cultivate a reputation.

Anna Kisselgoff's (1983) dismissal of national ballet styles as stereotypes is unique in the ballet world. Her article appeared in a collection which very few dancers seem to have read. The assumption that dancers express their national character or temperament when they dance is firmly grounded among dancers, choreographers, coaches, agents and other critics. Although top dancers and ballet companies are able to market themselves transnationally by way of the national ballet styles, with increased transnational mobility – such as tours, visits, competitions, galas and stays abroad to train or work with another company for a while – comes a contradictory awareness that ballet styles are not dependent on passports, but on training systems. Good dancers can learn to change styles, even switch back and forth between different national ballet styles, and between ballet styles and so-called choreographic styles, meaning those styles that contemporary choreographers such as Siobhan Davis and Matthew Bourne in Britain develop. Young dancers at the Royal Ballet talked about the growing mixture of styles, either approvingly as 'crossover' or disapprovingly as 'mish-mash'.[9]

Disciplined Ballet Bodies

As Howard Morphy (1996) astutely observes, the anthropology of the body needs to include an anthropology of clothing and bodily adornment, which should be treated as an area of inquiry in aesthetic anthropology. This can propel us to view the English ballet style as performed by more or less authentic 'English bodies', but otherwise there is not anything particularly English about constructions of the body at the Royal Ballet. Apart from differences in the national styles, the body is one of the homogeneous – and central – aspects of the transnational ballet world. Everywhere, however, the ballet body differs quite substantially from how bodies are constructed and perceived outside the ballet world in wider society.

It is the pervasive power of ballet discipline that moulds dancers' bodies into the special lines and language of classical ballet, which as stated by Michel Foucault's (1979) celebrated argument, implies subordination. Dancers work with their bodies, and they work very much: five to six days a week they do training class in the morning, rehearsals in the afternoon and frequently performances in the evening, often even at weekends and national holidays. An element of this intensity is that dancers should ideally keep getting fitter all the time – unlike athletes who work hard just before competitions, dancers cannot rely on some basic fitness. Because of the strenuous bodily nature of a dancing career, dancers consequently acquire an extreme body consciousness of both their own bodies and bodies around them, in particular of bodies in motion.

Dancers move distinctly even when they are not dancing, they are masters at proxemics and kinesthetics. They know, for instance, a lot about how to communicate without looking at each other even across the studio or the dressing-room, they carry on verbal or non-verbal conversations back and forth like a game of ping-pong even when they are out of each other's sight and hearing. Dancers are good at monitoring what is happening next to them without turning, and also 'talking' with their backs, since this is what they have to do on stage all the time. Another aspect of dancers' extraordinary sense of movement and form is their capacity to imitate, which they do when they learn new steps and choreography. This is transferred to social commentary both through imitating and ridiculing carriage and movement styles whether of skating star Nancy Kerrigan or a rival dancer. Dancers often 'converse' ironically or jokingly about a specific event, perhaps with a feared choreographer, by way of steps that they did at a particular rehearsal when something happened such as a row. But often the sheer routine, monotony, not least when ballets have to be rehearsed over and over again, can be referred to by way of a step when dancers run into each other during a break in the canteen. All this bodily awareness makes dancers 'send out' specialized 'intertextual' non-verbal messages, which are sometimes misinterpreted by non-dancers. I am not thinking of explicit ballet mime such as a hand going from the heart towards another person meaning 'I love you', but more detailed expressions such as dancers imitating the fragile flapping of swan wings in *Swan Lake*, or moving their arms upwards in a threatening gesture and grinning like Carabosse, the wicked fairy in *The Sleeping Beauty*.

Writing about dance as a non-verbal communication that can produce unique bodily experiences, both for performers and spectators, John Blacking (1977: 23) argued rightly that body and mind are ideally united in dancing. Yet for professional dancers, there is a lot of thinking behind those rare transcendental states of flow when they are 'able to move *without* thinking'.

In the ballet world, there are elaborate conceptualizations of body types and movement talents, which are often identified in relation to the mind. There are thus 'thinking dancers' who take an interest in choreographic structure and mental training including diet, in contrast to 'natural talents' or 'good bodies'. Different body types are also linked to the types of roles in classical ballets such as the *soubrette*, a small woman who dances with speed, and the *danseur noble*, an attractive man who dances with dignity, often the prince. The 'lyrical' dancer is his beautiful princess, the quintessential ballerina. Most *demi-caractères* or 'character dancers' are men, rather small but with a colourful stage presence, which is why they get to do roles such as the Jester in *Swan Lake*. There are, moreover, distinctions according to prestigious skills in classical ballet: a dancer is thus defined as 'a jumper' or 'a turner', or 'not a pirouetter'.

Dressed to Dance

The vision of an ethereal ballerina in a tutu and on pointe has become the generic representation of ballet outside the ballet world. Predictably, it has provoked a feminist critique in dance scholarship as a victimization of women, a stance which is beginning to be questioned in favour of an attribution of more female agency (Banes 1998). Because it is so well-known and associated with a certain delicate mood, this image of Western femininity is useful in parody, not least in drag and cross-dressing, also in contemporary ballets. One of the greatest successes in the 1990s transnational ballet world came out of London. It was a modern version of *Swan Lake* choreographed by Matthew Bourne with two Royal Ballet dancers in leading roles: Adam Cooper as the Swan and Fiona Chadwick as the Queen Mother. There was in fact a whole troupe of male barefoot swans imitating the fragile flapping of – the women dancers in the classical *Swan Lake,* rather than swans. Unlike other modern versions of *Swan Lake*, such as the one by Swedish choreographer Mats Ek, these male swans did not wear tutus, but feather trousers. They still evoked the image of the women swans wearing white tutus in the classical *Swan Lake*, gently making fun of them. Part of the parody was that these swans were barefoot and male, since that is as far as one can get from women dancing on pointe.

Because dancers constantly work with their feet, or as the saying goes they 'talk with their feet', dancers' shoes are highly significant. Different types of shoes, pointe shoes or soft ballet shoes, influence the dancing. Pink pointe shoes[10] made of satin are probably the most distinguishing feature of ballet, even more than the tutu. Pointe work dates back to the European Romantic movement in the arts in the nineteenth century with its focus on lightness and grace. It was Swedish-Italian Marie Taglioni who established pointe work as a basis for ballet when she dazzled in *La Sylphide* in Paris in 1832.[11] Worn pointe shoes, signed by famous dancers, are for sale at dance-wear and book shops such as Dance Books in London. There is an extensive lore about pointe shoes in the ballet world and how to 'break them in'. These fragile yet hard shoes are treated with glue, tacks and file (and even occasionally put in the oven) in order to soften and fit individual pairs of feet, as well as help the dancer to move silently on stage, even though this actually depends on the dancing rather than on the shoes. One strategy used to be to put raw meat in the front of the shoes, which was said to make them more comfortable. Pointe shoes do not last very long: leading ballerinas need two pairs for one full-length ballet, for instance. The sight of women dancers 'sewing their shoes' (e.g. attaching ribbons and taking off the silk on the pointe in order to get a good grip) is very common in the background of the studios or during breaks in the green room backstage at Covent Garden, as elsewhere in the ballet world. This is a continuous and never-ending task.

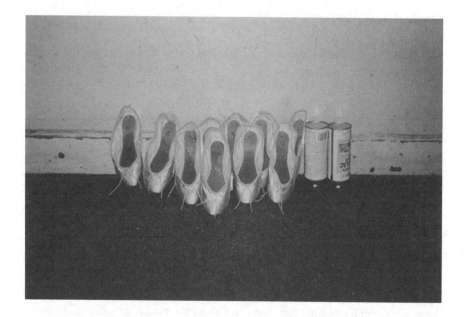

Figure 3.1 'Worn Pointe Shoes'. Photograph: Helena Wulff

Costumes are shared by dancers in different casts, and those that are used in classical ballets are often handed down from generation to generation. Some of the tutus and other costumes that dancers wore during my field study had been made in the 1950s. The last names of the dancers are written inside the costumes, so when there are one or two famous names in a garment, it is also a piece of ballet history. Just like pointe shoes that famous dancers have worn and then signed, the genealogy of these costumes, or artefacts (cf. Lubar and Kingerly 1993) that are second-, third- or even fourth- or fifth-hand give them a symbolic capital and patina that is quite different to the social meaning of most other used and tattered clothes and shoes. Both old pointe shoes and costumes (that are sometimes exhibited in dance museums) become celebrated artefacts for admiration by fans as well as by dancers, although the latter may also attribute a costume that has

Figure 3.2 Ballet Costume as Artefact. Photograph: Helena Wulff

been worn by an acclaimed dancer with the possibility of transferring some of the dancing powers of the previous wearer.

Dancers do not have much say about stage costumes, but they have to be able to move when they wear them. Costumes are often changed because they are in the way of movement or there is a risk that they will break (and potentially injure the dancer or someone else). I happened to witness a row between a male principal dancer at the Royal Ballet and a designer who had just delivered his new costume for the dancer. The dancer did not like the costume: the pair of trousers and a jacket were not tight enough. This hurt the designer who left the studio upset, yelling that he was not going to make any changes! The next day at the première the dancer wore his own personal trousers and the jacket which had been changed after all.

When dancers practice and rehearse, their appearance is usually far from that of ethereal sylphs or smart princes. Many dancers seem to indulge in individual expressions of practice clothes: comfortable multi-coloured layers of worn leotards, plastic trousers (to get warm quickly), tights with holes and ladders and old woollen sweaters made to fit with safety pins all manifest as well as symbolic evidence of the massive amount of hard work and physical pain that are not supposed to show in performance. Then on the other hand, neat and attractive practice clothes may be a way to get the attention of a coach who is in the process of selecting dancers for roles, and thus have an impact on dancers' careers.

Dancers also use t-shirts, sweatshirts and pants with company names printed on them, which is both a part of creating a sense of community, identity and belonging (cf. Cohen 1982) and a way to market the company. T-shirts that have been made to promote tours are kept by the dancers as souvenirs and used in rehearsals afterwards. Wearing a t-shirt from a company or a competition abroad is a statement about an individual transnational experience. T-shirts with general dance motifs such as 'Dance or Die. New York City' were also common. Apart from ironic or joking commentary there were serious messages about the necessity to prevent the spread of AIDS on a few t-shirts at the Royal Ballet.

Among the dancers the idea of 'street' (or 'private') clothing, make-up and hairstyle was prominent. This emphasis on what one wears away from work is a reminder of the fact that dancers spend most of their time dressed in practice clothes and stage costumes (often identical ones), make-up and hairstyles. Some of dancers' practice clothes periodically make it into fashion outside the theatre, as leg-warmers and tights did in the 1980s, and the shape of dance shoes which has inspired a special type of ladies' shoes. But the contemporary world of fashion also reaches into the theatre: choreographers commission fashion designers to create costumes for their dance productions.[12]

Contemporary dance may feature naked or, at Covent Garden, almost naked dancers on stage – for example the woman dancer wearing a see-through top in

Herman Schmerman choreographed by William Forsythe. In *Firstext*, which Forsythe created for the Royal Ballet during my fieldwork, dancers perform in costumes that look like practice clothes, thereby adhering to an aesthetic tradition in the ballet world which challenges the separation between rehearsal and performance, or reality and fantasy in the theatre room.

Ballet Aesthetics in Britain: From the Professional Point of View

The anthropology of art and aesthetics has mostly dealt with non-Western societies, or with problems around transformation or appropriation of non-Western objects and expressive forms in the West, yet this needs to be complemented with studies on art and aesthetics within the West (cf. Maquet 1986, Thomas 1997). This is so because of growing cultural exchange which makes the Western/non-Western distinction unclear, as Thomas (1997) argues, but also because of a changing political and cultural landscape in the West. There is, for instance, the European/ ex-East European distinction to investigate more fully, which includes ballet. The European integration is, moreover, changing the dynamics of power in Europe, not least in terms of nationalism.

Morphy (1996: 259) importantly puts forward the view of 'aesthetics as a field of discourse that operates generally in human cultural systems, since like cognitive processes it can be applied to all aspects of human action'. By way of Morphy's (1996) exhortation to consider clothing and bodily adornment as part of the anthropology of the body, and clothing as a field for an anthropology of aesthetics, I have analysed the visual affecting presence among people working with ballet in terms of constructions and meanings of the body and clothing at the Royal Ballet. Not always in search of beauty, these objects, bodies and clothing were also constructed as rugged, funny, touching, ugly, indecent, and imbued with someone else's dancing powers. They did not have very much to do with conceptions of 'Englishness', which on the other hand were quite prominent when it came to the dancing, especially the English national ballet style. I have discussed and contested the belief that national characters make people dance in a certain way, in particular the idea that the English are supposed to dance 'with reserve'. Yet there seems to be a grain of truth in this, at least in a transnational comparative perspective. At the same time, good dancers of any national origin can learn the style of another nation, which is one aspect of the ongoing symbolic construction of national difference in the transnational world of ballet.

Anthropological studies on nationalism seem to have focused on nation-building, political processes of unification of diverse ethnic groups in young nation-states, rather than on the disintegration of established nation states, or fundamentally changing nationalisms which may become the normal course of events in the future for many nations (cf. Hannerz 1993, Paxman 1999). It is curious that Britain itself, the heart of the postcolony, is absent in most social science discussions on nationalism, except as a past or present oppressor.

In the long run the idea and practice of classical ballet may fade away, not least because it seems to be difficult to find healthy training schemes and second-career options for dancers (who have to retire when they are around forty), but also because of the elitist label which parallel to popularizing efforts is still cultivated by the Royal Ballet. Just as British nationalism will have to reinvent itself, so will classical ballet. The questions remains, however: Is it possible to replace the etherealness of ballet aesthetics?

Acknowledgements

I wish to express my profound gratitude to Nigel Rapport for inviting me, a non-Brit, to write a chapter for this volume. I was much inspired by *The Prose and the Passion* (1994) and *Diverse World-Views in an English Village* (1993), both original and elegant books. And I got to read more Forster (1996). The major part of this chapter is new, but some sections are revised versions of Wulff (1998b).

Notes

1. Although the Royal Ballet is the most prestigious of the national ballet companies in Britain, there are three of them. The other two are Birmingham Royal Ballet and English National Ballet.
2. Nicholas Thomas (1997: 256) suggests that 'the emerging anthropology of the "visual" will incorporate the anthropology of art'. This emerging anthropology of the 'visual' is defined by Howard Morphy and Marcus Banks (1997: 5) as 'the anthropology of visual system or, more broadly, visible cultural forms'. This entails the visual in terms of cultural and social reproduction, problematizing the visual in cultural process, and investigating visual representations as well as indigenous ways of seeing.
3. Also music has been considered in terms of national music styles. See Stokes (1994) on the complexities of national music styles and political ideology, especially the chapters by Baily (1994) on bricolage music in Afghanistan, Mach (1994) on Chopin and Polish musical identity, and Reily (1994) on music as a projected unifying force among different ethnic groups in Brazil.
4. The black girls were immigrants in the second generation whose parents had come with the immigration wave in the late 1950s or early 1960s to Britain

from West Africa or the Caribbean. Theoretically this study was phrased in terms of ethnicity and youth culture, more specifically how these girls formed a microculture in order to make room for their own focal concerns and handle those of their parents, teachers, youth workers and the media that related to them, sometimes contradicting their own experiences of friendship in an ethnic mixture. I got to see the British class and race system from below: some of the teenagers lived in very simple accommodations with unemployed parents, and a few girls that I met briefly had run away from home or a hostel.

5. By then, the Stockholm school of anthropology was beginning to get systematically organized around work on culture theory and globalization, the media and occupational cultures, often involving multi-locale fieldwork since the communities that were being studied operated multi-locally.

6. In 1998 I began a study on dance in Ireland, north and south. It has provided me with yet another perspective on Britain, mostly as ex-colonizer, which still has an impact on Irish dance whether it is traditional dancing, dance theatre, or dance show such as *Riverdance*.

7. See Bourdieu (1977) on formative bodily experiences, body hexis, which I apply in my memoir of growing up in the ballet world and my account of returning to do fieldwork there (Wulff 1998b, 2000a).

8. Dancers put rosin on the soles of their shoes to prevent slipping.

9. Ideas about national dancing styles are also prominent in folk dance such as Irish dancing recently highlighted through the success of *Riverdance,* the Irish dance show, which introduced a more 'modern' version of Irish dancing. At *Riverdance,* 'Irish descent' is used in the marketing of the show, even though the management knows that an early start and intense training are even more important when it comes to learning Irish dancing than is Irish nationality. Still, nationalist notions such as 'it helps if there is Irish in the blood' keeps coming back. The majority of the dancers in *Riverdance* were born and grew up in Ireland, north and south, but quite a few come from England, the United States, Canada or Australia (Wulff 2000b).

10. Informed by a Lacanian perspective, Susan L. Foster (1996) has written about pointe shoes as 'the ballerina's phallic pointe'.

11. The scope of Taglioni's fame as a dancer, as well as the symbolic meaning of shoes in the ballet world, are illustrated by the anecdote about balletomanes in Russia who bought a pair of her shoes, cooked them and ate them for dinner (Clarke and Crisp 1992)!

12. Gianni Versace did costumes for the French choreographer Maurice Béjart, and the Americans Twyla Tharp and William Forsythe. The Japanese designer Issey Miyake has worked a number of times with William Forsythe. In 1992 dancers of Forsythe's company, Ballett Frankfurt, went on the catwalk modelling Miyake's summer collection in a fashion show.

Helena Wulff

References

Armstrong, R.P. (1971) *The Affecting Presence*, Urbana: University of Illinois Press.
Baily, J. (1994) 'The Role of Music in the Creation of an Afghan National Identity, 1923–73', in M. Stokes (ed.) *Ethnicity, Identity and Music*, Oxford: Berg.
Banes, S. (1998) *Dancing Women*, London: Routledge.
Blacking, J. (ed.) (1977) *The Anthropology of the Body*, ASA Monograph 15, London: Academic Press.
Bourdieu, P. (1977) *Outline of a Theory of Practice*, Cambridge: Cambridge University Press.
Clarke, M. and Crisp, C. (1992) *Ballet*, London: Hamish Hamilton.
Cohen, A.P. (ed.) (1982) *Belonging: Identity and Social Organization in British Rural Cultures*, Manchester: Manchester University Press.
Csikszentmihalyi, M. (1990) *Flow*, New York: Harper Perennial.
Denby, E. (1986) 'In the Abstract', in R. Cornfield and W. Mackay (eds) *Dance Writings*, New York: Knopf.
de Valois, Ninette (1959) *Come Dance with Me*, London: Hamish Hamilton.
Forster, E.M. (1996[1926]) 'Notes on the English Character', in *Abinger Harvest and England's Pleasant Land*, London: André Deutsch.
Foster, S.L. (1996) 'The Ballerina's Phallic Pointe', in S.L. Foster (ed.) *Corporealities*, London: Routledge.
Foucault, M. (1979) *Discipline and Punish*, New York: Vintage.
Hannerz, U. (1993) 'The Withering away of the Nation? An Afterword', *Ethnos*, 3–4: 377–391.
Hastrup, K. (1993) 'Native Anthropology: A Contradiction in Terms?', *Folk*, 35: 147-61.
Kisselgoff, A. (1983) 'There is Nothing "National" about Ballet Styles', in R. Copeland and M. Cohen (eds) *What Is Dance?*, Oxford: Oxford University Press.
Lubar, S. and Kingerly, W. (1993) 'Introduction', in S. Lubar and W. Kingerly (eds) *History from Things*, Washington: Smithsonian Institution Press.
Mach, Z. (1994) 'National Anthems: The Case of Chopin as a National Composer', in M. Stokes (ed.) *Ethnicity, Identity and Music*, Oxford: Berg.
Mackrell, J. (1997) *Reading Dance*, London: Michael Joseph.
Maquet, J. (1986) *The Aesthetic Experience*, New Haven: Yale University Press.
Meisner, N. (1998) 'Carlos Acosta: A Profile of the Royal Ballet's New Star', *Dance Now* 7(2): 74–6.
Morphy, H. (1996) 'Aesthetics is a Cross-Cultural Category', 'For the Motion(1)', in T. Ingold (ed.) *Key Debates in Anthropology*, London: Routledge.
—— and Banks, M. (1997) 'Introduction: Rethinking Visual Anthropology', in H. Morphy and M. Banks (eds) *Rethinking Visual Anthropology*, New Haven: Yale University Press.

Narayan, K. (1993) 'How Native Is a "Native" Anthropologist?', *American Anthropologist* 95(3): 671–86.

Paxman, J. (1999) *The English*, Harmondsworth: Penguin.

Rapport, N. (1993) *Diverse World-Views in an English Village*, Edinburgh: Edinburgh University Press.

—— (1994) *The Prose and the Passion*, Manchester: Manchester University Press.

—— and Dawson, A. (1998) 'The Topic and the Book', in N. Rapport and A. Dawson (eds) *Migrants of Identity*, Oxford: Berg.

Reily, S. (1994) 'Macunaíma's Music: National Identity and Ethnomusicological Research in Brazil', in M. Stokes (ed.) *Ethnicity, Identity and Music*, Oxford: Berg.

Stokes, M. (1994) 'Introduction: Ethnicity, Identity and Music', in M. Stokes (ed.) *Ethnicity, Identity and Music*, Oxford: Berg.

Thomas, N. (1997) 'Collectivity and Nationality in the Anthropology of Art', in M. Banks and H. Morphy (eds) *Rethinking Visual Anthropology*, New Haven: Yale University Press.

Wulff, H. (1988) *Twenty Girls*, Stockholm Studies in Social Anthropology, 21, Stockholm: Almqvist & Wiksell International.

—— (1995) 'Inter-racial Friendship: Consuming Youth Styles, Ethnicity and Teenage Femininity in South London', in V. Amit-Talai and H. Wulff (eds) *Youth Cultures*, London: Routledge.

—— (1998a) 'Perspectives toward Ballet Performance: Exploring, Repairing and Maintaining frames', in F. Hughes-Freeland (ed.) *Ritual, Performance, Media*, London: Routledge.

—— (1998b) *Ballet across Borders*, Oxford: Berg.

—— (2000a) 'Access to a Closed World: Methods for a Multi-Locale Study on Ballet as a Career', in V. Amit (ed.) *Constructing the Field*, London: Routledge.

—— (2000b) Reverberations of Riverdance: Irishness, Technology and the Global Marketplace', Paper for the 5th Nordic Forum of Dance Research (NOFOD) in Copenhagen, 27–30 January 2000.

Part III
Strategies of Modernity: Heritage, Leisure, Dissociation

Introduction to Part III
Nigel Rapport

The chapters in this section deal with practices and techniques which make up for some sense of deficit, loss or trauma in modern life in Britain: from overly rapid rates of change to the 'massification' of social life, entrepreneurial pressures to consume and succeed, and unemployment and retirement. Through a variety of 'strategies of modernity' may be achieved or regained a sense of personhood, of continuing local identity, of self-worth, resistance and self-control. Such strategies may span an arc from the institutional through the communitarian to the psychical; but all are characterized by attempts to come to terms with experience through some form of rationalization and to make it consequent and meaningful.

In Chapter Four, 'On "Old Things": The Fetishization of Past Everyday Life', Sharon Macdonald highlights some of the cultural specificities of 'British' ways of thinking about and performing 'the past'. Her particular focus is upon what she calls 'museums of everyday life' which set out to present to the visiting public recreations of the living conditions of past centuries: from the Science Museum, London, to the Skye Museum of Everyday Life. Public interest in these institutions amounts to something of a pilgrimage, according to Macdonald, and an extremely popular and widespread recreational practice since at least the 1960s.

Museums of everyday life must be understood in the wider context of gift and commodity exchange and of 'commodity fetishism', Macdonald argues. The objects placed in museums stop accumulating specific histories of their own but they provide symbolic capital through which people can compose a narrative of historical continuity and particularity. To the people of Skye the 'old things' in the local museum speak of local belonging and speak out against the threat to local identities of mass production and mass consumption. The 'old things' are used as part of the proof that modern, British personhood can evince inner depth and distinctiveness.

The heritage industry more generally may be understood as one of a set of cultural practices providing existential anchors in a time of social uncertainty. Against the fragmentation and disembeddedness of social life in post-war Britain, of inbuilt obsolescence and technological revolution, 'heritage' affords continuing individuality and longevity on a variety of levels: individual, communitarian, regional and national.

In Chapter Five, 'Leisure and Change in a Post-mining Mining Town', Andrew Dawson examines the role that leisure plays in the lives of retired and elderly ex-miners, their spouses and friends, in the former coal-mining town of Ashington. Leisure activities, he concludes, can be more properly regarded as a form of work: taking the place of work and carrying their own existential freight.

In its heyday, mining dominated the occupational landscape in Ashington. Indeed, nepotistic and familistic in its practice, mining ramified into many if not most aspects of local life. But the efforts and energies that went into mining, as both material and symbolic practice, can now be seen in transmuted form in such local leisure pursuits as rearing animals, partaking of clubs and lodges for the retired, spectating at football matches, and composing local, historical and personal narratives in poetry and song.

More precisely, Dawson describes leisure pursuits as providing a means by which individuals are able to come to terms more effectively with change – whether in occupational standing, in gender relations, in familial and other sites of sociality, or in the ethnic composition of their locale. Leisure – as has been argued more generally for 'play' as such – represents a medium through which change is both resisted and accommodated.

In Chapter Six, 'Dissociation, Social Technology and the Spiritual Domain', Tanya Luhrmann explores the phenomenon of psychic 'dissociation' as a cognitive strategy for both dealing with trauma and achieving ecstasy in everyday life. Dissociation is a means by which individuals instill 'magic' into 'modernity'.

Psychiatrists, Luhrmann explains, describe dissociation as a technique of self-hypnosis whereby individuals manipulate their senses of identity and consciousness and may, as a result, form unusual and (what seem to others) irrational interpretations of events. Dissociation may be deliberately employed in the service of religious experience, or spontaneously and pathologically deployed as a kind of psychical escape.

Both middle-class 'witches' in Britain and those who frequent American psychiatric clinics can, according to Luhrmann, be found exercising a capacity for dissociation which all people have but which most employ with less regularity and skill. Dissociation may be of high or low intensity – from daydreams to trances – and it can be subjected to training. It gives onto a change in experienced time, in I-Thou relations, in the sensed locus of control, and in a desired engagement with the world.

Far from simply a medical condition, dissociation may be more profitably approached as a psychological mechanism which receives cultural shaping and social institutionalization; between, say, London and California the 'trauma' to be exorcized may differ, as may the material artefacts which provide necessary transitional practices to psychological states – from witchcraft rituals to teddy bears.

–4–

On 'Old Things': The Fetishization of Past Everyday Life

Sharon Macdonald

Scattered throughout Britain are numerous small museums which focus on 'life gone by' in this or that area, island or village. Their subject matter is mostly the everyday life, at home and at work, of 'ordinary folk'. Everyday objects salvaged from past times summon up this world: blackened irons stand to warm on a recreated hearth, battered cooking pans hang by the range, there will be a mangle, a butter-churn, a spinning wheel (threaded up, a basket of sheep's wool nearby), several old ploughs – a little rusted, a three-legged stool and rough-hewn wooden bench. In some cases domestic interiors are recreated, complete with box-beds, framed cross-stitch samplers and shawl draped over the back of a rocking-chair, stuffed cat on the faded cushion, half-moon spectacles on the family Bible. In others, whole mills or factories are 'restored', waterwheels and steam-powered pistons being 'brought to life', heaving and creaking into non-productive action, especially on Sunday afternoons. 'Discover the past!' say the advertizing leaflets, 'History comes alive!'.

Why should so much effort be put into trying to recreate the living conditions of a previous century or persuading a decrepit old loom to work again? Why should people spend their Sunday afternoons visiting such places? Historically and cross-culturally, this public display of, and popular pilgrimage to, such mundane and everyday artefacts as old cooking and washing equipment, is surely remarkable. While certainly not exclusive to Britain, this phenomenon was, even here, relatively unusual prior to the 1960s (Lowenthal 1998, Urry 1995). Now brown signs indicating heritage sites and heritage trails dot the landscape. In this chapter my aim is to explore, from an anthropological viewpoint, aspects of this relatively recent form of cultural practice – the 'fetishization' of past everyday life.

To do so I look at such museums in relation to various anthropological literature concerned with objects. One of the main ways in which objects have been considered in anthropology is in analysis of gift and commodity exchange; and a good deal of work has been devoted to delineating differences between societies where exchange is based on 'gifting' and those where 'commodity' relations predominate (see for example Carrier 1994). Gifts, according to classical Maussian analysis, are fundamentally different from commodities in that they carry something of the spirit of their giver with them, as in the famous Maori *hau* (Mauss 1967). Gifts 'symbolize relationships', they implicate persons with one another and bind them into ongoing social relations. In commodity exchange, by contrast, objects do not bring their producers or sellers into ongoing relationships with those who buy. Instead, through money as an abstract means of according value, objects are 'lifted out' of matters of social obligation. As Mauss describes, they are disinvested of their *moral* dimension and are treated instead in purely 'economic' and 'rationalistic' terms. Since Mauss wrote his classic essay, there has been a good deal of sophisticated elaboration of his distinction, including attempts to highlight variations within each of the supposed societal 'types' and to deal with object relations which seem to evade the 'gift' versus 'commodity' distinction: Annette Weiner's concept of 'inalienable possessions' and Janet Hoskins's of 'biographical objects' are two to which I return below.

In trying to read a cultural practice – that of museums of everyday life – through some of the arguments and insights from this cross-cultural literature, my intention is to try to look at this practice in terms which I hope will highlight some of its aspects that we more usually take for granted. At the same time, by reading this literature in relation to a practice to which it is not usually applied, I hope also to provide some further considerations for ongoing debates in this area. In particular, I suggest that rather than focusing on specific types of 'object relations' and analysing each as separate spheres, we need to consider more how they relate semantically to one another and how certain practices may symbolically mediate between apparently discrete domains. More specifically, I argue that the collection and display of objects in museums, including museums of everyday life, far from being disconnected from the world of commodities, is intimately connected to it and plays an important role in its symbolic mediation. I suggest, moreover, that in trying to understand the object relations involved, we can come to understand better some of the ways in which other cultural formations are constituted in relation to this practice.

Approaching Britain

In what follows I refer especially, though not exclusively, to the Skye Museum of Island Life on the Isle of Skye, Scotland, a museum which I first came to visit during the 1980s as part of fieldwork concerned with matters of identity, cultural revival and history in the Scottish Highlands (Macdonald 1997a). I have also returned more recently to spend time at the Museum and to talk with those involved in running it, especially its creator, Jonathan Macdonald (who was born and brought up on the island). In addition, I have visited numerous other museums of everyday life and sites of industrial heritage in many parts of Britain, partly in connection with fieldwork which I have carried out in the Science Museum, London, and I have interviewed staff at many such museums and read literature produced by and about them. In my account below I draw on this material too, though without going into details of individual cases, for my aim in this chapter is to highlight a repertoire of what seem to me to be salient features that are found, to various extents, in many instances in this cultural field.

I should note that, in working at this fairly broad level of analytical resolution, I do not seek to deny significant differences between such museums and between the stories that they tell in different parts of Britain. As we shall see, telling *local* stories and articulating local or regional identities is, very often, central to these museums.[1] Here, however, rather than looking at the detailed content of such accounts, I want to look more at the fact that they do this, and more generally at the shared forms and idioms in which they say or do what they do. In other words, my interest here is not so much in the differences which such sites assert (though this is a perfectly legitimate interest) as in what Marilyn Strathern has expressed as 'the way their self acknowledged differences draw on common British ideas about difference' (1987: 32). Whether we are in the end talking about 'British ideas', however, remains to some extent an open question for there is undoubtedly much that these British cases share with other parts of Europe and beyond; and indeed we are dealing here with a cultural form which, while articulating the local, is itself increasingly transnational. Yet although the museum of everyday life is found in many parts of the world, and has emerged within similar (though not identical) historical time-frames, there may well also be significant differences between such developments (e.g. between the French eco-museums and the German Heimat museums to which we would surely look as comparisons with our British cases here). This would be a fully comprehensible outcome of, *inter alia*, the fact of the distinctive development of nation states, their differential patterns of industrialization, urbanization and social mobility, variable definitions and practices of 'citizenship', and different levels of centralization or regional-ization. Such an analysis is beyond the scope of the present chapter but it is hoped that the account here could prove useful to a later project of this kind. At the least, in trying to highlight some of the semantic constellations implicated in this particular case, I hope to provide some points of reference for investigating those sometimes specific cultural assumptions which may be masked under superficially similar cultural forms.

Ordinary Objects: Sacred Objects

Museums of everyday life, and museums more generally, typically contain objects, often in great numbers. The Skye Museum of Island Life expanded from one 'blackhouse' (single-storey thatch-roofed stone dwelling) opened in 1965 to five such houses full of the 'old things' with which its creator has filled it. Agricultural implements stack up in profusion, pottery crowds the dresser, photographs fill wall after wall. Some of these objects are historically unique and even precious – such as some mementoes of Flora MacDonald, of Bonnie Prince Charlie fame, who lived in this area – but what is especially characteristic of museums of everyday life is the ordinariness of many of the objects included and the fact that they are drawn not from grand or famous histories and events but from the daily life of the majority of the population.

Objects come to museums such as these after a previous life of regular use. This prior existence is a key aspect of their 'aura' or, following Mauss, of the *hau* that they carry with them. In one folklife museum in Scotland, the man running it directed my gaze to the handle of a peat-cutting implement where a shinier and slightly indented area of wood indicated years of use, and told me that I had to think of the back-breaking labour, out on the moorland in maybe poor weather, that this tool would have experienced. It was as though it was a witness, telling me, if I had the will to listen imaginatively, about what it had lived through. Not only have such objects previously been used, almost all were at some point in their biographies commodities (Kopytoff 1986). Although museums of rural life contain many craft items, most of these, as well as mass-produced goods (e.g. Staffordshire pottery, Sheffield cutlery, Oxo cube tins), would have been sold and bought. Some – a vase, an embroidered cushion perhaps – may also have been gifts. What is significant about museums, however, is that objects are removed from both circulation and daily use, and from the 'candidacy' (Appadurai 1986) to participate as such. Museums only occasionally sell objects from their collections, and this is nearly always accompanied by unease, criticism and self-justification (perhaps involving claims that this is being done out of dire necessity and to help preserve remaining objects in the collection). Demonstrating the use of their objects – of a spinning wheel or steam engine – is not itself generally taboo for these museums; and indeed some are to varying extents what are called 'living museums', where previous activities are acted out for visitors. (Jonathan Macdonald would like the Island Life Museum to be able to do this.) But to return something to ordinary daily use – to lend a farmer a scythe from the collections to help with the harvest, or to borrow a cup from the dresser to drink tea – are not to be done. Once they are in museums – such is the magic-conferring power of these institutions – objects are special. However mundane they were before, they are now to some extent sacred. Museums bestow such sanctity. They also anchor or stabilize objects: they remove them from daily use and transaction. A museum, for most objects, is a final resting place – a moment frozen in time for future contemplation – not a stop-over on a journey elsewhere.

'Inalienable Possessions' and 'Biographical Objects'

To help refine the nature of the object relations involved here let us briefly consider two particular 'special' cases: inalienable possessions, as formulated by Annette Weiner (1992); and Janet Hoskins' concept of biographical objects (1998). In an account partly based on a re-analysis of the famous Trobriand *Kula* described by Malinowski (1922), Weiner examines cases of what she terms the 'paradox of keeping while giving'. In *Kula* exchange, valuables (*vay'gua*) – shell arm-bands and necklaces – circulate around the islands in the *Kula* ring in a set of exchanges. Kept only until the next round of giving, each is treasured nevertheless. Contrasting this with commodity exchange and with more familiar (or less grand) gift exchange, Weiner emphasizes that in cases such as these, ownership is not wholly transferred but that the valuables are in a sense 'kept' in that they are 'imbued with the intrinsic and ineffable identities of their owners' (1992: 6). Inalienable possessions are regarded as special because of this accumulation of specific histories which make them 'subjectively unique' (1992: 10).

As noted, museum objects are not normally part of patterns of continuing exchange, and once they enter a museum they generally cease to accumulate specific histories.[2] This is particularly the case for the kind of ordinary objects discussed here, objects which, moreover, are often not imbued with detailed individual histories. Rather, these objects are mostly ones which collectively intimate a 'folk' and accompanying 'way of life': 'the Skye Museum of Island Life'. We are not usually told to whom this spade or that mantle-clock belonged – the idea that they belonged to 'people of the place' is crucial. Sets of photographs in the Skye Museum of Island Life are for the most part individually unidentified and headed with titles such as 'Crofters', 'People of the Place'.[3] Nevertheless, Weiner's attempt to identify particular types of object relations, and the notions of 'inalienability' and 'possession', can offer insights into the museum case, as can her perception that 'inalienable possessions' are not just a distinct category of objects but that they can inflect upon the meanings of other objects. The very fact that it is possible to have possessions that are *inalienable*, means that the transaction of other objects – which would normally be alienable – is imbued with special meaning. Thus the barter that accompanies a *Kula* exchange is not 'mere' barter but itself made to some degree special by its proximity to inalienable possessions. Moreover, Weiner's suggestion that 'inalienable possessions' – precisely because they are conceptualized as 'inalienable' and as 'possessions' – can play a special role in the articulation of notions of stability and identity, is also one which is suggestive for the case of objects in museums of everyday life. Before examining these suggestions in more detail, however, I turn to Hoskins's account of 'biographical objects', for this too will offer some conceptual keys and a useful framework for understanding the case in hand.

The category of 'biographical objects' is intended, writes Hoskins, to 'occupy one pole of the continuum between gifts and commodities' (1998: 7). Drawing upon the work of French sociologist Violette Morin, she contrasts 'biographical objects' (which, we should note, may have begun life as mass-produced goods) with 'public commodities' in terms of their mediating relationships to time, space and ownership or consumption:

> At the temporal level, the biographical object grows old, and may become worn and tattered along the life span of its owner, while the public commodity is eternally youthful and not used up but replaced. At the spatial level, the biographical object limits the concrete space of its owner and sinks its roots deeply into the soil. It anchors the owner to a particular time and place. The public commodity, on the other hand, is everywhere, marking not personal experience but a purchasing opportunity . . . Finally, the biographical object "imposes itself as the witness of the functional unity of its user, his or her everyday experience made into a thing" (*sa quotidienneté faite chose*) ([Morin] 1969: 137–8). The public commodity, on the other hand, is not formative of its owner's or user's identity, which is both singular and universal at the same time. Consumers of public commodities are decentred and fragmented by their acquisition of things, and do not use them as part of a narrative process of self-definition (1998: 8).

Daniel Miller's analysis of shopping in North London (1998) suggests that the characterization of 'public commodities' as depersonalized and not part of narrative processes of self-definition may be part of a prevalent stereotyped discourse about mass consumption rather than a reflection of the complex and more personalized relationships involved in practice. Nevertheless, the discourse of mass consumption as meaningless itself plays a part in formations of object relations. Moreover, the contrast invoked by Hoskins clearly highlights different possible permutations of relationships to everyday objects, though neither quite captures the nature of the museum objects considered here. This suggests that different types of object relations should be seen not so much as on a continuum as part of a more multidimensional complex of different possibilities. In order to explore this further, I look at the museum case through each of Morin's 'mediating relationships' – time, space and ownership/consumption – in turn.

Time

While 'biographical objects' age along with their owners, and 'public commodities' remain 'youthful', according to Hoskins and Morin, museum objects have previously aged as part of everyday lives but in the museum come to a temporal standstill. Here they are 'frozen' – fixed at the moment when they ceased to be part of such ordinary lives. Sometimes, museums seek to 'return' objects to their earlier state, to remove the rust or to repaint, though others leave them as they were found, even if this state is a consequence of years of neglect rather than of use itself. At the Museum of Island Life, there is evidence of both of these courses of action – houses have been rethatched and repaired but tools have an ever increasing patina of rust. However, from the way in which Jonathan Macdonald talks about the objects it is clear that what is most important is the fact that they are *old*: they have lived through time and been part of an earlier way of life. Here, for example, is how he describes how he started to collect and form the basis of the museum:

> Many, many years ago when I had just left school I started off doing weaving in the local weaving factory and . . . after that, around 1950 . . . I started a craft shop, a little craft shop down the road, and I had to buy crafts from various people. And part of that shop I put aside for old things because I had an interest in old things. And I began collecting around that time and it was an interest I had all my life – collecting old things, and hearing old stories and history and old songs and so on. And anything old interested me and I began a collection in a corner of that shop. And in 1965 . . . I moved the lot of the artefacts in here and it started from there. And of course ever since then I have always collected old things, collecting all the time. I never seemed to be far from old things and collecting more.

The 'old things' that Jonathan Macdonald collected were not confined to a very specific time-period and the museum itself contains artefacts ranging from several hundred years ago (as with some of the Flora MacDonald memorabilia) to fairly recent (e.g. coronation memorabilia of Elizabeth II). The majority, however, are from what he describes as 'the period before the white houses and the comforts that we have'. This is a world that he caught glimpses of as a child – for example at the ceilidh house (house for meeting, singing and telling stories) which he sometimes attended when young – and that his parents and grandparents had lived through. Gathering the artefacts of this period was a means of salvaging a way of life which was on the brink of vanishing:

> It was firstly a case of trying to keep together something that I saw disintegrating and *fast* disappearing. Because when I was a young boy growing up people were very very anxious to get new things – new houses, new comforts, everything new, piped water, roads, cars, tractors. Everything they could find, they were striving hard to get them so that they could get out of the old way of life and into a better and more comfortable way. And this [the museum] was something here that I believed would keep the best of what we had lost or were about to lose.

Weiner has suggested that 'inalienable possessions' may be help to articulate notions of stability and permanence through the fact that even though they are passed on, they remain somehow 'kept'. The transformation of 'ordinary objects' into 'museum objects' is likewise an expression of stability and, more specifically in the case of museums of everyday life, of stability in the face of change. The attempt to salvage a way of life which has just been swept away is characteristic of many such museums, whether they deal especially with rural life or with industrial heritage. By maintaining the objects of such lives through time – museumizing them – the ways of life themselves in a sense live on. 'History comes alive!' as the leaflets so often claim. Or, as Jonathan Macdonald puts it in talking about generations and the effect that he hopes his museum will have on young people:

> I thought of it as being a museum that people, young people of Skye, you see, who were coming through a major change, would see how their parents and their grandparents, and their forefathers lived. And I was hoping very much that people in Skye would come here and say this is how my people lived earlier on. And that would be something for them to keep alive, keep alive their history.

What we see in Jonathan Macdonald's account, and in his museum and so many others, is an attempt to rescue certain ways of life from transience. Rapid social change has rendered whole ways of life ready to be discarded like so many commodities. The constant emphasis on the 'new', which Jonathan Macdonald sees in the desires of so many people around him and which Morin sees as typical of 'public commodity' relations, risks, in this account, failing to hold on to anything of value from the past. By literally preserving 'old things' – artefacts which would otherwise be thrown away – it is as though the way of life and the people of that time are 'de-alienated', removed from kinds of social relations that are imagined as typical of a more modern 'consumerist' society. To be forgotten is conceptualized as a kind of death; but by employing objects as mnemonic devices, capable of 'carrying' the past, the past is brought into the present and, with the 'young' generations who are part of the museum creator's hoped-for audience, into the future. The museum is thus understood as a means of denying ephemerality – as a symbolic counter to the transience of a world in which 'the new' threatens to predominate and even overwhelm. In a period in which it is widely perceived that 'all that is solid melts into air', as Marx so famously expressed it, museums of everyday life, rather literally, attempt to 'resolidify'.

Space

Just as the 'past life' of museum objects is crucial to their temporal mediation, so too is the fact that they are 'of the place', or 'from here or hereabouts', to their mediation of space. The biographical object in Morin's and Hoskins' account 'limits the concrete space of its owner and sinks its roots deeply into the soil' (Hoskins 1998: 8). Because the objects in museums such as the Skye Museum of Island Life have already come *from* the local area, and may even have worked the local soil, they help conjure up a concrete and lived *space*: that is, a *place*.

In the case of the Skye Museum of Island Life, that 'place' is Skye, as the name of the museum implies, and as the museum's creator often invokes in his accounts. 'Placeness' is often also conceived at a still more local level, as when he talks of where the objects have come from and the significance of Flora MacDonald – here, it is the townships that most closely surround the museum that seem in fact to be the 'place' that is being imagined. As is particularly characteristic of the discourse of 'place' in the Scottish Highlands (see Macdonald 1997a) and to an extent in many parts of Britain (and in the anthropology of Britain), place is to a degree conflated with community. To be 'of the place', as would be said in Skye, is not simply to live in a particular area but to be bound into a set of social relationships. To be 'of the place' is to 'belong' – to use a possessive term which both is used indigenously and has been the focus for some insightful anthropological accounts of identity in various areas of Britain (Cohen 1982). The objects in the Museum of Island life are 'of the place' not so much because they have been made there – very many have not – but because they have been implicated in social lives in the locality. And just as people can 'belong' to a place, so too can 'objects'. Indeed, as in the case of the temporal mediation of objects, what is involved here is objects obliquely 'standing for' persons, not just as individuals but also as part of a collective. This evocation of identities through the medium of objects – property, belongings – is in turn part of a wider culturally prevalent mode of conceptualizing 'identity' itself as property; a mode which, in relation to persons, has been referred to as 'possessive individualism' (MacPherson 1962) but which, by extension, has also become typical of increasingly transnational modes of thinking 'cultures' and 'cultural identities' (Handler 1988; Hides 1997). Within this semantic web, museums – as repositories of 'a culture's' 'cultural property' – become manifestations of cultural identities (sometimes before the latter are widely acknowledged within localities).

One aspect of narratives of belonging, exemplified in such museums as well as in the anthropology of Britain, is an attempt to reclaim both difference and independence in the midst of changes which are widely believed to threaten both. In popular discourse this threat is often envisaged particularly in relation to material culture: mass production and mass consumption being cast as obliterating distinctive identities, as, for example, regionally distinctive clothing is replaced by jeans and tee-shirts, and local foodstuffs by burgers and cola. In Jonathan Macdonald's account, 'new' products and 'comforts' 'from outside' are regarded as threatening local integrity; and in his museum he wants to tell local people:

that it is always a good idea to hold on to the good things of the past. And to really show them, you see, how people were so ingenious and how they did things for themselves. They weren't dependent on the outside world. They were dependent on their own resources. But they relied on themselves, you see, and what was around them. You see, even in the building of a house there was nothing brought in except pieces of wood, perhaps, from the shore. Everything else, you see, was there and they used it. They had to be resourceful. I think that this is something that young people have to learn nowadays – to be more resourceful and to use what is available to them – to be more concerned really, not to really look to the outside world for everything. They should be more looking to themselves, to create and to use and to establish things from what they have . . . You see, I'm *ashamed* when I look at the island that we live in now. Even all of the milk that we drink every day is from outside; all our vegetables brought in, everything – butcher meat, bread, whatever, brought in from outside. And we do so very little for ourselves. We are so *reliant* on *other people*. And this is the example and lesson I think that this portrays, that people were very versatile and could put their hand to everything.

As is done in the museum, then, presenting a locality's 'own' objects – especially those which demonstrate local production (the weaving looms, the ploughs, the steam engines) – stands as a testament to local resourcefulness and independence from the 'outside' which is regarded as threatening to engulf the local.

At another level, however, museums of this type often simultaneously refer to a way of life that is broader than the locality – e.g. 'island life', 'rural life', 'the industrial age'. This has two dimensions. First, it metaphorically extends the significance of the local – a process that I have referred to previously as extending 'semantic reach' (1997b). Second, moving metonymically and 'intensionally' (as opposed to extensionally) this time, it makes broader ways of life and social processes visible and 'grasp-able' at a local level. The museum – located in a discrete and 'over-see-able' space – presents itself as a microcosm (cf. Proesler 1996); and the visitor is invited to enter not just a few old houses from a local township, or a mill from this particular industrial town, but something conceived as representative of a broader way of life. At the same time, this spatial mediation can serve to help 'de-alienate' those wider processes by inserting locality and the idea of human presence into them. In the museums, one aim is to remind us that we are not dealing with 'mere' objects or 'mere' technologies but with people's lives.

The fact that museums themselves occupy a terrain helps to convey this idea: the visitor literally inserts their presence into the space, and – in the words of the advertizing leaflets again – is invited to 'experience the past'. By physically moving through the space of the museum – strolling from one black house to another or between different parts of the mill – the visitor is conceptualized as being in proximity to (being 'in touch with') past lives. The recreation of domestic interiors, with their carefully constructed *Marie Celeste* impression of being only temporarily vacated (knitting still on the chair, a half-eaten meal on the table), is one of the most powerful ways in which this sense of proximity is effected. It is, moreover, characteristic of a cultural conception of spaces as relationally 'layered' in terms of belonging, with domestic space as the most intimate, followed by locality or community, and layering out to national and then global space. The depiction of an anonymous domestic interior in the museum – an interior which we are supposed to understand as representing many such interiors – is thus also one of the ways in which we are enabled to think layered space; and thus bring wider spaces 'home'. Furthermore, because 'the home' in Britain has (especially since the nineteenth century) widely come to be depicted as a 'haven' from public life (and even the 'heartless world') – and because, more broadly, personal and collective identities are conceptualized as analogous – domestic interiors represent the idea that the local identity has 'inner spaces' or 'inner depths'. The museum thus physically articulates certain key features of 'the modern identity': the possession of 'inner depths' and the expression of distinctiveness (Taylor 1989).

Ownership/Consumption

Who is the 'owner' of the museum object? Part of the museum effect is to move objects from individual ownership into what is conceived as a more collective ownership – ownership by the locality. Although the Skye Museum of Island Life, for example, has been conceived and executed largely by one person (with no external funding), he talks about doing this as though on behalf of 'the people of Skye'; and when people bring him artefacts for the museum, they do so not as a personal gift but as contributions to a local resource. Indeed, the establishment by the Museums and Galleries Commission in the 1980s of a museum's registration scheme was partly intended to try to deal with the potentially conflicting notions of 'ownership' involved in such donations in the face of the massive expansion of independent museums. In donating objects to museums, the Commission recognized, individuals did not regard these as becoming the property of the museum owners to do with whatever they wanted, but rather conceptualized their donations as in a sense 'public' and assumed that objects would be kept in the museum and preserved for ever.

In museums, ownership and consumption are potentially separate. However, they are almost always conceptualized as to a degree overlapping, and the imagined collective 'owners' are nearly always claimed as the most important audience. Talk of 'the community' and attempts to involve 'the community' are very widespread in these kinds of museum. Jonathan Macdonald, for example, recognizes (and values) that the Skye Museum of Island Life attracts tourists but he emphasizes that it was not *for* tourists that he began the museum: it was 'for the people of Skye'. And although the museum is a public space, it acts as a biographical object in just the way described by Morin: as a witness to the unity of its 'owners' and as a making of their everyday experience 'into a thing' (quoted in Hoskins 1998: 8). As a collection of objects which are 'kept' – which are 'inalienable' in Weiner's terms – the museum is a manifestation of the very existence of the locality to which it 'belongs'. Moreover, it literally 'objectifies' the everyday experience, and very existence, of the locality by representing it through a collection of things (the manifestation of 'possessive collectivism' mentioned above).

In museums of everyday life, then, objects are to some extent contrasted with the relationships that are stereotypically regarded as characteristic of 'public commodities'. Ownership is collective rather than individual, objects are salvaged and preserved rather than bought, sold and thrown away, and those who come to 'consume' – i.e. visit – the museum do not literally take the museum's objects away with them. In this way, I suggest, the act of collection and the institution of the museum serve as important symbolic counterpoints to – even as a kind of cultural commentary upon – other kinds of relationship to objects which are perceived as alienating and ephemeral. Moreover, because objects are associated with personal and collective identities, museums of everyday life can also stand for the possibility of retaining personal and collective values in an increasingly 'throw-away' society. Museums offer the promise of 're-enchantment' in the face of social processes which are widely perceived as 'disenchanting' (in Weberian terms).

The elision of 'owners' or 'producers' with 'viewers' or 'consumers', so important to the rhetoric of museum creators and managers, is important to this attempted re-enchantment. So too, I suggest, is an emphasis on *experience* which seems so often to be privileged in advertizing leaflets and museum-makers' accounts. Experience is not just looking: it is 'being in touch with', transcending the boundaries between past and present, viewers and viewed. The spatial layouts of such museums, entailing not just gazing upon a scene set out in a diorama behind glass but actually entering an original black-house, mill or factory – placing oneself *within* – configures the audience not as 'outside' (as in the 'window-ethic' mode of seeing (Adam 1995: 131)) but as 'implicated' (ibid.). The presence of *everyday* objects, and the representation of 'ordinary' lives ('we' as viewers would probably have lived or worked like this), is a further dimension of this subject:object implication. Viewers are being invited here not so much to gaze upon 'others' but on themselves as they might have been: they are being asked to *identify* rather than to position themselves as distanced subjects. The domestic interiors, and perhaps especially those artefacts that visitors remember from their own childhoods or from those told by their grandparents (those Oxo-cube tins, inhaling devices for Vick's Vapo-rub, an advert for Birds' Custard Powder, the mangles, the irons), are particularly effective in generating a sense of semi-familiarity and thus mediating the subject/object divide.[4] And even in what might seem to be unfamiliar contexts for most visitors, as a mill or pottery factory might be for younger visitors today, the exhibitionary strategies, accompanying text or guide will probably work, with varying degrees of success, at trying to generate a sense of imagined implication ('You lad, how old are you? Ten? Well, you'd have been working here, then. Up at six, not knocking off until six or after . . .').

The Skye Museum of Island Life began its own life as a collection in a craft shop. The presence of 'old things' that were not available to be bought or sold within a shop, the main purpose of which, by definition, was buying and selling, can itself be seen as an attempt to mediate some of the usual connotations involved in commodity relations. In her account of 'inalienable possessions', Weiner suggests that their presence can alter the meaning of other kinds of exchange or relations in their vicinity. So too, the 'old things' in the craft shop helped to transform this from being a site of 'mere commercial exchange' and the objects for sale from being 'mere' ephemeral goods. With their symbolic weight of age, stability and locality, the 'old things' helped to suggest that visitors too could buy something which might one day become an 'old thing' – unlike most mass-produced fast-discarded artefacts – as part of the personal collection of its purchaser perhaps.

Museums today nearly always have a shop, and museums of everyday life, including the Skye Museum of Island Life, are no exception. Within the perspective that has been pursued in this chapter, such shops can be seen not as a separate subject for analysis but within the same framework. It is notable that such shops do not contain just any objects: rather, these are specially selected and generally play upon similar sets of ideas to those represented in the museum, perhaps also within similar presentational styles. At the Skye Museum of Island Life, for example, the shop is also contained in a black house, and a dresser – similar to that in the reconstructed domestic interior – is used to present a selection of pottery, jams, shortbread and other products for sale. Almost all of the items displayed are in some sense 'local' even if this is construed here as more generically 'Scottish highland' (as in the tartan-boxed shortbread) – they may have been locally-produced, or may depict local scenes (postcards and watercolours of nearby landmarks), or at the least (as with key-rings, pencils, purses, miniature tool-kits) they have the name of the museum itself on them. In some museums of everyday life, reproduction (or in some cases real) 'old things' are on sale – as, for example, with bobbins in many mill towns in the North of England and crockery in museums in the Potteries; and occasionally products of the museums themselves can be bought (e.g. flour from a windmill in Nottinghamshire, scissors from a workshop located in a Sheffield industrial museum). This could, of course, be seen as a cynical marketing ploy but even if it is (and I suggest it only sometimes is), it draws nevertheless on a powerful popular drive to make consumption meaningful, to remove it from alienating social relations, to 'sacralize' it (cf. Miller 1998), to endow it with the *subjective*. Museums, which transform objects of everyday use into objects of devotion, are one space in which this can be effected; and their shops, which invite visitors to buy artefacts of the locality – objects which can themselves act as mementoes, carrying one time into another, even turning their owners into collectors – are another space in which objects can be rescued from the fate of being 'mere' commodities.

The Fetishization of Everyday Life

Taking 'ordinary', 'mundane' objects of the recent past and putting them on display in museums entails a kind of fetishization of everyday life. Key to the fetish is its 'irreducible materiality' (Pietz 1985: 7) which contributes to its capacity to cross borders (Spyer 1998) – of time, space or identities. And while fetishes often seem to be worthless to outsiders, and the objects of apparently 'irrational' devotion, anthropologists have sought to understand the meanings with which they may be imbued.

For Marx, one characteristic of capitalism, is 'commodity fetishism' (Marx 1976). As Peter Stallybrass notes, this was one of Marx's 'least understood jokes' (1998: 184), for what Marx was emphasizing was not the *material* nature of commodities but that capitalism entails a fetishization of 'the invisible, the immaterial', i.e. de-materialized pure monetary values (ibid.). It is against this – and the alienation that such fetishism of monetary exchange-value produces – that the fetishization of ordinary objects and lives described here is constructed. Marx's notion of 'commodity fetishism' purposefully couples two terms not usually considered together in order to highlight the historical and cultural specificity of the practice involved. The notion of 'everyday fetishism' is likewise intentionally paradoxical. The objects in museums of everyday life may not be 'strange' or 'exotic' either to those who collect them or to anthropologists of Britain, but this should not be allowed to obscure either the 'special' meanings with which they may be imbued or the more general significance of the cultural practice of which they are part.

Putting familiar everyday objects and everyday lives on museological display is, as noted above, especially characteristic of the post-1960s period in Britain; and it is, moreover, a practice which has flourished especially in parts of Britain which are relatively marginal within late capitalism (though which were perhaps once much more central). There has been a good deal of commentary from various disciplines on the post-War 'heritage boom' under which the cultural practice discussed here could be subsumed; and some of this has noted a frequent motif of 'ordinary' lives (e.g. Wright 1985; Samuel 1994). In this chapter my aim has not been to try to read this practice off from wider contextual change but to approach it both from 'within' (i.e. from the point of view of some of those involved) and comparatively (i.e. in relation to various other kinds of object-practice). One consequence of the former is that it enables understanding of the practice not simply as an *outcome* of certain broader developments but as an active commentary upon them. This commentary may be entail a familiar romantic allegory of resistance to potentially alienating social change, but this makes it no less deserving of anthropological attention. This attention – involving the comparative approach – highlights the web of knowledge and practice, entailing culturally-specific ideas about time, space, objects and identities, involved.

The idea that the post-Second World War period in Britain (and elsewhere) has been one of considerable and dislocating social change is widespread; and has been the subject of extensive social and cultural theorizing. Many of these accounts have suggested that this period (be it described as post-Fordist, post-Modern, late-Modern, the time of flows or whatever) is one in which our very conceptions of time, space and identities – the foci of this chapter – have been transformed. In a period in which time and space are 'compressed' (Harvey 1989) or 'distanciated' and identities 'fragmented' or 'disembedded' (Giddens 1991), an increase in cultural practices seeking to provide existential anchors is not surprising. What is of particular interest, however, is the forms in which this has flourished. In the case of museums of everyday life this has involved the 'irreducible materiality' of object fetishism – a form which, I have suggested here, should be understood at least partly in relation to other kinds of object relations, particularly 'commodity fetishism' and 'materialism' (as popularly understood, *contra* Marx, as an undue concentration upon superficial material things). The emphasis on *everyday* things (and lives) is an ultimate extension of this idea – *everything* can be salvaged, everything turned into a collector's item, and all lives given recognition (in an appropriate identity-displaying agency such as a museum). It is also a function of the rapidity of commodity obsolescence which generates ever more 'old things'; a phenomenon which also has a practical dimension in that it is now possible to start a museum with little more than a garage full of 'junk'.

Many factors, more than discussed here, are implicated in the fetishization of everyday life – some of them relatively long-standing (such as notions of possessive collectivism and the interiorization of identity), others more recent (such as the salvage of newly 'old' things and the attribution of all kinds of social ills to the lust for 'new' things). In attempting to read this cultural practice in relation to a selection of anthropological literature on objects, I hope that I have highlighted some of the particular cultural assumptions involved in the practice: e.g. that objects can stand for lives, that the past can be 'experienced', that identities can be expressed in material form, that commodities can be 'de-alienated'. In doing so, my aim has also been to assert that the collection of otherwise fairly mundane 'old things' into special places where they can, for a fee, be visited by whoever has a wish to do so, is surely as culturally a significant object practice in contemporary Britain as, for example, the potlatch or the Kula in other places about which anthropologists have written so much.

Acknowledgements

I am very grateful to all those working at museums, and most especially to Mr Jonathan Macdonald, for help given during the research for this chapter. It has also benefited from insightful comments from Michael Beaney, Mary Bouquet, Jeanette Edwards and Nigel Rapport.

Notes

1. See especially Edwards 1998 for insightful anthropological discussion of this; and also Edwards 2000.
2. Museums may in some circumstances exchange objects with other museums and, of course, once in museums objects may make all kinds of movements (e.g. between cabinets and storage spaces). For discussion of such movements and the continued accumulation of histories see Saumerez-Smith 1989.
3. Some museums do provide names of individuals depicted in photographs, even though these may not mean much to some of those who view. For local people, however, reading the museum in terms of more specific and personal knowledge is likely to take place with or without the provision of information by the museum (cf. Blaikie 2001; Clifford 1997, especially chapters 5 and 7). In the Skye Museum of Island Life, for example, local people could often point out just who a particular photograph was of, or who had donated a certain item, in relation to contemporary kinship links in the area. This was a practice that also occurred in relation to other media, for example published books about the area. Thus local neighbours would indicate to me in books that I had bought that, say, a picture headed 'a crofter cutting the peats' was in fact Murdina's grandfather (cf. Cohen 1987: 134) . Trying to make such identifications, and asking others for help in doing so, was a practice which I often witnessed.
4. In this respect these museums are like those middle-class television-owners discussed by Hirsch (1998) who try to work against the grain of the 'culture of the exhibition' which classically positions 'audiences, persons and objects' as separate 'bounded entities'.

References

Adam, B. (1995) *Timewatch: The Social Analysis of Time*, Cambridge: Polity.
Appadurai, A. (1986) 'Introduction: Commodities and the Politics of Value', in A. Appadurai (ed.) *The Social Life of Things: Commodities in Cultural Perspective*, Cambridge: Cambridge University Press.

Blaikie, A. (2001) 'Photographs in the Cultural Account: Contested Narratives and Collective Memory in the Scottish Islands', *Sociological Review* 49(3): 345–67.

Carrier, J. (1994) *Gifts and Commodities: Exchange and Western Capitalism since 1700*, London: Routledge.

Clifford, J. (1997) *Routes: Travel and Translation in the late Twentieth Century*, Cambridge, MA: Harvard University Press.

Cohen, A. P. (ed.) (1982) *Belonging: Identity and Social Organisation in British Rural Cultures*, Manchester: Manchester University Press.

—— (1987) *Whalsay: Symbol, Segment and Boundary in a Shetland Island Community*, Manchester: Manchester University Press.

Edwards, J. (1998) 'The Need for a "Bit of History": Place and Past in English Identity', in N. Lovell (ed.) *Locality and Belonging*, London: Routledge.

—— (2000) *Born and Bred. Idioms of Kinship and New Reproductive Technologies in England*, Oxford: Oxford University Press.

Giddens, A. (1991) *Modernity and Self-Identity: Self and Society in the Late Modern Age*, Cambridge: Polity.

Handler, R. (1988) *Nationalism and the Politics of Culture in Quebec*, Madison: University of Wisconsin Press.

Harvey, D. (1989) *The Condition of Postmodernity*, Oxford: Blackwell.

Hides, S. (1997) 'The Genealogy of Material Culture and Cultural Identity', in S. Pearce (ed.) *Experiencing Material Culture in the Western World*, London: Leicester University Press.

Hirsch, E. (1998) 'Bound and Unbound Entities: Reflections on the Ethnographic Perspectives of Anthropology vis-à-vis Media and Cultural Studies', in F. Hughes-Freeland (ed.) *Ritual, Performance, Media*, London: Routledge.

Hoskins, J. (1998) *Biographical Objects: How Things Tell the Stories of People's Lives*, London: Routledge.

Kirschenblatt-Gimblett, B. (1998) *Destination Culture: Tourism, Museums, and Heritage*, Berkeley: University of California Press.

Kopytoff, I. (1986) 'The Cultural Biography of Things', in A. Appadurai (ed.) *The Social Life of Things: Commodities in Cultural Perspective*, Cambridge: Cambridge University Press.

Lowenthal, D. (1998) *The Heritage Crusade and the Spoils of History*, Cambridge: Cambridge University Press.

Macdonald, S. (1997a) *Reimagining Culture: Histories, Identities and the Gaelic Renaissance*, Oxford: Berg.

—— (1997b) 'A People's Story: Heritage, Identity and Authenticity', in C. Rojek and J. Urry (eds) *Touring Cultures: Transformations of Travel and Theory*, London: Routledge.

MacPherson, C.B. (1962) *The Political Theory of Possessive Individualism*, Oxford: Oxford University Press.

Malinowski, B. (1922) *Argonauts of the Western Pacific*, London: Routledge.

Marx, K. (1976[1876]) *Capital: A Critique of Political Economy*, vol. 1, trans. Ben Fowkes, New York: Vintage.

Mauss, M. (1967[1925]) *The Gift: Forms and Functions of Exchange in Archaic Societies* trans. Ian Cunnison, London: Routledge.

Miller, D. (1998) *A Theory of Shopping*, Cambridge: Polity.

Morin, V. (1969) 'L'objet biographique', *Communications* 13: 131–9.

Pietz, W. (1985) 'The Problem of the Fetish', in *Res* 9: 5–17.

Proesler, M. (1996) 'Museums and Globalization', in S. Macdonald and G. Fyfe (eds) *Theorizing Museums: Representing Identity and Diversity in a Changing World*, Oxford: Blackwell.

Samuel, R. (1994) *Theatres of Memory*, London: Verso.

Saumerez-Smith, C. (1989) 'Museums, Artefacts and Meanings', in P. Vergo (ed.) *The New Museology*, London: Reaktion Books.

Spyer, P. (1998) 'Introduction', in P. Spyer (ed.) *Border Fetishisms: Material Objects in Unstable Places*, London: Routledge.

Stallybrass, P. (1998) 'Marx's Coat', in P. Spyer (ed.) *Border Fetishisms: Material Objects in Unstable Places*, London: Routledge.

Strathern, M. (1987) 'The Limits of Auto-anthropology', in A. Jackson (ed.) *Anthropology at Home*, London: Tavistock.

Taylor, C. (1989) *Sources of the Self: The Making of the Modern Identity*, Cambridge: Cambridge University Press.

Urry, J. (1995) *Consuming Places*, London: Routledge.

Weiner, A. (1992) *Inalienable Possessions: The Paradox of Keeping-while Giving*, Berkeley: University of California Press.

Wright, P. (1985) *On Living in an Old Country – the National Past in Contemporary Britain*, London: Verso.

–5–

Leisure and Change in a Post-mining Mining Town
Andrew Dawson

Introduction

For the elderly working-class men who still use them, Ashington's allotments are a haven from the vicissitudes of worldly events. They are protected physically. Six-foot high fences divide pit workings, a run-down council estate, a shopping centre and a busy main road from the green and tranquil space they encompass. The boundary between the two is permeated only by the constant chatter of transistor radios that accompanies the weeding, digging and planting. The radios bring in news and information that provides material for in-shed and over-the-fence conversation. Conversation, which focuses on a range of issues, but that of change in particular, is strikingly ambivalent in character. On one hand, it is highly individualized. As competition growing is the order of the day, sharing gardener's secrets is a no-no. Nevertheless, the ability to talk a good garden is at least as important as actually growing one (see also Herzfeld, 1986). While being careful not to divulge too much, men boast about their fail-safe recipes for success. Some of the knowledge extolled is based on tradition, other on experimentation and other on innovation in the horticultural sciences and beyond. On the other hand, conversation is highly consensual. Notably, with knowing nods and utterances of agreement, reflections on change, about which they are reminded by the radio news, are juxtaposed discursively to the certainties of the annual growing cycle, to the slow and sometimes years-long development of plants, to the values of patience and commitment required of the good gardener, and to the permanence of the allotments amidst the flux that surrounds them.

A basic starting point in most sociological writing on leisure is that it is 'non-work' (Clark 1992: 255). Beyond this there is little consensus. Indeed, scenes such as the one I have described, and the conversational ambivalence in particular, resonate with a schism in contemporary sociological accounts of the role of leisure. For theorists of postmodern society, individuals define themselves by leisure activities, creating styles and identities from the artefacts and cultures of a pluralist society (ibid.). For others leisure is structured by class, gender and ethnicity and is, above all, a central means of fostering community (ibid.: 268). The persistence of this schism is particularly woeful in the light of other developments in the sociology and anthropology generally. In particular, consideration of the theoretical tension between the roles of agency and structure in the constitution of society and the individual has been a defining contribution of the British ethnographic tradition. Empirically, exploration of this tension has often focused on the issue of the maintenance of social order, on how individuality is managed within the context of community, in times of rapid change (see for example Cohen 1978).

Focusing on the elderly residents of Ashington, a former coal-mining town in North East England, this chapter argues that leisure provides an important context through which people can respond effectively to or, in other words, 'work-out' change, and post-industrial change in particular. Central among these changes, particularly for older people, is a need to make new social networks and manage the potential for conflict within them. This 'working-out' of change through leisure also consists of a mode of communication in which the potential for conflict that would otherwise be wrought by the unfettered expression of individual views, about the changes that have beset the area in particular, is minimized.

Change: from Industrialism to Post-industrialism

Ashington, a town of almost 30,000 in North East England, was born on the back of coal-mining, and for much of its existence it was commonly referred to as 'the biggest coal-mining village in the world'. While the coal industry went into gradual decline after the end of the Second World War, it maintained its position of local economic centrality until the early 1980s. However, in the aftermath of the 1983–84 strike and within a period of merely three years all but one of the local pits closed. The closures brought with them rapid and massive social changes.

The dirt of the mining industry is both a symbol of the town's marginality and a central marker of its identity (Dawson 1998: 213). Thus, in the absence of any other significant source of local employment Ashington became, almost, 'a coal-mining town' without a coal-mine. More concretely, the closures brought large-scale unemployment and the eradication of a form of employment with highly particular social relations (Morgan 1989, Wight 1993, Dunk 1994). First, the pits were peculiarly nepotistic and familistic contexts of employment, where fathers eased the way for the employment of sons and, often, were responsible for their apprenticeship (Dennis, et al. 1956). Secondly, while the pits were almost exclusively male domains, the small-scale service and light industrial sectors that were left in their wake were staffed largely by women (see also Crompton 1997 and Walby 1999). Finally, the pits drew, except during times of strike action, almost exclusively on a local workforce (see also Bulmer 1975). Thus, despite its rapid early growth some two hundred years ago on the back of an influx of migrant labour, Ashington had for much of its history a very stable population. In recent years however, through outmigration and other processes, its population has changed noticeably. A most visible symbol of change is the growth of its immigrant population. In recent years the small Chinese, Italian and South Asian populations who work largely in the town's service sector have been added to periodically, by a small number of refugees. The earliest of these, from Vietnam and Cambodia, were resettled as part of a humanitarian gesture by local authorities. However, more recently, and in the light of opportunities wrought by government legislation[1], rumours are rife throughout the town that the local resettlement of refugees is being considered seriously as one avenue for local economic and social regeneration.

These themes of identity and change, particularly in terms of gender, inter-generational and ethnic relations, permeate the ethnographic vignettes of leisure activities in Ashington that follow.

Leisure

Rearing

One of the most ubiquitous sights in Ashington's allotments, gardens, parks and streets is the old man and his animals. In most instances the relationship is, in part at least, a working one. Horses are kept for prize showing. Horses, pigeons and dogs are kept for racing and betting. Dogs and cocks are kept for fighting and betting. Dogs and ferrets are kept for hunting. Relationships are established with feral cats for purposes of pest control. And, most commonly, rabbits, chickens and pigs are reared for food.

The commonality of animal rearing for food is rooted in the peculiarities of local history. Ashington's history as a significant urban centre dates back only to the early twentieth century. Rapid development of the local mining industry in this period required the colliery owners to import a labour force from outlying rural areas and from their agricultural estate lands in places as distant as Ulster. Continuity of the rural subsistence skills that these people brought to the area was facilitated principally by the emergence and resilience of the allotment movement and stimulated periodically by the shortages of war, recession and unemployment.

Having said this, rearing of animals is more than a mere matter of subsistence. These semi-domestic animals are subjects of an array of beliefs and practices whose logic is intimately related to local experience, and, in particular, to the threat of mining death. Above all, the pig is simultaneously the most revered and feared of animals. In some accounts it is attributed with the powers of prediction. Charlie Burnsey: 'You can tell when there's a storm comin' when a P.I.G. turns its arse to the breeze.' In other accounts it is characterized as the purest of animals. Jackie

Thompson: The pig eats nothing but 'rubbish, muck and shite, but when you cut it open it's as clean as a whistle'. Indeed, among the varied ingredients, the Guinness, the virgin's urine, and the rabbit droppings, that are used to nourish prize vegetables, pig's blood is regarded by many as the very best. Charlie Burnsey: 'A bucket of gissy blood on your leeks works wonders . . . it's like rocket fuel.'

Contrastively, for fear of inviting death many people refrain from using the word pig, referring to it instead as 'P.I.G.', 'gissy', 'grunter' or descriptively 'round fat thing with stumpy legs'. On a number of occasions the taboo has been used effectively. For example, one man relayed a story of the last days of the strike of 1928. Many of the men at Newbiggin pit were weakening and returning to work. In response, a group of men broke in and nailed the decapitated head of a pig to the entrance of the main shaft. Before the management had time to remove it, one of the returning men saw it and beat a hasty retreat. Word of the event spread and the strike remained firm for a while longer.

Buffing

'Buffs' clubs, whose name is taken from the organization to which they are affiliated, 'The Royal Antideluvian Order of the Buffaloes', have provided a key socializing context for local men since their inception at the beginning of the twentieth century. However, regarded widely as anachronistic, a poor man's version of the Masonic Lodge, with all the ritual but none of the power, they are fading gradually from the local scene. The dwindling of membership at North Seaton Lodge no. 1 was met by an eagerness to recruit. Joining is an ordeal, involving the learning of a complex pattern of secret door knocks and password exchanges, bodily exposure, a symbolic breaking and remaking of the self, smoking the Native American Indian peace pipe, swearing allegiance to the Queen and, finally, fulfilling the requirement to get roaring drunk.

The humiliating dimension within the rituals of aggregation is carried over into the monthly visit of Lodge no. 2, a lodge of considerably younger men. The evening consists largely of members of one lodge raising accusations about members of the other. The satin-robed 'City Policeman', from Lodge no. 1, weighs up evidence presented by either side, passes judgement and then levies a fine which is to be paid by the victor:

Brother Wayne (Lodge no. 2): City Policeman, Brother George's just tell us there's a dolphin behind the bar.
City Policeman: Do you wish to raise this as a charge Brother Wayne?
Brother Wayne: I do.
City Policeman: Then bring your charge brother.

Brother Wayne: City Policeman, I charge Brother George Reilly from North Seaton Lodge no. 1 with telling a falsehood, that there's a dolphin behind the bar.

City Policeman: What do you say to this charge Brother George?

Brother George (Lodge no. 1): City Policeman, I say that this is a false charge. I call Brother Billy Jeffries to give evidence in me defence. He'll prove beyond any reasonable doubt that Brother Wayne's nout but a lying little shite. In fact, it was Brother Wayne who started all this dolphin nonsense.

City Policeman: What do you say Brother Billy?

Brother Billy (Lodge no. 1): City Policeman, I say that they're both lying shites.

City Policeman: Ah well, there's only one thing to do to resolve this matter. Mr Thompson (barman), look behind the bar and see if there's a dolphin there.

Barman: Nee dolphin here your Lordship.

City Policeman: Right. There's nee dolphin behind the bar. Brother Wayne is indeed a lying little shite. The charge stands. Brother Wayne, do you have anything to say for yourself?

Brother Wayne: Yes. There's nee justice in this lodge. And the City Policeman likes to take it up the arse . . . (laughter) . . . look at the fancy dress man!

City Policeman: That may well be so. However, for lying and attempting to slander the name of the City Policeman I set the fine at one whole pound. This will be paid by Brother George on Brother Wayne's behalf and distributed in the traditional manner.

Brother Wayne: The City Policeman sniffs little girl's knickers an' aall.

City Policeman: Make that one pound fifty.

In usual fashion, Brother Wayne knelt at the feet of the Grand Master. The coins were distributed by Brother George and rained down on Brother Wayne with force by the members of Lodge no. 1. The City Treasurer collects the money from the floor and puts it into the 'box' for later distribution to charities.

Writing[2]

Ashington's clubs for the elderly are far from being the restive places that they are often stereotypically described as being (see, for example NCHC, 1987). There is a considerable creative and performative dimension to club life. Many of the largely elderly women participants engage in the making, writing and/or performance of handicrafts, sketches, songs and, above all, poetry.

As writers, participants are conscious of their expected role as perpetuators of a local tradition of artistic creativity that was established in the miners' welfare associations and championed by a modernist urban intellectual elite in the early part of the twentieth century (see Fever, 1988). More recently this expectation has been encouraged formally and principally by the measures of a local authority that has, in the face of pit closure and fears about the town's loss of identity, tried to incorporate the elderly within a series of mining-related heritage ventures (Dawson 1998: 215).

After community, gender is the most common subject of poetic celebration in the clubs.[3] The images that emerge are underpinned by a range of everyday referents, but above all by ideas about the threat of mining death. Importantly, and in contrast to images of men, the images of women are largely negative.

At one level, women are represented as powerless. Some imagery celebrates women's power within the home. This is personified in the common image of the domestic matriarch:

> He pulls the bed-claes ower his heed,
> (Some minutes mare he'll try),
> Buth muther's voice 'ud wake the deed,
> And he timidly answers, 'Aye',
> Off cums his linin's, vest and sark,
> He strips reit doon't the buff,
> Me muthor gi's his arse a yark,
> And, shoots, 'Oot noo yuv had enough'.

Having said this, other material qualifies such images. For example, one particularly popular sketch performed by the 'Evergreen's' concert party depicts humorously the financial dealings of an elderly couple on club night. Bessie hands Geordie the bingo money over the table, but only after Geordie passes it to Bessie under the table. Ultimately, such images represent women's domestic power as in the gift of men and, thus, at best as circumscribed or, at worst as not really power at all.

At another level, men and women are represented as displaying propensities for both communalism and individualism. This gives onto further contrasts between sociability and privatism, collaboration and competitiveness, and peaceability and antagonism. In the case of men the ambivalence is usually resolved. The resolution involves reference to a discourse of necessities and needs. Underlying this is the threat of mining death. For example, antagonism of the verbal kind is represented widely as a means of testing and strengthening the resilience of the cooperative and mutually responsible working relations required to minimize danger in the pit. Conversely, drunkenness and the physical antagonism (physical fighting is one of the most striking aspects of Ashington street life) that it fosters are represented widely as a necessary compensation for and release from the pressures of hard working lives. They foster the psychological well-being, 'the right fettle', required to work vigilantly and, therefore, safely:

Then buzzer blaas, and man to man
They queue infront o' the cage
For ten lang ooers belaa they'll gan
To mek a livin' wage.

Then who wad dare that man to judge
If Sat'day neet he boozes?
Aye who amang ye wad begrudge
That confort if he chooses.

At yet another level, women are represented as dangerous. No such resolution of the ambivalence between communalism and individualism is apparent in representations of women. Indeed, a counterpoint to the discourse of necessities and needs is a discourse of blame, and blame that is usually attributed to women. Again, underlying this is the threat of mining death. It should be clear that beyond natural causes human error is regarded as the main source of danger in the pit. Reckless pursuit of productivity and psychological ill-being, 'the wrang fettle', are regarded as the main sources of human error. Women, as bad housekeepers or as makers of excessive sexual, domestic and/or financial demands are represented widely as the main source of such conditions. The link between women and death infuses much of the content of entertainment within the clubs.

A nagging wife promotes the strife,
That *maims* and *kills* affection,
And *buries* it deep, in *lasting sleep,*
Past hope of *resurrection.*

The link also extends to depictions of men's social death. The privatism of men is represented widely as brought about at the behest of women. For example, the content of the many retirement parties that take place in the clubs is invariably consistent, emphasizing men's gradual lifetime extrication from the social world of other men to a life of social exclusion and sexual and domestic domination by demanding wives (Dawson 1990: 180–1).

Importantly, much of the entertainment goes further than this, associating women with the pit and thereby in another way with death. The pit is often spoken of as if it had human qualities. For example, the creaking and grinding of earth movement is commonly presented as the coal speaking to indicate its strengths and weaknesses. More often than not the pit is gendered:

I bide in the darkness,
With the silence of the grave,
Men may prey or beat me,
Yet never see me wave.

With boys toiling tortured,
And sweating till they're tired,
There above bright world you wait me,
I'll always be required.

I lie below without a voice,
No body, heart nor soul,
So mortals bend on your knees,
For I am black queen coal.

The idea of a symbolically female pit also informs practice. Coal carries a heavy symbolic load, and one of its many perceived qualities is the power of protection (Dawson, 1998: 116). Thus, during the course of the working week many miners refrained from washing their backs, the point of contact with the earth above them, that which must be prevented from collapse. Some such miners would keep what is referred to as a 'dirty working bed', sleeping with their wives in the marital bed only at weekends. Beyond the obvious question of hygiene few reasons were offered for the practice other than that failure to adhere to it would be tantamount to inviting pit accidents and death. However, using material reasoning, it was suggested to me that since sex is physically draining, it hinders the miner's productive potential and his vigilance. It could also be suggested that the practice expresses a kind of symbolic serial monogamy between the miner and the two women in his life, pit and wife. Clearly, at least, the practice expresses an association between women, and women's sexuality in particular, the pit and death. This matrix is reflected in other respects. For example, the local name given to the terrifying noise of settling seam roofs is the 'Banshee', a female spirit whose wail portends death.

Finally, women are represented widely as being in need of control. Keeping a 'dirty working bed' is one among the many taboos respected and practices adhered to by miners for fear that failure to do so would be tantamount to inviting pit accidents and death. Having said this, the most widely written about and celebrated taboo concerns the conduct of women. It was considered unlucky and dangerous to see any woman while on the way from home to the 'back shift' that began at 2 a.m. At one level the taboo serves to control potential sexual liaison outside marriage. More importantly, it represents the domestic sphere as the appropriate sphere within which women should operate. Its emphasis on their confinement to this domain, enforced by the threat of mining death if transgressed, symbolizes the imperative of women's necessary and uncritical devotion to their supportive role within this context. Fundamentally, it reinforces the representation of women as potential agents of death if out of place.

Spectating

The dwindling fortunes of Ashington Association Football Club do not prevent a group of die-hard elderly supporters from turning up to home matches every other week. The club lost its Football League status years ago and has plummeted inexorably into obscurity ever since. Spectating is now a dubious pleasure, not enhanced by the leaking terrace roofs and the freezing sea wind that blows in through the derelict East Stand. Rather, as each, usually incompetent, home performance unfolds it provides a contrasting backdrop for reminiscences about local football heritage.

Despite Ashington AFC's demise, local sporting pride had been maintained through the steady stream of local boys who have made the big time elsewhere, from Jackie Milburn of Newcastle United's last League Championship team to the Charlton brothers of World Cup winning fame. However, the stream has slowed to a trickle in recent years as changes in employment legislation, player transfer rules and the quality of international football have led to an increasing cosmopolitanization of the 'English game'. Newcastle United, the second love at least of most Ashington supporters, is exemplary of these changes. With promotion from Second Division to Premier League in successive seasons and appearances in two FA Cup finals, the 1990s saw the first major resurgence in its fortunes since the 1950s. Significantly, the team featured players largely from continental Europe and Latin America.

Despite the relative success of cosmopolitan Newcastle United, a media outcry caused by the sale of the team's last remaining local player did much to prompt the multi-million pound purchase of another. However, the arrival of Alan Shearer, the Newcastle-born England striker, was followed by another period of decline. Matters came to a head in the late 1990s in a thinly veiled struggle within the team between Shearer and its Surinamese-Dutch coach, Ruud Gullit. The struggle was presented, accurately in part, as a clash of footballing philosophies, between the English and Continental games. In the end, localism won out, but only in part. Gullit left and was replaced by Bobby Robson, a local man whose career had nevertheless been marked by dramatic conversion from the English to the Continental way of playing.

Events at Newcastle United, 'The Toon', provide the central topic of conversation on Ashington's terraces. In recent years this has focused greatly on two related issues. First, what's better, the English or the Continental way of playing football? Given the success in recent years of Continental teams and cosmopolitan English teams, for the many who answered 'Continental', the question was barely worth asking. For others, the dichotomy was a false one. Football has for many years been characterized by the international import and export of styles and staff. Indeed, the great Newcastle United team of the 1950s was built as much on the endeavours of the Chilean Ribledo brothers as it was on the those of Jackie Milburn. Secondly, can Newcastle United really be regarded as a local team if it is made up largely of foreigners? For many, answering in the affirmative is easy. Team loyalty, rootedness, local ways and local ways of playing in particular can be displayed by foreigners as much as by the born and bred. The point is reiterated again and again. What made Belgian Philippe Albert, the team captain, so popular was the club commitment he displayed through a willingness to eschew advances from other clubs. What made Ruud Gullit so unpopular was not his colour or nationality, but his eagerness to catch the first flight home to Amsterdam after every game. And, in an area that prides directness and physicality (Dawson 1990: 108) what made the Columbian Faustino Asprilla and the black British Andy 'Goal King/Coal King' Cole so popular was their aggressive style of play that bore similarities to that of other great Newcastle strikers through the ages.

Leisure, Change and Conflict

What such ethnographic vignettes demonstrate is the myriad ways in which leisure provides an important context through which people can respond effectively to – or, in other words, 'work out' – change, and post-industrial change in particular. In some instances change is resisted. The ability of the dirt of the mining industry to function both as a symbol of marginality and a cherished marker of identity rests upon a linguistic and symbolic distinction between types of dirt. Coal dust, termed 'duff', is pure. Other types of dirt, termed 'muck' or 'clarts' are impure (Dawson 1990). The distinction is central to local cultural practice in a number of ways. It informs ideas about health and the body (Dawson 2002), gender and sexuality (Dawson 2000), class and status (Dawson 1998: 213) and animal classification. The centrality of the pig within ideas about animal classification stems from its perceived ability to transform and thrive in the impure dirt that is represented locally as a threat to people. What matters in the context of this chapter is that, despite the closure of the pits, through rearing and ideas about animals such as the pig the centrality of coal (-mining) within local identity is reasserted.

In some instances, leisure pursuits provide a fund of cultural resources with which to negotiate the practicalities of change. The point can be illustrated in relation to the changes wrought within same-sex intergenerational relationships. Put most crudely, it is clear and recognized locally as such that the power of elders has diminished markedly. Most importantly for men, the dependent quality of the relationship between older and younger men that was created by the nepotistic and familistic nature of mining employment has been eroded. Most importantly for women, the deferential attitude of younger toward older women has been eroded by the greater financial independence that comes to younger women with the emergence of factors such as direct access to social security benefits and, crucially, the recent local salience of women's waged work.

In the responses through leisure to these situations that I have outlined above humiliation would appear to play a central role. Buffing consists largely of a mutually complicit ironic humiliation of younger men by their elders, and the women writers I have discussed construct largely negative self-imagery. However, this makes them no less effective as responses to change. Buffing makes light of the changing power relations between older and younger men. More importantly, the negative self-imagery that women construct through their writing provides a powerful means of linking their own personal experiences with those of younger women and a set of rationalizations of and normative responses to perceived social crises wrought by change and by post-industrialism in particular. Examples of this are profuse and diverse. Ideas about blame and images of the danger of women are used to rationalize the town's high child-crime rate. Images of the individualism of women are used to make sense of the single-parent families whose number is burgeoning as, during an era of unemployment, many women become increasingly aware of the declining role of men within the context of the family. Images of the powerlessness of women are used to convey sentiments about the futility of younger women pursuing the kind of personal aspirations that lie at the heart of their marital conflicts.

Finally, in some instances leisure constitutes a cultural resource with which to rationalize and come to terms with change. What became clear through the contrasting of fieldwork conversations conducted respectively in public and in more intimate contexts is that terrace talk which emphasizes the possibility of thinking of Newcastle United as a quintessentially local team of foreigners has as much to do with local race relations as it has with football. It is in many cases an indirect and essentially benign commentary on recent in-migrations and a welcoming commentary on recent in-migrants. Not coincidentally, this resonates with fairly commonplace associations of migrancy, locality and belonging. Some versions emphasize that travel, of the many formerly itinerant long-term residents of the town who left in periods of economic depression and later returned and, in some cases, of more recent migrants, enables a consciousness of locality whose distinctiveness derives from juxtaposition with the world beyond its boundaries. Others emphasize the fact that Ashington, like many other mining places, is a relatively new town made up principally of migrant settlers. In this vein, that most local of local attributes, local dialect, is often referred to as the 'Polyglottal Buzz' (Dawson 1998: 218).

All this begs the question why there may be a need for such indirection (Hendry and Watson 2001) in relation to matters such as ethnic relations and in some instances for that matter, issues of intergenerational relations, gender, identity and change. The elderly in Ashington, as in many other places, face a situation of increasing marginalization from their former sites of sociality. For example, poverty prevents participation in working men's clubs and pubs. Poor health and death in this area where because of mining-related disease mortality rates are high, erodes and fragments life-long social networks. Post-industrial transformation also plays its part. Notably, for example, with the closure of the pits, the relative lack of alternative employment and, in turn, a strikingly high rate of out-migration, many elderly people have effectively been deprived of family as a site of regular sociality.

In these circumstances, many local elderly people turn to free or subsidized leisure contexts for social contact. These include the many Darby and Joan and Over-55s clubs, as well as the allotments, the Buffs and the sports stadia. Commonly, the former provide initial contact points for the development of new social networks in the latter. Importantly, the potential for conflict within such networks resulting from the unfettered expression of individual views is high (Dawson 1990: 223–59). This is not simply a matter of unfamiliarity or of the fact that unlike in the pubs and clubs there are no unwritten but well-established rules about tolerance of one's right to express opinion and make subjective assertion (ibid.). It relates also to the fact that Ashington is a highly politicized context. In particular, local divisions run deep when it comes to the roles that local people played either as supporters or detractors of industrial action during the strike of 1983–84. In local historical accounts there is a clear narrative break between 'before' and 'after' the strike and in most cases, all that is seen as problematic about contemporary post-industrial Ashington is put down to mining's demise.

It is then clear that leisure performs a key role within the local social context. Not merely 'non-work', it provides a context through which people can respond effectively to or, in other words, 'work out' change, and post-industrial change in particular. Moreover, in an era when many social networks, and particularly those of older people, are increasingly fragmented, leisure provides a key context for the development of new social networks. However, for a range of reasons, including the political tensions that have emerged as a consequence of post-industrialism, these networks are threatened by the unfettered expression of individual views, and views about post-industrial change in particular. The 'working-out' of change through leisure also consists of a mode of communication in which the potential for conflict that would otherwise be wrought by the unfettered expression of individual views, about the changes that have beset the area, is minimized.

Notes

1. The 'national dispersal policy' forms a central strand of the 'Immigration and Asylum Act 1999'. This policy, designed largely to relieve pressure on local

authorities in London and the South East, enables 'local consortia' to bid to the Home Office for refugees and asylum-seekers who are then compulsorily dispersed. Successful bids result in significant financial remuneration.

2. See also Dawson (2000) for a full discussion of writing about gender.
3. The poems presented here were written by club participants and other local poets. Most such poems have been in circulation for several years and the details of their authorship is rarely known.

References

Bulmer, M. (1975) 'Sociological models of the mining community', *Sociological Review* 23: 61–92.

Clark, S. (1992) 'Leisure – *jeux sans frontiers* or major European industry?', in J. Boulder (ed.) *Social Europe*, London and New York: Longman.

Cohen, Anthony P. (1978) '"The Same – but Different!": The Allocation of Identity in Whalsay, Scotland', *Sociological Review* 6(3): 449–69.

Crompton, R. (1997) *Women and Work in Modern Britain,* Oxford: Oxford University Press.

Dawson, A. (1990) '*Ageing and Change in Pit Villages of North East England*', Unpublished PhD thesis, University of Essex.

—— (1998) 'The Dislocation of Identity: Contestations of 'Home Community' in Northern England', in N. Rapport and A. Dawson (eds) *Migrants of Identity: Perceptions of Home in a World of Movement*, New York and Oxford: Berg.

—— (2000) 'The Poetics of Self-Depreciation: Images of Womanhood amongst Elderly Women in an English Former Coal Mining Town', *Journal of European Societies and Cultures* 9(1): 37–52.

—— (2002) 'Towards a Phenomenology of Community', in V. Amit (ed.) *Realizing Community*, London: Routledge.

Dennis, N., Henriques, F. and Slaughter, C. (1956) *Coal is Our Life: An Analysis of a Yorkshire Mining Community*, London: Eyre and Spottiswood.

Dunk, T. (1994) *It's a Working Man's Town: Male Working-Class Culture*, Montreal and Kingston: McGill-Queen's University Press.

Fever, W. (1988) *The Pitmen Painters: the Ashington Group, 1934–84,* London: Chatto & Windus.

Hendry, J. and Watson, C.W. (eds) (2001) *An Anthropology of Indirect Communication*, London: Routledge.

Herzfeld, M. (1986) *The Poetics of Manhood: Contest and Identity in a Cretan Mountain Village*, Princeton: Princeton University Press.

Jansen, S. (2001) '*Anti-Nationalism: Post-Yugoslav Resistance and Narratives of Self*', Unpublished PhD Thesis, University of Hull.

Morgan, W.J. (1989) *Social Welfare in the British and West German Coal Industries*, London: Anglo-German Foundation for the Study of Industrial Society.

Northumberland Community Health Council (1987) *Guide Around: Local Services for the Elderly*, Newcastle-Upon-Tyne: NCHC.

Walby, S. (1999) *Gender Transformations*, London: Routledge.

Wight, D. (1993) *Workers not Wasters*: *Masculine Respectability, Consumption and Unemployment in Central Scotland*, Edinburgh: Edinburgh University Press.

–6–

Dissociation, Social Technology and the Spiritual Domain

Tanya Luhrmann

In 1983 I took myself off to London to conduct fieldwork among a subculture of people – several thousands at least – who thought of themselves as, or as inspired by, the witches, wizards, druids, kabbalists and shamans of mostly European lore. They met in different kinds of group: 'covens', 'lodges', 'brotherhoods' – which all ultimately descended from a nineteenth-century group – the Golden Dawn – created by three dissident Freemasons in the heyday of spiritualism and psychical research. In magical rituals, magicians sink into meditative states and visualize images described by the leader. The central image usually represents the ritual's goal, and the assumption is that group concentration on the image makes the goal more likely to be realized. The theory behind this practice is that subtle 'energies' pervade the universe and directly influence the way events unfold. These interconnections are sensed and affected by the non-rational in human psychology: feelings, intuitions, dreams and so forth. In a ritual, magicians deliberately try to bypass their 'rational minds' and stimulate these non-rational responses. In using imagery as a focus for concentration, magicians think that they can alter the flow of these energies and interconnections in the directions suggested by the image: a good job, a healthy relationship, world peace. They also tend to be educated, middle-class, and sane.

I set out to explain what made their spells and rituals persuasive to them, what made apparently reasonable people talk and act as if they believed in apparently unreasonable beliefs. In 1989, in a book entitled *Persuasions of the Witch's Craft*, I presented a model which I called 'interpretive drift' to make sense of the fact that after joining these groups, people seem to drift from one way of making sense of the world into another through the process of becoming experts in magical practice. I argued that there were three interwoven parts to this process: first, shifts in the basic identification and analysis of events; second, powerful, compelling, phenomenological experiences; and third, the emergence of common intellectual strategies to handle the disjunction between involvement in magic and in what these magicians called science, or the scientific way of understanding.

Yet for me, the surprise lay in recognizing that cognitive commitments seemed to trail after the phenomenology of the practice. It was as if I had thought about religion as a propositional commitment – either you believed in God, or you did not – and I had discovered that whether you believed was really less important than whether you felt God's presence. I discovered, in short, that there were indeed what Mircea Eliade called techniques of ecstasy and that, to my astonishment, the techniques worked.

The goal of the present chapter is to argue that these techniques manipulate a bodily capacity in a manner familiar to us from religious practices the world over and, I will suggest, newly familiar to us from the psychiatric trauma disorders. This is the ability to go into altered states of consciousness, or hypnotic states. That these states exist, and that most people have the capacity to experience them, is more or less widely accepted. What is less appreciated is that these states are profoundly shaped by what we might call 'social technologies', and that those social technologies mold them in particular ways.

Magical Practice

When I was doing my fieldwork, the people who called themselves magicians, or saw themselves as practicing magic, held ordinary jobs – they worked with computers, or in business, or as psychologists. None of them had been born into the practice. They came across an ad – 'Susan is forming a coven, if interested please call . . .' – pinned to the wall in an occult bookshop, or they met someone who knew someone, or they went to a New Age fair and struck up a conversation. Usually, even before that, they bought a book, on witchcraft, tarot cards, candle magic, that told them what it was and how to practice it. Such books served as manuals to teach people how to perform the rituals through which the magical power will supposedly flow, and they set the framework in which someone learned about magic.

Home study courses, advertised in books and magazines, offer the most structured form for the training which most magicians assume that a neophyte needs. Most of these courses are quite similar. They provide a series of fortnightly or monthly lessons for which the student does daily exercises and writes short essays on assigned themes. Courses explain magical theory, and the nature and purpose of magical practice. They then teach the student to meditate and to visualize magical images, guide him or her through the rudiments of ritual technique, and encourage him or her to develop an elaborate, personalized symbolism. These courses are structured like English university courses. There are Directors of Studies, and supervisors, and revision essays. Each 'student' is assigned to a supervisor who comments on the 'lessons'. And upon finishing the course, the student is often initiated as having attained the first 'degree'.

Marion Green's course had handled 500–600 people in the first five years or so of its existence, by the time I took it in 1984. Green did not advertise her course as the precursor to initiation, but she sometimes wrote to promising students to invite them to join small 'working' groups. Magical groups often required potential members to take their home-study course. Most lasted for between one and five years. None of them that I encountered in Britain were money-making institutions. I paid twelve pounds for a one-year course of twelve lessons, and thirty pounds for a ten-month, each with considerable attention from my supervisors.

Here is a partial sample lesson from Marian Green's course. It is typical in its amalgam of 'feeling' and 'explaining':

Work To Do

1. There are small illustrations on pgs 7 and 31. Meditate on each of these for six days and write a brief report on your findings. Choose two sentences from Chapter V and meditate on them and report.
2. Try out the self-blessing on pages 33/34 and explain what seemed to happen. If you don't like the words or gestures make up your own self-blessing and use that. Say what you experienced.
3. Briefly explain some traditional happening you have seen and say how you think it is continuing the old traditions of the Mysteries . . .

Here is another lesson, from another course, a published manual which offers a guide to the 'Western Way' – 'a body of esoteric teaching and knowledge which constitutes a system of magical belief and practice, dating from the beginning of time'. Each chapter of the course manual talks about different concepts-the 'old religion', the 'magic earth', 'meeting the gods' – and suggests meditations and imaginative exercises at the end to let the reader experience these things directly.

This is the Two Trees exercise. To do it properly, you would memorize the imagery or record it on cassette, and play it to yourself while you relaxed into a meditative state:

You are standing at the top of a low hill. Below you is a shallow valley at the center of which lies a lake. Beside are two trees – silver birches – which are reflected upside down in the water. Walk down from the hill and around the margin of the lake until you pass between two trees. As you do so, focus

---

your attention on the sky well above the horizon. There you will see either the sun or the moon: is it day or night? When you have established which, lower your gaze and see a figure approaching. It may be male or female, veiled or unveiled. This is your guide. Follow the instructions he or she gives to you. Your guide may accompany you or appoint a companion, or you may be sent on alone. Remember that no actual harm can come to you. Follow the way laid down for you and seek the goal to which you will be led. (Matthews and Matthews 1985: 129–30)

The remarkable feature of this training is that through the course students have experiences which they come to call 'spiritual', they 'see' mental images more clearly, their dreams become more vivid, their reveries become filled with the moon, Isis, the archangel Gabriel. At least part of this impact is the result of the specific self-manipulative techniques taught in the training.

There are two main techniques in magical practice: meditation and visualization. Meditation entered Western popular culture with love beads in the 1960s. In a loose sense, meditation involves a 'stilling' of the mind, in which the meditator concentrates on an object, or a word, or an image, or on thoughts themselves. There are a variety of more or less complex religious systems which teach meditation. In the Western magic I encountered, the teaching and use of meditation is relatively haphazard. Nevertheless, the magical use of meditation in conjunction with the second technique would sometimes produce the results for which the serious meditator strives. The end of most serious meditational practices such as Zazen or Therevada Buddhism, in which the meditator sits, usually non-speaking and non-moving, for perhaps an hour or more a day, is a significantly altered state of mind during that period, with perceptible changes in mind and body alertness in the hours after the meditation. The most dramatic of these states is a mystical experience which, as described by William James (1902), is a highly intense, short-lived experience in which one feels suspended in space and time, immortal, at one with the universe and often surrounded by light and love. Serious meditators rarely elicit this state through deliberate practice. Nevertheless they do experience very real physiological changes and what, for want of a better term, are often called 'changes in consciousness' in which time passes more slowly and the individual feels distinctly different (cf. Goleman 1977). I became persuaded that two or three of the hundred or so people I knew reasonably well could have semi-mystical experiences more or less at will. These were the 'adepts', designated by other practitioners as highly competent, and I was convinced from the way they behaved in ritual and talked about their experiences, and from the diaries of other highly involved 'adepts', that they were able to induce states that are rare, and usually spontaneous, in the wider population.

The second and more important magical technique is visualization. Visualization is the ability to 'see' mental images. I hold up my hand, I look at it, I shut my eyes and then try to see 'in my mind's eye' the image of my hand. Kosslyn (1980) argues that the process of visualization involves at least four separate abilities working in combination – the ability to generate an image, to inspect the image, to manipulate the image and then to transform it. Individuals vary widely in the pictorial clarity of their mental imagery. Some people experience themselves as 'seeing' their hand; others experience themselves as thinking of the idea of their hand. For most, or all, of them, it is possible to develop the precision, clarity and intensity of the image with practice, and there is good evidence that magicians do so. Certainly I did. My own training in visualization demanded that I develop an 'internal garden' (echoes of a spiritual garden in many religious traditions) which I would visit every day for fifteen minutes, for a minimal period of nine months. I was instructed to enter a meditational state, to shut my eyes, and to imagine that I was leaving the room and my body, and travelling to my garden. Once there, I was instructed to use all my senses imaginatively to experience the garden. I was to smell the flowers, hear the bees, feel the warm summer heat and the cold damp inside the temple I built in the garden; I tasted the wine in the chalice in the temple, and of course, I saw the garden.

As far as I am aware, most serious magical rituals in the West have as their central structure some visualization sequence, whether they be those of Giordano Bruno, Marsilius Ficino, John Dee, or my friends in London. In modern magic the most powerful visualization sequences are called 'pathworkings': you go away, you arrive somewhere else in the middle of some story, you do something for yourself in the course of the story which is emotionally powerful for you, and you return. Throughout all this you aim within the greatest motivation to *see* the images in the narration. Typically, a pathworking ritual will include sentences like this: 'the boat bumps against the shore. We disembark, feeling the grass beneath our feet. Day has just broken, and the birds trill from the trees. We walk up the path. The stones scrunch as we move . . . The goddess appears from behind the temple . . . She gives you something of your childhood which you hide within your heart.' Whereas the technique of meditation works to dampen sensory stimulation, the technique of visualization uses our most powerful sense, in conjunction with the others, to overwhelm everyday awareness with imagined sensory stimulation.

There are two important points to note about visualization. First, it is very frequently involved in powerful religious experiences around the world and particularly in religious enterprises whose aim is the conversion of the neophyte. The Spiritual Exercises of Ignatius Loyola, for example, are identical in structure to magical pathworkings, down to the involvement of the five senses, the narrative structure, and the emotional involvement of the exercitant within the imaginative frame. These exercises are intended to create a deep spiritual conversion:

Fifth exercise: a meditation on Hell

First preliminary. The picture. In this case it is a vivid portrayal in the imagination of the length, breadth and depth of hell.

Second preliminary. Asking for what I want. Here it will be to obtain a deep-felt consciousness of the suffering of those who are damned, so that, should my faults cause me to forget my love for the eternal Lord, at least the fear of these sufferings will help to keep me out of sin.

First heading. To see in the imagination those enormous fires and the souls, as it were, with bodies of fire.

Second heading. To hear in imagination the shrieks and groans and the blasphemous shouts against Christ our Lord and all the saints.

Third heading. To smell in imagination the fumes of sulphur and the stench of filth and corruption.

Fourth heading: To taste in imagination all the bitterness of tears and melancholy and a gnawing conscience.

Fifth heading. To feel in imagination the heat of the flames that play on and burn the souls . . .

The vision quest of the Native Americans, which is an initiatory experience, or the initial experiences of the South American shaman, which again are initiatory experiences, are used to involve the neophyte in the religious undertaking with a kind of skill that he then uses within the religious practice. Crocker (1985) describes not only the vivid imaginative experience of the new Bororo shaman, but the older man who sits by the side of the neophyte, asking him what he sees and hears, interpreting his visions for him, suggesting what he might see. Nevertheless, Crocker reports, the new shaman earnestly reproduces the established genre of shamanic experience with the private, personal sense that he has seen the stump move and heard the monkey talk.

Second, those who have had this kind of training seem to me to have a much easier time having rich, spontaneous experiences which they call religious. Far more of my magicians had spontaneous mystical experiences than non-religious friends: often, they would describe these as elicited by an off-the-cuff paradoxical question, like the man who was tucking his child into bed and suddenly thought, I wonder if God loves me the way I love my son, and suddenly was suspended in space and time, overwhelmed by love, and so forth, with the classic afterglow of 'saintliness' which often accompanies these events. Far more of my magicians than my non-religious friends had visions, like the woman who was trying on a dress in front of the mirror and suddenly saw the Goddess. I myself, after I had been learning these techniques for a year, and was immersed in a 'magical' novel, awoke early one morning and saw six druids standing by the window. I felt myself possessed by an Egyptian cat goddess as the worshippers drummed and chanted during a ritual; I felt myself 'rising' on the 'planes', I felt power course through me like a current. I hasten to say that in having these experiences, I was demonstrating my membership in the tribe. People spoke of feeling the touch of the Goddess, of leaving their bodies to hunt on the astral plane, of smelling and hearing and tasting (but mostly seeing) things that were not there. Sometimes they seemed to have genuine hallucinations, and other times, vivid imaginations. But they spoke of specific kinds of experiences and, often, with those experiences there were associated specific kinds of practices. It was accepted that you could, for example, learn to leave your body, or to see auras, or to scry – to see an image in black obsidian. To leave your body you visualized a small geometric shape, or a tarot card, and you saw it getting larger and larger, and then you stepped through it. If you succeeded, you felt yourself leaving your body at the solar plexus, and you turned around to look at yourself before you left to travel.

Trauma and Dissociation

From 1989 to 1994 I spent from 10 to 80 hours a week in an American psychiatric setting, studying psychiatry, psychiatrists, and psychiatric patients. During that time, 'dissociation' came to the fore as a response associated with trauma, and as I listened to the doctors and their patients, I began to realize that I had heard something like these stories before. (The British interest in dissociation has been somewhat different than the American – the scare about Satanic ritual abuse, for example, focused on children rather than on adults remembering their lives as children – but the broad structure of the American thinking on trauma is effectively transAtlantic.)

'Dissociation' is a word used in many different ways to describe a phenomenon that no one really understands. The word is in effect a code word for altered states. In the standard American psychiatric nosology, the DSM IV, a dissociative symptom is defined as 'a disruption in the usually integrated functions of consciousness, memory, identity, or perception of the environment'. The international nosology, the ICD 10, shares this descriptive language.

An identified trauma is not one of the criteria for a diagnosis of a dissociative disorder. However, dissociation is understood as a psychological capacity which works as an escape mechanism when bodily flight is impossible. The classic dissociative symptoms which can also be identified as disorders are amnesia, fugue and depersonalization. In amnesia, the individual is unable to recall important personal information, usually of a stressful nature, with loss too extensive to be explained by ordinary forgetfulness. For example, an estimated 5–14 per cent of all military casualties experience amnesia (Andreasen and Black 1995: 364). In fugue, the individual suddenly and unexpectedly travels away from home, forgets the past and assumes a new identity, usually as the result of severe psychological stress; fugue states have been reported during war and natural disasters. In depersonalization, the person feels detached from his or her own body and mental process. Many of us have experienced transient depersonalization as the result of sleep deprivation, medication, or travel; the disorder is diagnosed only when depersonalization is severe and persistent.

Unlike the dissociative disorders, post-traumatic stress disorder (PTSD) is listed as anxiety disorder in the DSM IV, a distinction that has generated much debate. Also unlike the dissociative disorders, an identified trauma is one of the required criteria for diagnosis. Nevertheless, the response to adult trauma is thought to be often dissociative. PTSD is understood as a response to actual or threatened death (or serious injury) to self or others with intense fear, helplessness or horror. These patients are thought to re-experience the trauma through intrusive memories, recurrent dreams, intense distress at cues that symbolize the trauma and, most famously, flashbacks, in which the trauma is relived through a hallucination which passes like a movie before the person's eyes. Patients may also persistently avoid reminders of the trauma, may go numb; socially withdraw; forget aspects of the trauma; feel detached from others; be unable to have loving feelings; not expect to have a career, marriage, children, or a normal lifespan. They may also experience persistent symptoms of increased arousal – insomnia, intense irritability, difficulty concentrating, hypervigilance, an exaggerated startle response.

Virginia Woolf's character Septimus, in her novel *Mrs Dalloway*, would be a classic example of such a patient. Septimus' suicide is the shadow that falls across Mrs Dalloway's party. Septimus had been a sensitive adolescent. The First World War had toughened him, made him brave and independent, so that he didn't even mourn much, just at the end, when his best comrade died. Then, perhaps six months later, he began having horrible dreams. He was unable to concentrate, unable to deal with his wife or for that matter with anyone else, unable to sleep, unable to think about the future. He began to hear his comrade, see him walk across the grass to him and die. He began to know that in the rustlings of mice the dead were waiting and that they and the universe judged him guilty. He saw these dead men, whose deaths he had done nothing to prevent, not as memories but as live events in front of him, in Hyde Park, on the sidewalk, in the sitting room, until he killed himself to stop the scenes from coming.

The most severe dissociative disorder is Dissociative Identity Disorder, once called Multiple Personality Disorder or MPD. Again the dominant theme is escape. The child sees his drunken father coming with the belt and he escapes in fantasy.

When the stepfather opens the little girl's door at night, she simply goes somewhere else in her head. The child is thought to dissociate as a way of coping with overwhelming negative affect, and with what is perceived as a threat to bodily or psychological integrity, and the experience is sometimes characterized as a fragmentation of the self, with a physiological impact on memory and emotional process.

When the trauma is repeated and the dissociative response becomes habituated, the dissociative state is thought to automatize behaviour, compartmentalize information and affect, and estrange identity from body. The dissociation thus becomes a way to separate distressing knowledge and upsetting emotions into a domain where the memory of the trauma remains psychologically powerful but is somehow held separately from the individual's primary sense of self. The child develops the dissociative style as an effective response to her circumstances, but she finds herself in the psychiatric consulting room years later because she dissociates easily and uncontrollably without understanding what she is doing, and she loses time, gets confused, gets fired, and in general falls apart. The typical argument is that the children of sexual abuse do well throughout later childhood and only find themselves in trouble when they try to develop sexual intimacy as adults.

Let me provide an example of the kind of patient. A basic psychiatric textbook gives this as a 'typical' case history:

Cindy, a 24 yr old, had been well until three years before admission, when she developed 'voices.' She also developed other symptoms, including multiple somatic complaints, periods of amnesia, and self-abusive behaviours. He family and friends noticed abrupt changes in personality and mood and thought that Cindy had become a pathological liar because she would do or say things that she would later deny. She became chronically ill, was in and out of hospitals, and was puzzling to her doctors. She had received trials of antipsychotic medications, antidepressants, lithium carbonate, and anxiolytics with little or no benefit. She continued to get worse.

Cindy was a friendly, diminutive young woman, who was clean and neatly groomed. There was no evidence of a formal thought disorder, but Cindy carefully described the voices that she had heard for many years. She reported that these voices were from nine separate personalities that, with the help of a therapist, she had learned about during her prior hospitalization. The personalities ranged in age from 2 to 48 years, and two of the personalities were masculine. Her problem, she said, was to control the switches among the personalities, which made her feel out of control. Cindy reported that she had been sexually abused by her father as a child and made to perform unspeakable acts. She also reported visual hallucinations of her father coming at her with a knife. Although we were not able to confirm the history of sexual abuse, it was felt to be likely, on the basis of what we had learned about her father . . .". (Andreasen and Black 1995: 370)

Patients like Cindy have sometimes been treated by therapists by hypnosis, in which the memory of the trauma is recalled; the therapist uses hypnotic induction to bring forth the other identities, or alters, in the patient. Whether hypnosis is used or not, the therapeutic goal is to help the patient control the 'switch' to different alters and back again. There are complex and politically charged arguments about the validity of the memories these patients recall under hypnosis. My inclination is to treat many of the memories as indications of past terror and distress, but to be agnostic about the specific kind of distress involved, and about the relationship between the historical past and the narrative past. People can recover memories that are not true; they can also recover memories that are, and without external evidence there is no way to determine the difference (see the discussions in Putnam 1997). The patient experiences these memories as true, and so the therapist, entering the patient's world, tends to accept them; and indeed, patients often insist on acceptance as a condition of therapy. It is important, however, that these vividly remembered events often have characteristics unlike other memory experiences: patients often speak of 'seeing', rather than 'remembering' particular scenes.

In situations that give rise to traumatic dissociation as it is modelled in the psychiatric literature, the person feels helpless. Often there is a time lag. Immediately following the trauma, the person may do well, and only later, when the immediate danger is past, and when the stimuli crop up in different settings, does he fall apart. Visual phenomena like hallucinations are common, as are high hypnotizability, high persuadability, and a fuzzy line between fantasy and reality. Finally, these dissociative experiences are unwanted, intrusive and disruptive. People come into the psychiatrist's consulting room because they are in pain.

From the standard psychiatric perspective, dissociation is commonly seen as pathological. Some researchers, such as Putnam (1997), will mention as an aside that there is 'normal' dissociation, but the default assumption tends to be the one summarized in a recent article on a psychological instrument called the 'Dissociative Experiences Scale'. That article begins with the following definition: 'Dissociation is typically defined as some incapacity to integrate one's thoughts, feelings or experiences into one's present consciousness'; 'dissociative symptoms have been implicated in . . . diverse psychopathological conditions'. Having evaluated a revised DES scale in an American community, the article comments that 'as would be expected, most of the items [of the scale] describe experiences beyond those likely to be reported by the relatively normal individuals in this community sample' (Goldberg 1999: 134–5).

On the basis of my fieldwork in London, I think that this is a mistake, and that the two different ethnographic studies, even situated as they are on different sides of the ocean, can teach us something about human bodies and human experience.

The Model

I suggest that the specific kinds of magico-religious and psychiatric experiences I've described here express more or less the same kind of psychophysiological shift; for convenience's sake, we can call it dissociation. Both the psychiatric and the religious experiences involve at least four characteristics: first, a change in experienced time; second, a change in the self/other/I–Thou relationship (either the self feels extremely fragmented, or absent, or the self finds itself in relation with divinity); third, a change in the locus of control; these states feel passive, although the passivity in the religious domain is usually pleasurable, while in the trauma domain it is a terrifying loss of agency; and fourth, an increased degree of absorption, so that the person seems to have withdrawn into his or her own world. From that perspective, dissociation is not pathological but neutral. It is a human capacity associated with imagination and play. In essence, in a dissociative state an individual's attention retreats from the surrounding reality into an imagined domain which becomes more important that the surrounding world.

The attention withdraws, however, along a continuum, from low intensity to high intensity, and it withdraws differently under different conditions. First of all, most of us daydream, sometimes with great absorption. Most of us have low-intensity dissociative experiences of being so caught up in a book or a film that we lose track of time, we live in the story, and even once we put down the book or leave the cinema the characters stay with us all day, haunting our daydreams and thoughts. Most academics experience what Mihaly Czichzemihaly calls flow: when we are writing well, we lose track of time, the words flow through us as if of their own accord, we pay little attention to the outside world and jump when the phone rings, our sense of separateness and selfhood tends to diminish and afterwards, we don't know quite how we did it. Boredom may also be a low-intensity dissociative state which can serve as a defence against anxiety. Boredom is a state of slowed time, disconnection, disengagement from activity, and great passivity; we speak of 'snapping' out of boredom.

Dissociation can also be trained. Athletes are often taught to visualize themselves as winning their competitions, and superb athletes sometimes report experiencing successful performances as altered states: they see the tennis ball move slowly across the net, and they plan their response as if the film of life were slowed down to a frame-by-frame viewing. Religious practice often involves some kind of disciplined concentration through prayer. At the high end of this continuum, there are a set of striking 'bells and whistles' experiences which I suspect have somewhat different psychophysiological features and seem to be elicited in somewhat different ways. Jamesian mystical experiences are associated with epilepsy, and can be elicited by meditation or by physical trauma too sudden to be frightening (as when Rousseau, for example, was knocked down by a dog on a walk outside of Paris, and regained consciousness in the surety of transcendent bliss); out-of-body experiences, in which the person turns around and sees his or her body after 'leaving' it, tend to be reported in near-death experiences, surgery and epilepsy, and are in my experience more often associated with visualization; there are possession states (including speaking in tongues) in which the person becomes a 'channel' for a spirit and often reports amnesia; and shamanic states, in which the person acts as the spiritual agent and does not report amnesia.

I suggest that the best way to understand the psychiatric data is that the person's dissociative capacity has become overwhelmed, and when overwhelmed it some-how impacts emotional processing and memory, in which fantasy may be used to avoid the memory of an upsetting reality. It is not clear how this works but it is, I think, important to distinguish between pathological dissociation, which involves intense negative affect and a terrifying ego-dystonic loss of agency, and non-pathological dissociation, which is more often controllable and ego-syntonic. Both pathological and non-pathological dissociation are, however, culturally shaped. Ian Hacking (1995) and Allan Young (1995) are only two of the most prominent of social commentators to point to the way contemporary trauma memories reflect contemporary notions of gender, self, information processing, memory, and so forth. There appears to be pathological dissociation in other cultures which similarly reflects local cultural concerns. Latah, for example, is a Malaysian elaboration of a startle response in which an individual laughs uncontrollably, strikes out, and comically mimics those who tease him or her (primarily 'her'). A latah is not held legally responsible for what she does in this state, although, as is true of most dissociation states, she clearly has some degree of volitional control. One of the important points about dissociative states in general is that it is difficult to distinguish between someone who is 'really' dissociated, and someone who is theatrically faking it.

The anthropological data suggest that when the dissociative capacity is trained, it can make the imaginative or religious domain real to people. It also seems to be the case that if someone has dissociated in response to trauma, training can make the unwanted intrusions of traumatic dissociation more controllable; in fact, one way to understand the way therapists have worked with MPD patients is that they are teaching them to be possessed by themselves. The therapists identify intrusive states as alters, and teach the patient how to control their presence and absence. Such patients may also be able to use religious practice to manage their distress. Recent work in Bali and Sri Lanka (Suryani and Jensen 1993) suggests that ritual trance experts are particularly likely to have been traumatized as children, although not all ritual trance experts have been traumatized. The following example illustrates the way in which someone who has been traumatized may use the techniques taught in religious domains and avoid experiencing him- or herself as ill.

Case Study

Sara is 34. She works in an occult bookstore and practices magic, although she is more likely to think of herself as a shaman than a witch. She is an American, but she reads the same genre of literature as the British magicians, and she practises the same techniques of meditation and visualization as they do. She seems sensible, smart and psychologically astute. In the store, she manages a staff of ten and has become a primary buyer for the store. She has been in a stable relationship for seventeen years, and has been married for most of them. She is neither flamboyant nor attention-seeking. By ordinary criteria, she is doing just fine.

Yet she had the kind of childhood that precedes major problems with dissociative pathology. When she was ten, her mother became psychotic and has remained so intermittently since. When psychotic, her mother tried to kill her on at least three occasions, at least one of them with a kitchen knife. I find this believable, although I have no external evidence. When she was seventeen, she thought she was going crazy, right on cue for a dissociative disorder due to childhood trauma. She saw things that were not there, heard things other people could not hear, and felt as if her life was fragmenting around her. She told me that two things helped her. Apparently, since her mid-teens she had been a member of what sounds like a New Age version of a grandmotherly bridge group, except that instead of playing cards, they played with ouija boards, crystals and automatic writing. Most of the other members were thirty or more years older than she was, and she gives them the credit for parenting her through adolescence. She felt safe with them. As she tells the story, though, what really made a difference at 17 was that her boyfriend took an anthropology course on shamanism, albeit one influenced by the New Age/ occult writings of Michael Harner (1980), and one afternoon he came home and told her that she wasn't going crazy; she was becoming a shaman. To this Sara attributes the fact that she began sleeping soundly, although she also told me, as an aside, that this was also when she moved out of her mother's house. The next term Sara took the shamanism course herself, and since then she has considered shamanism to be her natural spirituality. By this she means shamanism as conceived by Michael Harner. She talks comfortably of 'journeying', and of 'spirit animals'.

These days Sara experiences herself as shifting in and out of dissociative states all the time. She recognizes these states as dissociative because, she says, they don't feel like her, or because she loses time, or because she 'snaps back' and realizes that she was 'gone'. They are not distressing and they make her life richer.

Discussion

Why did Sara become a shaman rather than an MPD patient? Part of the story is temperamental and psychodynamically individual. She has a resilient personality.

She has what a clinician might call 'good ego strength'. She is capable of attachment. However, mostly Sara seems to me to be someone who began to dissociate in order to escape from and to manage her mother's chaos and who did so in a social environment that she could use to transform that escape into a productive and soothing spirituality. 'Social environment', however, is a fairly broad category. I suggest that an anthropologist can identify at least four features of a social environment that could play a role in a person's interpretation and experience of a dissociative state.

The first is knowledge. Typically, the identification of the individual's condition lies in someone else's hands. The individual anxiously seeks counsel about these strange experiences, and at some point someone will offer a diagnosis. That diagnosis may or may not be accepted, but some diagnosis probably will be, and that diagnosis will presume a body of knowledge which accounts for suffering and ecstasy, be it biomedical, Christian, magical, and so forth. Sara was 'diagnosed' by her boyfriend, and then later by a charismatic professor, at a point when she might have found herself in a psychiatrist's office. Had she seen the psychiatrist first, and been persuaded by him, her relationship to these states might well have been different. Distraught patients would be diagnosed with different diagnoses in different periods, and might well have found their symptoms conforming more to that dominant understanding.

Also there are common discourses and narratives. There will be local cultural models about what the unusual state is: whether a spirit enters the body, whether the state is the consequence of sexual trauma, whether the state is due to a frisky and flirtatious demoness. Sara acquired books and a teacher and a complex set of ideas around shamanism, and as she learned more about shamanism, that knowledge will have deeply shaped her further experiences. Similarly, the common cultural ideas about Satanic ritual abuse emerged around 1980 and faded in the early 1990s. During this period, there was an explosion of dissociative patients, particularly in America, who remembered having been tortured within Satanic pentagrams, impregnated by cult members and forced to kill and eat the babies they bore, and so forth. The stories were repetitive and stereotypical, and yet therapists believed them because the patients experienced them as true. Curiously, there was no such explosion in Britain. Instead, social workers caught an epidemic of Satanic child-abusers, a phenomenon which, as La Fontaine (1998) explains, is more like the witchcraft accusations of the past than the dissociative patients of the present.

Second, there are methods of bodily discipline to induce dissociative states and to control their duration. The course Sara took on shamanism not only gave 'meaning' to the dissociative state that frightened her, but gave her specific visual and linguistic technologies to control them. There are also ritual bodily procedures that mark the states, so that if the ritual demands a group it is unlikely that possession will occur outside it. And there is social mimicry, or mimesis. William James argued that we feel fear because we flee; Asad (1993) might say that we discipline the body to experience the soul. Initiates in possession learn to become possessed in part through going to rituals and acting as if they are possessed. Similarly, dissociative patients are often encouraged to discover hierarchies of 'alters' and then asked repeatedly to shift from one to another in therapy. The physical experience of being one person, or alter, and then another, may help the patient to differentiate the states; the experience of shifting probably helps the patient to master them.

Third, there are the larger social institutions that surround the specific practice. For example, there is a socially established payoff, or secondary gain, for certain kinds of states. To have multiple personality disorder gives you status as a victim and as part of a large feminist social movement; it may provide you a disability pension as well, but its cost is being 'crazy'. The advantage of getting possessed in the Northern Sudan is that a woman may be released from an undesirable marriage, but caring for a spirit can be quite expensive; the advantage of becoming a shaman among the Amazonian Bororo is that as a shaman you are well fed and in effect handsomely paid, but the cost is that your neighbours find you terrifying. The social context establishes what is rewarded and how. Sara liked her shamanic diagnosis; she was familiar with alternative spiritualities so that the diagnosis seemed plausible; moreover, it promised her power and self-mastery and preserved her from being crazy.

Fourth is the taught nature of the self-other relationship, and particularly, the I–Thou relationship with divinity, which shapes the self–other framing of the state. This I think is the most fascinating of these cultural artefacts. In a relationship with God, or with spirit or animal or however divine being is conceived, divinity is experienced as different from the self. In both Britain and America, where I have done fieldwork on religion, people talk about God as if that relationship is intimate. God touches, communicates, responds, informs. God is mysterious, to be sure, but you cannot do justice to the religious experience without appreciating that God is not experienced as the projection of some internalized ideal, but as a being with intentions and desires which are not immediately evident and who exists in a relationship of what Erikson called 'mutuality' with the worshipper. Sara says that she has always been an atheist, and that the world is unreliable, not to be trusted, and certainly not fundamentally good. Yet through her shamanism she has power animals, spirit helpers, and a few intimate ancestors who counsel her, care for her, and keep her safe. Although she doesn't trust the world, she trusts that she will be safe within it.

In psychiatric settings one might think not of God, but of the relationship established between therapist and patient. Dissociative patients have relatively good prognoses, but the prognosis is often said to depend upon the nature of the patient's relationship with the therapist, and on whether the patient can trust the therapist sufficiently so that he or she can feel safe within a relationship.

Social Technology

I want to talk about this social environment as 'social technology'. By that I mean something not so far from what Jack Goody (1977) meant when he argued that the kind of technology a society uses has a profound impact on its social organization, its culture and its cognitive performance. For example, Goody (1976) and Stock (1983), Street (1984), Anderson (1983) and others, have argued that the technology of writing externalizes memory, shifts 'truth' from the mind of an authoritative elder into an independent reality, and changes the nature of collective identity. The pencil, the printing press, the computer – all these technologies become part of what Hutchins (1995) calls the 'functional system' of our cognitive capacities, and the cognitive performance of the group depends not on the individual's brain but on social management technologies. When we unpack, we use the space around us to organize our piles and make ourselves more efficient, just as when we take a bicycle apart we use the floor to keep all the pieces in order so that we don't forget what nut goes with which bolt. When pilots pilot planes, they use the navigational control panel to provide more information than they could keep in their minds without its help. Michael Cole (1996) identifies these activities as cultural 'artifacts', by which he means something changed by prior human activity which mediates human experience in the world.

Technologies which are not tangible (like pencils) but social (like ritual) are, I suggest, equally important, and to focus on specific types of action as specific social technologies can be helpful in an intellectual domain where the concept of culture makes so many people so anxious. The point of calling a set of actions a 'social technology' is to draw attention to the fact that the actions are more or less socially organized and more or less systematically learned, just as a technology such as writing is socially organized (who writes, how they write, what they write) and systematically learned (by schoolchildren, by monks, by merchants, and in a classroom). The advantage of thinking in terms of a learning process is that the fieldworker can actually collect this information, and then later analyse the way it matters.

But it is not the learned social process which is the social technology, but the interaction between social process, psychic experience, and bodily vulnerability. An individual chooses which diagnostician to hear, consciously or not; he or she has a body that does or does not struggle with the neurobiological consequences of trauma. The social environment can mediate his or her psychological state only if his or her body is responsive and his or her psyche accepting.

Another way to describe this approach is through the psychodynamic lens of Donald Winnicott's (1971) concept of the transitional object as a symbolic intermediate between the me and the not-me as the child developmentally matures. The child recognizes the teddy bear as an external object, and yet the bear is also subjectively held. Winnicott wrote of an intermediate area of experiencing, to which reality and external life both contribute. For him the world of fantasy, play and illusion become the arena of development because through it the individual can manipulate, reaffirm, and experience a sense of mastery over the reality that the mother is absent and the father is distant, or other sharp edges of the real world. This intermediate area is first the area of the transitional object, then of play, then of artistic creativity and religion, and then ultimately of cultural experience in general.

I think about the theory of social technology as a kind of transitional phenomenon writ large. There are constraints on the external objects a local world provides to its struggling individuals. A true transitional object is under the control of its child; but teddy bears fall apart. A child who grows up in a house where the teddy bear is always eaten by the pet dog may perhaps develop somewhat differently than one who does not; a child whose teddy bear is ripped apart by a drunken mother to make a cruel point about authority will likely develop differently than one whose is not. There are constraints on the psychic architecture with which the child learns to be in the world – constraints on the experience of self and emotion and empathy and other structures and habits of internal process. And finally there are constraints on bodies. Not everyone can flow easily into an altered state; not everyone can recover from maternal rejection. I have always studied the way a world becomes real for people, the way that as an ethnographer one can point to the specific domains of learning through which people develop their experience of the world. My goal here has been to consider ways of making more explicit the interaction of body, psychological structure and cultural artefact through which this happens.

References

Anderson, B. (1983) *Imagined Communities*, London: Verso.

Andreasen, N. and Black, D. (1995) *Introductory Textbook of Psychiatry*, Washington, D.C.: American Psychiatric Press.

Asad, T. (1993) *Genealogies of Religion*, Baltimore: Johns Hopkins University Press.

Cole, M. (1996) *Cultural Psychology*, Cambridge MA: Harvard University Press.

Crocker, C. (1985) *Vital Souls*, Tucson: University of Arizona Press.

Goldberg, L. (1999) 'The Curious Experiences Survey, a Revised Version of the Dissociative Experiences Scale', *Psychological Assessment* 11(2): 134–45.

Goleman, D. (1977) *The Varieties of the Mystical Experience*, New York: Irvington.

Goody, J. (1977) *The Domestication of the Savage Mind*, Cambridge: Cambridge University Press.

Hacking, I. (1995) *Rewriting the Soul*, Princeton: Princeton University Press.

Harner, M. (1980) *The Way of the Shaman*, San Francisco: Harper and Row.

Hutchins, E. (1995) *Cognition in the Wild*, Cambridge MA: MIT Press.

James, W. (1902) *The Varieties of Religious Experience*, London: Longman, Green.

Kosslyn, S. (1980) *Imagery and Mind*, Cambridge MA: Harvard University Press.

La Fontaine, J. (1998) *Speak of the Devil: Tales of Satanic Abuse in England*, Cambridge: Cambridge University Press.

Loyola, I. (1973) *The Spiritual Exercises of Ignatius Loyola*, trans. T. Corbishey, Wheathampstead, Herts: Clarke.

Luhrmann, T.M. (1989) *Persuasions of the Witch's Craft*, Cambridge MA: Harvard University Press.

Matthews, C. and Matthews, J. (1985) *The Western Way*, London: Arkana.

Putnam, F. (1997) *Dissociation in Children and Adolescents*, New York: Guilford.

Stock, B. (1983) *The Implications of Literacy*, Princeton: Princeton University Press.

Street, B. (1984) *Literacy in Theory and Practice*, Cambridge: Cambridge University Press.

Suryani, L.K. and Jensen, G. (1993) *Trance and Possession in Bali*, Oxford: Oxford University Press.

Winnicott, D. (1971) *Playing and Reality*, London: Tavistock.

Young, A. (1995) *The Harmony of Illusions*, Princeton: Princeton University Press.

Part IV
The Appropriation of Discourse

Introduction to Part IV
Nigel Rapport

The chapters in this section treat alike cases of 'global' discourses being locally and individually employed in the informing of 'ordinary' and everyday British lives. The argument made is that whether the discourse stems from government policy, from the big business of 'big science', or from the ubiquitous computer-ization of social life, through a process of appropriation the discourse comes to be used in a locally contextualized way to say localized things. Indeed, in interpreting and reproducing the discourse, an agency and an autobiography come to fulfilment whose logic and purpose may borrow from the discourse's ubiquity and authority but be subversive of them, tangential and ultimately distinct. Hence, a discourse of immaturity is used to bespeak autonomy, a discourse of infertility to bespeak family, a discourse of connectivity to bespeak fragmentation.

In Chapter Seven, 'The English Child: Towards a Cultural Politics of Childhood Identities', Allison James argues for a non-essentialistic understanding of 'the child' and for children to be seen, in a sense, as authors of their own childhoods. Identity-politics should not only concern such issues as gender, race and sexuality, she contends, but also age and a sensitivity to the ways in which age is socially and institutionally constructed – hence, her call for children to be recognized as individual agents whose self-identity emerges from their instrumental engagement with cultural assumptions and political milieux around them.

More precisely, James's chapter is an examination of the ways in which children interact with those discourses which would claim to define them: how, for instance, social policies to do with family and parenting in contemporary Britain assume precise forms in particular children's everyday lives; how children actually experience and respond to the archetypally defined 'children' they encounter in school and abroad. The relationship, James contends, is dynamic and symbiotic; however definitionally powerless and discursively silenced, children employ tactics of resistance – deceit, special pleading and emotional blackmail – whereby they gain a measure of control over their lives, writing their own narratives of maturation.

In Chapter Eight, 'Bits and Bytes of Information', Jeanette Edwards examines the nature of 'scientific' knowledge and, by implication, what may be the appropriate terms for delineating relations among it, anthropology and 'lay beliefs'.

The chapter begins with a description of a prevalent Western ethos of 'scientism' wherein it is assumed that a certain scientific literacy, an ability to retain bits and bytes of objective information, underlies a rightful claim to citizenship in a contemporary democracy; a measure of public understanding of science is taken to be indicative of British subjects' modernity and rationality. By contrast, Edwards contends, anthropological incursions into the Western laboratory, and studies of the politico-industrial complex in late twentieth-century techno-science, have revealed 'big science' to be at core contradictory, relational and contingent in nature: its knowledge no more scientistic than any other.

Edwards' project is further to 'culturalize' scientific knowledge by focusing specifically on New Reproductive Technologies (NRTs) as these impinge on the lives of individual inhabitants in the north-west English town of Bacup. How do advances in reproductive and genetic science connect with 'ordinary people'?

The picture Edwards paints is one of assimilation. The public understanding of science comes about by individuals embedding New Reproductive Technologies within existing local, social, moral and spiritual universes; they make sense of new science by way of old idioms such as kinship, and as they engage with it and in the context of habitual social interactions. They succeed, Edwards concludes, in melding 'science' and ordinary or 'commonsensical' understandings into one universe of knowledge – as may we all, scientist and anthropologist alike.

In Chapter Nine, 'Culture in a Network: Dykes, Webs and Women in London and Manchester', Sarah Green reflects on the use of new Information and Communication Technologies (ICTs) among two distinct groupings of people: lesbian-feminist separatists in London in the 1980s, and a computer-skills training centre for women in Manchester in the 1990s. How, she asks, have these women variously incorporated the use of ICTs into their ongoing interrelations with one another and with the wider urban milieux?

Green's finding is that while talk about these technologies is widespread – in everyday life as in the media, in policy statements and in academia – the substance of individuals' talk is often old fears, assumptions and obsessions: old topics of self, relationships and world. Nor does the ethos and practice of connectivity of the new technologies seem to affect the substance of the talk. For, while fashioning new and alternative electronic connections, locations and networks, the overriding life experience made manifest is a sense of disconnection. The women are both spurred by and ultimately unable to escape the feeling of fragmentation in their lives; a surfeit of connections transmogrifies into an understanding that there is no core either to their socio-electronic networks or to their common womanhood. Electronic connectedness translates into memberships of networks that are open-ended and ultimately incoherent.

The English Child: Toward a Cultural Politics of Childhood Identities

Allison James

In her book *Children and the Politics of Culture*, the anthropologist Sharon Stephens addressed the tremendous changes which have occurred not only in the social and economic status of children worldwide but also in attitudes toward and discourses about childhood itself, arguing that children do not – and indeed cannot – escape the political climate of the particular cultural contexts in which they find themselves. She writes:

> As representatives of the contested future and subjects of cultural policies children stand at the crossroads of divergent cultural projects. Their minds and bodies are at stake in debates about the transition of fundamental cultural values in the schools. The very nature of their senses, language, social networks, world-views and material futures are at stake in debates about ethnic purity, national identity, minority self-expression and self-rule. (1995: 23)

Childhood, for Stephens is a site upon which both national and international politics impinge and where the rights of children are put at risk or exploited by particular government and state regimes. Here, however, I want to invert this proposition and take a slightly different tack to suggest that such processes be theorized in terms of an identity politics for children. Rather than seeing children as passively positioned in relation to the political process, this new perspective emphasizes their agency. It draws attention to the ways in which a child's own conceptualization of self-identity as a 'child' emerges and develops through his or her practical engagement with the political and cultural practices through which childhood is inscribed in everyday life in particular cultural settings. In this sense I want to explore the politics of policy-making which is encountered by children in and through the micro-politics of their everyday lives. Here envisaged as a social actor, the child is understood, therefore, to share in the authorship of the childhood he or she inhabits and in the child identity which follows from it.

The theoretical value to be gained from adopting such an agency-centred approach can be seen from Roseneil and Seymour's (1999) depiction of contemporary identity politics, which argues that there has been an increasing questioning of identity in late modernity:

In the contemporary era, globalization and rapid social change disturb the temporal and spatial certainties which had continued to be offered through modernity by community and place, stable employment and class structures and the nuclear family. The variety of life choices facing us increases and our knowledge about these choices explodes in a media-saturated world. Less and less seems to be determined by tradition and social structure and establishing our identity becomes both more important and more difficult, as our identities are subject to ever more frequent and complex challenges. Attempting to anchor our sense of self in this maelstrom of social life, to create ontological security in a world of rapid social change we each as individuals face the task of constructing for ourselves our biographical narrative. (1999: 3–4)

As an account of *adults'* engagement with processes of social change, this explains well why issues of identity have become politicized in late modernity, giving rise to new social movements of various kinds. However, the transformation and processes it describes are, when read from within the framework of the new social studies of childhood (James and Prout 1990; James, Jenks and Prout 1998), perhaps less remarkable: making life choices, receiving identity challenges, seeking anchorage for the self, facing rapid social change and constructing biographical narratives for the self are what all children do as a matter of course! These processes are what have traditionally been regarded as key features of childhood socialization. For every child, growing into adulthood involves precisely such risks, challenges and social learning. To the list of the new identity politics of gender, race and sexuality might be added, therefore, that of age. The groundworks for this are set out in this chapter.

In brief, the chapter represents an initial exploration of the theoretical benefit to be derived from reframing questions of childhood socialization in terms of a cultural politics of childhood identities. This involves, first, seeking out how it is that discourses of 'childhood' and 'the child' – for example those evident in the law, in social policies about family and parenting, in educational policy and political rhetoric – are given practical form in children's day-to-day experiences through the shaping and reshaping of the category of 'child' and the generational space of 'childhood' (James and James 2001). Second, it involves asking how children encounter and respond to these versions of the self as 'child' and of 'childhood' itself that they meet on an everyday basis in their relationships with adults and, indeed, with their peers. Framed in this way, such a cultural politics of childhood identities gives sensible documentation of the process – rather than simply of the outcome – of socialization. And it does so through positing children as active participants in it, rather than as mere passive bystanders (James 1993).

On the face of it such a standpoint is hardly new. First, the proposal is quite simply to put some ethnographic flesh on the bare bones of theories of cultural reproduction – to find some empirical evidence for Giddens' 'structuration theory' or Bourdieu's theorizing about the 'habitus'. Second, within the new social studies of childhood, research which gives children's perspectives on social life a prominent place is by now quite commonplace. Indeed, it is precisely this approach to the study of children's lives which I pursued over the last twenty years or so in my own quest to understand not just what happens during socialization but *how* it takes place and is experienced by children themselves. As a raw postgraduate I explored child-to-child socialization through a detailed ethnographic study of children's cultural life among their peers. Here I glimpsed children teaching one another about the adult – as well as the child's – world through language games and competitions of a more physical kind; through teases, insults, nicknames, jokes and fights; through their utilization of outdoor space and their consumption of sweets, tobacco and alcohol (James 1979, 1986). In these different cultural practices, I argued, it was possible to see how children participate in shaping the form and process of their everyday social relationships and thereby gain, or indeed in some instances fail to achieve, the kind of ontological security which as Giddens (1991) has argued provides the foundations for social identity.

A later study (James 1993), focused on children's experiences of difference and disability. This extended my questioning of children's experiences of social-ization into the more adult-governed spaces of the home and the classroom. In these contexts children were necessarily encountering and engaging with adults, as well as with their peers; and from parents, teachers and members of the medical profession they experienced different forms of instruction and knowledge about 'the child' they were or might become and the kind of 'childhood' that it was appropriate for them to inhabit.

Central to these understandings were stereotypes of the 'normal' child, stereotypes which children had to deal with and manage on a day-to-day basis in the formation of their social relationships (Armstrong 1983). This process was particularly significant for children with disabilities; but for other children, too, concepts of 'ordinary childhood' and the 'normal child' provided an implicit and yet quite insidious framing of their childhood identities. As I have detailed elsewhere (James 1998), for example, children who were transferring from nursery to primary school were already 'known' to their teachers through summative assessments made on the basis of their pre-school visits to the children's own homes. Jim and Kirsty, for instance, were both regarded as potentially vulnerable and problematic children, an opinion formed largely though the teachers' reading of their home environments as abnormal. According to his teacher, Jim's house

> was dreadful . . . complete with large manky dog. There were rosettes all over the wall
> – her husband's dog is some kind of champion.

Kirsty's house, by contrast,

> *was plastered with photographs of the new baby and her mother's recent wedding. There were none of Kirsty and her elder sister.*

Such shorthand judgments about these and other children's potential difficulties as school pupils were, during their first few days at school, reinforced for the teachers who critically observed their parents' (usually mother's) behaviour and attitudes towards their children:

> *Sally's mother still wants to keep her a baby*
>
> *Kim's mother has not told us her new phone number*
>
> *She's very pushy . . . Donna's mother.*

Rarely positive, the teachers' comments focused intensively on the hidden dangers lurking in a child's family background that would make their job of teaching more difficult and it was against these stereotypes that teachers evaluated the children's behaviour and abilities during their first few weeks at school. However, although in many cases the teachers did have their worst fears confirmed, in some instances children confounded their teachers by behaving in ways which they had not predicted. The teachers were forced to adjust their opinions and to move such children metaphorically up or down the implicit scale of normality against which the child's trajectory towards adulthood had been calibrated.

Two lessons can be drawn from this. First, that discourses of normal childhood are not simply discourses; they are enacted and given practical realization and material form through the minutiae of the everyday social practices which take place between adults and children in the home, at school or in the doctor's surgery. Moreover, such discourses about 'normal childhood' do not stand alone; they represent the culminated history of social policy-making with regard to the protection and welfare of children, policies both predicated upon and helping to promote particular ideas of children's needs, ideas of what children are or normally should be (see Hendrick 1990; Stainton-Rogers and Stainton-Rogers 1992). Thus, what can be seen sedimented out, in for example the everyday cultural practice of teachers' assessment of children's vulnerability, is a particular distillation of the accumulated history of policy-making with regard to children in British society. A second lesson can be drawn from this study. As noted, it was through their own actions that some children forced the teachers to reconsider their initial judgments, giving weight to the suggestion that it is through detailed observation and analysis of such day-to-day encounters that one might indeed begin to map out a cultural politics of childhood identities.

At a theoretical level, therefore, what I wish to argue here is that there is a highly dynamic and symbiotic relationship between the conceptualization of childhood as a particular generational and cultural space and children's actions as the occupants of that space; that children are social members of the category 'child' who, through their interactions and engagement with the adult world, help form both the categorical identity of 'child' with which they are ascribed and the generational space of 'childhood' to which they belong; and that this relationship delineates the 'how' of the socialization process. This chapter begins to map out the dynamics of the relationship between structure and agency which lie at the heart of such a cultural politics of childhood by considering children's understandings and experiences of just one aspect of the socialization process: the ways in which English children learn of and about their relative powerlessness vis-à-vis adults.

Discoursing on British Childhood

The discursive properties of Western conceptions of the child and childhood have been well remarked (Jenks 1996; Gittens 1998). Childhood as a period of innocent dependency, with children often denied responsibility for themselves and seen to have only partial competence, is constantly attested to in the literature of developmental psychology, in popular and scientific representations as well as in common parlance. All that is easy is deemed childish, and irresponsible adults are charged with an immaturity akin to that of children; children's main value lies in their future potential but childhood's appeal lies in its present portrayal of innocence (James, Jenks and Prout 1998). And such discursive representations take on material form, with practical outcomes for children. Within the English legal system, for example, the status of child is largely demarcated by age and although the Children Act 1989 makes clear that incompetence should not be automatically assumed for children, and that adults must take account of children's wishes and feelings in any decisions they might take on their behalf, in the end ultimate responsibility and judgement about any *particular* child's competence to decide rests with the adult (see also Alderson 1993). Similarly, despite the rhetoric of the UN Convention on children's rights, which on the face of it would seem to offer children more scope for participation and citizenship, this often fails to be realized in practice (Archard 1993). Indeed, as I shall show here, the definition of themselves which British children most often encounter in their mundane and everyday interactions with adults continues to be one which stresses their powerlessness, their dependency and their incompetence.

Such global, universalistic conceptions of childhood and children's needs are, however, refracted and enacted in and through different localities. A cultural politics of childhood acknowledges therefore the importance of locality for children with regard to their biographical narratives and life-projects – a child is always a child of and within a particular setting – but considers that, *even within one locality*, children will have different kinds of social experience as they move across and between its different spheres. Each 'institutional context' (Giddens) or 'social field' (Bourdieu) will be shaped by slightly different, though often overlapping, concerns about what children should be. Differing sets of 'rules and resources' (Giddens) will enable the 'habitus' (Bourdieu) so that the child can be son or daughter; future citizen; schoolchild; playmate; patient; consumer. A key question for the cultural politics of childhood is, then, what do children understand by and how do they respond to such *localized* and changing identity ascriptions, and what consequences does this have for a child's sense of self, as child?

Looking back on my own work I now realize that this is a question I have so far failed to address. The Britishness of my own ethnographic accounts – the Yorkshireness, the Midlandsness, the North-easternness – has never been dramatic-ally foregrounded. Rather, these different locales have been the taken-for-granted backdrop against which other, broader questions about childhood identity and belonging could be asked.[1] It is only of late that their 'Britishness' – well, actually the Englishness – has become apparent and it was precisely the recognition of this omission which encouraged me to think theoretically about what I am here calling the cultural politics of childhood identities.

One explanation for this absence lies in the history of childhood studies. The challenge, begun in the late 1970s, to foreground children as social actors – as people with views, competencies and opinions which are worthy of study in their own right and which are not simply replicating those given to them by adults (James and Prout 1990) – has been hard-won. It involved the contestation of universalizing models of childhood and child development through resort to small-scale and detailed studies of children's everyday lives in order to demonstrate the socially constructed character of childhood. Such studies showed up the diversity of children's childhoods and called into question universal models. However, the great irony here is that, in order to make this argument, the Englishness or Frenchness of the cultural context was effectively downplayed, if not at times written out altogether. The greater challenge was to demonstrate the importance of the categorical position of children vis-à-vis the adult world, and to insist that children can be informants in their own right who take an active part in shaping the course of their own lives. Thus, in my own work, I explored the local context of children's everyday lives in order to argue *for* a more universal recognition of the compet-encies that all children share while, at the same time, using the same particular local examples of child lives to argue *against* traditional, universalizing discourses of children's dependency and incompetencies. But in all of this, the precise character of an 'English' childhood was never fully articulated nor explored through these snapshots of children's lives in England.

Pleading mitigation, this was perhaps because such an endeavour is in some ways impossible. The massive social stratification of contemporary Britain – stratification by ethnicity, class, health status, gender and, of course, age – defeats such an intent at the outset. As an English anthropologist I cannot write sensibly about an English childhood, though I might talk broadly of English childhoods (cf. Qvortrup 1994). And yet, such accounts of childhood in other cultures are produced by anthropologists (see Stafford 1995) and within sociology and psychology 'the child' is still often held to constitute an effective and useful symbolic representation of all children's everyday lives. What then accounts for this difference and my omission? Part of the explanation may simply be an effect of anthropology at home – a lifetime's familiarity breeds not only a certain disaffection, but perhaps a contempt! However, it also provides abundant implicit knowledge of the intricacies of *intra*-cultural difference which make it less possible to generalize and to talk with confidence about the cultural patterns and regularities constraining a whole category of people. In my omission therefore lie the seeds of a cultural politics of childhood identities, a politics which I shall now explore through the detailing of children's relative powerlessness, at home and at school, in one particular region of Britain.

Ethnographic Settings and the Self

The fieldwork on which I draw dealt with 10-11-year-old children in the north of England in the late 1990s. They all attended one of three local primary schools, two in a rural area and one in the inner city. The research project was intended to explore children's perception and understanding of time, including both clock time and biographical time,[2] and in order to enable these perceptions and understandings to be revealed the children talked with us about their everyday lives at school and at home, about the nature of family life, about their own biographies and about their aspirations for the future.

The ethnographic examples analysed in detail in this chapter, however, are snapshots taken from only the urban primary school. The school draws on a catchment area of relatively poor families, reflected in the high number of free school meals provided for the children. The school also has high numbers of children living in lone-parent or reconstituted families. Thus the disputes about family life which the children endlessly related to us during fieldwork reflected, in part, the often crowded nature of the household environments in which many of them were living. They shared their homes with step-sibs, half-sibs and real sibs; sometimes with grandparents, aunts and married elder brothers; some children did not live in the family home but stayed most nights at their grandparents' house or lived with an aunt. Bedrooms were often shared, leading to sibling arguments about the use of that space, and the TV in the living room was the focus for many familial disputes. Most of these children spent at least an hour every evening after school playing outside the family home with their neighbourhood friends. This is, then, a particular form of child street-and-family life in Britain which contrasts strongly with the lives led by other children in the study who lived in the rural areas. Many of these rural children belonged to smaller, more middle class, intact families and had larger houses and gardens. For them, living where they did and coming from such families as they did, playing after school out in the street with friends was not possible because of the distances involved. Sometimes it was not even permitted, for parents were anxious about the risks children might face when out alone. Thus, the home experiences the inner-city children had were rather different from those of other children involved in the study who lived just some twenty miles distant.

On the other hand there were also many potential continuities of experience across the group of children. All the children had to learn under the broad framework and rubric of the National Curriculum which, increasingly, constricted both children's and teachers' time during the day (Christensen and James 2001). In all the schools both staff and children complained of the relentless pressure caused by the SATs testing system, whose outcome would yield a ranked standardization of individual pupils and, through the publication of national league tables, of the attainments and quality of the school itself. Similarly all the children, precisely through their designation as children, were subject to the broad sweep of the British legal and welfare system whose practices work to homogenize childhood's very heterogeneity and are designed to help eradicate the stigmatizing differences between children brought about by, for example, family structure, poverty or ill health.[3]

Threaded through the children's narratives, therefore, are glimpses of these many different, sometimes conflicting, ideas of what childhood is or what children should be and the ways in which children encounter them in the course of their everyday socializing relationships with adults at home, at school and in the street. Embedded in the narratives also are children's varied responses to and modes of integration of these images in the making of their childhood identity. As Giddens notes:

> A person may make use of diversity in order to create a distinctive self-identity which positively incorporates elements from different settings into an integrated narrative. (1991: 190)

Thus, I suggest, the different versions of 'the self as child' with which children engage in their everyday social encounters and which they are endeavouring to weave into a coherent narrative for the self can tell us not only about their individual experiences of being socialized into the category 'child', but also about the formation of the conceptual space of 'childhood' as part of the life course in contemporary British society.

Adults' Power and Children's Powerlessness

To enable the children to think more concretely about how they spent their time, a set of participatory tools was devised which, variously, asked the children to draw or tabulate the ways in which time is divided up during the week and who has control over decisions about their use of time (see Christensen and James 2000). Most children thought time could be divided broadly into 'time in school' and 'time outside school' , with the latter being detailed into discrete blocks of time spent doing different kinds of activity – football, housework, shopping, swimming, watching TV. In all but one example, however, time in school was simply represented as a blank space (Figure 7.1). Only one girl differentiated blocks of time within 'school time' but did so in a most revealing fashion (Figure 7.2). The times she marked out are the only times during the school day when children themselves have some control over what they do: going home from school, lunchtime and break time (see also for example Blatchford 1998). At an analytic level, therefore, this diagram suggests that children's experience of schooling in Britain is an experience of relative powerlessness when compared to their experiences outside school; that the role of schoolchild subtly changes between different spaces within the school – between the classroom and the playground; that it changes at different times within the school day – between playtime and lunchtime;[4] that therefore the boundaries to childhood which are mapped out and enacted even within one very particular and limited locale such as the school are relatively fluid, making the idea of a 'child' temporally and spatially contextual; and finally that children themselves are highly cognizant of the potential which such differences might have for themselves as children, the local inhabitants of this childhood space. All of which seems perhaps rather a large claim to make from one small diagram! The rest of the chapter enlarges and develops these themes.

The Continuities of Adult Power

Describing her daily experience of school, Amy vehemently denounced it as follows:

> *BAD BAD BAD BAD BAD BAD BAD BAD BAD BAD I wish they'd never had invented it*

And when later she was asked to complete a chart about the decisions she was allowed to take at school she commented:

> *There's no point [in putting herself on the chart] because they never let you do anything that you say anyway*

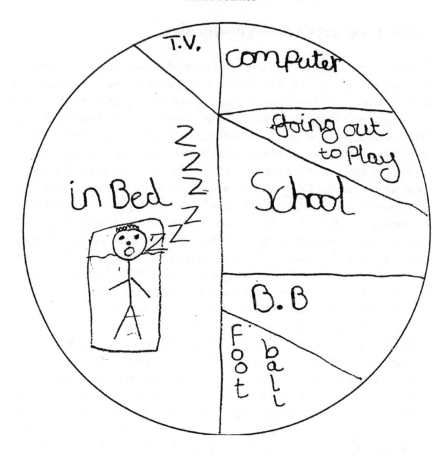

Figure 7.1 Use of time: I

'They' the teachers control what children do, as children see it. However, it is not just at school that children experience a relative powerlessness over how they spend their time. Thus, for example, also in Figure 7.2, we can see the graphic portrayal of the decision-making and arguments that take place for many children at home over bedtime. GO TO BED is written in large capital letters and indeed occupies a large space in the diagram, thus pictorially recalling the verbal descriptions other children offered about disputes with their parents over bedtime.

Parents not only set time limits but, as teachers do, also endeavour to influence *how* children spend their time, as is revealed in children's common detailing of familial conflicts over time use – for example, over the amount of time spent watching TV or playing on the computer. Such activities may not be regarded by parents as beneficial for children and thus, as Harry observes, parents – who are legally deemed to know what is in their best interests – often try to insist that their children spend their time more effectively:

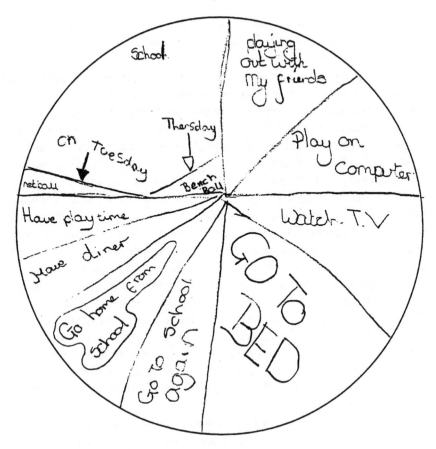

Figure 7.2 Use of time: II

*my mam she always tells me to move or go and get something to do while I'm sitting
there watching the telly*

And similarly at school, adults insist that there are right and wrong ways to spend
one's time. Even the dinner-ladies, who are known by the children not to have the
same kind of power as teachers, endeavour to control what children do at dinner-
time:

She bangs on the table with spoons like that. She tells people off for no reason at all

At home, to punish children for bad behaviour, parents may further usurp children's
own time by 'grounding' them within the family and disallowing contact with
their friends, a practice paralleled in schools by teachers not letting children have
their playtime (Christensen, James and Jenks 2000). Darrel explains what happens
if he has been naughty at home:

If I've been naughty I'm not allowed to play out so . . . until I've apologized and, erm, I've got to stay in for one night and then I've got to apologize.

Thus, through the minute detailing of particular examples children revealingly commented on their everyday experience of relative powerlessness at school and at home. At the same time, however, they indicated their awareness of its general-izable potential across localities and over time. Thus, Harry described his mother as *always* interrupting what he does. Through the use of the conditional *if* and the illustrative *like* Tim and Darrel similarly drew broader generalizations to evaluate their relationships with their mothers: *She's like bossy; if I'm naughty . . . I've got to stay in.* But, more significantly, it is through the common use of the present tense that children offer reflexive generalizations about the nature of their everyday encounters with adults. The use of the present tense – *she is, she bangs, she tells, they never* – makes a past incident into simply one among many of a kind, an on-going and repetitive patterning of the relationships children have with adults.

Such continuities between home and school are further exemplified in children's narratives by their broad categorization of parents and teachers as '*they*', a distinctive group apart from the '*we*' who are children. '*They*', the adults, are people who '*tell*' you or '*make*' you do things; alternatively, '*they*' are also people who '*let*' and '*allow*' children certain privileges. Thus, even if children are not being made to do things they dislike, nonetheless they still see themselves as having only a restricted say over how they spend their time: to be allowed to go to town is rather different from deciding for oneself to do so. In their own words, children *have to* or have *got to* comply with the demands adults make of them.

Thus, the events about which the children in the study complained were not one-offs, nor yet did their articulation represent the sudden dawning of a realization that such generational power differentials existed. On the contrary, as the children sat comparing notes about these incidents – or ones very much like them – it was clear that this was very much a shared experience; that having no say, being told what to do, being interrupted, receiving orders, being chastised and reprimanded and being unable to offer much resistance were themes patterning most children's everyday relationships with most adults. At an analytic level, therefore, it could be said that adults are seen by children as those by whom permission to act can be granted or withheld and, indeed, as those who are in positions of authority to instruct and coerce them to behave.

It is in these diverse and implicit ways, then, that children experience their identity as 'children' being inscribed and ascribed through the flow of the everyday power politics which comprise the process of socialization at home and at school. And, indeed, it may be that this perception of their own powerlessness accounts for the fact that in self-ascription, or when describing their peers, children never use the term 'children'. They always use instead the more positive term 'people'.

Particularizing Adult Power

Although as noted above adults are categorized by children into a homogeneous group with respect to the power that they can potentially wield, children nonetheless recognize that, in practice, there is a differentiated hierarchy of authority among the adults. The head teacher, for example, is regarded as having an authority which extends beyond the spatial boundaries of the school into the home:

> *he's like in charge of the behaviour of us and what we do . . . chows at us and sends a letter round to our parents or rings them up.*

The authority of ordinary class teachers, by contrast, is much more limited and in some instances their control is not perceived to extend legitimately beyond the walls of the classroom. Thus, Jon, with a good deal of grievance in his voice, complained bitterly of his class teacher who had told him off for bringing a rugby ball into school to play with at playtime, time which he considered his own time at school.

The fact that the attenuated sphere of influence and control of the head teacher into time outside of school is not questioned by the children is, however, significant. It provides a clear exposition of how children are experiencing the current refashioning of childhood in contemporary Britain. The legal and regulatory frameworks surrounding current educational policy have considerably tightened the links between home and school – through, for example, the introduction of truancy-watch schemes and the encouragement of parental policing of homework (James and James 2001) – and it is the role of the head teacher to ensure the effectiveness of such policies. And at home it is mothers who help the school forge these links by supervising how children spend their time. Tim, relating an everyday story of his life at home, mimics his mother:

> *'Your bedroom's looking untidy, tidy it up now, do your homework.' I'll come in, like I'm real tired: 'I'm off to bed'. 'No, you have to do your homework.' She's like bossy.*

Fathers seem to take little part in such forms of regulation at home.

That children perceive different adults to have different kinds of authority over them allows children to see themselves as being able to exercise some decision-making power. Knowledge of how do this is shared by a community of children through recounting tales based on their own experiences. These provide them with examples from which to generalize. In the following conversation, for example, two friends discuss the relative powers that the head teacher and their class teacher have over their actions at school. Maureen, more confident than Gemma, boldly asserts that, although the head teacher has very extensive powers, there are structural and institutional limits to even his control over what she does – for example, he cannot control whom she talks with:

> *Do you think Mr Brown (head teacher) has any say in who I talk to? He don't really. It's up to me who I talk to.*

Gemma is less sanguine about this for, although she would like to acknowledge the truth of Maureen's assertion, as she knows well from her own daily experiences in the classroom, in practice teachers – even ordinary teachers – continually manage to assert their control:

> *No, Miss Martin (class teacher) tells you who to talk to quite a lot, 'cus she always tells you not to talk to me!*

Gemma was looking forward to moving to secondary school because then Mr Brown's sphere of influence would be curtailed:

> *He told them (the teachers at the new school) that we'd not to go together... But it's got nowt to do with him, 'cus he's not looking after us no more.*

In her analysis of Mr Brown's authority Gemma reveals her understanding and experience of both the explicit and implicit regulation of contemporary British childhood. As head of the primary school Mr Brown's control over what she does officially ends when she moves to secondary school. Gemma is therefore angry that he should have abused his power by trying to influence the new teachers' opinions of the friends with whom she should be allowed to associate. As she says: '*it's got nowt to do with him*'. However, in her defiant stance Gemma reveals a deeper, more implicit understanding of the more generalized nature of child–adult relations which, though often experienced as controlling, are always assumed to be framed within and by a more overarching ethic of care (Neale, Wade and Smart 1998) and to be in the child's best interests.

Negotiating Adult Power at Home and School

That this ethic of caring/control is often experienced by children as overarching may mean that for some children there is little room for negotiation in their every-day relationships with teachers at school and, as noted elsewhere (Hockey and James 1993), this is a marked feature of the familial ideology through which the dependency of children is naturalized within Western societies:

> Care, control and abuse all represent the exercise of power, and reflect the presence of structured inequalities within the family along gender and generational lines ... Thus while the child's relationship with its parents may be seen to provide an acceptable

ideological model of dependency, that relationship, in practice, is one which can be both painful and dehumanizing as well as caring and protective. (1993: 125)

For some children, therefore, it may only be possible to gain control over time-use by deliberately choosing to misbehave or disobey and thus, through confrontation, to assert their rights as independent social actors:

> *Chris*: playtime . . . there's usually a teacher on play times, so you (if you) get into trouble, so, they decide what you do at playtime. **They don't decide if you're gonna play football, or if you don't behave.** (our emphasis)
>
> *Kerry*: they can't like *make* me do work.
>
> *Allison*: So that's when you think you've got some control . . . cos you can actually choose whether you do it . . . and if you choose not to do it and you get into trouble, that's your choice. Is that what you mean?
>
> *Kerry*: Yeah . . . You can do, in some work you can decide what I want to do. [sic]

That children see teachers, who are in loco parentis, taking on a role comparable to that of parents is not surprising for, in many ways, primary schools mirror family systems in their institutional structuring of generational inequalities. In this sense it could be argued that there is a continuum of socialization across these domains. However, in that such control *is* exercized through an ethic of care does permit some children greater room for negotiation at home where care is, or ideally should be, foregrounded.

Adults' power over children at home is perceived by the children to be differentiated and, more importantly, more differentiable than at school, as is clear from the following observations about familial decision-making over bedtime:

> *Sam*: My dad let's me go about ten 'cus my mum and dad's divorced. My mum lets me go about nine.
>
> *Diana*: And granddad makes me go about eight, my other nana and granddad whenever I want.
>
> *Jim*: My dad tells me to go to bed at nine and mam tells me to go to bed at half past eight, step-mum at nine.

Children shared among themselves the strategies they used in such negotiations and their observations underscore the particularities of the social locality in which they live. For these children, as opposed to the children from intact and more middle-class rural families who also participated in the study, it was the existence of a range of adult care-takers at home which enabled them a marginally greater space for negotiation. Here not only are mums played off against dads as occurs in many families, but the possible conflict between parents is open to further emotional exploitation. Sam says: *My dad let's me go about ten 'cus my mum and dad's divorced*. The implication is that there are different rules pertaining in his father's house as opposed to in his mother's; moreover, he implies that his father lets him go later than his mother does, precisely *because* they are divorced. Whether this is in fact a truthful account of his father's motivation matters not; this is how Sam understands it and explains it to himself. In his eyes his father is more lenient; he is more tolerant of later bedtimes and by implication less strict than his mother; and he behaves like this because they are divorced. Jim in similar family circumstances, by contrast, simply acknowledged rather glumly that different rules apply in different places and that control is exercized over him by three different adults: by his dad, by his mum and by his step-mum.

Diana, on the other hand, lives in a single-parent household with her mother but spends much time at her grandparents' houses. For her, negotiating space is achieved less by exploiting the potential of the emotional competition between warring parents but by recognizing the differences between the ways in which adult power *can* be exercized. Thus one of her granddads is a strong disciplinarian who *makes* her go to bed at eight, while her other grandparents are much more easy-going, allowing her to make her own decisions about bedtime, and it is this nana and granddad, her mother's parents, with whom she spends most of her time.

Children's responses to their ascribed powerlessness thus take different forms and analysis reveals how the generalized dependency of children becomes subtly transformed through the locality of the local context. Strategies of pleading, deceit and emotional blackmail are used opportunistically by children to gain some say over what they do. Sally describes one occasion when the simple technique of insistent pleading and begging eventually paid off and she was permitted to have her ears multiply pierced:

> *My mum won't let me get my ears pierced up there and I begged her into, please, mam, please, please and she let me, I was always begging my mam.*

Keith, who shares a bedroom with his brother and who, like the majority of these children, had their own television in their bedroom, reveals how as siblings they collude against their parents' bedtime strictures to gain access to forbidden late-night TV. Once in bed his parents do not come upstairs to see them so,

> *my little brother turns the sound down (on the TV) so mam can't hear it.*

Penny, who lives alone with her mum and senses that perhaps her mother finds looking after her rather difficult, for she often spends weeks living with her aunt and uncle rather than her mother, readily uses emotional blackmail to get her way:

> *'cus when mam don't let me do things I go off in a mood so she let's me.*

Conclusion

For any individual child, therefore, this chapter has argued that the categorical identity and experience of being a child, and belonging to the universal category of 'children', is tempered in and through the negotiations they manage to personally achieve with particular adults in particular locales. These negotiations take place around the ways in which contemporary child-centred policies are being implemented by adults on children's behalf, such as those which shape classroom encounters between teachers and their pupils. Less specific, though no less critical, are the negotiations which take place, often at home, over broader cultural attitudes to and ideas about what children are, which can be said to be the sedimented and accumulated cultural history of past policy-making on the behalf of children.

As I have tried to show, through the detailed ethnographic examples above, it is by negotiating their way through these versions of the self they encounter at home and at school that children gain a sense of self-identity and have some control over their personal biographical life-project as an English child. The variations which they encounter permit children different opportunities for and degrees of participation in decision-making, with different competencies being ascribed to them and different responsibilities allocated. Thus Barbara, for example, comes from a family where the generational separation between adults and children at home may be less than is common in other English families and is certainly far less than she experiences at school. Ten-year-old Barbara describes her relationship with her mum as follows:

like me and my mum can have, like, a good talk, so we will tell each other things.

But on another occasion Barbara was highly critical of her mother's behaviour and the way she dressed, describing her as being *like a tart*. Perhaps in part a consequence of her parents' divorce, the generational line between child and parent is continually down-played in her home:

If my dad rings, I spend like a lot of time on the telephone but he don't talk much. I've got to do all the talking, 'cus he's just like 'Hi' and 'Bye' and he don't talk much. I have a good conversation with his girlfriend (who is French) She speaks real good English.

But once at school, Barbara has to be like any other ten-year-old English school girl and to submit to the more overall controlling power of teachers through which teacher and pupil identities are enacted and through which English educational policy is pursued.

Therefore, in realizing and exploiting the heterogeneity of power which in practice shapes their everyday relations with adults, children come to see the structural space of childhood as, in some respects, also heterogeneous. On the one hand, as I have shown, childhood is a shared experience, a separate and separating generational space which unites children into a 'we' which daily is enacted and set against the 'they' which adults comprise. On the other hand, this cultural space can be experienced differently between and across different local sites by a child as he or she moves between home and school; or, indeed, individual children may have rather different experiences of what is ostensibly a shared cultural and generational locale. Thus the *cultural* politics of childhood identities are revealed as central to the ways in which socialization is experienced by children.

Geertz argues that 'the important thing about the anthropologist's findings is their complex specificness, their circumstantiality' for it is through this that grander theories and concepts can be thought 'realistically and concretely about . . . and creatively and imaginatively with' (1973: 23). It is to be hoped that in this chapter, through the presentation of children's perspectives on just one aspect of their everyday dealings with adults, some insight has been shed on the ways in which, for children, the categorical identity of child acquires some less than categorical meanings during the process of socialization.

Notes

1. In this sense my own work represents a rather different tradition to the earlier British community studies.
2. This project 'Changing Times' was part of the ESRC Children 5–16 Programme, and was carried out by me, Pia Christensen and Chris Jenks, with Sally McNamee as a research assistant.
3. There is no room here to look comparatively across these groups of children but it is clear that, for example, many of the inner-city children would have had more personal experience of the law than those in the rural areas through, say, the divorce of their parents. They were also more likely to be subject to 'welfarist' policies in school in relation to truancy or school exclusion.
4. Aspects of this powerlessness at school are further explored in P. Christensen and A. James (2001).

References

Alderson, P. (1993) *Children's Consent to Surgery*, Buckingham: Open University.
Archard, D. (1993) *Children: Rights and Childhood*, London: Routledge.

Armstrong, D. (1983) *Political Anatomy of the Body: Medical Knowledge in Britain in the Twentieth Century*, Cambridge: Cambridge University Press.

Blatchford, P. (1998) *Social Life in School*, London: Falmer Press.

Christensen, P. and James, A. (2000) 'Childhood Diversity and Commonality: Some Methodological Insights', in P. Christensen and A. James (eds) *Research with Children: Perspectives and Practices*, London: Falmer Press.

—— (2001) 'What are Schools for? The Temporal Experience of Children's Learning', in B. Mayall and L. Allanen (eds) *Conceptualising Child-adult Relations*, London: Falmer.

—— and Jenks, C. (forthcoming) '"All We Needed to do was to Blow the Whistle": Children's Embodiment of Time', in S. Cunningham Burley (ed.) *Exploring the Body*, London: Macmillan.

Geertz, C. (1975) *The Interpretation of Cultures*, London: Hutchinson.

Giddens, A. (1991) *Modernity and Self-Identity*, Cambridge: Polity.

Gittens, D. (1998) *The Child in Question*, London: Macmillan.

Hendrick, H. (1990) 'Constructions and Reconstructions of British Childhood: An Interpretive Survey, 1800 to the Present', in A. James and A. Prout (eds) *Constructing and Reconstructing Childhood*, London: Falmer Press.

Hockey, J. and James, A. (1993) *Growing Up and Growing Old*, London: Sage.

James, A. (1979) 'Confections, Concoctions and Conceptions', *Journal of the Anthropology Society of Oxford* 10(2): 83–95.

—— (1986) 'Learning to Belong: The Boundaries of Adolescence', in A.P. Cohen (ed.) *Symbolising Boundaries*, Manchester: Manchester University Press.

—— (1993) *Childhood Identities: Self and Social Relationships in the Experience of the Child*, Edinburgh: Edinburgh University Press.

—— (1998) 'Imaging Children "At home", "In the Family" and "At School": Movement between the Spatial and Temporal Markers of Childhood identity in Britain', in N.J. Rapport and A. Dawson (eds) *Migrants of Identity: Perceptions of Home in a World of Movement*, Oxford: Berg.

——, Jenks, C. and Prout, A. (1998) *Theorising Childhood*, Cambridge: Polity.

—— and Prout, A. (1990) (eds) *Constructing and Reconstructing Childhood*, Basingstoke: Falmer Press.

James, A. L. and James, A. (2001) 'Tightening the Net: Children, Community and Control', *British Journal of Sociology* 52 (2): 211–28.

Jenks, C. (1996) *Childhood*, London: Routledge.

Neale, B., Wade, A. and Smart, C. (1998) '"I just get on with it": Children's Experiences of Family Life following Parental Separation and Divorce', *Working Paper 1*, Centre for Research on Family, Kinship and Childhood, University of Leeds.

Qvortrup, J. (1994) 'Childhood matters: An Introduction', in J. Qvortrup, M. Bardy, G. Sgritta and H. Wintersberger (eds.) *Childhood Matters*, Aldershot: Avebury.

Roseneil, S. and Seymour, J. (1999) *Practising Identities: Power and Resistance*, London: Macmillan.

Stafford, C. (1995) *The Roads of Chinese Childhood*, Cambridge: Cambridge University Press.

Stainton-Rogers, R. and Stainton-Rogers, W. (1992) *Stories of Childhood: Shifting Agendas of Child Concern*, London: Harvester Wheatsheaf.

Stephens, S. (ed.) (1995) *Children and the Politics of Culture*, Princeton: Princeton University Press.

–8–

Bits and Bytes of Information
Jeanette Edwards

Brigitte Jordan's book *Birth in Four Cultures* was first published in 1978. It is a comparison of childbirth in Yucatan, Holland, Sweden and the United States, and its early editions were mostly ignored by a 'mainstream' anthropology that appeared neither ready nor willing to take childbirth as a serious and 'proper' focus of anthropological enquiry, or to recognize its potential to contribute to core anthropological theory (Ginsburg and Rapp 1995). This resonates with the fate of the anthropology of Britain in and around the same era. I think it fair to say that the doyens of social anthropology, with notable exceptions, turned their back on the anthropology of Britain. Things have changed. A fourth edition of *Birth in Four Cultures* appeared in 1993, testimony to the tenacity of its core thesis and the foresight of the author. Jordan had put her finger on a concern that went to the heart of anthropology: a concern with what constitutes knowledge. 'Why and how', she asked, did women's knowledge about their own pregnancies not count, while medical knowledge 'carried the day'. Her comment that 'in any particular social situation a multitude of ways of knowing exist, but some carry more weight than others' might appear today to state the obvious, but we are still a long way from charting systematically ways in which '[s]ome kinds of knowledge become discredited and devalued, while others become socially sanctioned, consequential, even "official", and are accepted as grounds for legitimate inference and action' (1993: 150). This chapter is concerned with what counts as 'scientific knowledge' and begins by looking at the relationship between social anthropology and science.

Anthropology and Science: An Awkward Relationship?

Social anthropology has an ambivalent and intimate relationship with science. Certain anthropologists have been preoccupied, at different times, with the question of whether anthropology is or is not a science. They have asked whether the process of rendering human worlds anthropologically meaningful is axiomatically an imposition of a scientific sensibility. The question rests on an understanding of science as a way of conceptually ordering the world and as a set of practices which include empirical observation and generalization. Some anthropologists have argued the case for placing anthropology firmly in the scientific camp and in so doing have promoted its 'proper' (social) scientific credentials (e.g. Kuznar 1997; Barnard 1994; D'Andrade 1995). Others have distanced themselves from science and aligned themselves with artistic and literary effort (e.g. Wolcott 1995; Geertz 1988); while some argue that anthropology inevitably 'zig-zags' (Rapport 1997: 1–11) between the two (and see Ingold 1998). Debate which pitches art and science against each other, however, relies on assumptions about what constitutes, and is constitutive of, each and it is clear that such a crude dichotomy belongs more to the realm of polemic than to practice.[1] It also clear that the academic custom of cutting up its practice into disciplines, then clumping them together into distinct categories of, say, natural sciences, social sciences and humanities, aids and abets such polemic. For Tim Ingold (1998), the placing of anthropology in the social sciences and, for example, biology in the natural sciences has thwarted an adequate understanding of human beings in the world. He argues 'against the idea that human beings participate concurrently in two distinct worlds of nature and society' (1998: 48), and rejects the dichotomy which separates biophysical and sociocultural components of human life. But what of the cultural thinking that generates and maintains the dichotomy? There is evidently, to borrow a felicitous phrase from Marilyn Strathern (1987), 'an awkward relationship' between science and anthropology, and it is this awkwardness which is itself of anthropological interest.

According to Michael Carrithers (1990), the literary turn in anthropology which brought into focus writing as a core anthropological practice and drew analogies between ethnography and fiction and between the anthropologist and novelist could only be effective by relying on an unrealistic and stereotyped notion of science (and see Latour 1996). In order to see anthropology as 'creative fiction', science was constructed as positivist and objective. For Carrithers, defining science as a positivist pursuit and anthropology as interpretivist denied the everyday reality of both scientific *and* ethnographic practice. His answer is to trace the generalizing turns in the making of ethnography from the process of fieldwork, and to show thus the affinity between science and anthropology. I am less interested in the question of whether anthropology is or is not a science than in the fact that the question can be asked at all. This chapter is concerned more with scientism than it is with science itself: with a culturally specific celebration and reverence of the rational and empirical and an assumption that these things *belong* to the scientific endeavour (and see Okely 1996; Lave 1996).

Ballast to the 'anthropology as science' thesis is that of 'science as everyday practice'. Anthropological, social and historical studies of science have revealed not only the social, political and economic forces at play in the pursuit of science but also the social relations of 'laboratory life' and of 'discovery' (e.g. Rabinow 1996; Kay 1993; Latour 1987; Traweek 1988; Haraway 1989; Latour and Woolgar 1979).

Social studies of science have focused on the mundane rather than the sacred, and the ethnographic detail emerging shows multiple trajectories, some of which are far from positivist, and a diversity of practitioners who are far from homogenous. We know about 'feelings' for the organism, intuition, hunches and prescience (e.g. Barr and Birke 1998; Rose 1994; Keller 1983), and about the social relations of experimentation and verification. Metaphors that have shaped what can be discovered and how have been unpacked to good effect.[2] The contingency of scientific practice and progress is by now well documented.[3] Yet the idea of science as rational, objective and relying on 'plain observation' prevails, and begs the question of how such an idea is sustained. In its myth of 'factual account', science is purged of impurities and the fuzziness of human affairs.

To ask 'what is science?' from an anthropological perspective is to ask about the status and place of scientific knowledge in culturally diverse ways of knowing the world. Is it culturally specific (peculiarly Western perhaps[4]) or universal (a human way of reasoning[5])? Certain scholars have found the distinction between 'big science' (Big Science [Fuller 1996]) and 'little science', or between techno-science and ethnoscience, useful (Nader 1996). Others reject such contrasts. Donna Haraway, for example, points out that the distinction between science and ethnoscience is meaningless as 'science is knowledge-crafting practice that is always historically specific' (1997: 140). It is argued on the one hand that all people understand the world scientifically, and on the other that science is culturally specific (but has been successful at inserting itself and dominating other ways of knowing[6]). If science is a system of practices and scientists its practitioners, it is also a way of imposing conceptual order on the world. As such, it is both contrasted with and likened to other forms of knowledge. It is defined by what it is not – and it is not for example 'indigenous' 'local' or 'native' knowledge – and by what it is: particular (Western), global (its tendrils reach everywhere), and universal (all people think scientifically).[7] At the same time, it is thought that those who live in what are deemed to be scientifically motivated societies do not think scientifically all the time. Western cosmopolitans, for example, like to think of themselves as multi-faceted, creative, independent actors who deploy a wide range of ways of thinking about, and being in, the social worlds they create for themselves.

From almost the inception of British social anthropology, anthropologists (and others) have argued that people the world over deploy principles of observation, experimentation and deduction: principles which, from some quarters, were considered not only the sole preserve of science but also its particular and crowning achievement. For Malinowski, in the language of the time:

> There are no peoples however primitive without religion and magic. Nor are there, it must be added at once, any savage races lacking either in the scientific attitude or in science, though this lack has frequently been attributed to them (1948: 17).

When this was first published in 1925, models of science relied on a distinction between 'primitive' and 'civilized', and each was associated with 'concrete' and 'abstract' thought, respectively (Lewis 1994; Malinowski 1948). Levy-Bruhl had firmed-up the difference by 1910, legitimating his theory of the 'primitive mind' with science, and arguing for a difference in cognitive ability (Lave 1996). Europeans were 'analytical' and Africans, among others, incapable of being so. We know that such notions were part and parcel of strategies of domination, and the assertion that 'primitive peoples' were incapable of 'analytical' thought is stark today in its racism. Yet although 'the primitive mind' thesis has been exposed as artifice of the time, it has proven robust as a model of knowledge. Rather than being displaced and replaced, it has merely mutated. The protagonists might have been substituted (for 'primitive' read 'ordinary') but the ranking of knowledge, and consequently of categories of person, remains.

There appears to be a growing acknowledgement of the place and value of non-Western indigenous knowledge (even if cynical readings – of which there are many – point to this as lip-service or unchecked romanticism) and, at the same time, a diminishing respect for Western non-scientific knowledge. In Britain, it is not very often that 'ordinary people', or what Jean Lave calls in a North American context jpfs (just plain folks), are deemed to have anything to offer science. Instead their lack of 'scientific literacy' is noted and mourned, and the boundary between punter and scientist vigilantly patrolled. Scientists are understood to have a special kind of knowledge which can be imparted, more or less successfully, to non-scientists ('the public') via education. The traffic is decidedly one-way.

It is no accident that, at the beginning of the twenty-first century, in Britain (but not only), there is a burgeoning interest in 'the public understanding of science' (PUS[8]). Each of the terms in PUS – 'public', 'understanding' and 'science' – is loaded. They beg immediate questions of which 'public' and what kind of 'understanding', while the problem of defining 'science' has already been noted.[9] The newly awakened interest in PUS relies on a category of 'ordinary people' who are deemed, generally speaking, to be 'scientifically illiterate'. Quizzes and questionnaires which fail to elicit correct answers are used to prove the point. Scientific knowledge is measured and assessed in the ability of people to retain and regurgitate bits and bytes of information. Now rather than some sort of innate or inborn cognitive inability which prevents abstract thought, shortfalls in scientific understanding are said to be due to lack of education, or to access to 'proper' information, or to a short attention span. Indeed 'the public' are thought to have the ability to 'think scientifically' but they need to be trained/educated to do so. But 'thinking scientifically', as in all conceptually creative endeavours, entails the making of connections. If scientific literacy, a new emblem of citizenship, is marked only by people's ability to retain bits and bytes of information, the analogies people make and the alacrity with which they make connections across different domains of social life are ignored (Strathern 1992). This chapter is concerned with the links people make when talking science. It focuses in from 'science' as a broad generic activity, and dwells on one specific (albeit huge) field of scientific activity, namely genetics.

There have been a number of important and influential studies from a psychosocial perspective on 'the public understanding' of 'new genetics'.[10] Martin Richards, a prominent figure in the debate, argues that 'lay beliefs' (in this case, of kinship) obstruct a scientific understanding of genetic inheritance. In his view, lay people do not easily assimilate Mendelian (scientific) genetics because it conflicts with their pre-existing knowledge and beliefs (Richards 1996; 1998). When they do apprehend Mendelian genetics, they do so as a new domain of knowledge which then exists separate from, and parallel to, their everyday ideas of inheritance (Richards 1997). Richard's impetus is in the imperative of the clinic, and in the need for patients to have a clear understanding of 'scientific genetics' in order to make informed and difficult decisions (and see Green 1992).[11] In this model 'lay belief' co-exists with 'scientific understanding', and the two impinge on each other only insofar as the former 'gets in the way' of the latter.[12]

The anthropology of Britain is well placed to put together what easily gets separated out: to move between clinics, homes, work and meeting places, and to dwell in the borderlands, in what Kathleen Stewart (1996) calls 'the space in the gap'. I am interested in placing reproductive *and* genetic technologies in the same frame, in order to discern the 'patterns that connect' (even if molecular biologists, geneticists, embryologists and obstetricians, with their own fields of expertise, would for good reason object to their being lumped together in this way [Stacey 1992]).[13] The links different publics, including scientists, make or do not make across different scientific domains is crucial to an anthropological perspective on science. The point to make is that if, as many commentators note, new reproductive and genetic technologies appear to tap 'deep-seated fears' or mobilize 'background assumptions and premises', then what connects them is of anthropological interest.

There is a danger in this model that 'understanding' and 'belief' (like 'culture') are treated as if bounded and immutable. But neither exists in isolation; they are both communicated and formulated in interaction with persons and institutions (such as mass media and biomedicine). An anthropological study of genetic technology must ultimately tell us something about the appropriation, negotiation and rejection of science and the contexts in which this occurs. It is in the process of engagement with, for example, the science of genes that 'public understanding' is formulated. It is common to pull out one thread of such understanding and call it 'public opinion'. Of interest is which thread is unbraided when, and for what purpose. Anthropology focuses attention on the connections people make and the things they are reminded of when they engage with possibilities presented by science, in this case 'new reproductive technologies' (NRT[14]).

Participating in Kinship

In 1990, I spoke with Mrs Lawson in her home in Alltown.[15] It was the first time I had met her. She offered me tea and biscuits and we sat in her living room. She said she did not mind me tape-recording our conversation and had heard that I was interested in 'test-tube babies' and things like that.[16] At the time, Mrs Lawson was in her mid-forties, she told me she had seven children and 'two families'. She had three children with her first husband, from whom she was divorced; one with her second husband; and three from her second husband's previous marriage. She looked after and was 'mother' to all seven children, although three of them, she said, had two mothers. Her second husband had died, and she was now married for the third time to Mr Lawson. One of her daughters (with her daughter) lived with them, and Mrs Lawson looked after two other grandchildren during the week. I, at that time, was in my mid-thirties, had one child, and had never been married. Mrs Lawson knew this, and a little more, from her conversations with the woman who had introduced us.

Mrs Lawson told me that initially she had not wanted to marry her present husband because she knew he wanted children and, when they met, she had already gone through 'the change'. She had considered leaving him so he could meet somebody else and start a family of his own, but he persuaded her not to. This led me to ask her about the possibility of post-menopausal women being able to conceive a child through medical intervention. The excerpts from the transcription of our recorded conversation are deliberately lengthy and retain my questions and comments in an attempt to show how ideas lead on to other ideas and to make a point about the way in which 'scientific understanding' is co-produced and cannot be plucked and isolated from the contexts in which it is significant.[17]

> JE: . . . there's all kinds of intervention and assistance given to people who, for whatever reasons, are infertile. So, one latest idea has been that actually you can allow women . . . that have actually had a – gone through the change and are not having periods any more – erm (*pause*) you can have hormone treatment, create a situation whereby eggs are produced and then fertilize them in a test tube and then re-implant them. And clinicians are saying that this is actually one – a way of women to choose whether they can have children when they are older or not. So, I mean, I wondered _
>
> ML: Having thought about it since, I don't think I would want one now.
>
> JE: mm
>
> ML: For the simple reason, not for me, for the child. Because a woman having a child at forty has got a child who's got grandparents the same age. When I was thirty-eight, I had grandchildren.
>
> JE: mm

ML: And the kids would be going, 'And who's that old lady? Your gran?' 'No, it's me mum'.

JE: You'd think there'd be a stigma?

ML: Yeah. *I know* there would. Because I know such a case. Locally as well.

JE: So if women have children older _

ML: Yeah.

JE: _ there's a stigma attached to the children?

ML: To the child, not to the parent.

JE: What about children that are born through these techniques, through artificial insemination or test tubes or – do you think there's a stigma attached to them?

ML: No

JE: That would be different?

ML: Not unless it was to an older parent.

JE: So it's the age that's important?

ML: It's the age that's important. I mean if I thought, when I was a young woman, if I couldn't bear any children, I would have done *anything*, anything at all to have children.

JE: Would you?

ML: Yeah. I always wanted children. I wanted to be a nursery nurse and as I couldn't be I thought I'd have as many as I could. Have me own nursery. No, children are – even now, I mean, I'm on holiday really, because five days a week I look after two of me daughter's children, and we have a baby that lives here as well.

Mrs Lawson identifies age as a limiting factor on possibilities presented by technologies of assisted conception. A child with an older mother will be ridiculed, and this is good reason for not making fertility treatments available to older women. From the perspective of the child, mothers can be too old. But thinking of age reminds Mrs Lawson that when she was younger she would have given *anything* to have children. She extends her self-knowledge to other women; age now becomes the reason for making fertility services available. Age comes up again, later in our conversation, when I ask Mrs Lawson directly what kind of criteria should be used to assess priority.

JE: What kind of criteria can people use to say 'well, okay'_

ML: _'they should go first'?

JE: mm.

ML: There again, I think with that age would have to be a big concern. Because if a woman has been trying for years. I mean, some women get married twenty, twenty-one, they're getting to thirty and they still haven't succeeded and they've tried every other method.

JE: Um.

ML: I think age must be the main thing there. I mean a younger woman's _

JE: _ You mean age, as what? Thirty? Around there?

ML: Yeah. Because it – that is sort of their last hope, isn't it? Their last chance. Whereas a younger woman, can afford to wait longer. Whereas a woman of thirty can't afford to wait too long. She doesn't have too long to wait. She could be going through the change at thirty-eight.

JE: Right.

ML: I mean that's what the doctor told me. I was on the pill for fifteen years. I don't think I even had my blood pressure taken in most of that time. And I came off the pill and found I was already on the change.

Mrs Lawson extends her experience of menopause to other women: it was unexpected, premature. For her, it coincided with her being a grandparent. A biological and social marker of age collided; an age beyond which pregnancy could and should not occur. It is clear for Mrs Lawson that when menopause can occur at the age of thirty-eight, time is short. Age becomes a prominent factor in assessing the immediacy of who should have access to NRT.

Thinking of the urgency of pregnancy and of how it might be achieved when there are problems leads Mrs Lawson to think about surrogacy. In her words, 'even' using a 'host mother' is possible. The excerpt below begins where Mrs Lawson makes the interesting and significant distinction between a host mother and a surrogate. In Mrs Lawson's terms, the child is conceived with the egg of the surrogate and here she draws the line. A host mother, like a surrogate, is a woman who carries a baby on behalf of a woman unable to do so, but unlike a surrogate the child is not conceived from her egg (in other words, the host mother is not genetically related to the foetus). Mrs Lawson knows the experience of being unable to carry a foetus to term; she tells of the experience of her daughter-in-law and her son: she knows what it is like through them. She has participated in their trauma and heartache. My attempts, on several occasions, to shift the conversation back to anonymous NRT and an abstract everyperson fail, and eventually I succumb and tell what I know of my mother's experience.

JE: Right. So if you couldn't have had children, you can actually see that for people that can't have children now, that these kinds of developments, advances as it were, in technology, if they can help them, they should be used?

ML: Oh definitely. Even the host mother, you know, erm (pause)

JE: Surrogacy?

ML: Yeah. I mean, I would have done it for any of my sisters that wanted children. I don't see it as wrong, that (pause) especially, not so much surrogacy as the host mother, because that is – it is both their eggs, isn't it?[18] And um, a[nother] woman that carries them, [when they] can't carry a baby.

JE: Right.

ML: I mean I've got a daughter-in-law like that. She had that child there (points to a photograph). Gorgeous little thing. That was taken two weeks before he died.

JE: aww

ML: Cot death. That was her first son. She had five miscarriages.

JE: After that?

ML: After. She's now got a daughter that the sun shines out of her bottom and she's a horror. (laughter) No, she's not that bad.

JE: Did they know why she kept miscarrying? Was there something?

ML: They were amazed she carried him. She didn't carry him full term. This last one she carried full term and do you know how she did it? She stayed in bed, all day, every day. Twice she nearly miscarried, at, erm, four and a half months she nearly miscarried, and six and a half months she nearly miscarried.

JE: ahh

ML: If she got out of bed, she couldn't even walk to the shop and she'd start to bleed. But that's after all the others. And the experiences she had, she knew if she could lay on her back. And she was so determined to have this baby.

JE: It is amazing what people go through. Because none of these – a lot of these treatments of extracting eggs are very painful and risky.

ML: Um.

JE: And it's amazing what women do actually _

ML: Um.

JE: _ go through to have _

ML: The suffering that girl's gone through. I mean she had babies born at four and a half months. Twins. And, ah, this is the most horrible thing, you know, I've ever heard of. I mean, because they knew that these twins had only a fraction of a chance of living – and there was a baby born – I mean they only weighed one pound, one pound a few ounces, you know, three ounces, something like that.

JE: Right.

ML: And, at the hospital, there was a baby born that was six pound but had breathing problems and only one incubator so they asked Carol could they take her baby out the incubator and [said] 'you can sit and nurse it till it dies'. That is what they told her and that is what she did. They had no right to do that. I mean babies at four and a half months have lived before now. And tiny babies.

JE: Well, you can't ask the mother _

ML: You can't play God, can you? Not when they're in such a bad state. I mean one baby'd just died. It only lived a few minutes and then they asked her to play God on the life of the other one.

JE: She must have been heartbroken.

ML: Well we didn't think she'd have any more after that. And she went two years and then Lucy got pregnant and it's, it must have just triggered off something, and she got pregnant and they both had their babies at the same time practically.

JE: Did they?

ML: Weeks. There's twenty-three days between her and . . .

JE: So is this your son's_

ML: _Yeah, David's wife.

JE: This is your next to eldest?

ML: Yeah. But *that* broke their heart.

JE: mm.

ML: Several months. I mean there was nothing wrong with him. He just went to sleep and died. It – cot death, it's a terrible thing (pause)

JE: Yes. (pause) My mum had one. And she still now, even after thirty-five years, it still brings her, you know, it still brings a tear to her eye. She's, because, them days, you weren't allowed to mourn it really. You know, it was taken away from the house and she never saw it again. And there was always a sort of slight suggestion from different people _

ML: Stigma. There is _

JE: _that you've done something wrong.

ML: There is *now*. It's just the same. Kath went through hell with people saying, 'Oh, what happened?' Somebody said she suffocated it. She got notes through the door, child murderer. All sorts. The grief it caused.

JE: Oh my _

ML: She moved. There are people that are so stupid.

This last piece of our conversation provides a context for Mrs Lawson's earlier comments on stigma. She knows what neighbourhood gossip can come up with. She talks movingly of the anxiety generated by the sudden, unpredictable death of an infant: cause unknown. The conduit it provided for community hostility. The experience of stigma in one domain of social life (having an older parent) is extended to another (having a baby die); and each provides the context for the other. No event is isolated. Mrs Lawson talks of the economics and politics of health care, and the decisions of life and death she thinks God, and God alone, should make. She talks of the tenacity and courage of individuals, as well as their maliciousness. Mrs Lawson embeds NRT in a social, moral and spiritual universe, and kinship is the idiom through which she does so.

And so . . .

This chapter has focused on scientific understanding as processual and formulated in interaction. It is not to be found 'in people's heads' from where it can be retrieved: it cannot be tapped with the right tools, and consequently it is not quantitatively present or absent. Formulated in interaction, co-produced for particular reasons and with intention, understanding is contingent. I have wanted to highlight the way in which so called 'public understanding' of new reproductive and genetic technologies, for example, are formulated in conceptual engagement with them. It is in their engagement with science, the questions it poses and the possibilities it presents, that people make sense of its potential. It is not so much that different knowledges lie side by side, or that they merely collide, they also partially meld.

However much we trace the complexities of *all* knowledge systems, and attempt to break down and break through the prejudiced and biased ways in which they are hierarchically ordered (more often than not with Western scientific knowledge placed at the pinnacle of human achievement, but increasingly, and no less insidiously, with a romanticization of 'indigenous' knowledge of the third- and fourth-world kind packaged for Western consumption), it behoves us to keep power and capital (no matter how slippery the concepts) in the frame. Mrs Lawson knows the economics of caring for premature babies in incubators, and the emotional cost of decisions made to ration and rationalize such care. She has an attuned understanding of the ups and downs of scientific innovation. Clearly the Western scientific enterprise has been successful in all kinds of ways, and not least in disseminating its worth. Eric Grace, like many commentators on the rapid changes in biotechnology, argues that '[s]cience is *merely* a way of understanding how the world works' (Grace 1997: 223, my emphasis). On the same page he quotes Sir Peter Medwar, as saying that science is 'incomparably the most successful enterprise human beings have ever engaged upon'. My aim is not to quibble with its achievements, but to note that it is undoubtedly all the more successful for its imperialistic tendencies which include consistently downgrading alternative ways of understanding how the world works.

A complex political, economic and scientific alliance has fuelled a speeded-up pursuit of biotechnology. This is resulting in an unprecedented plethora of both life-enhancing and life-degrading possibilities.[19] Biotechnology is both feared and lauded: invested with both negative and positive potential. Dystopian and utopian visions surround it.[20] The solution often given for unrealistic expectations is 'more education' (of the 'proper' kind). 'More education', from this perspective, rarely means educating populations on the political, social and economic production of science or its place as one among many ways of ordering the world (and see Claeson et al. 1996). Scientific literacy is measured in terms of the information one has to hand; of the facts that can be recalled. It is no accident that, at the beginning of the twenty-first century, when knowledge is rendered tangible as bits and bytes of information, there is the tendency to lay 'the essence' of humanity at the door of the genome. While there might be little in the way of genetic difference between human beings and between humans and other animals, there is a palpable intrigue with the genetic basis of human beingness.

I draw on my conversation with Mrs Lawson as one example of an engagement with science. The study of science as part of the fabric of daily lives (be they professional or lay) is needed to counteract the tendency of scientific understanding to be analysed as if it were only esoteric and bounded knowledge that can be tapped and collected in survey or interview. An anthropology of Britain which dwells on connection and the in-betweens will reveal that in the laboratory there is no less contradiction and no more creativity than at home.

Notes

1. Notwithstanding C.P. Snow's (1959) still pertinent observations on two incommensurable cultures, and see contributors to Ross (1996).
2. To give an example: What is identified as a present-day confidence in the pervasive power and agency of genes is said to have stemmed from the metaphors in which genetic explanation is couched. For Evelyn Fox Keller (1995), the metaphor of *information*, and its co-metaphors of *programme* and *instruction*, were crucial to genetics becoming a central biological discipline. Such metaphors, she argues, spurred the search for genes: 'If our genes make us what we are – it ma[de] perfect sense to set the identification of these sequences as the primary and, indeed ultimate, goal of biology' (1995: 21). Such analysis clearly needs to be placed within the complex economic, political and technoscientific alliances that have been formed in pushing forward projects such as the mapping of the human genome.
3. What is surprising is that we could have been persuaded otherwise (cf. Leach 1969).
4. I use the term Western science with all the caveats proposed by the history of science, not least in imagining its origins in the West and ignoring the influence of the Middle and Far East on classical Greek thinking (Nader 1996). It is science with a big S, and it is at home on the industrial and military milieu of capitalism.
5. Writing of Cree hunters, Colin Scott refers to science in this way: 'If one means by science a social activity that draws deductive inferences from first premises, that these inferences are deliberately and systematically verified in relation to experience, and that models of the world are reflexively adjusted to conform to observed regularities in the course of events, then, yes, Cree hunters practice science – as surely as all human societies do' (Scott 1996: 69).
6. The power of Western science has often been related to its metaphors of domination and control over 'nature': but again metaphors require economic and political clout if not to fall on deaf ears.
7. A recent conference of the Association of Social Anthropologists of Britain and the Commonwealth took 'Indigenous Knowledge' (IK) as its theme (SOAS, April 2000). In this multidisciplinary meeting, several speakers underlined the complexity of IK and, in a spirit of cultural relativism, argued it was different from, not inferior to, Western scientific knowledge (which was not to deny that the latter often has more clout and has been overbearingly successful in its hegemony). It was acknowledged (particularly with reference to 'environmental issues') that 'local experts' were more knowledgeable about local conditions than cosmopolitan scientists and that one of the major problems of development projects (as we know them) has been the reluctance of 'developers' to take

'indigenous knowledge' seriously. By now this must be a truism in anthropology. The consequences of not listening to local people has been charted with depressing regularity (see, for example, Chambers 1983; Hobart 1993). But listening, while a good start, is not an end in itself, and what also emerged in conference was just how difficult it is to maintain a distinction between indigenous and scientific knowledge (and see Green 2000).

8. After the Royal Society report in the mid-1980s which called for improved public understanding of science and improved communication from scientists, several new chairs in the Public Understanding of Science were established in major British universities and filled by prominent scientists. I think it is useful to retain the ugly acronym PUS, despite the problematic terms, in order to distinguish between *the study* of the 'public understanding of science' (PUS) and its subject matter. PUS appears to be rapidly becoming a discipline in its own right, at least in Britain.

9. This is not the place to unpack what is invested in the contemporary focus on PUS. As my history of science colleagues point out, such an analysis requires a historical perspective which addresses a series of crises that have questioned the legitimacy of science.

10. The term 'new genetics' has been coined for developments in genetic science since techniques of recombining DNA.

11. Social scientific research on, for example, prenatal screening (e.g. amniocentesis, maternal serum alpha-fetoprotein – MSAFP), on genetic testing (for disease such as Huntington's and breast and ovarian cancer), and on carrier screening (for cystic fibrosis and sickle cell anaemia) has focused on issues such as informed consent, processes of decision-making and risk-assessment. Significant insights from these studies have clear implications for policy and practice. They go from strength to strength, particularly as more robust collaborations are forged between social and biological scientists. Such studies importantly discern a range of situated knowledges from differently positioned populations who have specific questions and motivations in mind. The problem is when they get congealed as 'public understanding'.

12. There have been a number of studies of 'the public understanding of genetics' in biomedical settings, and the need for research outside the clinic is recognized but often couched in instrumental terms. For example, in order to improve the clinical outcome it is argued that we need to know more about 'the beliefs' people bring to the clinical encounter, or because genetic medicine is focusing increasingly on multi-factorial conditions, it will encroach on more and more people (Richards 1998; Durant et al. 1996).

13. The connections made between technologies of assisted conception and of 'new genetics' allow for the understanding of one area of science to be contextualized in another and thus analysed as part of a dense social fabric rather than as isolated and separate threads.

14. I'll use this acronym loosely as shorthand for technologies of assisted conception.
15. Alltown is in the north of England and has a population of about 15,000 people. I carried out residential fieldwork in Alltown 1987–88, and returned in 1990 with a particular interest in new reproductive technologies (NRT) (see Edwards et al. 1999; Edwards 1999; Edwards and Strathern 2000).
16. I was advised to go and speak to Mrs Lawson by another Alltown woman with whom I had been working. Mrs Lawson was the woman's ex-husband's dead brother's wife. She also told Mrs Lawson about me, what I did and what I was interested in and asked her whether it would be all right if I got in touch. I was often referred on to people who were thought to have a particular and relevant kind of expertise when it came to NRT: their expertise invariably turned on their experience of kinship.
17. Transcription conventions: . . . material omitted
    _ at the end of an utterance indicates the speaker has been interrupted
    – in the middle of an utterance is used in place of a comma, usually to indicate where the speaker changes direction mid-sentence
    [ ] encloses my addition
18. The gametes of both the man and the woman who will be the parents.
19. In the words of Laura Nader, we have 'developed technologies that are life shaping, that have the potential of irreversible destruction, and that do not recognize international boundaries' (1996: 274).
20. For David Suzuki '[b]iotechnological research serves the desires of the rich rather than the needs of humanity' (also quoted in Grace 1997: 228).

References

Barnard, R. (1994) *Research Methods in Anthropology: Qualitative and Quantitative Approaches*, London: Sage.

Barr, J. and Birke, L. (1998) *Common Science: Women, Science and Knowledge*, Bloomington and Indianapolis: Indiana University Press.

Carrithers, M. (1990) 'Is anthropology art or science?', *Current Anthropology* 31: 263–82.

Chambers, R. (1983) *Rural Development: Putting the Last First*, London: Longman.

Claeson, B., Martin, E., Richardson, W., Schoch-Spana, M., and Taussig, K. (1996) 'Scientific Literacy, What it is, Why it's Important and Why Scientists Think We Don't Have it', in L. Nader (ed.) *Naked Science: Anthropological Inquiry into Boundaries, Power and Knowledge*, New York: Routledge.

D'Andrade. R, (1995) 'What *do* you think you're doing?', *Anthropology Newsletter* 36(7).

Durant, J., Hansen, A. and Bauer, M. (1996) 'Public Understanding of New Genetics', in Marteau, T. and Richards, M. (eds) *The Troubled Helix: Social and Psychological Implications of New Human Genetics*, Cambridge: Cambridge University Press.

Edwards, J. (1999) 'Why Dolly Matters: Kinship, Culture and Cloning', *Ethnos* 64(3): 301–24.

—— (2000) *Born and Bred: Idioms of Kinship and New Reproductive Technologies in England*, Oxford: Oxford University Press.

—— and Strathern, M. (2000) 'Including our own', in J. Carsten (ed.) *Cultures of Relatedness: New Directions in Kinship*, Cambridge: Cambridge University Press.

——, Hirsch, E., Franklin, S., Price, F., and Strathern, M. (1999) *Technologies of Procreation: Kinship in the Age of Assisted Conception*, 2nd edn, London: Routledge.

Fuller, S. (1996) 'Does Science Put an End to History, or History to Science? Or Why Being Pro-science is Harder than you Think', in A. Ross (ed.) *Science Wars*, Durham, NC: Duke University Press.

Geertz, C. (1988) *Works and Lives: The Anthropologist as Author*, Cambridge: Polity.

Ginsburg, F. and Rapp, R. (eds) (1995) *Conceiving the New World Order: The Global Politics of Reproduction*, Berkeley: University of California Press.

Grace, E. (1997) *Biotechnology Unzipped: Promises and Realities*, Washington D.C.: Joseph Henry Press.

Green, J. (1992) 'Principles and Practicalities of Carrier Screening: Attitudes of Recent Parents', *Journal of Medical Genetics* 29: 313–19.

Green, M. (2000) 'Participatory Development and the Appropriation of Agency in Southern Tanzania', *Critique of Anthropology* 20(1): 67–89.

Haraway, D. (1989) *Primate Visions: Gender, Race and Nature in the World of Modern Science*, New York: Routledge.

—— (1997) *Modest_Witness@Second_Millennium.FemaleMan©_Meets_ OncoMouse*™, New York: Routledge.

Hobart, M. (ed.) (1993) *An Anthropological Critique of Development: The Growth of Ignorance*, London: Routledge.

Ingold, T. (1998) 'From Complementarity to Obviation: On Dissolving the Boundaries between Social and Biological Anthropology, Archaeology and Psychology', *Zeitschrift für Ethnologie* 123: 21–52.

Jordan, B. (1993) *Birth in Four Cultures: a Crosscultural Investigation of Childbirth in Yucatan, Holland, Sweden, and the United States*, 4th edn, Prospect Heights: Waveland Press.

Kay, L. (1993) *The Molecular Vision of Life: Caltech, the Rockefeller Foundation, and the Rise of the New Biology*, New York: Oxford.

Keller, E.F. (1983) *A Feeling for the Organism: The Life and Work of Barbara McClintock*, New York: W.H. Freeman.

—— (1995) *Refiguring Life: Metaphors of Twentieth-century Biology*, New York: Colombia University Press.

Kuznar, L. (1997) *Reclaiming a Scientific Anthropology*, Walnut Creek: Altimira Press.

Lambert, H. and Rose, H. (1996) 'Disembodied Knowledge? Making Sense of Medical Science', in A. Irwin and B. Wynne (eds), *Misunderstanding Science: The public Reconstruction of Science and Technology*, Cambridge: Cambridge University Press.

Latour, B. (1987) *Science in Action: How to Follow Scientists and Engineers through Society*, Cambridge, Mass.: Harvard University Press.

—— (1996) 'Not the Question', *Anthropology Newsletter* 3(3).

—— and Woolgar, S. (1979) *Laboratory Life: The Social Construction of Scientific Facts*, Beverley Hills, CA: Sage.

Lave, J. (1996) 'The Savagery of the Domestic Mind', in L. Nader (ed.) *Naked Science: Anthropological Inquiry into Boundaries, Power, and Knowledge*, New York: Routledge.

Leach. E. (1969) *Genesis as Myth and Other Essays*, London: Cape.

Lewis, G. (1994) 'Magic, Religion and the Rationality of Belief', in T. Ingold (ed.) *Companion Encyclopedia of Anthropology: Humanity, Culture and Social Life*, London: Routledge.

Malinowski, B. (1954 [1948]) *Magic, Science and Religion and Other Essays*, New York: Doubleday Anchor Books.

Nader, L. (ed.) (1996) *Naked Science: Anthropological Inquiry into Boundaries, Power, and Knowledge*, New York: Routledge.

Okely, J. (1996) *Own or Other Culture*, London: Routledge.

Rabinow, P. (1996) *Making PCR: A Story of Biotechnology*, Chicago: University of Chicago Press.

Rapport, N. (1997) *Transcendent Individual: Towards a Literary and Liberal Anthropology*, London: Routledge.

Richards, M.P.M. (1993) 'The New Genetics: Some Issues for Social Scientists', *Sociology of Health and Illness* 15: 567–86.

—— (1996) 'Lay and Professional Knowledge of Genetics and Inheritance', *Public Understanding of Science* 5: 217–30.

—— (1997) 'It Runs in the Family: Lay Knowledge about Inheritance', in A. Clarke and E. Parsons (eds) *Culture, Kinship and Genes: Towards Cross-Cultural Genetics*, London: Macmillan

—— (1998) 'Lay Understanding of Mendelian Genetics', *Endeavour* 22(3): 93–4.

Rose, H. (1994) *Love, Power and Knowledge: Towards a Feminist Transformation of the Social Sciences*, Cambridge: Polity Press.

Ross, A. (ed.) (1996) *Science Wars*, Durham, NC: Duke University Press.

Scott, C. (1996) 'Science for the West, Myth for the Rest? The case of James Bay Cree Knowledge Construction', in L. Nader (ed.) *Naked Science: Anthropological Inquiry into Boundaries, Power, and Knowledge*, New York: Routledge.

Snow, C.P. (1959) *The Two Cultures and the Scientific Revolution*, New York: Cambridge University Press.

Stacey, M. (1992) *Changing Human Reproduction: Social Science Perspectives*, London: Sage.

Stewart, K. (1996) *A Space on the Side of the Road: Cultural Poetics in an 'Other' America*, Princeton: Princeton University Press.

Strathern, M. (1987) 'An Awkward Relationship: The Case of Feminism and Anthropology', *SIGNS* 12(2): 276–92.

—— (1992) *After Nature: English Kinship in the Late Twentieth Century*, Cambridge: Cambridge University Press.

Traweek, S. (1988) *Beamtimes and Lifetimes: The World of High Energy Physicists*, Cambridge, Mass: Harvard University Press.

Wolcott, H.F. (1995) *The Art of Fieldwork*, Walnut Creek: Altimira (Sage).

Culture in a Network: Dykes, Webs and Women in London and Manchester[1]

Sarah Green

Introduction

In the past few years, networks have come to be regarded as *the* form of postmodern sociality: they imply no essential or fixed boundaries and no necessary hierarchies, which results in a tendency to allow overlaps, hybrids, transitions and transformations, apparently with little disturbance.[2] Within networks, people can make their own webs, connecting anything with anything else. However, some puzzles arise here: within this networked sociality, what is culture (as opposed to 'cultural') and, more to the point, where is it? Can one speak of 'British ethnography' and actually mean anything by the phrase in a networked world?

The problem, I suggest, is a lack of attention to three elements of sociality in most discussions of networks: first, the importance of *disconnection* as well as connection in social relations; secondly, the fact that connection must have some substance – in crude terms, people need a reason to connect and the connection must be meaningful to them, which implies there must be something beyond the connection itself, and upon which the connection is based; and finally, lack of attention to the way people make use of the *idea* of networks (as opposed, say, to 'society' or 'group' or, indeed, 'culture') to generate an understanding of social relations. In short, focusing on networked connections has tended to lose sight of the conditions that make networks possible, and thinkable.

This chapter will address these gaps by using two ethnographic research projects carried out ten years apart, the first in London and the second in Manchester, to explore experiences of 'network' in practice, and it uses sexuality as an issue around which to develop the argument. The first project, on lesbian feminists in London, was carried out pre-Internet; the second was based on looking into the introduction of new *i*nformation and *c*ommunications *t*echnologies (ICTs)[3] in various organizations in Manchester. Both cases involved women's organizations, and it was notable that in both, the women involved expressed a sense of fragmentation, or disconnection, in their lives. The interesting element here is that this sense of disconnection was expressed in much the same way by both groups of women, despite the lack of Internet and 'network mania' in the earlier project.

Through looking at these two examples, I argue both that disconnection is as important an element of networks as is connection, and that culture is indeed in the network, in three ways: first, by showing that networked relations need to be meaningful and relevant, for otherwise they become empty connections; secondly, by arguing that people are using the idea of network as a metaphor to discuss other things (i.e. network is good to think); and thirdly, by arguing that network is a familiar and culturally marked concept, and one that is a popular way to view sociality at the moment, at least in Britain. In short, networks in themselves are not new phenomena, they do not constitute the only or even main basis for sociality today in Britain, and they are not only about connection, but also about disconnection. I am not suggesting that the notion of network is therefore ontologically meaningless; I am suggesting that culture intervenes to make it meaningful in a particular way, and that there is clear continuity between earlier and current meanings of the term, which implies that it is not the new technologies – or, indeed, any other 'globalizing' process – that are at the bottom of the idea that networks are currently at the centre of things.

Lesbian Feminists in London and Cyber-women in Manchester

Both the ethnographic projects discussed here have at times given me the impression of being somewhat off-centre within anthropology. However, this was only mildly because they involved 'anthropology at home' in Britain; more to the point was *what* they were about. In the late 1980s, it was lesbian feminist separatists, their attempts to carve out a space for themselves in London and to make sense of the rapidly changing contexts in which gender and sexuality were being debated, both intellectually and in the 'alternative scene' of London (Green 1997); in the late 1990s, it was the introduction of information and communications technologies (ICTs) across a range of sectors in Manchester, exploring how these technologies became interwoven with the historical and social specificities of Manchester.[4] The research included looking at the voluntary sector and in particular spending some time at the Manchester Women's Electronic Village Hall (WEVH), a computer-skills training centre for women, one aspect of which will particularly concern me here.

The first project was slightly off-centre because it focused on an issue almost invisible within anthropology at the time: political activism based on sexuality. That shifted sexuality at least partially out of its usual anthropological location within kinship and/or gender relations,[5] though remaining centrally linked to these themes. The research concerned women who explicitly challenged the kinship and gender relations existent within their own social context (i.e., contemporary Britain), and tried to construct different forms of sociality for themselves. The broad lesbian feminist argument behind that effort was this: the sexualities normally available to women ('compulsory heterosexuality', 'abjected lesbianism') were read as politically constructed to produce women as self-perpetuating subordinate persons. These sexualities were generated at the level of interpersonal relationships, particularly but not exclusively between men and women; they constantly informed those relationships, maintaining and reinforcing the inevitability and 'naturalness' of the resulting oppressive, and by some readings often violent, relations between men and women.[6] An alternative reading of sexuality was needed in order to escape this self-perpetuating cycle, and this alternative had to be put into practice within personal interrelations in order to be effective in producing different kinds of persons.[7] It was not possible simply to think your way out of (hetero-)patriarchal oppression, by altering your consciousness; it was also necessary to alter the kinds of relationships you had, with both yourself and others, because those relationships (re-)produced and maintained both the consciousness and the oppression.

For feminist separatists, this implied dislocating oneself from prior relationships, and in particular any relationships with men, and generating new kinds of connections between women, would simultaneously be both a personal and a political project. It was the attempt to put these alternative connections into practice within London that was a main focus of the research. The aim was to try to understand how being somewhere in particular (in this case, late 1980s London) would articulate with an abstraction (in this case, lesbian feminist theories of sexuality and sexual relations) in the generation of alternative connections in practice.

The second project, carried out jointly with Penny Harvey and Jon Agar, created an occasional sense of being off-centre in a different way. The first indication of a problem was that discussing the research project in seminars generated an air of biliousness in anthropological audiences: the question of the Internet and its associated electronic technologies seemed altogether too close to 'home' for many, as the increasing pressures to deal with emails, machines that crash and the impossibility of finding something useful on the Internet within a reasonable space of time (not to mention the incessant and ad nauseam public debates about the Internet) was causing many an anthropologist to glaze over when the topic was mentioned.

This casual observation will become relevant later, but more importantly here, information and communications technologies (ICTs) were commonly understood to be about globalization and the creation of new kinds of spaces and places for sociality ('virtual' or 'cyber' spaces). Yet the Manchester project was firmly focused on Manchester, contained a strong historical rather than future-oriented slant, and was not conducted on-line, but in the more usual way of spending time with people as they went about their business – in this case, the business of trying to cope with the hardware and software that had entered their lives in one way or another.

In this sense, both the London and Manchester projects deliberately brought an abstraction about connection together with located connection: lesbian feminist abstractions about sexual relations were brought together with located connections within London, and abstractions about the capacity of ICTs to connect anything with anything else irrespective of the distances and differences between them was brought together with located connections in Manchester.

The Manchester research began with the expectation that the way ICTs became involved in people's lives would be linked to factors that introduced ICTs to Manchester in ways particular to that city and the groups within it. It seemed highly likely that people would draw upon the rest of their lives, their other connections, to provide this basis for on-line connection, including having a reason to connect at all. This approach was in distinct contrast to the main social research focus for ICTs in the late 1990s, which concerned the abstract ('virtual') connection capacities of ICTs, and in particular, the ability to hold connection in place within a separate electronic ('virtual') space long enough for social interaction to develop.[8] In that approach, where you are in the world ought not to matter, because the 'place' made through on-line connection is always already somewhere else. In contrast, the Manchester project started from the view that whether or not this is the case, on-line connection will always already incorporate other kinds of connections, because connection between people (as opposed to computers) must have some content and meaning in order to exist.

The Manchester Women's Electronic Village Hall (WEVH) was studied as one kind of transformation of that. Its formal aims were to provide ICT training for women in Manchester, which was intended to reconfigure the relations women had with such technologies, for whatever purpose women wished. Interesting as that is, it is not the aspect which concerns me here: rather, an additional element of the WEVH was to generate and maintain a network of connections between women and organizations involved in ICTs in Manchester, and to link these to other organizations elsewhere. Partly, this was so as to be free of dependence upon established public institutions within Manchester (and in particular, the city council) in the continual search for funding to maintain women's ICT organizations; partly, it was to build up a network of supportive connections between women who wished to use ICTs in ways that did not particularly resonate with current commercial or political policies. These connecting activities inevitably drew upon the particular links WEVH members and staff had with people, groups, organizations and other things in Manchester, and therefore the connections ebbed and flowed in different directions as people came and went. The underlying point, though, was always the same: to create and maintain an 'alternative' web of connections between women. In this, and as might be expected, the use of email and the Internet was easily blended with other kinds of connection.

Connections and Disconnections

In one sense then, the research in both cases was an exploration of how people fashion alternative located connections, of conscious intent to create practical social links that are different from those already available, and based on ideas about sociality that are, at least in part, in opposition to those available. The studies were also about the creation of networks between diverse scales of experience – of deliberately linking abstractions with practices, and of bringing together different groups and types of people in order to pursue the alternative sociality imagined. The aim in both studies was to look at the practice of theory, as it were, rather than to consider the theory of practice (Bourdieu 1977).

However, in both cases, the focus on located connection turned out, in practice, to be more about *disconnections*, in two senses. First, in the straightforward sense that a major concern for women in both projects, though for different reasons, was an increasing sense of fragmentation in their lives that led to a sense of disconnection, a feeling of the different aspects of their lives being fragmented rather than coherent in some way. And secondly, in the more indirect sense that something has shifted in dominant understandings of what actually constitutes connection between persons in the ten years that separated the London project from the Manchester one. The shift was already implied in the London project, but has now become so commonplace that there is less of a sense of shift, and more of a sense of 'the way things are'. The 'way things are', the sense of general disconnectedness, seems to be due to an increased involvement in open networks that ultimately have no underlying coherence – or, alternatively, that can have many different coherences simultaneously, but in any event lack closure. This is where a return to sexuality is useful, as a means to explore the disconnections implied in the proliferation of possible 'alternative' webs of located connection; too much connection, it turns out, can cause one to lose connections. I will take each case in turn.

Lesbian Feminist Separatism and Disconnection through Diversity: the Postmodern Challenge

To put the situation briefly for the case of lesbian feminist separatists in London: some women's groups and individuals, involved in the social networks that lesbian feminists were attempting to transform, directly challenged the lesbian feminist reading of sexuality and proposed different kinds of 'alternative' connections between lesbians. These challenges came particularly from two sources: groups involved in anti-racism of various types, and groups involved in experimenting with visual representations of sexuality, especially in film and photography, but also in their own choices of fashion and style. Many groups representing black women were by the late 1980s regularly attacking separatists, accusing them of being racist by default, because their conception of women did not appear to include any recognition of the differences in experience of black women in white-dominated cultures. The groups experimenting with representations of sexuality (often called 'libertarians' by lesbian feminists)[9] argued that identities were complexly constructed culturally and historically and were continually being reconstructed, and therefore lesbian feminist readings of sexuality were as restrictive as what they opposed, and also probably missed the point.[10]

Those kinds of challenge had the effect of fragmenting the coherence of social networks generated by the lesbian feminist reading, through offering both a critique and a range of possible alternatives. Moreover, the fact that the challenges came mostly from postmodern readings of sexuality – that is, readings that resisted closure, so that there were no longer any clear boundaries between sexualities (this later became queer theory) – meant that the reasoning behind creating the alternative networks in the first place began to unravel. In short, too much con- nection between differences generated disconnection in located networks. Let me expand on this a bit.

During the late 1980s, the increasing number of challenges to lesbian feminist approaches indicated to many lesbian feminists I met that something fundamental was changing, but they did not know quite what, and that was deeply unsettling. In 1989, all that most of these women knew was that criticisms against them no longer came solely from their 'natural' opponents – anti-feminists, homophobes, the moral majority – but from their own ranks, and from others who separatists thought should be their allies. A few prominent hard-line separatists had publicly abandoned the separatist cause and declared that the thinking behind separatism had been fundamentally wrong. And on the whole, these women were relatively young, energetic, often well-read in the latest feminist theory, and they took their feminism seriously. In other words, they had not become bored of, or burned out by, feminism; rather, they had changed their minds in some way. Both the anti-racist and the 'libertarian' challenges were part of the ongoing assault on the coherence of the concept 'woman', which had been crucial to separatist readings of sexuality.

The conflict between 'libertarians' and separatists was particularly bitterly expressed. The 'libertarians' were not a group as such, but a disparate collection of young women, who had only recently begun to be noticed around 'alternative' London. As briefly outlined above, they were experimenting – playfully if seriously as they saw it, and dangerously as separatists saw it – with sartorial and bodily styles and performances. Some of these women were especially interested in experimenting with concepts of dominance and subordination in sexual relation- ships. What is more, not only were they putting these experimental ideas into practice themselves, but they were taking photographs and making films about it as well.[11] One of the more famous of these women was Della Grace, whose photographs became more and more extreme explorations of sex- and gender-bending, with prominent use of leather, chains, body piercing and so on.

Nothing could provoke and upset separatists more than that combination of activities: sexual domination of women, their objectification through dress and style, and their abuse in the pornography industry had been at the core of feminist separatist conceptions of what patriarchy is all about, and the reason they were dedicated to fighting it. For separatists, patriarchy was fundamentally about structural, embedded injustice towards women based on the sexual exploitation of women; a patriarchal society did not treat women as full social beings, but as subordinate beings. So, to have women, particularly those who engaged in relationships with other women, as most of these young women did, *experimenting* with such sexual practices, styles and representations rather than attempting to eradicate them was appalling to most separatists.[12]

The younger women were adamant that they were politically aware, but that their approach reflected a different politics from that offered by separatists: one drawn from the still fairly nascent influence, in this context, of postmodernist thought; an approach drawn from the world of signs and simulacra, which increasingly argued that experience is made up of linguistic and visual manipulation and nothing but that: no hope of finding authenticity beneath the metonymic web. And if that was the case, then experimenting with these manipulations could change the world – or at least, change these women's experience of the world. In short, they were dealing with ideas that focused on *diversity* rather than on *difference*. The concept of difference always implied a stable difference between one kind of person and another kind of person: you either are or are not a woman; are or are not black; are or are not gay. Even if these categories were regarded as being socially constructed, they had an experiential reality. The concept of diversity, however, implied something very different: it focused more on the continual process through which categories are constructed, and argued that these apparently stable categories were in fact constantly having to be constructed and maintained in order to continue to exist. In the fight against oppression, therefore, the thing to do was to reject any categorization and to treat yourself as a project, creating and re-creating different mixtures and hybrids of identity as you yourself saw fit. That shift from difference to diversity was the crucial one, though at the time, most women felt that what they were doing was experimenting with something to see where it went.

In this sense, lesbian feminists had been confronted directly, and rather early, with the possible implications of trying to break modernist assumptions apart by living in a world of signs and images. However, most of the women I met, even the ones who were doing the experimenting, also felt that it was a personally fragmenting, even if occasionally liberating, experience. Even though previous assumptions about the fixity and authenticity of gender, sexuality and the body had to be rejected (both on the grounds that these assumptions appeared to leave out many people who did not quite fit these identities as defined, and on the grounds that analytically, such assumptions could no longer be supported), women commonly expressed a sense of disconnection, both personal and social. They were not entirely sure why or how a perspective that appeared to offer them infinite connection, and infinite combinations of connection, could leave them feeling they had lost something, in terms of a sense of belonging to a network of women in London, in terms of a sense of purpose, and in terms of a sense of themselves in the world, as opposed to a sense of themselves, in themselves, as an endless project.

Strathern, by way of introduction to her own critique of the notion that all women everywhere have something inherently in common (i.e. that there is closure in what constitutes womanhood), said that, 'In Hagen, netbags certainly stand for womanness; it is what womanness stands for that we should ask' (Strathern 1981: 674). She followed this with a detailed exploration of how gender constructions are cross-culturally variable and therefore there can be no such thing as a 'universal woman'. This same critique directed against lesbian feminists in London in the late 1980s undermined the reason to close their networks around a coherent reading of sexuality and gender. The network opened, became plural and lost its location, as it were. It became disconnected.

The Manchester Women's Electronic Village Hall and Disconnection through Over-connection

The case of the Manchester WEVH was different from the lesbian feminist experience, but the outcome, the sense of disconnection, was the same. The continual ebb and flow, and expansion, of connections led to the networks, as imagined coherent entities, becoming relatively invisible to women, or rather, chaotically and excessively visible, which comes to the same thing. The effort involved in maintaining the connections seemed to take increasing amounts of time and work, while at the same time, the relevance of maintaining them seemed to become less and less obvious. The result, again, was disconnection: a reduction of connections to those of immediate relevance and interest.

The experience of one multimedia trainer at the WEVH, Pat, provides both an overlap with the London project and an example of this in practice. Pat combined personal interests in art, sexuality and ICTs; she read widely on the interrelations between all these themes, particularly queer theory, kept in touch with those involved in one or all of these interests in Manchester, used ICTs to experiment with both sexuality and art (often in combination), and incorporated her reading of these themes in her teaching at the WEVH. In many ways, she had the kind of perspective on sexuality that had so seriously challenged lesbian feminist readings in London in previous years: one that aimed to break down boundaries and generate connections between diverse expressions of gender and sexuality. For a time, she experimented with being a drag king (though never at work at the WEVH), and commented ruefully on the negative reception she received in public lesbian and gay places about this – in contrast to drag queens, who cause hardly a second look these days, let alone any attempts to eject them from bars and clubs, as Pat had frequently experienced.

In sum, Pat combined use of websites, email and other ICT applications, experiments with her own presentation and style, personal social networks and links with a variety of places and organizations in constructing her connections within Manchester and elsewhere. Over time, however, the sheer quantity of connections this generated caused severe pressures on Pat's time, and increasingly, the demands of her made by the WEVH began to seem onerous. She started to feel distanced from the WEVH, and eventually, after repeated requests for time off to do research were turned down on the grounds that the WEVH could not spare her teaching skills, she found another job in London. In this instance, the disconnection was dramatic.

Losing Connection and Imagining Networks

The irony of these repeated disconnections, both in London and Manchester, is twofold. First, once connections lose closure, once being linked to others is opened up to any kind of connection, it is easy to shift toward making connection itself the reason for being connected. However, that is unsustainable in terms of generating and maintaining located networks, for the reason outlined earlier: connection between persons must carry with it some meaningful content; connection for connection's sake therefore tends to generate disconnections – people drop out, because there is nothing to be 'in', as such. The shift in the nature of connection between persons from the time of the London project to the more recent Manchester project thus seems to be in the incoherence of these networks: meanings and content, where they exist, are often short-lived and constantly competing both with other meanings and against the threat of being reduced to connection itself. People end up connecting and then disconnecting, repeatedly.

Intriguingly, where ICTs did directly come into this in Manchester was as a means to express views about such forms of connection and disconnection. The Internet and email easily provided the symbolic baggage to talk about re-imagining the world, and particularly to talk about connection, disconnection, and about images and simulacra. People in community ICT projects, small e-commerce companies and even most of the women in the WEVH were not wondering which theoretical approach on postmodernity would be most appropriate to use to guide their lives, as was the case among separatists in London; but similar issues were being debated. As already implied, the question seemed to circulate around how seemingly infinite connection can simultaneously feel like disconnection. The technologies did not in themselves produce this effect in Manchester any more than they did in pre-Internet London; but these technologies were most certainly used to discuss it in Manchester.

The second irony is that far from removing the relevance of location, the tendency for over-connection to generate disconnection makes the specific and the located all the more important. Sometimes, it is all that people in both London and Manchester felt they had left. A number of lesbian feminists in London commented, while discussing the fragmentation caused by challenges to their understanding of sexuality, that they had 'retreated' to their close friends and their area of London, having become exhausted with being continually challenged elsewhere. In the WEVH, many had reduced their links – electronic and otherwise – to their immediate social and work-related connections and a few special interests, and had rapidly learned the art of deleting emails without reading them. Too much (dis)connection had led many to seek more coherent connection in their immediate social networks and surroundings.

I referred to this shift in terms of the London project as one that moved from a focus on difference to a focus on diversity. That was about an intellectual debate, representing a transition in social theory away from a focus on the *differences between people* (seen in the earlier 'identity politics' range of perspectives),[13] which placed the analytical gaze on boundaries; and towards a focus on the (loose and contingent) *connections between differences*, which placed the analytical gaze on overlaps – hybrids, cyborgs, trans-everything – which celebrated the (apparently infinite) diversity of ways such overlaps can be made between differences.

This is where the observation that ICTs were being used to discuss the sense of over-connection and disconnection in Manchester comes in. The emerging consensus and popular rhetoric about what ICTs are and what effects they may be having appears to be the most effective source of metaphors for popular discussions about Harvey's 'postmodern condition' (Harvey 1990). That has generated an elision between the technologies themselves and the presumed causes of social over-connection and disconnection (easily enough done in the context of wide-spread technological determinism). But more interesting for my purposes here is how the rhetoric about ICTs has come to achieve this status: in short, how the digital networks have come to contain the cultural substance to talk about other things.

I suggest the answer is that ICTs have been imagined, and thus created, from the social contexts that both groups of women discussed here were dealing with: a shift in social connection from one of imagined closure to both imagined and experienced lack of closure. The first part of that assertion is a rather banal statement, in that it is difficult to see how any technology could come into being outside of the social conditions in which it was both developed and became popular;[14] the more interesting point is what it is that these technologies are used to imagine. The Internet and email came to typify that shift in sociality in concentrated form: for many, in the Manchester case study at least, ICTs came to represent entirely open connection par excellence. Yet ICTs did not start life as that kind of technology, but rather as a series of professional tools, used both for military purposes and in more obscure academic pursuits such as the astronomy element of particle physics, which needed to track the activities of the heavens from various points around the globe.[15] An enormous effort had to be put into making the Internet and email what they are today, including developing the hardware and software, laying thousands of miles of special cabling as higher connection speeds have been demanded (many more thousands of miles are still needed), formulating international protocols and legal conditions (many of which still remain to be agreed), and so on. That level of effort and investment, both commercial and political, is astonishing. That is by the by here, except to note that ICTs did not appear magically out of the ether, and that the form they have taken was neither random nor dictated by technological capacity itself (something made particularly clear by recent disputes between Microsoft and the US federal courts); more to the point is what resulted from this orgy of ICT development: a powerful set of imaginings and assertions about ICTs that made them represent, and apparently actually produce, something like concentrated super-diversity within apparently limitless connection potential. The outcome looks remarkably like a cardboard cut-out image of the kinds of shifts in sociality noted in the two ethnographies discussed. The Internet and associated technologies have become – that is to say, have been made into – a stereotype, in the terms suggested by Herzfeld (1997: 15).

In short, I am arguing that the emergence of ICTs has not caused the host of imaginings about what is happening in the world, it is the other way around: the social (and political and economic) contexts in which ICTs emerged brought them into existence in a particular form, and that form became ideal for use as a stereotype – by governments, by commerce, but also by other people to discuss their conditions of life, the universe and everything, as it were. The culture was always in the network.

What remains is to go through some of these stereotypical renderings, the underlying assumptions, fears, obsessions and leitmotifs of the world for which ICTs are being used as both metaphor and metonym, which illustrate some of what people are telling themselves about themselves, a way of understanding how they see themselves, as persons, in relation to the world. This includes going through political, media and academic assertions, for these constitute a good deal of the substantive material that people used in Manchester to think through these issues; it was available, and use was made of it.

The Structure of the ICT Hype

I will briefly take the media hype about ICTs seriously (initially rather a difficult step, I have to admit). What marks this hype out is its character of radical doubt: the possibility that the structure of social and material connections, their form as opposed to their content, is radically changing. And as outlined above, the net has rapidly become both metaphor and metonym for this postmodern condition, while also being regarded as one of its ultimate products and one of the driving forces that makes it possible.[16]

Of course, the internet and its associated digital methods of communication is not the only technology involved in this kind of story people are telling about themselves. In addition, there is also digital television and multimedia in terms of things that manipulate signs, information and images; but more than that, there are the technologies that manipulate flesh and the material world: the new reproductive technologies, genetic engineering and the human genome project, genetic modification of plants, cloning of sheep. In the strongest expression of the hype, both within the media and in the literature, all of these are connected to one another, and implicated in some fundamental change. A restructuring of everything is under way, and in particular the interrelationship between nature and culture, people and machines, minds and bodies. All those old modernist chestnuts are being thrown up in the air and reconfigured, this time not as dichotomies, but somehow as inter-subjectively linked entities with fuzzy boundaries. In this respect, it is somewhat ironic that the debate about the effects of these changes have, on the whole, remained stubbornly dichotomous: nirvana or armageddon, global utopia or dystopia. But I will pass over that for the moment, except to note that the question of inequality between persons has been reconfigured as well: in the shift from an identity politics of difference to the pursuit of the self in diversity, inequality comes to seem a bit of an anachronism, in this kind of debate at least.

Fragmentation

Paul Rabinow tried to identify this transition in how new technologies were being related to the world a few years ago in his paper, 'From Sociobiology to Biosociality' (1992). In it, he claimed that the new techno-scientific paradigm generated by these technologies is focused on a metaphor of information for understanding the human condition, rather than, as had been the case before, a metaphor of machine. Everything can now be reduced to codes rather than to the nuts and bolts, cogs and wheels. And unlike physical bits and pieces, codes look much the same whether they are the genetic code of a human being or the structural code of the videotape containing an episode of *The Simpsons*. Suddenly, the ability to tell the difference between objects and subjects, between the social and the natural, between the body and the mind, between an image and the object it depicts, becomes something of a problem. This is indeed a deeper shift than that suggested by the young women in London: for them, images and codes might re-create experience of the world, but they did not physically make the world.

Since Rabinow's article, there has been an exponential increase in literature on the issue of how these kinds of technology, the ones that seem to particularly mess with the relationship between human flesh, the mind, machines, the places humans live, the things humans eat and the way humans interrelate, are revolution-izing the experience and understanding of being human. Donna Haraway, who has been paying attention to this kind of thing since the late 1970s, has recently suggested that indeed, our connections have been reconfigured. She analyses this in some detail in her new book, *Modest_Witness@Second_Millennium.Female Man©_Meets_OncoMouse™: Feminism and Technoscience* (1997). She says, for example,

> ... in the wombs of technoscience, as well as of postfetal science studies, chimeras of humans and nonhumans, machines and organisms, subjects and objects, are the obligatory passage points, the embodiments and articulations, through which travellers must pass to get much of anywhere in the world. The chip, gene, bomb, fetus, seed, brain, ecosystem, and database are the wormholes that dump contemporary travellers out into contemporary worlds (Haraway 1997: 43).

In short, Haraway is claiming that people's images, their connections (articulations), and the way people move around in the world, are today either created, or at least mediated, by the kind of 'technoscience' that blends flesh, mind and computers with everything else. And in breaking down all those nature/culture dichotomies, the raw categorical distinctions and differences created by them, the essentialisms upon which inequalities, most especially gender inequalities, were based, are thrown up in the air, become almost meaningless. Another view is the opposite of this: that all those technologies do is reinforce whatever assumptions we previously had, and give us the opportunity to embed them ever deeper into our very beings.[17]

Simulacra

So much for fragmentation, for the breaking down of boundaries between things that the modern world kept separate. There are also the commentaries about images and signs, claims that the image has become all-powerful. According to that perspective, we now live in a world of glitzy images and copies of things, a world of the inauthentic, and we rarely get the opportunity to see or experience the original. Ranging from Jean Baudrillard (1994) through to David Harvey (1990) and a whole host of commentators on postmodernity in between, the centrality of signs, of images, of copies and simulations has been regarded as the hallmark of postmodernity. In the fragments of postmodern deconstructions of any claim to authenticity or ontology, we find signs, codes, metaphors, images, which had been used to construct a modernist reality, used even to make flesh. Today, according to the likes of Baudrillard, it does not much matter whether we are interacting with an image or an object, the 'real thing' or a projection, or a copy of it. Since aesthetics is more important than ethics these days, it is how it looks that is the point, not how it is. Marc Augé makes a similar point in his most recent attention to this issue:

> . . . a culture dissolving in quotations, copies and plagiarism, of an identity losing itself in images and reflections, of a history which is swallowed up in the here-and-now of a here-and-now which is itself indefinable (modern, postmodern?) because we perceive it only piecemeal, without any organising principle which can enable us to give meaning to the clichés, advertizing commercials and commentaries which stand in for our reality (Augé 1999: 10).

Augé's earlier concept of 'non-places' also draws close connections between an obsession with images and 'realistic' copies with the generation of inauthenticity in everyday experience (Augé 1995). 'Non-places' include airports, freeway service stations, supermarkets, hotel chains, and buildings constructed using Computer Aided Design software, so that the end result looks much the same in London as it does in Tokyo. Note that for Augé technology here is producing the inauthenticity through the removal of difference: through standardization, processing, its capacity to produce identical copies. That is the mark of technology in the modernist perspective, of course: it is the key difference between human persons, who can never make completely identical copies of anything and also can never be completely identically copied themselves, and machines, which can hardly do other than make identical copies, except when they break down.

In any event, Augé suggests we are all living most of our lives in 'non-places' these days. There are some 'places' left, spaces which were made through people using them, moving through them, building things in them, interacting within them repeatedly, and over time coming to identify themselves with them. But such places, Augé suggests, are not where we live anymore: they are cordoned off, floodlit, signs are put up explaining what these places once were, and we are often charged for visiting them. Our postmodern lives (Augé calls it 'supermodernity') are too ephemeral to allow us to create places anymore: instead, we copy past places, we borrow things from anywhere and everywhere, to create hybrids, chimera and cyborgs. We are and live within simulacra according to this perspective, and are incapable of creating our own places anymore.

Now it is easy to see how people point to the power of today's computers to manipulate, infinitely copy and reproduce, mutate, collage, and transform into three-dimensional moving entities any image fed to them, as being central to the world of simulacra. There is no denying our environment is chock full of images today as never before, and that the seams of alteration of those images do not show anymore. The power of ICTs in this respect is widely regarded as both a perfect metaphor and creator of the image-obsessed world. Somewhat more extreme writers such as Mark Slouka (1996) have argued that most people have become so used to images being the same as the objects they depict that they are beginning not to be able to tell the difference. Slouka says: 'More and more of us, whether we realize it or not, accept the copy as the original . . . We seem more and more willing to put our trust in intermediaries who 're-present' the world to us.' (1996: 1–2). And there is nothing more dangerous to our sense of reality, for Slouka, than virtual space and cyberspace, which he refers to as 'that strange non place beyond the computer screen' (ibid.: 5), which is controlled by 'net religionists' who believe that the real world ought to be downloaded onto a computer (ibid.: 9). Slouka concludes: 'Cyberspace, I realized, represented the marriage of deconstruction and computer technology – a mating of monsters if ever there was one' (ibid.: 30). Why monsters? Because, Slouka says, post-modernism has the theories which suggest nothing is authentic or real in the world, and, quotes, 'cyberists had machines that could make it so' (ibid.: 32).

I have to say that as I was reading this book, I was also spending some time visiting the WEVH in Manchester. I could see little connection between Slouka's nightmare and my experience at the WEVH; the women there seemed entirely capable of telling the difference between an email message and talking to someone in the same room. Perhaps I missed something, but it seemed to me as though, for most of these women, seeking out the WEVH was in order to deal with mundane matters such as having to make a living, and wanting to expand their possibilities and experiences of the world around them. Their practical, located, experience of the technology itself (which was often very positive in the WEVH) was not in fact the subject of their abstract discussions about the effects of ICTs, and the problem was not difficulties in telling image from 'reality': the subject and the problem was a sense of over-connection and disconnection in the way they experienced their lives, and popularly available rhetoric about what ICTs do were used to express this, a point I shall return to in a minute.

In any event, I think have provided enough of a flavour of that particular discursive leitmotif: that ICTs have made the world into a simulacrum of itself. The positive reading of it is the notion of transcendence, the ability to move beyond the restrictions of apparently fixed identities, fixed locations, fixed states of mind, body and being, and move instead into a much more flexible world of signs and choice. Ironically, from the same technology that generates the standardization and homogeneity of our inhabited spaces we can also apparently produce infinite diversity. If there is no one truth, nothing original anymore, we can all produce our own truths – and what could be more democratic or free-market than that? The price to be paid for this – according to a good deal of the literature – is a sense that things are not, and can never be, entirely what they seem to be, because it is never possible to sense them in more than a partial way: knowledge of diversity, and of diverse truths in particular, has ensured this.

Manchester fragments and simulacra

There were echoes of this kind of thing being discussed in Manchester, but it was related in more practical terms to experienced life rather than to some notion of 'cyberspace' or 'virtual reality', and that made the implications drawn some-what less extreme. The use of this kind of fragmentation, transcendence and/or simulacrum idea was often related directly to what were perceived as new forms of sociality. An example – and this was the most notable way in which both women at the EVH and others in ICT organizations in Manchester drew upon these kinds of idea – was in discussing the confusion generated by the increasingly common network structure of organizations, as opposed to the more familiar pyramid-style hierarchical structure of businesses and institutions. Network structures emerged in making collaborative links between different organizations (e.g. between universities, local city councils and local healthcare organizations); usually, each collaborating organization had quite different interests, ways of working, hierarchies and structures from those of other organizations. As a result, in the 'meta-networks' that linked them together, people found it difficult to locate any centre or any boundaries and, in practical terms, that meant it was difficult to know who or what to contact when the organization was needed for something. This had two effects: first, an increasing reliance upon personal and informal knowledge, so as to know where to go and whom to speak to. This is an example of how the 'virtual' networks relied on face-to-face networks in order to work; there was no reduction in the need for located knowledge in order to operate within such new organizational structures, and in fact the opposite was often the case. And secondly, which is more relevant here, it increasingly generated a sense that each organization involved in such links and collaborations was losing its own boundaries and centre; the diversity was producing a greater focus on the connections between organizations, rather than on the self-contained, internal structure of the organization itself, and it led to a sense that there would only ever be a partial grasp of what the entity itself constituted.

The case of the women's EVH is an interesting example. It was linked to a range of 'meta-networks' of this kind, both because of the need to continually search for new funding, and because of a desire to keep informed of new developments within the city and elsewhere, so as to assist women who came to the service in finding jobs and so on. Such networks consisted both of 'web-rings' and of various outreach projects, where members of the WEVH attempted to develop links between organizations and individuals across a variety of sectors in Manchester, and then to link those links in with other organizations, both in Britain and Europe. These projects were grant-aided, usually by the European Union, but also by various British government programmes; usually the aim of such grants was precisely to encourage cross-sector links.

This kind of continual linking activity had the double effect of both highlighting the particularities of the 'image' of the EVH – as a voluntary organization, physically located on the fringes of central Manchester, focused on providing services for women, and represented as such in its links with others – and making the organization feel itself lacking closure for both staff and students. The range of projects underway in the EVH at any one time (anything up to fifteen), all of which had incomprehensible acronyms, were extremely hard to keep track of for those not directly involved, and the women managing those projects were often fairly disconnected from other women within the organization. Moreover, it was quickly realized by most project co-ordinators that any hope of reducing confusion must involve fairly regular and structured face-to-face meetings of people and organizations linked to their particular projects, which in itself was a difficult thing to arrange, because of the diversity of interests and working conditions of those organizations and people. And as a result of all that, women thinking of becoming involved in the EVH were often confronted with what seemed to them an enigma – there was no direct, and certainly no complete, answer to the question: what exactly is the WEVH?

It is not too surprising that under such circumstances, the rhetoric surrounding ICTs and what they represented were used regularly by WEVH members to discuss what was happening. In such discussions, the technologies themselves were blamed for having generated much of the incoherence, confusion and mirrors-within-mirrors experiences of trying to work in this new sector, with its proliferation of 'meta-networks' (another form of too much connection). However, this location of blame at the doors of the technology was not because of any sense of these technologies having generated some kind of 'cyberspace' or 'virtual reality'; rather, it was seen more pragmatically as a combination of what grant-funding bodies imagined these technologies ought to be able to achieve in terms of new connections, contrasted with the reality, which generally speaking failed to do any such thing. Using the technology both as a metaphor and causal explanation for these political and practical conditions seemed almost unavoidable.

Conclusion

I am suggesting that digital networks have become a sort of paradigm for talking about culture, both within social theory literature and among people using ICTs in Manchester (one of Strathern's 'straw people', as outlined in 'Culture in a Netbag'). At the same time, the culture is 'in' the network, both in terms of being represented as causing cultural change, and in terms of reflecting the kinds of shifts in connection and disconnection that are occurring elsewhere. The London research, conducted before the Internet became a trope of postmodernity, picked up on the beginnings of these shifts, in the rather unusual context of women who explicitly abstracted certain ideas about persons and their connections, and were therefore aware of the possible implications that challenges to their readings of sexuality could have. That suggests, if this is needed, that the technologies themselves, as technologies, are not at the core of this matter. It is the cultural work that the technologies are being made to do that is at the core.

Notes

1. The title is borrowed from Strathern's 'Culture in a Netbag' (1981). This (mis)use of the phrase is wordplay on two themes: critiques of some feminist positions on the notion of 'woman' (a theme in Strathern's paper), and the popular use of information and communications technologies ('networks') as a means to generate a discourse on perceived cultural change.
2. I am not here concerned with the analytical study of 'network' as a concept. See Riles (2000) for a critical analysis of the use of the term, particularly the notion that 'network' is a self-evident concept that is principally concerned with links, or connections.
3. The acronym 'ICTs' began to be used in the late 1990s. It replaced both 'IT' (information technology) and 'telematics' (referring to multimedia communication across a distance). It refers to all telecommunications and computer-based technologies and techniques used to manage, organize, transmit and translate information, and it refers to the use of these technologies to communicate.
4. This was a joint research project with Penny Harvey and Jon Agar, 'The Social Contexts of Virtual Manchester', part of the ESRC's *Virtual Society?* programme.
5. See for example, Ortner (1988), Herdt (1984), Rubin (1975). Obviously, there have since been many changes in theorizing sexuality within anthropology (e.g. Stoler (1991) and Lancaster & di Leonardo (1997)).

6. e.g. Jackson (1987), Leeds Revolutionary Feminist Group (1981), Hanmer (1987), Brownmiller (1975).
7. e.g. Hoagland (1986a, 1986b), Jeffreys (1990).
8. e.g. Hayles (1999), Heim (1993), Jones (1997), Rheingold (1995), Mitchell (1995), Slouka (1996), Springer (1996), Featherstone (1995), Shields (1996).
9. See Leidholdt and Raymond (1990) for lesbian feminist counter-attacks against his approach.
10. See Blackman (1990), Egerton (1985), and Rubin (1982) for examples.
11. For a range of views reflecting this perspective and the controversy it provoked, see Sheba Collective (1989), Vance (1984), Ardill (1986), Blackman (1990), Nestle (1987).
12. For examples of such a dispute, see Ardill (1989) and L.I.S. (1988).
13. For feminism, this is excellently described in Echols (1989).
14. For various versions of theories suggesting this, see Bijker (1992, 1997, 1987), Woolgar (1988), Law (1991). For a critical assessment of these theories, see Downey (1998, pp. 21–31).
15. For a summary of the development of ICTs, see Beniger (1986) and Winston (1998).
16. Some of the more extreme examples include Slouka (1996), Mitchell (1995), Springer (1996), Hayles (1999).
17. See for example, Boal (1995), Moore (1995), Wynn (1997), Anderson (1996).

References

Anderson, J. (1996) 'On the Social Order of Cyberspace – Knowledge Workers and New Creoles', *Social Science Computer Review* 14: 7–9.

Ardill, S., and Sullivan, S.O. (1986) 'Upsetting an Applecart: Difference, Desire and Lesbian Sadomasochism', *Feminist Review* 31–57.

—— (1989) 'Sex in the Summer of 88', *Feminist Review* 127–34.

Augé, M. (1995) *Non-places: Introduction to an Anthropology of Supermodernity*, London: Verso.

—— (1999) *The War of Dreams: Studies in Ethno Fiction*, London: Pluto.

Baudrillard, J. (1994) *Simulacra and Simulation. The Body, in Theory: Histories of Cultural Materialism*, Ann Arbor: University of Michigan Press.

Beniger, J.R. (1986) *The Control Revolution: Technological and Economic Origins of the Information Society*, Cambridge, Mass. and London: Harvard University Press.

Bijker, W.E. (1997) *Of Bicycles, Bakelites, and Bulbs: Toward a Theory of Sociotechnical Change. Inside Technology*, Cambridge, Mass. and London: MIT Press.

Bijker, W.E. and Law, J. (eds) (1992) *Shaping Technology/Building Society: Studies in Sociotechnical Change. Inside Technology*, Cambridge, Mass. and London: MIT Press.

Bijker, W.E., Hughes, T.P. and Pinch, T.J. (eds) (1987) *The Social Construction of Technological Systems: New Directions in the Sociology and History of Technology*, Cambridge, Mass. and London: MIT Press.

Blackman, I. and Perry, K. (1990) 'Skirting the Issue: Lesbian Fashion for the 1990s', *Feminist Review* 67–78.

Boal, I.A. and Brook, J. (eds) (1995) *Resisting the Virtual Life: The Culture and Politics of Information*, San Francisco and Monroe OR City Lights: Subterranean Company [distributor].

Bourdieu, P. (1977) *Outline of a Theory of Practice*, Cambridge: Cambridge University Press.

Brownmiller, S. (1975) *Against Our Will: Men, Women and Rape*, New York: Simon and Schuster.

Downey, G.L. (1998) *The Machine in Me: An Anthropologist Sits among Computer Engineers*, New York and London: Routledge.

Echols, A. (1989) *Daring to be Bad: Radical Feminism in America, 1967–1975*, Minneapolis: University of Minnesota Press.

Ettore, E. (1980) *Lesbians, Women and Society*, London: Routledge & Kegan Paul.

Faderman, L. (1991) *Odd Girls and Twilight Lovers: A History of Lesbian Life in Twentieth-Century America*, Harmondsworth: Penguin.

Featherstone, M. and Burrows, R. (ed.) (1995) *Cyberspace/Cyberbodies/Cyber-punk: Cultures of Technological Embodiment*, London: Sage.

Green, S. (1997) *Urban Amazons: Lesbian Feminism and Beyond in the Gender, Sexuality and Identity Battles of London*, London: Macmillan.

Hanmer, J. and Maynard, M. (eds) (1987) *Women, Violence and Social Control*, London: Macmillan.

Haraway, D.J. (1997) *Modest_Witness@Second_Millennium.FemaleMan©_Meets_OncoMouse™. Feminism and Technoscience*, New York and London: Routledge.

Harvey, D. (1990) *The Condition of Postmodernity: An Enquiry into the Origins of Cultural Change*, Oxford: Blackwell.

Hayles, N.K. (1999) *How We Became Posthuman: Virtual Bodies in Cybernetics, Literature, and Informatics*, Chicago and London: University of Chicago Press.

Heim, M. (1993) *The Metaphysics of Virtual Reality*, Oxford: Oxford University Press.

Herdt, G. (1984) *Ritualized Homosexuality in Melanesia*, Berkeley: University of California Press.

Herzfeld, M. (1997) *Cultural Intimacy: Social Poetics in the Nation-State*, London: Routledge.

Hoagland, S. (1986a) 'Lesbian Ethics: Some Thoughts on Power in Our Interactions', *Lesbian Ethics* 2: 5–31.

—— (1986b) 'Lesbian Separatism: An Empowering Reality', *Gossip* 24–36.

Jackson, Margaret (1987) 'Facts of Life or the Eroticization of Women's
Oppression? Sexology and the Social Construction of Heterosexuality,' in
P. Caplan (ed.) *The Cultural Construction of Sexuality*, London: Tavistock.

Jeffreys, S. (1990) *Anticlimax: A Feminist Perspective on the Sexual Revolution*,
London: The Women's Press.

Jones, S. (ed.) (1997) *Virtual Culture: Identity and Communication in Cybersociety*,
London: Sage Publications.

Lancaster, R. and di Leonardo, M. (eds) (1997) *The Gender/Sexuality Reader:
Culture, History, Political Economy*, New York and London: Routledge.

Law, J. (ed.) (1991) *A Sociology of Monsters: Essays on Power, Technology, and
Domination*, London and New York: Routledge.

Leeds Revolutionary Feminist Group, The (1981) 'Political Lesbianism: The
Case Against Heterosexuality,' in O. Press (ed.) *Love Your Enemy? The Debate
Between Political Lesbianism and Heterosexual Feminism*, London: Onlywomen
Press.

Leidholdt, D. and Raymond, J. (eds) (1990) *The Sexual Liberals and the Attack
on Feminism*, New York: Pergamon.

Lesbian Information Service (1988) 'Treachery at the Lesbian Summer School',
Lesbian Information Service Newsletter 13: 5–9.

Mitchell, W. (1995) *City of Bits: Space, Place, and the Infobahn*, Cambridge, Mass.
and London: MIT Press.

Moore, D. (1995) *The Emperor's Virtual Clothes: The Naked Truth About Internet
Culture*, Chapel Hill: Algonquin Books.

Nestle, J. (1987) *A Restricted Country*, London: Sheba Feminist Publishers.

Ortner, S. and Whitehead, H. (eds) (1988) *Sexual Meanings: The Cultural
Construction of Gender and Sexuality*, Cambridge: Cambridge University Press.

Rabinow, P. (1992) 'Artificiality and Enlightenment: From Sociobiology to
Biosociality,' in J. Crary and S. Kwinter (eds) *Incorporations*, New York: Zone
Books.

Rheingold, H. (1995) *The Virtual Community: Finding Connection in a Computer-
ized World*, London: Secker and Warburg.

Riles, A. (2000) *The Network Inside Out*, Ann Arbor: Michigan University Press.

Rubin, G. (1975) 'The Traffic in Women: Notes on the Political Economy of Sex,'
in R. Reiter (ed.) *Toward an Anthropology of Women*, New York: Monthly
Review Press.

Rubin, G. (1982) 'Thinking Sex: Notes for a Radical Theory of the Politics of
Sexuality,' in C. Vance (ed.) *Pleasure and Danger: Exploring Female Sexuality*,
London: Routledge & Kegan Paul.

Sheba Collective (ed.) (1989) *Serious Pleasure: Lesbian Erotic Stories and Poetry*, London: Sheba Feminist Publishers.

Shields, R. (1996) *Cultures of Internet: Virtual Spaces, Real Histories, Living Bodies*, London: Sage.

Slouka, M. (1996) *War of the Worlds: Cyberspace and the High-tech Assault on Reality*, London: Abacus.

Springer, C. (1996) *Electronic Eros: Bodies and Desire in the Postindustrial Age*, London: Athlone Press.

Stein, A. (1997) 'Sisters and Queers: The Decentering of Lesbian Feminism', in R. Lancaster and M. di Leonardo (eds) *The Gender/Sexuality Reader*, London and New York: Routledge.

Stoler, L. (1991) 'Carnal Knowledge and Imperial Power: Gender, Race, and Morality in Colonial Asia,' in M. di Leonardo (ed.) *Gender and the Crossroads of Knowledge: Feminist Anthropology in the Postmodern Era*, Berkeley: University of California Press.

Strathern, M. (1981) 'Culture in a Netbag: The Manufacture of a Subdiscipline in Anthropology', *Man* (n.s.) 16: 665–88.

Vance, C. (ed.) (1984) *Pleasure and Danger: Exploring Female Sexuality*, London: Routledge & Kegan Paul.

Winston, B. (1998) *Media Technology and Society: A History from the Telegraph to the Internet*, London and New York: Routledge.

Woolgar, S. (1988) *Science: The Very Idea*, Chichester: Horwood.

Wynn, E. and Katz, J. (1997) 'Hyperbole over Cyberspace: Self-presentation and Social Boundaries in Internet Home Pages and Discourse', *Information Society* 13: 297–327.

Part V
Methodologies and
Ethnomethodologies

Introduction to Part V
Nigel Rapport

The chapters in this section focus on the close connection between processes of data-acquisition and particular social setting. The methodologies of anthropological data-collection and interpretation exist in a wider context of meaning-making which includes the 'ethnomethodologies' which individuals (anthropologists and non-anthropologists alike) employ in construing their everyday lives. Indeed, the fuzziness of the boundaries between social-scientific, 'specialist' or 'expert' methodologies, and 'lay', 'everyday' or 'folk' ones, and the way practitioners draw severally and strategically upon these, provide these chapters with their tension.

The chapters also tell of the negotiations that take place, both in the minds of practitioners and in public exchanges, regarding the pertinent and rightful methodologies to employ in particular settings. Further fuzziness, indeed, concerns the ways in which these negotiations might not themselves be seen as part of the research process, for data-collection takes place as the very decisions are being made, and are ongoingly made, about what constitutes the data of the project. Whether determining to interview informants, or to play the language-games of ethics committees, or to employ computational sampling packages, one is already playing the 'field-anthropologist' by an avowed sensitivity to local knowledge-practices and a reflexivity towards one's own.

In Chapter Ten, 'Interviews as Ethnography? Disembodied Social Interaction in Britain', Jenny Hockey argues for a reappraisal of the interview as means of accruing ethnographic data. In anthropology, Hockey feels, the interview is conventionally disparaged. Disadvantageous distinctions are said to exist between what gets relayed in interviews and what 'really' transpired such that interview data represent limited commentaries on lived experience, taking place at a distance from remembered events.

Instead of an approximation to participant-observation, however, Hockey would call for the interview to be recognized as a particular kind of social interaction – one with its own ethos, habitus and practicality. Rather than something simply abstracted from the temporal flow of the life-course, the interview may be said to partake of its own kind of experiential and sensual dimension: something which goes beyond the observable world, for instance, to an inner one of individual informants' thoughts, memories and imaginations. Interviews may be described as a kind of punctuation point, a moment of being, in which to engage with aspects of life which may not surface elsewhere (to create space for what has been left unsaid or remains invisible); interviews are one of a number of reflexive means of making-strange the present.

Nor is this merely a matter of pragmatics, moreover, for the interview may be found to be a particularly appropriate form of participation for sociocultural research in Britain. Recognizing the routine nature of transient social interaction in Britain – with its geographically dispersed relationships, and the predominantly mediated way in which personal data on others is accessed via advice columns, tabloid newspapers and published autobiographies – significant and instructive parallels may be drawn between interviewing and 'real life' as such.

In Chapter Eleven, 'Entering Secure Psychiatric Settings', Christine Brown tells the story of the method she had to employ, the 'language-game' she had to play, in order to attempt to interview a group of 'mentally disordered offenders' held in secure medico-legal institutions. The processes involved in applying for ethical approval from the appropriate committees, Brown argues, are significantly revelatory of the bureaucratic procedure whereby British society comes initially to define otherwise socioculturally and ethnically diverse people as specifically 'other'. Her chapter is an account of the dialectical workings of a medico-legal bureaucracy whose administering of a certain kind of person is at the same time an on-going construction of their categorial distinctiveness.

British attitudes to the criminally insane are highly ambivalent, Brown asserts. The division between 'bad' and 'mad' is fuzzy, and how this difference is to translate into legal as distinct from medical institutionalization is fraught with contingency. How are responsibility, treatment, care and blame to be allocated? Furthermore, are mentally disordered offenders patients to be protected (and whose consent to be studied is to be carefully sought), or prisoners of the state whose inducements to be studied are to be carefully regulated?

The 'gatekeepers' on medical ethics committees Brown likens to officiants at an esoteric rite. They partake of their own formal language and practised expertise, and they must be approached and persuaded by way of a harangue which accords with their own discursive tenets. The researcher's methodology and manner must, in short, accord with and be grounded in a set of prejudices already constitutive of his or her research subjects, of him- or herself and of his or her possible treatment of data.

In Chapter Twelve, 'Cultural Values and Social Organization in Wales: Is Ethnicity the Locus of Culture?', Carol Trosset and Douglas Caulkins set out to reassess the workings of ethnicity by exploring the variation in values held within an ostensibly singular cultural group: the Welsh. An appreciation of 'value themes' is necessary, they argue, for an understanding not only of the formation of ethnic and local identities but also of the construction of occupational and recreational strategies. Key values are implicated in the performance of identity and social practice, affecting individual lives and also those of communities. A method must be devised, however, to measure and not corrupt the intrinsically distributive nature of cultural values in a population.

Trosset's and Caulkins' chapter is an exercise in computational sampling. Factoring by way of an ANTHROPAC Consensus Analysis Module enables the researcher to look beyond the surface rhetoric of hegemonic discourses to the values that actually inform behaviour, mapping both the diversity and the agreement among a large number of residents in two Welsh towns (Machynlleth and Lampeter) who might claim a variety of political, class, gender and ethnic ('Welsh', 'English', 'Anglo-Welsh') affiliations.

Trosset's and Caulkins' findings are that values of 'egalitarianism', 'martyrdom', 'aesthetic performance', 'emotionalism' and 'nostalgia' are more contested ideologies of Welshness than shared cultural truths. And that people's engagement with these ideologies itself spans an arc from commitment, through criticalness and rebelliousness, to disseverment.

–10–

Interviews as Ethnography? Disembodied Social Interaction in Britain
Jenny Hockey

This chapter takes up the question of an appropriate methodology for an anthropology of Britain; and in so doing explores methodological issues which ethnographic work in the UK raises for the discipline as a whole. Research questions which stem from and address the British social environment often seem unamenable to the fieldwork methods described in the classic monographs of traditional non-Western anthropology. Research sites are heterogeneous and scattered, the weather is dire and everything interesting seems to be going on behind closed doors. Decisions made by funding councils and external examiners play their part here. Faced with a research proposal form, we may cage the fluidity and openness of participant-observation, reducing it to no more than a prescribed number of 'semi-structured interviews' and 'focus groups', with the possible addition of some documentary research. Conversely, if we encourage post-graduate students registered in cognate disciplines to read anthropology, we may then find them reluctant to describe their rich qualitative interviews as ethnography, fearful that an external examiner might judge their methods inadequate when measured against this term. As a discipline, we may have become less apologetic about the study of locally produced 'exotica', but participant-observation continues to occupy the methodological high ground. When the anthropology of Britain is practised primarily by interviewing, its method risks being seen as a second choice, imposed by force of circumstances.

Speaking of Ethnography

Invited to contribute to a conference stream on new British ethnographies in 1999,[1] I initially limited myself to my 1981 participant-observation study within the old people's home. Inhabiting the role of 'care aid' on a daily basis, my work conformed to traditional ethnography in a way which my subsequent interview-based studies did not seem to. This prompted me to reflect on the issues which this chapter now explores. To produce data in a British 'field site' and to persuade funding bodies that research projects are sufficiently 'structured', many anthropologists make extensive use of interviews. Yet, like me, they may sense that their disciplinary identity is slipping. They are prioritizing a method which occupies a secondary position within a traditional hierarchy where extended, face-to-face fieldwork is privileged. Here I question the discouraging perception that doing the anthropology of Britain means that participant-observation must yield to pragmatism.

Though participant-observation can often encompass interviews, these tend to be represented as but one part of a seamless whole. Thus, for example, when I came to transcribe the taped life-history interviews I had conducted at old people's bedsides, dressed in my care aid's overall, I integrated these texts into the body of my field notes. By contrast, a series of stand-alone interviews is often regarded as the poor relation or handmaiden of a participant-observation study. This view underpins a methodological hierarchy which urgently requires reconsideration. Without this, the practice of anthropology is in danger of restricting itself to traditional field sites and methods, a position which risks impoverishing its disciplinary identity in the following ways. First, the full breadth of an anthropology of Britain which moves beyond islands and isolates will remain compromised. Second, the contributions of those whose professional duties and funding sources militate against extended participant-observation may be lost to the discipline. And, third, empirically informed dialogue with those who work within different disciplines but draw upon anthropological theory and methods may be constrained since the status of their data is likely to be questioned.

Arguments to say that skilled interviewing can yield material of a quality which almost matches the products of participant-observation are persuasive, but do little to disrupt a hierarchical model of anthropological field methods. Instead, I suggest, we need to question the distinction between interview data and 'what really happened' and acknowledge parallels between interviewing and 'real life'. The aim of this chapter, therefore, is to demonstrate that the research interview is a culturally appropriate form of participation in Britain. This is not to undermine the value of fieldwork and the expertise which anthropologists have built up in this area, nor to pit one approach against another. Rather, I am taking qualitative interviewing out of the wings to put it centre stage and explore its relationship with other aspects of social life in Western cultures. The tradition of ethnographic fieldwork uniquely endows us with the capacity to 'make strange' the familiar. Here I am asking for a reconsideration of both a familiar social science research method, 'interviewing', and its relationship with the changing nature of our everyday patterns of social interaction in Britain. I am suggesting that interviewing might be particularly suited to a Western setting for more than just pragmatic reasons.

Anthropologists often feel that interviews by themselves can only take us to the periphery of what we might better investigate through participant-observation. They leave us problematically reliant upon our interviewees, as gatekeepers to their own experience. And we worry that we have extracted them from their everyday worlds, our data being just the accounts of singleton exiles. While this apologetic stance is common, it may be unhelpful. Many of the field settings in which Western researchers conduct 'anthropology at home' are very different from those in which our discipline developed its distinctive approach. Everyday social interaction in the West is often spatially dislocated, time-bounded and characterized by intimacy at a distance. At the same time, 'anthropology at home' requires us to participate in the flow of ordinary encounters, but often without the spatial and temporal boundaries which traditionally separate the field from academia. Ethical issues to do with confidentiality, the relevance of research for 'users' and its potential to do harm to informants are challenges which have acquired new urgency with the development of research within our own environments. Introducing the ASA monograph *Anthropology at Home*, Jackson said, 'The main distinctive characteristic of anthropology as a discipline is that the fieldworkers go and live with the people under investigation' (1987: 13). He meant that they packed their bags and moved in. Living with people while actually staying at home was not part of this picture. However, it is the potential of the interview in settings where the researcher's participation is not mediated by a distantiated relationship between 'them' and 'us' which this chapter considers. How shall we proceed in a deeply familiar social world of fleeting encounters and geographically dispersed relationships?

First we need to be clear what we understand by the term 'interview'. Textbooks describe the use of qualitative interviewing to sample larger populations in order to come up with 'lay' definitions of key terms, to identify themes and issues and get at process and negotiation in everyday life. In this context, interviewees are chosen mechanically according to systems of social stratification which are assumed to be relevant. Tapes and transcripts pile up, often analysed in a similarly mechanical fashion weeks or months after interviews took place, not necessarily by the person who conducted them. As words typed onto pages, these data fore-ground the verbal dimensions of experience. Though conscientious interviewers augment the transcribed data with a record of the 'body language' or 'non-verbal communication' which the tape fails to pick up, the use of these terms is itself telling. Language and communication remain pre-eminent, even when words are not being used. I suggest that this approach diverts attention from the more holistic aspects of the research interview, although these in turn are often upstaged by the capacity of participant-observation to privilege experience over language, action over dialogue, the senses over cognition.

Hastrup and Hervik argue that 'ethnographic material is composed of so much more than words' (1994: 5) and fieldwork is valued for its capacity to incorporate sensory experience. I found this out when I began work on death and dying (Hockey 1990). In my role as care aid in an old people's home, I recorded the following at the end of day one: 'As I write the strong, distinctive smell of elderly urine collects in my nostrils, even though it was not overpowering at the time'. Some days later, after taking a resident to the toilet for the first time, I wrote, 'I led her off, worried that I hadn't washed her hands (although I'd noticed that other care staff didn't do this). Again I felt the repeated desire to wash my own hands – between bed-making and table-laying for instance, which no one else seems bothered about.' Material of this kind, gathered across time, documented my gradual acquisition of the embodied skills through which care workers managed the deterioration and death which the residential home served to contain.

However, while remaining within my hands-on role in the old people's home, I found an additional field site – as a befriender/counsellor for a bereavement organization. My engagement with widowed clients resembled interviewing in that I sat and listened to people talk freely about their loss. With their permission, case notes became fieldnotes and fed into my academic work. As people spoke about their grief, they engaged in performances which took us back into the past time of the marriage. My visits were powerful gestures which disrupted the often solitary space which the bereaved person occupied and evoked memories of the embodied presences of earlier years (Hockey 1990: 53). They focused attention upon the deafening silences which people drowned out with radios in every room and the constant murmur of television in the background.

In these encounters the chair occupied by the bereaved person and the chair offered to the befriender are often those in which a couple once sat together to talk or watch television. As the researcher animates these spaces of remembered intimacy, performances can be stimulated, the incomer being used as a kind of body double for the lost person. For example, after I had unknowingly chosen her dead husband's place on the settee, one widow re-enacted the time when her husband had stood before the mirror over the fireplace, telling her how dreadful he thought he looked, throwing his arms around her neck and asking her to reassure him that death was not as dreadful as he feared. Similarly, a widower showed me how he had had to lift his wife from her bed, coming over to mime his remembered gestures in relation to my own body. Again I had chosen to sit in the spot where her bed had been set up in the downstairs room.

More recent taped interviews which I conducted with elderly people bereaved of their partner provide additional examples of how 'being there' can be fruitful. I wanted to find out about changes in older widowed people's use of private and public space now that they were living alone. Entering their homes did not just reveal where they sat, what objects or which view provided the main focus for their gaze – but also how the space of home related to the world outside. For example, among a group of well-off widows, getting access was difficult in every sense. When I finally approached their homes I observed fortresses with drawn Venetian blinds and gardens pared down to an austere minimum. Burglar alarms had to be negotiated and signs were fastened onto a succession of porches and internal doors, forbidding smoking and warning of dogs. Mavis,[2] a widow in her seventies, said, 'I really think we're frightened to go out at night and you're in your home, the doors locked, you feel safe, except last night I did not feel safe . . . (after a visit to the theatre) . . . no sooner had I got back inside than my son-in-law phoned and he says "the Police have been down to your house . . . your burglar alarm went off". Now I thought if I got a burglar alarm fitted I would . . . be happy, content when I was away and this had done it twice in six months . . .'. Mavis recognized herself as lucky in being able to drive but this mobile extension of her home space also stimulated a defensive attitude: 'then it comes dark and you think, "Ooh, I've got to go through Dunton and Woodley and driving my old banger, what will happen if I break down?" You daren't put your hazard lights, you don't know what Tom, Dick and Harry's gonna stop and say, "Are you all right?" I mean you daren't even open your door, dare you?'

By contrast with these defended spaces I found easy access to the homes of elderly men. In one case a widower had a ground-floor sheltered flat at the corner of a busy intersection. Just outside his front door, under an external staircase which led up to a neighbour's flat, he had installed a bench and half a dozen plant tubs: 'and if it's anything like (fine weather), I sit out there and sit, watch the traffic go by, happy as a pig in . . . happy as a pig in muck', he said. He had also colonized the communal gardens immediately surrounding his 'patch' and a bed of unofficial annuals were in place. Few people were able to pass the flat without being noticed and many were stopped for a chat. During the interview he continued surveillance activities through his living room window, while neighbours and relatives came and went on small matters of business through his front door which stood open to the road throughout my visit (Hockey, Sibley and Penhale 1999).

This kind of interview was not just a mechanical matter of sampling and recording. The elderly widower had been recommended to me by a neighbour of his whom I knew socially. Hearing I was having difficulties with access, she said, 'Try Bill. He'll talk to you. He's a right gas bag'. During the time spent in his flat I was introduced to his upstairs neighbour and let into the secret of the man's cancer which Bill felt he was not facing up to. I was shown the vegetable patch the two men had set up behind the flats as well as the tiny collection of shabby rooms which made up the flat itself. Bill explained his difficulties with managing a bowel problem and I was aware of the long-familiar smell of slight incontinence. What was subsequently transcribed from the tape is therefore located within a complex social and physical environment. Cases such as this show the scope of the interview. My encounter with Bill is not unusual.

However, as indicated earlier, my aim is not to 'talk up' interviews. Instead I'm questioning the view that by themselves they can only offer a limited commentary on lived experience, taking place at a distance from remembered events. Not only did my field role as a bereavement befriender/counsellor resemble an interview but, as argued, both relationships shared experiential and sensory dimensions and went far beyond the spoken word. Data reveal bereavement visits as occasions which are not simply abstracted from the temporal flow of the life-course. Rather they are situated moments in which people engage with aspects of life which may not surface elsewhere. They allow past and future to be accessed via the present and create space for what has been left unsaid and what remains invisible. There is a sense, therefore, in which the bereavement visit, like the interview, makes strange the informant's life to them, providing a punctuation point from which to stand aside and generate meanings which then feed back into future life.

The data produced in these encounters disturb assumptions about the familiar categories of 'the research interview' and 'the counselling session'. They suggest that neither of them constitute mere snapshots abstracted from the present. Both involve spatialized performance and the embodied recovery of the past. In addition, while an outside observer might perceive the visit as a sequestrated encounter between two people, the data belie this view. In the moment of the one-to-one interview, not only the past but also the dead are present. Rather than a materiality which is limited to the body of the deceased, objects, space and other bodies become props in emergent dramas. Indeed the dead have agency in that they make a difference and acquire empowerment at particular sites as aspects of heterogeneous assemblages of people and things (Hallam et al. 1999).

In his ethnography of divorce and separation Simpson (1998) provides a similar description of the research interview. Here absent previous partners came to participate via mimicry and reported speech. Indeed, informants would 'address all manner of absent audiences such as a former partner, estranged children, the courts and public opinion in ways which went beyond the direct interaction between interviewer and interviewee' (1998: 128). This is evident in an extract he presents from an interviewee's account of a meeting with the Court Welfare Officer:

> I took Edward down (to the Welfare Officer) and I said 'don't say you want to stay with me cos I want you to' I says, 'I'll not come in the room' and they (Welfare Officers) says 'no stay' and I says 'you speak your mind it's not what I want or what your dad wants'. And he said what I knew he'd say 'I don't want to live with one or the other, I want to live half and half' and his dad says 'oh no, I'm having him' . . . (Simpson 1998: 128).

Destabilizing the 'outer:inner' Dichotomy

This line of argument seems to suggest that interviews are a good enough approximation of participant-observation. But this misses the point that privileging participant-observation keeps in place a notion that our proper disciplinary terrain is the observable world of human behaviour and face-to-face interaction. What people think about relationships, how the dead and the divorced make their entries into social life via the imaginations of others, are questions which are all too often relinquished to disciplines such as psychology or psychoanalysis (Simpson, 1998). The outer world of what is said and seen continues to be separated off from the inner world of consciousness, with the result that society's sources in the thoughts and actions of intentional human beings become obscured (Cohen and Rapport, 1995: 4). The notion that research interviews are limited or two-dimensional reflects this view. Misguidedly they are perceived to be an off stage commentary which takes place in the wings, rather than a centre-stage set, complete with scenery and props, which an entire cast of players can enter and exit. Interviewers are often reminded that their data may not match what actually happened but is valuable as an account in its own right. But does this distinction between the research interview and 'real life' actually hold up?

Classic participant-observation studies 'abroad', such as Malinowski's work among the Trobrianders (1922) or Evans-Pritchard's among the Nuer (1940), took place in societies where notions of home did not map onto Western models of differentiated private and public space with any precision. Many were sited in environments where social and economic activity often took place in shared out-door space, in climates warm enough to permit extended conversation. Though subsequent monographs reflect a greater diversity of methods and sites, the classic works stemmed largely from extended, embodied interaction within the field. Their distinctive method became one of the discipline's hallmarks. Anthropology 'at home' uses this method to valuable effect, but in a limited range of settings: in institutions, in organizations and among people whose lives unfold outside domestic space. Work on aspects of Westerners' lives which are secluded within the home – sex, housework, family relationships, informal healthcare – tends to use interviews. It seems like the only practical solution in the context of occupational and residential fragmentation, strong boundaries to private space and a miserably cold and damp climate for up to ten months of the year. But I'm arguing that something more than pragmatism is at work here.

In many respects the interview is an encounter which resembles many others in societies where important relationships can have a 'disembodied' quality, being conducted in bounded time slots via phone and email. As we know, communities no longer cohere simply on the ground but, increasingly, around occupational, leisure or cultural interests which transcend space, both locally and globally. Place, as Giddens argues, has ceased to be the site at which time and space connect, a change which 'provides the very basis for their recombination in ways that co-ordinate social activities without necessary reference to the particularities of place' (1991: 17). Lash and Urry echo this point in their description of a postmodernist political economy in which 'time and space "empty out", become more abstract and in which things and people become "disembedded" from concrete space and time' (1996, cited in Norris and Armstrong 1999: 22). Increasing recognition is also being given to imagined communities – as noted, Simpson's work on post-divorce families describes an imagined world populated with characters 'felt to be there', which continually splices into the real world (1998: 129). In relation to these data, he argues, 'it is important that we are aware not only of the actual face-to-face dimensions of social life but also of absent relationships which, in circumstances of conflict and limited communication, become highly significant . . . out of sight does not necessarily mean out of mind' (1998: 129).

Technology intertwines with the workings of memory and the imagination in these contexts. It makes a growing contribution to the unfolding of social relation-ships which, to the observer, consist of solitary individuals holding a mobile phone, reading a computer screen or tapping a keyboard. Such relationships are not thought strange, being experienced between geographically distant grandparents and grandchildren, parents and children in families where commuting and long working hours are the norm, punters who call for telephone sex, people with problems who talk with counsellors or clairvoyants and internet chat room users. All the elderly bereaved people I interviewed about their uses of public and private space were living alone in the homes they had once shared with embodied family members: husbands, children, elderly parents. Many interviews were punctuated by phone calls, often between neighbours. Edie, a widow in her seventies, referred to 'a lady across the road . . . she's a widow and we have each other's phone numbers in case either one's poorly during the night . . . you can't get in, but at least she could get help. I mean you could ring and they would ring my people and I would ring hers and we'd get help to each other and she's in her seventies too is Doreen, but she been on her own quite . . . a long time'. This technology-based reciprocity was echoed by Jocelyn who maintained a relationship with a relative living at a distance through weekly phone calls: 'what we usually do is I ring her and then after we've been on quarter of an hour, we put the phone down and she rings me back, or we do it the other way, so that's nice'. Mavis, whose car journeys meant the threat of contact with a dangerous outside world, had found a part solution to the problem in the mobile phone: 'I'd rather go with somebody, than go on me own, you know . . . in fact somebody that I know . . . four ladies now, we've all bought mobile phones'. Mavis also felt that the isolation of living alone could bring on senile dementia. A phone call might represent the first social exchange of a solitary day: 'I'll answer the phone and people will say "Have you got a cold?" I say, "No. You're the first person I've spoke to today. I haven't really cleared me throat". And then some of the others'll say that they talk to themselves, and I think, "Oh, I haven't got as bad as that yet."'

As well as a sense of security, the phone also provided these older widowed women with scope for intimacy at moments which fell outside the accepted times for social interaction between people who do not share the same home. It allowed emotional expressiveness in the moments of distress. Carrie was another widow in her seventies and she had joined a local friendship group for bereaved people. She said:

> I've two or three that have become close friends and we ring each other up and, you know, if we need any help or any . . . if we just feel like talking because of the loneliness, you know, and feeling a bit down in the dumps, which you do now and again, we'll ring one another up because we know at the other end of the line she understands how I'm feeling, you know. There's one little old lady . . . was saying yesterday that she nearly rang me up during the week because she was feeling down in the dumps. 'Well why didn't you?' 'Well, I didn't know what you might be doing.' I said, 'It dun't matter what I'm doing. I'll make time to talk to you. Ring me up. I've told you, you know'.

Draper's study of men's experience of becoming parents (2000) provides another example of the role of technology in mediating 'disembodied' social relationships. Using traditional anthropological theories of transition, her research was stimulated by personal awareness of the ambiguous position of British men who were becoming fathers. While enjoined to 'participate' in pregnancy and childbirth, they were simultaneously distanced from the cultural category 'pregnancy' in that it was constituted as a series of medicalized processes which took place within the separate, bounded space of someone else's body. One member of the group of men she interviewed said, 'I think you try to be involved and you try to ascertain how the pregnancies feel from your partner, but you're always going to be that one step removed from it and therefore you're going to be remote' (2000: 110). Draper's choice of method was qualitative interviewing but in her account she describes it not as 'doing ethnography' but, more guardedly, as the use of 'the *principles* of ethnographic research' (my italics). Yet her series of interviews parallels the experience of men who were 'one step removed' and achieved engagement only via a sequence of 'body mediated moments': the pregnancy test, the ultrasound scan, the baby's movements, labour and delivery' (2000: 143).

While the email and the mobile phone might be used to link individuals who relate to one another at considerable spatial distance, here technology allows connections to be sought within what is represented as one of the most physically proximate and intimate of social relationships – that between parents and their unborn child. Ultrasonography provided an important medium for men seeking to overcome their experience of distance at a time when they felt an imperative to join in, yet could be left marginalized. Just as the dead enter the time and space of the bereavement visit, not as the living bodies they once were but through other forms of materiality, so the unborn take on agency via their representation on the ultrasound screen, 'a cultural symbol, a familiar and yet exotic, secular and yet sacred, representation' (Boulter, cited in Draper 2000: 172). One interviewee reported actually addressing the image as if it were the embodied child: 'the scan was the point at which . . . I really felt it's my child in there, sort of thing, and there it is. I can remember the first time keeping looking at that scan photo "Yeh, you're real aren't you?"' (Draper 2000: 163). Yet as Sawday argues, 'modern medicine, for all its seeming ability to map and then to conquer the formerly hidden terrain of the interior landscape, in fact renders it visible only through scenes of representation' (1995: 11).

While net access and mobile phones may be the media for middle-class social interaction, 97 per cent of British men attend the birth of their child and we can reasonably infer that many of them will have had prior technological contact with their baby via ultrasonography (Smith, cited in Draper, 2000: 66). The embodied social interaction which, for example, characterized cohesive single-occupation working-class communities during the first half of the twentieth century has been supplanted by other forms of connection. Diminished street policing, cross-generational tension and fear of crime have helped empty terraced streets and the public spaces of housing estates. This urban 'stranger society' is characterized by anonymity and the absence of trust. Reputations have to be established, either by credentials such as certificates and licences or by ordeals such as DNA or drug testing (Norris and Armstrong, 1999). Where people do encounter one another in embodied form – on public transport, at shopping and leisure venues – personal interaction may therefore be avoided for safety's sake. Toddlers out of sight are toddlers at risk. To promote failing city-centre economies, for example, the concept of Town Centre Management has developed and along with it another technological intervention, closed circuit television cameras (CCTV). Backed by businesses, it is sold as a way of promoting a 'feel-good factor' in urban environments where shoppers are likely to be strangers to one another (Norris and Armstrong, 1999: 38–9).

The workplace might seem to offer more by way of embodied encounters between individuals whose reputations are known to one another, yet time pressure has eroded coffee and meal breaks and the use of technology diminishes the need for teamwork. For all that embodiment has become a key focus of interest within the social sciences, social relationships of the kind described here often have a somewhat disembodied quality to them. Featherstone, whose work has been an extended exploration of the body in society, acknowledges the shift towards social interactions which bypass corporeality. In an account entitled, 'Post-bodies, aging and virtual reality' (1995), he focuses on bodily deterioration or betrayal in later life, arguing that developments in new information technology promise the experience of realistic out-of-body social interaction. Referring to the notion of an 'abstract society', he describes the possibility of interpersonal communication mediated by abstract systems. These could benefit the older adult whose body militates against easy face-to-face interaction, the lack of co-presence and visibility actually constituting an asset. He concludes his discussion by suggesting that, 'rather than abstract technological modes of interchange being regarded as "de-humanizing" in a negative sense through the loss of visibility, tactility and the alleged warmth of "full-blooded" face-to-face encounters, they may open up new possibilities for intimacy and self expression' (1995: 233). Featherstone's recognition of the expansiveness and depth of relationships which technology can offer mirrors this chapter's exploration of the complex but often unacknowledged intimacies of the research interview.

Ways of Knowing

In addition to contact between individuals who are known to each other, new technologies are also used as vehicles for ever more 'personalized' representations of people and events which have never been encountered face-to-face. As long ago as 1971, Lofland differentiated between 'knowing about' other people and 'knowing' them, arguing that in complex urban industrial societies, individuals expect to know about far wider categories of others than they can ever know directly: 'to be modern, then, is to have one's awareness of other people's worlds vastly expanded' (1971: 2). In the process a breach opens up between the expansion of 'known-about' worlds and an awareness of not actually knowing the people who inhabit them. In this breach, he argues, substitutes or mediated forms of knowing have appeared: 'reporters, novelists, film-makers, social scientists . . .' (1971: 3). As the twentieth century came to an end, mediators provided increasingly intimate accounts of people we only 'know about'. We feel grief when people die in disasters. We are shown their homes and communities and have a feel for the gap they have left behind from the testimonies of the bereaved. We know, intimately, the circumstances of their deaths and what is not visually accessible to the camera is described first-hand by survivors and rescue workers. We cannot miss it. It is repeated endlessly in the media. If we refuse to get involved and call it sensationalism we may still feel uneasy in our avoidance, like crossing the street to sidestep a recently bereaved neighbour when we are not in the mood for an awkward confrontation. Participant-observation in such settings is not just impracticable but in some senses culturally inappropriate. The anthropologist as 'other' cannot be incorporated into embodied life spaces and times which no longer exist. The anthropologist's role as mediators between people who only 'know about' one another therefore needs to be played out in different kinds of spaces, some of which may be 'virtual' and others 'internal' to the memories and imaginations of interviewees.

The research interview and the data we produce through it are therefore situated within societies where mediators of all kinds ensure the proliferation of personal data: in advice columns; the confessional autobiographies of the sick, the dying,

the royal and the criminal; sensational stories sold to tabloids and in-depth interviews in colour supplements. Like temporally bounded moments of family intimacy
or personal counselling, these data describe spatially differentiated fragments
of whole lives. In 1999 we could visit the Tate and see Tracey Emin's menstrual
knickers cast aside by her bed; or we can surf the net and see Diana, Princess of
Wales, dying in her limousine. In a world of consultants and confessional chat
shows, interviewing begins to resemble a form of participant-observation. As a
practice it conforms closely to Western categories of experience. The perceived
'inadequacies' of interviewing – that it extracts a fragment of time from an
individual's life, allows no embodied access to other life-worlds and relies upon
accounts rather than direct experience – these are the ordinary features of everyday
social interactions which Westerners currently live with and negotiate. As shown
in my exploration of the research interview and data produced, an apparently
distanced and disjointed process of visiting, interviewing and leaving turns out to
be a spatially and temporally complex encounter. Older women, physically isolated
within their own homes, are similarly sustaining intense, interdependent social
relationships via the truncated moments of phone calls.

Not Group but Category

My argument has suggested that what is seen as the experience-far method of
interviewing may actually be experience-near in Western settings. I now want to
conclude by highlighting some additional aspects of distance – whether social,
spatial or temporal – which are particular to anthropologists whose work involves
living within a culture while staying at home. The Western academic who interviews
locally is seen to jet into someone else's front room, bag some data and hotfoot
it to the secretary who transcribes the tape. The interviewer goes in and comes
out. This perception echoes a prevailing view of anthropology as the study of
spatially located social groups. In *Anthropology at Home* (1987), Jackson refers
to anthropology's need to find a bounded unit of some kind. Over ten years later
Watson introduces *Being There* with a discussion of what the researcher does 'pre'
and 'post' fieldwork. He says, 'reflection at a temporal and spatial distance from
our experience within a different cognitive and experiential context inevitably
brings about further reformulations and recastings of our thoughts and ideas'
(1999: 1). The spatiality underpinning these perspectives is inescapable. Our focus,
as social anthropologists, is people or a people. We go among them and we leave,
even if their degree of strangeness to us varies.

My fieldwork in the old people's home was dogged by this myth, my relief at
finding a bounded social group blinding me to the insights which became possible
only when I realized that I was studying social categories – aging and death –
which transcended the bounds of space and are all about time. Anthropology has

now set category alongside group as a focus, whether social, experiential or cognitive. When we work at home, through interviewing, those categories are likely to be ones we inhabit or think with or belong to. This makes it difficult to see our fieldwork and writing as distinctive narratives, separate from those 'other narratives which constitute our consciousness' (Cohen and Rapport 1995: 9). We are obliged to encounter and reflect on our own consciousness along with that of our informants. While this makes the research process particularly demanding, the insights derived from fieldwork 'at home' speak to the discipline of anthropology as a whole. In working on death and dying for over 20 years I have found few ways of distancing myself from my own material. I may grow more familiar with the category 'death' but as I age, death becomes an ever more pressing personal concern. Interviews confront me with my extinction, sometime in the next 30 years, my stark alternative to an eternal life lecturing at Hull University. The topic pervades all aspects of my life, from interrogating my unidentifiable aches and pains to rehearsing the death of every member of my family by turn.

In addition to the immediacy of my topic, the people among whom I work remain stubbornly embodied presences in my life. Since I do not seek a bounded community or large-scale population, those I interview may be neighbours or colleagues. Like other friends, family and acquaintances, they are absent much of the time but they do turn up – in research seminars or out walking on the common. Every weekday night I cycle home past Bill's ground-floor flat. He's not out on his bench any more and I wonder if his fragile health is holding up.

Acknowledgements

I am grateful to Elizabeth Hallam, University of Aberdeen, and Allison James and Clive Norris, University of Hull, for very helpful discussions during the preparation of this chapter.

Notes

1. Voices and Visions Conference, Department of Anthropology, University of Manchester, October, 1999.
2. All first names used are fictitious to preserve confidentiality.

References

Cohen, A.P. and Rapport, N. (1995) 'Introduction: Consciousness in Anthropology', in A.P. Cohen and N. Rapport (eds) *Questions of Consciousness*, London: Routledge.

Draper, J. (2000) 'Fathers in the Making: Men, Bodies and Babies', unpublished PhD thesis, University of Hull.

Evans-Pritchard, E.E. (1940) *The Nuer*, Oxford: Clarendon.

Featherstone, M. (1995) 'Post-bodies, Aging and Virtual Reality', in M. Featherstone and A. Wernick (eds) *Images of Aging*, London: Routledge.

Giddens, A. (1991) *Modernity and Self-Identity*, Cambridge: Polity.

Hallam, E., Hockey, J. and Howarth, G. (1999) *Beyond the Body: Death and Social Identity*, London: Routledge.

Hastrup, K. and Hervik, P. (eds) (1994) *Social Experience and Anthropological Knowledge*, London: Routledge.

Hockey, J. (1990) *Experiences of Death: An Anthropological Account*, Edinburgh: Edinburgh University Press.

Hockey, J., Sibley, D. and Penhale, B. (1999) 'Living Differently: Space, Memory and Bereavement', Paper given at the British Society for Gerontology Conference, Bournemouth.

Jackson, A. (ed.) (1987) *Anthropology at Home*, London: Tavistock.

Lofland, J. (1971) *Analysing Social Settings*, Belmont, CA: Wadsworth.

Malinowski, B. (1922) *Argonauts of the Western Pacific*, London: Routledge & Kegan Paul.

Norris, C. and Armstrong, G. (1999) *The Maximum Surveillance Society: The Rise of CCTV*, Oxford: Berg.

Sawday, J. (1995) *The Body Emblazoned: Dissection and the Human Body in Renaissance Culture*, London: Routledge.

Simpson, B. (1998) *Changing Families*, Oxford: Berg.

Watson, C.W. (1999) *Being There: Fieldwork in Anthropology*, London: Pluto.

–11–

Entering Secure Psychiatric Settings
Christine Brown

Fieldwork in Britain is easy (cf. Bloch 1988). The natives are readily available for study at the researcher's convenience and there are no communication difficulties for those fluent in the English language. British ethnography is what undergraduate students do to practise before attempting the real thing (cf. Richards and Robin 1975).

In this chapter, my aim is to question these assumptions and demonstrate that gaining access to a group of people or settings in one's 'home' country is not always straightforward. In Britain, research carried out in National Health Service settings first has to be approved by the Local Research Ethics Committee. Subtle differences in language-use between the researcher and the authorities permitting research can lead to misunderstandings. For example, what may sound like a well-reasoned argument to an anthropologist may seem an outrageous proposal to the members of the ethics committee. This process can be viewed merely as an obstacle to the anthropologist's pursuit of his or her object: 'they won't let me talk to my people'.

Anthropology, however, is not the study of objects but of humans, their relation-ships, interactions and social structure. The objectification of the hindrance, the obstacle between oneself and one's intended study, can be successfully resisted and itself brought into the field of subjectivities to be approached. The formal procedures of the ethics committee are one of the starting-points for the researcher in constructing the identity of the group of people under study. Such procedures are open to detailed analysis and should not be dismissed as pieces of bureaucratic nonsense that happen before the real fieldwork starts. In the example presented here, the processes of applying for ethical approval to speak to people detained in high and medium secure psychiatric care revealed much about their context in British society. Getting there can be as informative as arriving.

This chapter begins with a description of medical research ethics committees in Britain, setting out their historical context and the workings of the current day system. Leading on from this is an exploration of what the committees perceive as their duties and the conflicting value systems of various participants that are negotiated. In this specialist setting, certain words have particular significance that is different from their ordinary language-use. In order to negotiate successfully, the applicant must pay attention to this and not assume that because he or she is talking English that the words used will be understood. These observations add weight to the voices of a growing number of anthropologists questioning the assumption that 'own' language or culture is automatically 'known' by all persons originating from and sharing the same geographical space (Okely 1996).

The process of applying to an ethics committee, proposing an ethnographic study of people in a secure psychiatric hospital setting, resulted in deliberations that reflected the perception of this group by wider British society. The chapter argues that insights gained by considering the ethics committee application as part of the ethnographic process requiring analysis (rather than a mere technical hitch) are inherently valuable for elucidating the contemporary creation and maintenance of social groups in Britain. The research ethics committee is an institutional order that creates and maintains boundaries between different groups of people and thus fertile ground for anthropological study. It is also a place of negotiation between privileged knowledge and the moral values of British society.

The ethnographic example presented in this chapter is an instantiation and extension of anthropological insights into the working of bureaucracies in contemporary society (Herzfeld 1992). It also examines the dialectic between administering social processes and constructing them and their member parts. International policy directives such as European Conventions on Human Rights are here seen interacting with the bureaucratic process at a local level in shaping and reinforcing social boundaries that exist to keep separate a particular group of people in British society. This account of the application of international policy in local practice and the indigenous interpretations that impact upon such directives along the way draws on the anthropological literature of organizations and policy (Britan and Cohen 1980; Grillo 1980; Donnan and McFarlane 1989; Shore and Wright 1997). The purpose of this examination is to uncover the pre-existing perceptions and definitions inherent in the organizational processes involved and to reflect on the impact of these definitions on the ethnographic method.

Research Ethics Committees: History and International Context

Concerns about the ethics of medical research have existed throughout the development of specialist medical knowledge (Lock 1995). These focus on the morality of doing things to living people that have never been done before and whether the potential harm outweighs potential benefit. One of the earliest examples of legal intervention in human research dates from 1898. Albert Neisser, professor of dermatology and venereology at the University of Breslau was fined by the Royal Disciplinary Court of Prussia for injecting syphilis serum into prostitutes without their knowledge as part of a vaccination trial (Vollman and Winau 1996).

Formalized written codes specifically dealing with medical research date from the Nuremberg Trials in December 1946 of twenty-three German physicians and medical administrators whose defence to the charge of genocide was dressed up as legitimate scientific experimentation (Annas and Grodin 1992). As a direct result, the Nuremberg Code was published in August 1947 setting out ten principles governing permissible medical experiments on human beings. These included voluntary consent of research subjects, the advancement of knowledge for the public good and the agreement that all experiments should be sanctioned by the scientific community (Mitscherlich and Mielke 1949).

Though the Nuremberg Code never became enshrined in the laws of the countries participating in the Trials, it had a considerable impact on scientific communities in the western world. The World Medical Association held its inaugural meeting in September 1947, where the crimes of the Nazi doctors were condemned and a resolution passed to make reports of those crimes available to all medical professionals. The culmination of these resolutions came some years later with the Declaration of Helsinki by the World Medical Association in 1964. The principles outlined in this document have been the basis for international treaties. For example, within Europe the Convention on Human Rights and Biomedicine was opened for signature in 1997. The rhetoric of these documents is interesting:

> It is the mission of the physician to safeguard the health of the people. His or her knowledge and conscience are dedicated to the fulfilment of this mission . . .
>
> The purpose of biomedical research involving human subjects must be to improve diagnostic, therapeutic and prophylactic procedures and the understanding of the aetiology and pathogenesis of disease . . .
>
> In research on man, the interest of science and society should never take precedence over considerations related to the well-being of the subject (Declaration of Helsinki, revised 1996).

> Parties to this Convention shall protect the dignity and identity of all human beings and guarantee everyone, without discrimination, respect for their integrity and other rights and fundamental freedoms with regard to the application of biology and medicine (Council of Europe, Convention on Human Rights and Biomedicine, 1997).

These documents are set out as the basis for the research ethics committee structure in Britain and are very much part of the day-to-day workings of ethics committees. Every member of the committee will have a copy of the Declaration of Helsinki and be expected to have detailed knowledge of it. On research ethics committee forms, the proviso above the applicant's signature reads 'I undertake to carry out the work in accordance with the principles of the Declaration of Helsinki and its amendments'. The committee's business, as they see it, is to ensure that the principles enshrined in such international agreements are upheld across their provincial domain.

In fact, the local interpretation of apparently universal beliefs can still be consistent with diverse practice (Leach 1968). We can draw an analogy between the way that the Declaration of Helsinki is used here and other 'sacred' texts. For example, the written word of Hindu scriptures is a constant in modern Indian Law. However, the same words are interpreted in different ways in different places and times resulting in diversity of practice (Fuller 1988). The research committees also have written doctrines in the form of international conventions, but in practice these universal morals are given particular meaning by the specific local context and interpreted accordingly. Thus the members of a local research ethics committee are engaged in making judgements and negotiating between grand principles and everyday practice. This tension between the ideal of standardization and the diversity of practice has influenced the development of the research ethics committee structure in Britain.

Research Ethics Committees in Britain

The UK Medical Research Council published a report on research ethics in 1963 that emphasized the moral responsibility of researchers for their subjects (Medical Research Council 1964). By 1967 the Royal College of Physicians recommended that all clinical research should be subject to ethical review (Royal College of Physicians 1967). The following year this statement was copied by the Ministry of Health to all regional hospital boards, hospital management committees and boards of governors, along with a memorandum suggesting that hospital authorities should set up ethical review boards on an informal, advisory basis (Ministry of Health 1968). However, no guidelines on the composition and remit of these committees were issued. This resulted in a haphazard system of ethics committees with widely different procedures. Obvious regional variations in supposedly universal ethical standards led to concern expressed by researchers (Gilbert, Fulford and Parker 1989). In 1991 a Department of Health circular directed District Health Authorities to set up and provide administrative support for Local Research Ethics Committees (LRECs) as independent groups to advise the authority on the ethics of research proposals to be undertaken on their premises.

However, after the establishment of the LREC network, criticism about the idiosyncratic approach of different localities continued (Harries 1994, Alberti 1995, Ahmed 1996). Large-scale clinical trials result in the same ethics committee application being submitted to many LRECs nationwide, with each one giving different ethical opinions and requiring separate changes. Researchers complained that beneficial progress was being inhibited by the ethics committee process. In 1997, Multicentre Research Ethics Committees (MRECs) were established to facilitate ethical review procedures in studies involving five or more LRECs (NHS Executive 1997). The idea was that large studies would be dealt with by one of eleven committees corresponding to health-care regions covering England, Wales, Scotland and Northern Ireland. Once MREC approval had been granted, LREC approval would still have to be sought but the study should be 'fast-tracked' and only locally relevant changes to the study could be requested. At the time of writing, this system is still in operation but is under review following continuing complaints from medical researchers that 'the cure has been worse than the disease' (Lux et al. 2000; Alberti 2000). For example, one national study with MREC approval submitted 125 LREC applications, each consisting of 15 separate documents totalling 96 pages. Different LRECs required up to 21 copies of the application, resulting in a grand total for the study of 105 888 pages costing £6133 in photo-copying, postage and paper. Replies from nine LRECs were still awaited six months later (Tulley et al. 2000).

Why do researchers bother with this system when there is no legal requirement for ethics committees to exist and no obligation in law for a researcher to apply for ethical approval? After all, the authority of such committees is informal and extra-legal. Their purpose is solely to advise National Health Service bodies such as NHS Trusts and family health service authorities on the ethics of proposed research projects.

The answer is that in practice, despite this quasi-legal status, ethics committees can wield considerable power. LRECS can veto any research on human subjects that come under their remit regardless of whether or not that research has been approved by any other ethics review body. Their decisions cannot be overruled by a higher authority, be it legal or professional. Funding bodies stipulate ethical approval as a mandatory condition of awarding grants and medical journals will not publish papers resulting from studies without ethical approval (International Committee of Medical Journal Editors 1991). The consequences to individual researchers of conducting research without ethical approval in Britain depends on their professional body and employers. For example, doctors in the UK can expect to be struck off the General Medical Register and lose their employment. In the USA, legislation is under way that will result in $250,000 fines for individual unauthorized researchers and $1,000,000 for their associated academic estab-lishments. The justification for these substantial powers rests in the principle of non-maleficence, that is, researchers must demonstrate to committees that they will not cause harm to subjects. The process of granting ethical approval seeks to apply internationally agreed 'safety' standards to the enormously varied remit of 'medical research'.

Research Ethics Committees: Current Practice

The guidelines state that an LREC must be consulted about any research proposal involving National Health Service (NHS) patient, past or present, including those treated under contracts with private-sector providers; foetal material and IVF involving NHS patients; the recently dead in NHS premises; access to records of past or present NHS patients and the use of, or potential access to, NHS premises or facilities (Department of Health 1991). How these categories came about is not clear, though the circular's origin from the government department responsible for the National Health Service explains the emphasis on this setting as the main remit of the powers of the LRECs. As the committees were established in order to advise district health authorities, it follows that their domain closely mirrors NHS boundaries as they seek to ensure that unethical practices are not carried out on their premises.

However, the fact that an ethics committee has been consulted does not protect the health authority or individual researchers from claims for damages arising from research projects. In theory, committee members could be held personally liable for injury to patients participating in research projects if it could be demonstrated that they did not make a reasonable enquiry of the research proposal. In practice, most members of the committee are employees of the NHS (see below) and so are covered by NHS indemnity arrangements. Those who are not NHS employees are advised to secure an undertaking that the health authority will take responsibility for their actions as a member of the LREC in any liability claim (Kennedy 1997). In recent inquiries into harm resulting from research studies (NHS Executive West Midlands Regional Office (Griffiths Report) 2000), attention has focused on the health authority and NHS Trust involved, with resulting disciplinary proceedings brought against four individual researchers via their professional bodies (General Medical Council and United Kingdom Central Council for Nursing, Midwifery and Health Visiting). Members of the LREC in this case were interviewed by the review panel and subsequently criticized in the report, but no further action was taken against them.

The remit for LRECs as defined by published guidelines emphasizes the identity of the subject of research as the primary concern. This is in line with international codes placing concern for 'the well-being of the subject' as the overriding principle. It is not the academic background of the researcher that marks the boundaries of the committee's jurisdiction but the subjects and settings of that research. However, this is confused by the Declaration of Helsinki also stating that:

> Biomedical research involving human subjects should be conducted only by scientifically qualified persons and under the supervision of a clinically competent medical person (World Medical Association 1964 [1996]).

There are no written definitions of these categories, such who is an NHS patient or a scientifically qualified person, or what is biomedical research. This is up to the committee members, as 'a reasonable body of independent experts', to judge.

Appointing members of the committee is essentially the task of the District Health Authority which has the responsibility for establishing the LREC and who also provides administrative support. Originally the specifications were eight to twelve people drawn from both sexes and a wide range of age groups including hospital medical staff, nursing staff, general practitioners and two or more lay persons (Department of Health 1991). Current guidelines include members with expertise in specific areas of research such as statisticians and qualitative researchers (*Manual for Research Ethics Committees*, Department of Health 1997). Health professionals are selected following consultation with local professional advisory committees (for example the hospital Trust management) and lay members after consultation with the Community Health Council (which itself consists of twenty-four members drawn from County and Local Authorities, voluntary organizations and private individuals appointed by the NHS Regional Executive). It is stipulated in the guidelines that at least one member 'should be unconnected professionally with health care and be neither an employee nor adviser of any NHS body'. The District health authority appoints a chair and vice-chair from the committee members, of which at least one must be a lay member. The appointments to the committee are all on a voluntary basis; members are paid for the work they do.

The LREC meets regularly to consider research proposals submitted on standard application forms, including a copy of the research protocol and other documents relevant to the research, such as consent forms, interview schedules, patient information sheets and invitation letters. They keep a register of all applications and produce an annual written report to the District Health Authority which is available for public inspection. The deliberations and minutes of the committee meetings are confidential though applicants are sometimes invited to submit evidence to the committee in person to clarify certain points. All applications are responded to in writing and reasons are given for decisions made by the committee.

The main points on which the Committee members must satisfy themselves are the scientific merit of the proposal; the effect on the health of the research subjects; that potential benefit is not outweighed by potential harm; the competence and responsibility of the researchers; the recruitment of subjects and inducements to participants such as payment; and procedures for obtaining consent, including adequate provision of information for the subject and ensuring confidentiality.

The Language of Ethics Committees

The language used by the ethics committees is rooted in the dialect of bio-medical research and the health service setting. This permeates the entire process through application on a standardized form to the decisions made by the committee members. An understanding and fluency in this language aids communication with the committee and lessens the likelihood of rejection resulting from mis-interpretation. The particularities of the context need to be attended to and handled with according respect.

Modernist ideology still dominates the discourse of medical knowledge as it does the Nuremberg Code and other international declarations, little changed since 1948. Research is taken to mean the advancement of scientific knowledge by experiment and the gathering of empirical data. All study protocols are expected to be in a traditional format with subheadings of aims, hypothesis, methods, expected results and clinical implications. The standardized forms require details aimed at assessing the statistical validity of results such as power calculations, outcome measures, inclusion and exclusion criteria. There are annexes devoted to the administration of radio-active substances and medical product licences. Because of this peculiar local dialect, applications written by non-medical researchers tend to be at a disadvantage.

The application forms for ethical approval reveal the expectation that the research methodology will be from biomedical rather than social sciences. For example, study design is selected from a list consisting of options such as random-ized controlled trial, cohort, case control or epidemiological analysis. There must be included in the application a protocol stating hypothesis, methods and relevance of results. Emphasis is placed on statistical power calculations, which indicate whether the study's results are generalizable from the sample to the general population. It is easy for the social scientist to become affronted by the constant querying of what he or she as an applicant believes to be obviously valid methods of inquiry. This can lead to oppositional stances and accusations of intellectual fascism, with haughty responses such as 'anthropologists don't need power calculations'. However, the consequences of this position is often rejection by the committee. I found it helpful to approach the ethics committee as if they were a group of 'tribal' elders who had a right to ask questions and expect responses to be couched in their own dialect. Respecting aboriginal beliefs is just as important in Britain as it is in more conventionally exotic settings.

The ethics committee application does emphasize the negotiation between participant and researcher in the research process. Being sensitive to the past history of abuse of medical power in this relationship, the ethics committee requires formal scrutiny and explicit statements from researchers regarding exactly what they want to do and why. Along with consent forms that are always a part of the application, the researcher has to write a participant information sheet and a separate invitation letter in simple, clear language. These are to be given to potential participants and must explain the purpose of the study, who is funding it, what will happen on agreeing to participate, the risks and benefits of taking part and what will happen to the results. It is not just the ethics committee that have the opportunity to judge whether or not the study is worthwhile; the participants themselves have that same opportunity.

Research proposals are divided into two groups based on whether the study is 'therapeutic' with the potential of direct benefit to the individual concerned (such as drug trials) or 'non-therapeutic', that is, of no immediate benefit to the individual but rather to society in general by improving the state of knowledge. There are greater restrictions on non-therapeutic research, the risk of harm to the subject must be 'no more than minimal'. This could be seen as privileging interventionist research such as pharmacological trials over investigative inquiry. The other side of the argument is that individuals should be protected from unnecessary experimentation particularly if they are not going to benefit personally from the results. Research proposals must clearly demonstrate the potential benefits, for both the individual and society, to be gained from the study. If this is not done the proposal is likely to be rejected as irrelevant and a waste of the subject's time and society's resources. Answering the 'so what?' question is crucial.

For researchers coming from a specialist world of their own where particular theoretical points are of great significance (such as anthropology), these concerns can seem crass. From the utilitarian perspective however, the argument is strong. LRECs tread a delicate line across duty, rights and pragmatism, seeking to balance the potential use of research for the 'greater good' with the principle of protecting an individual's rights over and above the concerns of society. These moral positions and their consequences are addressed in the *Manual for Research Ethics Committees* (Botros 1997) and in training sessions, though there is no requirement for LRECs to include a member with formal qualifications in ethics or moral philosophy. The majority of committee members come from a health-services profession background and undoubtedly their own personal experiences from clinical work will inform their preferences in moral reasoning.

The deliberations of the committee often centre around key terms which have other layers of meaning in this specialized setting in addition to their everyday English-language use. An example of this is the issue of 'consent'. The process of giving or withholding consent is the direct negotiation between the interests of the individual subject and the agenda of the researcher. The LREC's perspective on consent comes from the medical world of their origin. In this context, the word means more than agreement. Consent to taking part in research is seen by the ethics committee as equivalent to consent for medical treatment. From this model comes the traditional practice of formally recording this negotiation in writing by means of the subject's signature on a consent form. LRECs will expect researchers to ask all the people they approach in the course of their study to sign a consent form.

This view of consent is rooted in medical and legal definitions from English case-law. In Britain today, consent is considered legally valid only if it is based on adequate information, if it is voluntarily given and if the person consenting is competent to do so. If it can be demonstrated that any of these criteria are not met, there is a basis for a criminal prosecution for assault or a claim for damages in the tort of battery. All three of these conditions have been the subject of court proceedings arising from clinical cases over the last two decades of the twentieth century, resulting in specific definitions that are based on the wordings of these judgments. Such definitions are subject to change as legal challenges from individual cases result in new case-law. For example, the issue of whether a child under the age of sixteen has the capacity to give valid consent is currently directed by the case of Gillick v. West Norfolk and Wisbech AHA, 1986. This says that a child will be able to give consent providing he or she is sufficiently mature and intelligent enough to be able to understand what is involved in the treatment. However, a more recent case has established that while a competent child may have the capacity to consent and so accept treatment, his or her refusal to consent for treatment may be overridden by a parent (Re W, 1992). Case-law developments are summarized and updated in the *Manual for Research Ethics Committees*, so that members can refer to them in the course of their discussions.

Making an Application for Ethical Approval

My research concerns the category of people known in the British health profession as 'mentally disordered offenders'. This group crosses two boundaries, that of English law and that of ill health. The social demarcation of these borders is currently contested by different experts from the medical and legal professions, a matter of public debate in the media and the subject of policy proposals by the government. As members of this group are partly defined by contact with health services, they are 'patients' in the eyes of the LREC, regardless of the setting or conclusion of their psychiatric assessment. Also, the fact that I am a registered medical practitioner defined my proposed activity as medical research, though I had planned only to talk to people in an unstructured way and not to administer any experimental treatment. Without ethical approval, contact with my 'chosen people' would simply not be possible. However, the study also presented particular challenges in terms of gaining ethical approval. Subjects were complicated first by their legal status as convicted criminals or detainees under the Mental Health Act, and secondly in terms of their implied mental disorder impairing their capacity to consent. The proposal also presented the problem of using qualitative methodology in the form of unstructured in-depth interviews rather than standard quantitative measures.

The concerns of the ethics committee when confronted with a research proposal involving law-breaking people are a complex balance of protecting individuals' rights and recognizing that these people have, in the eyes of British society, forfeited those rights by violating others, and that the victims of their crimes also have rights. A prisoner is, from the perspective of the legal system, property of

Her Majesty's Government. If my research involved only talking to prisoners, I could have circumvented the entire ethics committee process since 'prisoners' are not 'patients'. The procedure for researchers gaining access to prisoners is by permission of the prison governor. This principle holds as long as researchers do not cross into the health-care wing of the prison, or look at inmates' medical records, as this transforms them into patients and brings them under the jurisdiction of the LREC. People's identity from the point of view of the LREC is here concretely defined by their place of residence and the professional background of those locking them up.

That aside, the LREC's concerns are that people within a state system of detention are vulnerable to exploitation by researchers and that the principle of voluntary participation might be compromised. Echoes from the Nuremberg trials here are strong. Inmates may think that if they do what researchers want, they may be treated differently so their consent is likely to be invalidated by coercion, be it real or imagined. This is compounded by the idea that these bad people may in some way benefit from the research process and so 'profit' from their crimes. In many medical research studies, payment is offered to subjects to compensate for their time or discomfort. This is always a tricky point for the committees, one person's compensation may be another's inducement affecting their voluntary consent. Guidelines are strict that there must never be payment for risk-taking. The idea of payment to prisoners in any form is likely to be hotly debated by the ethics committee. The British media's outraged reaction to the revelation that a life prisoner released on licence was paid by her biographer (Sereny 1998) illustrates the state of current public opinion on this subject. It is likely that the value-systems of individual committee members will be influenced by the dominant discourse of morality operating in British society and that this will impact upon decisions made.

Another concern raised by the committee in regard to the subject's criminal status was that of confidentiality. 'What if,' the committee asked me, 'when you were talking to one of these people they told you about a crime they had committed that no-one else knew about?' The dilemma is whether to respect the confidentiality of the individual over the rights of others to be protected from harm. It is taken for granted in medical research that all data obtained is confidential, and researchers are under a legal obligation not to reveal any information that may result in the identity of a research subject becoming known. Exceptions to this can occur with the subject's permission, or when disclosure is thought to be in the public's interest if they are at risk from the subject (W v. Egdell, 1989). The ethics committee was clear that I had to let people know before they agreed to talk to me that if they said certain things, I would not be able to guarantee their confidentiality. This again highlighted the fine differences operating in the perception of the person as patient or criminal and the underlying tension of moral judgements surrounding the mad::bad dichotomy.

Not all of the people that make up this group are imprisoned. Some have committed offences but received a Mental Health Act disposal and are sent to medium or high secure hospital instead of prison. Others have been violent but never charged with an offence and are detained in hospital, again under the terms of the Mental Health Act. In order for this to happen in Britain, a person must be suffering from a mental illness, mental impairment or psychopathic disorder in the opinion of two independent doctors and a social worker, all approved under the Mental Health Act 1983. This procedure of course raises all sorts of interesting questions on definitions of illness and rationality but from the perspective of the LREC, detention under the Mental Health Act implies a vulnerable person who may not have the capacity to give valid consent.

Ethics committees have specific guidelines on research proposals involving people detained under the Mental Health Act from both the Mental Health Act Commission and the Royal College of Psychiatrists. Both of these organizations take the view that if a person is detained under the Mental Health Act it does not necessarily follow that the person cannot give valid consent. Each person must be individually assessed, preferably each time he or she is involved in the study, as that person's capacity may fluctuate over time. There is intense current debate in the field of mental health over the definition of capacity to consent, provoked by the 'Bournewood' case (Re L, 1997). This judgment ruled against Bournewood Community and Mental Health NHS Trust to state that if persons did not have the capacity to consent they could only be admitted to hospital under a section of the Mental Health Act (as opposed to voluntary admission). This had enormous impact on the way psychiatric services operate in practice and was controversially overturned by the House of Lords (Ex parte L, 1998). Current case-law dictates that in order to have the capacity to consent you must be able to understand and retain information, be able to believe the information (although you can disagree with it), and be able to weigh the information as part of the process of arriving at a decision (Re C, 1994). Thus the concept of consent differs from its ordinary English-language use when used in the context of an LREC application, and then acquires a further level of meaning when referring to the consent of subjects from a mental health services setting.

The LREC expects this process to be attended to for all research involving patients detained in hospital under the Mental Health Act. If, after an assessment of his or her capacity to consent, a patient is found to be incompetent, then he or she cannot be involved in non-therapeutic research as this, by virtue of being non-therapeutic, can never be in the individual's best interest (Re F, 1990). In practice, this means that research applications involving detained psychiatric patients need to reassure the Committee that they have addressed this issue with each subject prior to the research event. In practice LRECs are usually happy with the proviso that subjects will not be approached without the agreement of their clinical team as they are seen as the experts on each individual's capacity to consent and the guardians of their patients from research exploitation. Indeed, committees nearly always stipulate that the first approach to the subject about the study must come from somebody they already know, usually their own doctor. Thus even if ethical approval has been granted, negotiations to gain access continue.

Conclusion

Applying for ethical approval of this study seemed a prolonged uphill struggle to achieve meaningful contact with my 'people' for the purpose of research data that could be processed within academic anthropology. To which, 'Well, what do you expect if your people are criminally insane?' might be a typical response. But this crude label demonstrates the point. The difference between talking to a native of the British Isles and a native of the British Isles who is also a patient in a high-security hospital is determined by British social structure as well as by the individual's past actions. The bureaucratic procedures that make such people different from others has to be part of an analysis of this group. If we look closely we can see the social structure is a complex interweaving of medical and legal discourse that shape and are shaped by individual people or 'cases'.

The very fact that institutions such as the LRECs exist in Britain and encompass this particular group of people (so as to contain and regulate ordinary contact) is part of the boundary that makes them a distinct group. The layers of medical and legal procedures help to constitute their identities as different individuals in our society. The process of the ethics committee application mirrors the conflicting position of mentally disordered offenders in British society as both victim and perpetrator. Most of the time medical research ethics committees perceive patients as vulnerable sick people disadvantaged in their interactions with powerful doctors. In the case of psychiatric patients, this vulnerability is further compounded by their assumed mental incompetence. However, mentally disordered offenders detained in secure psychiatric hospitals are also people who have 'dangerous, violent or criminal propensities' (NHS Act 1977) confined in order to protect the public. Hence the ethics committee's ambivalence towards this group over issues such as confidentiality, balancing the rights of the patient with the rights of the public. In this way, the ethics committee application became an enactment on a small scale of the moral concerns of British society attempting to negotiate the rights of the individual with those of others.

The existence of the LREC structure in Britain certainly constructs the production of medical knowledge. There are restrictions placed on research carried out in British health-services settings that are determined by a local committee's interpretation of international codes and English case-law in the light of individual members' experiences. This can cause practical problems for researchers from disciplines such as anthropology. The LRECs have particular value-systems and use certain words in a way that is specific to their specialist context. If these are not understood then communication and negotiation to enter a setting may fail. Fieldwork in a health-care setting is not as straightforward as many assume.

However LRECs are not only a mechanism for the wielding of power by a specialist group but also an attempt by society to limit the power of specialists and hold them accountable. The process of gaining permission to carry out a study is not simply the equivalent of a prolonged, bureaucratically laden journey to an exotic location. Fieldwork in Britain begins with the process of recognizing how the category of the other is created and maintained. Formal procedures involved in making these distinctions, such as the research ethics committee system, can be an invaluable guide to the position of both the researcher and the subject in that society. The ethics committee is more than a technical hitch, it is a group that polices the borders between many different types of 'us' and 'them'.

References

Ahmed, A. and Nicholson, K. (1996) 'Delays and Diversity in the Practice of Local Research Ethics Committees', *Journal of Medical Ethics* 22: 263–6.
Alberti, K. (1995) 'Local Research Ethics Committees, *BMJ* 311:639–40.
—— (2000) 'Multicentre Research Ethics Committees: Has the Cure been Worse than the Disease?', *BMJ* 320: 1157–8.
Annas, G. and Grodin, M. (1992) *The Nazi Doctors and the Nuremberg Code*, New York: Oxford University Press.
Bloch, M. (1988) 'Interview with G. Houtman', *Anthropology Today* 4(1): 18–21.
Botros, S. (1997) 'Ethics in Medical Research: Uncovering the Conflicting Approaches', in *Manual for Research Ethics Committees*, London: Centre of Medical Law and Ethics.
Britan, G. and Cohen, R. (eds) (1980) *Hierarchy and Society: Anthropological Perspectives on Bureaucracy,* Philadelphia: Institute for the Study of Human Issues.
Charatan, F. (2000) 'Clinton Seeks Heavy Fines for Breaching Research Ethics', *BMJ* 320: 1491.
Council of Europe (1997) *Convention for the Protection of Human Rights and Dignity of the Human Being with regard to the Application of Biology and Medicine (Convention on Human Rights and Biomedicine)*, Oviedo: Council of Europe.
Department of Health (1991) *Local Research Ethics Committees*, HSG (91)5, London: HMSO.
Donnan, H. and McFarlane, G. (1989) *Social Anthropology and Public Policy in Northern Ireland*, Aldershot: Avebury.

Fuller, C. (1988) 'Hinduism and Scriptural Authority in Modern Indian Law', *Comparative Studies in Society and History* 30: 225–48.

Gilbert, C., Fulford, K. and Parker, C. (1989) 'Diversity in the Practice of District Ethics Committees, *BMJ* 299: 1437–9.

Gillick v. West Norfolk and Wisbech AHA [1986] AC 112.

Grillo, R. (ed.) (1980) *'Nation' and 'State' in Europe: Anthropological Perspectives*, London: Academic Press.

Harries, U., Fentem, P., Tuxworth, W. and Hoinville, G. (1994) 'Local Research Ethics Committees: Widely Differing Responses to a National Survey Protocol', *Journal of the Royal College of Physicians* 28:150–4.

Herzfeld, M. (1992) *The Social Production of Indifference: Exploring the Symbolic Roots of Western Bureaucracy*, Oxford: Berg.

International Committee of Medical Journal Editors (1991) 'Uniform Requirements for Manuscripts Submitted to Biomedical Journals', *New England Medical Journal* 324: 424–8.

Kennedy, I., (1997) 'Research Ethics Committees and the Law', in: *Manual for Research Ethics Committees*, London: Centre of Medical Law and Ethics.

Leach E. R. (ed.) (1968) *Dialectic in Practical Religion*, London: Cambridge University Press.

Lock, S. (1995) 'Research Ethics – A Brief Historical Review to 1965', *Journal of International Medicine* 238 (6): 513–20.

Lux, A., Edwards, S. and Osbourne, J. (2000) 'Responses of Local Research Ethics Committees (LRECs) to a Study with Multicentre Research Ethics Committee Approval', *BMJ* 320: 1182–3.

Medical Research Council, (1964) *Responsibility in Investigations on Human Subjects: Report of the MRC for the year 1962–1963,* London: HMSO.

Ministry of Health (1968) 'Supervision of the Ethics of Clinical Research', *HM* (68) 33, London: HMSO.

Mitscherlich, M. and Mielke, F. (1949) *Doctors of Infamy: The Story of the Nazi Medical Crimes,* New York: Schuman.

NHS Act 1977.

NHS Executive (1997) 'Ethics Committee Review of Multicentre Research. Establishment of Multicentre Research Ethics Committees', *HSG* (97)23, Leeds: NHSE.

NHS Executive (2000) *Report of a Review of the Research Framework In North Staffordshire Hospital NHS Trust (Griffiths Report)*, West Midlands: NHSE.

Okely, J. (1996) *Own or Other Culture,* London: Routledge.

R v Bournewood Community and Mental Health NHS Trust. Ex part L. House of Lords judgement 25 June 1998.

Re C (Adult: Refusal of Medical Treatment) [1994] 1 All ER 819.

Re F (a mental patient: sterilization) [1990] 2 AC 1.

Re L [1997] EWCA 4485 (2nd December, 1997)

Re W (a minor) (refusal of treatment) [1992] 4 All ER 33.

Richards, A. and Robin, J. (1975) *Some Elmdon Families*, Saffron Walden: Audrey Richards.

Royal College of Physicians (1967, updated 1973) *Supervision of the Ethics of Clinical Research Investigations in Institutions*, London: HMSO.

Sereny, G., (1998) *Cries Unheard: The Story of Mary Bell*, London: Macmillan.

Shore, C. and Wright, S. (eds.) (1997) *Anthropology of Policy: Perspectives on Governance and Power,* London: Routledge.

Tulley, J., Ninis, N., Booy, R., Viner, R. (2000) 'The New System of Review by Multicentre Research Ethics Committees: Prospective Study', *BMJ* 320: 1179–82.

Vollmann, J. and Winau, R. (1996) 'Informed Consent in Human Experimentation before the Nuremberg Code', *BMJ* 313: 1945–7.

W v. Egdell [1990] 1 All ER 835.

World Medical Association (1964, amended Tokyo 1975, Venice 1983, Hong Kong 1989 and South Africa 1996) *Declaration of Helsinki: Recommendations Guiding Physicians in Biomedical Research Involving Human Subjects,* Helsinki: World Medical Association.

–12–

Cultural Values and Social Organization in Wales: Is Ethnicity the Locus of Culture?

Carol Trosset and *Douglas Caulkins*

In recent years, the study of values has assumed a more central place in social science (Huntington and Lawrence 2000; Inglehardt 1998). For anthropologists, however, values are frequently subsumed under notions of cultural and behavioural norms. Something like values have reappeared as psychological anthropologists have paid increasing attention to concepts of personhood (the social meanings of being a good human individual in a particular culture), and to the ways that these vary between cultures. Much fascinating work has been done on these topics, but little has been said about how these concepts vary within a single culture. For example, one question left unanswered by Abu-Lughod (1986) is that of variability with respect to the value on honour; when Awlad 'Ali individuals are described as being criticized for lacking honour, we are not told whether they see themselves as lacking or if they as individuals have different priorities. Riesman (1992) speaks of *pulaaku* (self-restraint, acting Fulani) as if it had a fixed definition, yet presents evidence of shifting meanings and values (people can be distinguished from one another by the extent of *pulaaku* shown).

When confronted with untypical or negatively valued acts, most Welsh people tend to assume that the actor shares their values but fails to realize them in behaviour. This is not always correct. Anthropologists often also tacitly assume that individuals differ in their behaviours but not in their motivating concepts and values. Avoiding this error requires that the study of values be empirically grounded at the level of the individual, and that it be situated in theories that assume the presence of diversity and contestation. Cultural Marxist approaches to the study of hegemonic ideologies (see Brow 1996: 10–32) are well suited to the study of values. In Wales, the positive valuing of egalitarianism, martyrdom, performance, emotionalism, and nostalgia are central to people's experiences of life (Trosset 1993). However, their significance is not that of underlying cultural 'truths' but that of dominant, though contested, ideologies. The hegemonic discourse about these values not only assumes them to be universal among the Welsh, but makes the further assumption that attitudes toward these values vary with ethnic identity. Our research was designed to test both the hegemonic status of particular values in Wales, and the native assumption that these values are correlated with ethnic identity.

Background

We begin with brief descriptions of four hegemonic Welsh cultural values identified by Trosset:

Egalitarianism.   Here all people are seen as equal and as linked by personal relationships rather than by their status roles. This concept is in some sense an idealization of how Welsh people like to think of themselves. However, otherwise important status differences are effectively minimized in everyday life by various prescribed ways of acting. This relative lack of attention to social hierarchy is something many Welsh people value about their culture and which they cite as making them better people than the English, with their self-avowed class-consciousness.

Martyrdom.   The most highly valued personal acts are those done on behalf of the group. Ideas about the relationship of the individual to the group suggest a preference for people to be predictable and potentially controllable by the community. Self-sacrifice on behalf of others is idealized. Sacrificial actions need not be successful; in fact success is often suspect as a possible indication that a person has been acting, not on behalf of the group, but in the pursuit of his or her own gain.

Emotionalism.   The expression of emotional bonds and commitments is often taken as a sign that a person is fully human in an appropriately Welsh way. The governing value might be stated as 'Anything to do with people should be approached emotionally', or 'Emotional engagement is the correct approach to people'. Despite the belief that public performance may not accurately reflect inner experience, expressions of feelings are generally taken as proof that a person has had a strong emotional response to a situation rather than remaining detached (which is considered bad). Emotion is also an approved motive for many types of action, and the emotional intensity of many such actions is considered a uniquely Welsh attribute.

Performance.   It is generally believed that people's behaviours, including many of their expressions of emotion, do not accurately reflect their inner experiences, but that people intentionally behave very differently in public than in private. It is also assumed that Welsh people are predisposed to be good at certain types of public artistic performance. The ability to control one's public presentation of self may be prized as useful, but it also makes possible what is termed 'artificial' behaviour, in which public behaviour and private feelings are seen as diverging 'too' widely and which is severely criticized.

Trosset does not argue that any of these views is uniquely Welsh, or that every Welsh person supports these views of personhood. Her claim is (1) that each is considered by many Welsh people to be intimately related to notions of Welshness, and (2) that each sufficiently dominates the cultural ethos that everyone, even those who do not share them, must confront them in everyday life and conduct discourses about Welshness in a way that acknowledges the dominance of these assumptions and values.

In the summer of 1993, we returned to Wales as a research team, to investigate how the concepts defined by Trosset were distributed among residents of Wales of all ethnic and linguistic groups. We decided to employ methods that contrasted with Trosset's prior ethnographic immersion study, and which included consensus analysis (described below), as it is a statistical technique designed to measure levels of agreement between subjects. For research settings we selected two towns in the Western Welsh-speaking area (Bowie 1993), one ('Llanwyn') in the northern and one (Lampeter) in the southern region. With a population of several thousand each, both were large enough for diversity and were minor sites of Trosset's original study. Trosset's book (*Welshness Performed*, 1993) had not yet been published and no one in these towns was familiar with her interpretations of Welsh person-hood. Caulkins had previously worked in Wales studying high-technology entrepreneurs but none of the firms he had studied were located in these towns. The senior researchers recruited six undergraduate student assistants who had special training for the project. Three worked with Trosset in the northern site and three with Caulkins in the southern site. Trosset interviewed Welsh-speakers in Welsh; the rest of the team interviewed in English. The team followed a snowball sampling strategy, asking consultants to suggest other potential interviewees who might have a different perspective. We also developed a sampling frame that represented diversity of class, gender, and ethnic identity, obtaining a sample of 152 residents, approximately half from each location.

Designing a structured interview made it necessary that we identify features of the four concepts that could be evaluated by people in Wales. We decided not to use descriptive statements characterizing the concepts, as these would be subject to multiple (mis)interpretations (by Trosset in the original description, by Trosset and Caulkins together in the framing of the interview, and by each Welsh person being interviewed). Instead, we developed scenarios that illustrated the concepts. Most of these described events that Trosset had observed during her earlier fieldwork. Thus, in the triangulation study we asked interviewees to re-examine directly data used to formulate Trosset's original interpretations of Welsh concepts and values. We also introduced a few scenarios drawn from our lives in America, which illustrated behaviour we believed to be uncharacteristic of Welsh culture.

We also added a fifth concept. Egalitarianism, martyrdom, performance, and emotionalism are, in our view, observable in Welsh culture and are, to varying degrees, consciously associated with Welsh ethnicity, but none of the four is a marked category in the Welsh language or in ordinary speech about the culture. (Emotionalism is the most consciously salient, and martyrdom the least so.) However, there is one emotion word, *hiraeth,* that is frequently used and is considered so closely linked to the Welsh character and experience as to be untranslatable. It refers to the sadness felt for something that has been lost, and will be glossed here as 'nostalgia'. It has many possible objects, including dead or otherwise distanced people, or the cultural past of Wales. Feeling *hiraeth* for certain objects, such as one's family, is taken to be a sign of being fully human. As such, nostalgia should be viewed as a subset of emotionalism, as one of the several emotions that is considered appropriate both to experience and to enact. In our interview and in this analysis, however, it has been treated as a distinct concept.

Our eventual interview, then, consisted of the following scenarios, here grouped by the relevant concept:

Egalitarianism

1. Members of a small community assume that a newcomer with aristocratic family connections will not be a likeable person.
2. A schoolteacher, while shopping, modifies her speech in an attempt to avoid sounding more educated than the shop employees.
3. A university professor has tea in his kitchen with the workers who are repairing his garden wall.
4. An employee of a firm is pleased because he wins a promotion which gives him authority over other workers.
5. A child is discovered in tears after receiving third prize in a local competition.

Martyrdom

6. A woman regularly buys petrol at the higher of two available local prices, because the owner of that shop is a member of the same religious denomination.
7. A mother, who needs a new winter coat, goes without so that her not-very-talented daughter can continue her piano lessons.
8. A young man goes dancing and has a good time. The next day he feels guilty about having enjoyed himself so much.

9. A person chooses a career and a place to live based on the opportunity they provide for a high salary and job advancement.

Emotionalism

10. A middle-aged farmer speaks in hushed tones about how moved he is by the words of a hymn.
11. A young man decides to study singing after hearing an outstanding performance by a local tenor.
12. Two women fight bitterly because of their opposing political views.
13. A published letter from a newspaper reader asserts that one should argue social policy from the heart, not from the head.

Nostalgia

14. An older couple returns every year to their childhood community to visit the graves of their parents.
15. After five years in the city, a bank clerk still feels a bit homesick every Sunday as he thinks about his parents and sister having dinner without him.
16. A farmer often drives up at sunset to look at the ruins of an old fortress that stands on his property.
17. When an old couple dies, their adult children clear out the house before selling it, and toss old things like family photographs in the dustbin.

Performance

18. A family unloads their removal van from the back alley to prevent the neighbours from seeing their belongings.
19. At her parents' request, a small child stands on a kitchen stool, smiles at the family guests, and sings a song she recently learned at school.
20. A man, who wants to be the president of a local organization, disclaims any interest in power or prestige.
21. A shop owner often tells his customers that he is not interested in making a large profit.

In our interview we asked residents of the two Welsh towns two questions for each scenario: to describe the degree to which the behaviour and attitudes displayed seemed 'Welsh' to them, and to rate the degree to which they personally valued each behaviour (how 'good' it seemed). Ratings were done using an ascending 5-point Likert scale: a scenario rated 4 or 5 would be considered 'very good behaviour' (or very Welsh) while another scenario rated 1 or 2 would be considered not highly valued (or not very Welsh).

The design enabled us to analyse the aggregated results using consensus analysis, a technique that describes patterns of agreement or disagreement among individuals concerning a domain or category of knowledge (Romney, Weller and Batchelder 1986). A high level of agreement about the positive or negative value of each scenario would indicate a shared cultural understanding of that domain. In contrast, however, opinions about this domain might not be shared. They could be contested, distributed in different subcultures, characterized by weak agreement, or randomly distributed (Caulkins and Hyatt 1999). In the present case, however, we found a single-culture level of agreement about both the positive value and the Welshness of the concepts exemplified in the scenarios.

Using the ANTHROPAC (Borgatti 1992) consensus analysis module, we factor analysed the similarity matrix of the ratings of the 152 consultants from the two towns. For Welshness, the first factor accounted for 64.1 per cent of the variance while the second, and much smaller, factor accounted for only 18.4 per cent of the variance (Table 12.1). According to the interpretive conventions adopted in consensus analysis, if the first factor is three times larger than the second factor, we can say that there is a cultural level of agreement about the domain in the sampled population. As shown in Table 12.1, the ratio between the first and second factors is 3.481, so we can say that we have evidence of a widespread cultural level of agreement about Welsh behaviour.

Table 12.1 Factor Analysis of Ratings of 'Welshness' of Scenarios of Combined Samples (N=152)

Factor	Eigenvalue	Percent of variance explained	Cumulative Percentage	Ratio
1	39	64.1	64.1	3.481
2	11.204	18.4	82.6	1.057
3	10.605	17.4	100.0	
Total	60.809	100.0		

Average knowledge score = 0.460

Table 12.2 Factor Analysis of Ratings of Desirability of Scenarios in Combined Samples (N=151)

Factor	Eigenvalue	Percent of variance explained	Cumulative Percentage	Ratio
1	59.105	77.8	77.8	6.418
2	9.209	12.1	89.9	1.204
3	7.646	10.1	100.0	
Total	75.961	100.0		

Average knowledge score = 0.460

We found a much stronger level of agreement about what constituted good, highly valued, behaviour (Table 12.2). Here, the first factor accounted for 77.8 per cent of the variance, while the second accounted for only 12.1 per cent. The ratio between the first and second factors was a very high 6.418, showing a remarkable degree of shared values in the society. Put simply, residents in our research communities tend to agree on the ratings of each of the scenarios. ANTHROPAC produces a list of the 'culturally correct' ratings for each of the scenarios. These 'culture keys', combined with explanatory comments by inter-viewees, enabled us to refine our understandings of the concepts. These did not, however, change substantially from the descriptions given above.

The Search for Subcultures

Given a strong central tendency in both personal values and perceptions of Welshness, our next step was to search for any sociological variables that might define subcultures with distinct views. This analysis was limited to data from the northern site, since Lampeter, as a college town, has a demographic profile that is less typical of Welsh towns in general. This left the southern town on which to test any theories we developed from the analysis of the northern data.[1]

Residents of Wales make frequent distinctions between three groups: Welsh-speakers, non-Welsh-speakers of Welsh ancestry (often referred to as Anglo-Welsh), and English immigrants. The respective 'Welshness' of the Welsh-speakers and the Anglo-Welsh is a common topic of debate, and some immigrants claim a Welsh identity by virtue of residence. The three groups are often assumed to differ not only in their degree of Welshness but also in their personal qualities and preferred styles of interaction. Therefore, we began by testing the native hypothesis that these three groups would form subcultures with respect to their views of the concepts measured by our interview.

We found very little support for the existence of ethnic subcultures. Each of the three groups showed a single-culture level of agreement with respect to the value they placed on the scenarios, but their ratings correlated at over 0.9 (significant at p<.01). In other words, the three ethnic subgroups value the same behaviours. In their definitions of Welshness, slight differences were apparent, but not significant. Fifty Welsh-speakers and 41 English immigrants each showed single-culture agreement (with ratios of 4.3 and 3.2, respectively), but the 35 Anglo-Welsh did not form a single culture. This makes ethnographic sense, since the widespread use of language-based definitions of Welsh identity leave non-Welsh-speaking people of Welsh ancestry in a somewhat ambiguous position, sometimes reflected in their self-images. The ratings of Welshness that describe the central views of the Anglo-Welsh and the English correlated highly significantly at 0.983. The central views of Welsh-speakers correlated less highly (0.709 with the

Anglo-Welsh and 0.722 with the English), but these were still highly significant at p<.05. The English tended to value the behaviours less than the other two groups, but these differences were minor.

Turning to other demographic differences that might prove culturally salient, we failed to find any differences between the 58 males and the 72 females in the sample. Males did not quite demonstrate single-culture agreement on their views of Welshness (ratio 2.67), but the central views of the sexes on both parameters were highly significantly correlated. Age also proved insignificant, though we did find some evidence of change over time by dividing the sample into generations (age 60+, 40–59, 23–39, and 11–22). For example, only the older generations remembered the days when someone might have felt guilty about having a good time dancing. These few differences, however, were not sufficient to define the generations as distinct subcultures.

Turning to religion, our sample in this town included 44 members of the Church in Wales (affiliated with the English Anglican Church), 34 members of various chapel (Protestant) denominations, and 37 who did not claim any religious identity. The values profiles of all three groups were very highly correlated, as were their definitions of Welshness. The individuals from no particular religious affiliation had slightly less than single-culture agreement about Welshness, which is not surprising since, with neither church nor chapel membership, they were likely to have a less structured experience of the community. It was interesting that the chapelgoers gave the lowest rating of the Welshness of scenario no. 10, in which a middle-aged farmer speaks emotionally about the moving words of a hymn. Since chapel membership is steadily declining, it seems likely that these respondents were perceiving the farmer in question as part of a shrinking minority and therefore no longer particularly Welsh. This interpretation is supported by the fact that this scenario's Welshness received progressively lower ratings from each younger generation. (The behaviour was also less valued by younger respondents, though to a lesser degree.)

The distinction between the middle and working classes is certainly salient in Wales, though its significance is not the same as in England (Trosset 1993: 79–89; Williams 1978: 253–67). Nevertheless, here again we found no major differences, except that the 25 working-class individuals were slightly less in agreement about their views of Welshness than were the 66 middle-class members of the sample. Local members of Rotary (men) and Inner Wheel (women) were identifiable as a sort of higher-class network, and the 15 individuals we interviewed were one of the only subgroups that did not show single-culture agreement (as defined technically in consensus analysis) in the values they placed on the scenarios. They did, however, agree as a single culture on the Welshness of the behaviours described, showing that these individuals, despite their ethnic and other differences, have at least this aspect of cultural perceptions in common. (Members of Rotary come from all three ethnic/linguistic groups but all hold professional jobs, which place them and their spouses high on the local social scale.)

Class is closely linked to education level in Britain, so we evaluated education as a separate sociological distinction. The group of 36 individuals who left school at age fifteen, and the group of 31 individuals with a university degree each formed a single culture with respect both to the value of the scenarios and to their Welshness. Their central views were highly correlated, but showed a few interesting differences. Most notable was the tendency of the university-educated to rate both the positive value and the Welshness of the 'homesickness' scenario (no. 15) more highly. Since these people are the most likely to be living at some distance from their families of origin, they may have more experience of being homesick and therefore also see it as more typical of the Welsh experience. Though valuing nostalgia highly, the university-educated were less likely to value being motivated by emotions (expressed in scenario no. 13), or to consider such motivation as highly Welsh.

Our education analysis included a third 'group' made up of the 32 individuals who had completed either A-levels, technical college, or teacher's college but not gone on to university. These people were the least convergent of any sociologically defined group that we investigated. Their definitions of Welshness showed less than single-culture agreement, and their personal values regarding the scenarios failed to converge at all, an astonishing finding given the extremely high factor ratio (4.95) for the entire 132-person sample. This was the only group we found with such low convergence. However, as for the people with no religious affiliation, there is no apparent reason why those who have completed one of several unrelated intermediate levels of education should be expected to hold the same views of anything.

Many people refused to tell us which political party they supported, but we did interview 17 Conservatives, 20 Labour supporters, 21 Liberals, and 15 Welsh Nationalists. Here at last we find groups with different interview results. Labour supporters and Liberals show very high levels of internal agreement about values (factor ratios of 5.5 and 6.1, respectively). Conservatives fall just below single-culture agreement (2.9), but Welsh Nationalists are definitely divided subculturally in their values, with a ratio of 2.05. Conversely, Conservative, Labour and Liberal party supporters all fail to reach single-culture agreement in their views of Welshness, while nationalists are highly unified with a ratio of 4.89.

Political affiliation is itself a measure of views and values, but it only correlates some of the time with the five concepts we were measuring. The Nationalists, with their high agreement on Welshness and somewhat divergent personal values, formed the most visible subculture. In general, we see a trend for ascribed statuses such as age, sex, and ethnicity to be insignificant indicators of differences; partially

ascribed statuses such as religion and class (heavily influenced by family background, but also subject to individual actions) to be slightly more significant;
and fully achieved statuses such as Rotary membership, education level, and
political affiliation to be the most related to personal values and perceptions of
Welshness.

It seems clear that demographic distinctions are inadequate to account for
internal cultural diversity in this case. The very high agreement ratios for the
interview sample as a whole suggest that perhaps there is no diversity that needs
to be accounted for, but this is not the case. Besides giving factor ratios defining
levels of internal agreement, ANTHROPAC consensus analysis software also
assigns a 'cultural knowledge' or 'cultural centrality' score to each individual,
indicating how close his or her views are to the general consensus. For Welshness,
the mean cultural knowledge score is 0.46 (standard deviation = 0.213), indicating
that, on average, individuals were in agreement with the consensus answers slightly
less than one half of the time. For the values profile, however, the mean cultural
knowledge or cultural centrality score was higher, 0.58 (standard deviation = 0.224),
indicating that, on average, individuals were in agreement with the consensus
score slightly more than half of the time. Given this range of divergence on both
the Welshness and values scales, we need to look more carefully at the meaning
of high and low knowledge scores on these scales.

A Better Way to Describe Intra-cultural Diversity

By eliminating any assumptions about the significance of demographic groups,
and focusing instead on the views of individuals, we were able to use the centrality
scores of respondents to determine where each was situated with respect to the
local hegemonic values and views of Welshness. We can think of each person as
having a position on each of these two dimensions. One might be very close to the
cultural consensus on both dimensions, on one or the other of the dimensions, or
on neither. In the first case, the individual is responding with commitment to or
engagement with both cultural models (the culturally committed). In the second
and third cases the individual is responding in ways that either affirm the hegemonic
values and deny the accuracy of the shared description of Welshness (culture
critics), or affirm the shared description of Welshness and reject the shared values
(culture rebels). In the final case, the individual rejects both cultural models
and offers an idiosyncratic vision of both Welshness and values (the culturally
disengaged). These four responses are not just logically possible ways of being
situated ideologically in the local culture; they occur empirically. By comparing
individuals' knowledge scores on the two parameters, we were able to identify
individuals with each of the four ideological orientations.

When placed in rank order, centrality scores showed a natural gap in both categories at between 0.50 and 0.55. This supported our intuition that it is possible to classify some people as central in their views and others as marginal. Out of 130 respondents in the northern town, 100 had highly central personal values and 80 had highly central views of Welshness. When we combined the two positions of each individual, 65 (50 per cent) were highly central in both areas, 35 (27 per cent) had central personal values but divergent views of Welshness, 14 (11 per cent) had central views of Welshness but divergent personal values, and 16 (12 per cent) were marginal in both domains.

The Culturally Committed

This group, with highly central values and views of Welshness, is closest to the consensus view for the entire community sample. Like the sample overall, the culturally committed see good behaviour and Welshness in very similar terms, with characteristic Welshness slightly exceeding what is considered desirable (except with respect to egalitarianism, where the Welsh are seen as falling slightly short of the ideal). Their view might be expressed by saying 'This is how people should be, and the Welsh are like that and more so'.

Members of all ethnic groups are found in this quadrant. However, nearly half are Welsh-speakers, and more than half of all Welsh-speakers are situated here. These statistics define the culture to which these people are committed as a demonstrably *Welsh* culture. Other sociological groups that are overrepresented here, besides Welsh-speakers, include women, people over age 60, chapelgoers, the university-educated, and Nationalists. The most noticeably underrepresented group is the young adults (age 23–39).

The Culture Critics

These people share the values of the culturally committed, but do not agree with them that the Welsh live up to these values. Unlike most other subgroups we measured, this 27 per cent of the total sample thinks the Welsh are *under*-doing it. They hold the view that 'yes, that's how people should be, but the Welsh aren't as much that way as I'd like'.

In general, the critics see the Welsh as less emotional than the committed do, and also as less emotional than would be desirable. This view is particularly evidenced by their views of the mother, hymn, heart, and photo scenarios (nos 7, 10, 13 and 17). Welsh-speakers are fairly evenly represented in this quadrant, while the Anglo-Welsh are overrepresented.

The Culture Rebels

These people agree with the committed in their description of Welshness. However, they do not agree that this behaviour is desirable, nor do they agree with each other about any other definition of valued behaviour. They each seem to be saying, 'The Welsh are like that, but I have my own agenda'.

The one value clearly shared by this group is a dislike of performance. They give scenario no. 19, in which a child sings while standing on a stool, a typically high Welshness score, but valued it by far the lowest of any subgroup. Their views on other values are too divergent to be described meaningfully.

Welsh-speakers are found here in representative numbers, while Nationalists are overrepresented. This might be expected in a group of rebels (people who understand the culture but wish to change it). There are many underrepresented sociological groups, mostly those who dominate in the previous quadrants, as well as the working class and those who left school at age 15.

The Culturally Disengaged

These people agree neither about their own values nor about how to describe Welshness. They seem almost uninterested in the local culture that surrounds them. Predictably, Welsh-speakers are underrepresented, as are the other groups heavily represented among the committed. The three Welsh-speakers who appear in this quadrant come close to sharing the views of the committed.

We found only two types of people who are significantly likely to be disengaged in this community, sharing neither each other's values nor their views of Welshness. One such group is shop owners. Of 14 shop owners interviewed in this town, six (43 per cent) were culturally disengaged (as opposed to only 12 per cent of the entire sample). These six were a mix of Anglo-Welsh, English and foreigners, and did not share their other sociological descriptors either. What they shared was their entrepreneurial energy, an unusual commodity in Welsh towns. Many people of all three ethnic groups pointed out to us that most of the shop owners in this town were not Welsh, and even Welsh-speakers tended to attribute this imbalance to 'the Welsh' being unwilling to take risks. It seems likely that to be a capitalist in a small Welsh community may actually require one to disengage from certain dominant cultural values, especially martyrdom and the idea that one should be motivated by emotion.

The underrepresentation of culturally committed Welsh within the management levels of business and industry is also reflected in a long-term study of high technology entrepreneurs in mid-Wales in which few native Welsh entrepreneurs were found (Caulkins 1992, Caulkins and Weiner 1999). The majority of the entrepreneurs in mid-Wales were English immigrants from the Midlands. The barriers to technological business and manufacturing for Welsh-speakers seem to be cultural as well as structural. This problem has not escaped the notice of Welsh development agencies, which have helped establish *Menter a Busnes,* a Welsh-speaking organization dedicated to creating a 'long term action based programme to make sure that Welsh language culture adapts itself creatively in terms of economic attitudes and activities' (*Menter a Busnes* 1996). Studies funded by *Menter a Busnes* reveal that Welsh-speakers are unlikely to go into commerce unless their families are already in business and that 'Welsh-speakers are more likely [than others] to see their business in subjective terms' (*Menter a Busnes* 1993: 1).

New arrivals form the other heavily disengaged group. A full half of all those who had lived in mid-Wales for less than two years were disengaged, while none were culturally committed. Among those present for three or four years, only 14 per cent were disengaged, while 29 per cent were committed and 57 per cent were critics. The proportion of disengaged drops to only 6 per cent among those resident for 5–10 years, while half of this group are committed. Most members of our sample had lived in the region for more than ten years, and of them 55 per cent were committed, with only 11 per cent (a representative number) disengaged. This figures suggest that some process of acculturation may be taking place, perhaps in combination with a process of self-selection. Those who do not come to share the local values are presumably less likely to stay, unless they are sufficiently committed to Welsh culture to remain as rebels, or sufficiently indifferent to it to disengage from other people's concerns. Few people fall into either of these categories.

Benefits of the Quadrant Model for Describing Intra-cultural Diversity

Applying the quadrant model to the southern town helps to illuminate both the cultural differences between the two research sites and the usefulness of this way of describing cultural diversity. The first thing we find is that the quadrants assume different proportions in the two towns (Table 12.3). The northern, more 'typical' town, has proportionally more committed and critics (who all share the dominant values), while the southern town has many more disengaged members.

The relationship between quadrant membership and ethnic identity further illuminates the differences between the two towns. Table 12.4 shows, for each site, how many of the members of each quadrant belong to each ethnic group.

In the northern site, committed, critics and rebels are all comprised of fairly balanced numbers of the three ethnic groups. Most of the disengaged, who appear quite detached from the dominant local culture, are themselves ethnically Welsh and speak the language. The socio-cultural makeup of the southern town is quite different. Here, committed and critics, who share the dominant cultural values,

Table 12.3 Distribution of Persons Within Quadrants for Two Towns

Quadrant Types	Combined 21 scenarios	Northern town 21 scenarios	Northern town 10 scenarios	Southern town 21 scenarios
Committed	38%	43%	50%	34%
Critics	36%	39%	27%	32%
Rebels	5%	2%	11%	7%
Disengaged	21%	16%	12%	27%

Table 12.4 Distribution of Ethnic Groups by Quadrant (21-scenario data)

	Northern Town			Southern Town		
	Welsh	Anglo-Welsh	English	Welsh	Anglo-Welsh	English
Committed	36%	28%	36%	78%	0%	22%
Critics	34%	28%	38%	48%	23%	29%
Rebels	50%	0%	50%	20%	0%	80%
Disengaged	55%	27%	18%	35%	25%	41%

are predominantly Welsh-speakers. Rebels and the disengaged are mostly English, though the latter group is the most ethnically balanced of the four.

A further difference between the sites is the location of shop-owner entrepreneurs. In the northern town, shop owners were disproportionately disengaged, and none was Welsh-speaking. In the southern town, all the shop owners interviewed were Welsh-speakers, with half being committed and the other half critics.

These results are not unexpected if one is ethnographically familiar with the two towns. The northern site is widely considered 'very Welsh' by Welsh-speakers across the country. Though Trosset's network in that town was predominantly Welsh-speaking, it was clear that local social networks cross-cut ethnic distinctions. Conversely, while the southern site is in a very Welsh area, it has an untypical population structure. Caulkins's experience there was that ethnic groups moved in largely distinct social networks.

The description of a town as 'very Welsh' generally refers to its large Welsh-speaking population. Our analysis, however, suggests a different feature that can be used to characterize a town's 'Welshness'. In the 'very Welsh' northern site, Anglo-Welsh and English residents are fully integrated into the local culture of values and perceptions. In the southern site, we find Welsh and English residents located differently with respect to these parameters.

Concluding Remarks on the Significance of Ethnicity and Values

Others have drawn attention to the complexity and shifting nature of Welsh ethnicity while claiming that all of the diverse strands of membership and experience contribute to an identity that is 'distinctively and assertively Welsh' (Bowie 1993: 191). Our use of consensus analysis allowed us to map the distinctive Welsh identity that is dominant or hegemonic. That broad consensus on the components of Welsh identity could be considered a cultural model (Strauss and Quinn 1997). The dominant discourse in the region tends to equate the category of Welsh ethnicity with the boundaries of the Welsh-speaking community. Baumann (1996) describes a somewhat similar situation for the multi-ethnic population of Southall, London, in which the dominant discourse equates three concepts: ethnicity, community and culture. Southall residents speak as though these three concepts map onto each other. Just as Baumann's Southall residents all use (and sometimes contest) the dominant discourse, the Welsh residents in this study are collectively competent in this discourse but often position themselves differently in it.

Our classification of the social positioning of individuals is empirically grounded, rather than theoretically motivated by a belief in the importance of standard demographic and sociological categories. We have shown that a variety of these categories fail to reflect cultural differences: culture cross-cuts the categories (see also Baumann 1996: 190–5). Therefore, we conclude with the following thoughts:

1. Our analysis of the cross-cutting configurations of values and cultural knowledge of Welshness suggests a distributed notion of culture that envisions diverse positions along these two dimensions. There is no justification for assuming that the two will always be correlated, or that members of certain demographic groups will always hold a particular view. These are matters for empirical investigation.

2. Although we recognize that an almost infinite number of positional comb- inations can occur, we find it helpful to gloss four major strategies as culturally committed, culture critics, culture rebels, and culturally disengaged. In any community with a hegemonic set of values, it should be possible to classify individuals according to these four cultural positions. The relative size and composition of these 'groups' can then illuminate the nature of a particular community.

3. When different ethnic (for example) groups are consistently positioned differently with respect to values and cultural knowledge, the cultural significance of that demographic category will have been empirically demonstrated. But

ethnicity is not always the locus of culture. There are cases in which even a category of great importance to members of the community (such as being a native Welsh speaker) is not itself a significant factor in determining how individuals are culturally situated in other important respects.

4.   The 'lived experience' of all individuals is strongly influenced by the fact that they hold different values. Some know, for example, that the value they place on emotional expression is widely sanctioned by the community, while others have the experience of knowing that they are widely perceived as unusually reserved. These experiences are further complicated by an awareness that the perception of one's degree of emotionalism often affects perceptions of whether one is properly enacting one's other social niches, as Welsh, or perhaps as female, or as working-class.

5.   Values, and variation across the values of different individuals, have far-reaching significance for the study of communities and national groups. We have shown that only through the empirical study of cultural values and knowledge can the social organization of a community be clearly understood. Although ethnic and nationalist ideologies and cultural politics are generally seen as belonging to a different subfield of anthropology from the study of ethnopsychological attitudes, the two areas are often closely related, and should be integrated more often.

6.   When individuals take action with respect to political ideologies and goals, their behaviour is both grounded in and judged according to the same values of personhood that are used and debated in other spheres of life such as family relations. The values examined in our study all have implications for the politics of social interaction in Wales. Egalitarianism limits the extent to which any individual can appear to seek power or to exercise it over others. Martyrdom discourages success and achievement, affecting domains such as entrepreneurial activity. Performance values support certain aesthetic styles for the presentation of self. Emotionalism, including nostalgia, encourages the presentation of certain rationales for actions, while discouraging the open espousal of pragmatic motives. It is a community's hegemonic values that enable people to identify culturally relevant ways of pursuing their life goals and enacting their positions in society.

Acknowledgements

National Science Foundation grant (DBS-9213430) to co-principal investigators D. Douglas Caulkins and Carol Trosset is gratefully acknowledged, as is the generous support of the Grinnell College Grant Board, which helped fund the participation of our research assistants Kurt Dorschel, Kendra Hillman, Karen

Kulbe, Jennifer Paine, Jason Reynolds, and Stephanie Schmidt. We are greatly indebted to all of our Welsh consultants who gave so generously of their time.

Note

1. Many of the data in this section combine the 80 individuals from the northern site who completed the 21-scenario interview with an additional 50 who responded to a shorter 10-scenario interview. We developed this condensed 10-scenario interview to allow time to interview more people. Using the 152 21-scenario interviews from the northern and southern sites combined, we found that our results held constant if we used only two scenarios representing each of the five concepts. The ten scenarios used were numbers 2, 3, 6, 7, 10, 13, 15, 17, 18, and 19. The analysis of 130 10-scenario interviews showed a culture key similar to that resulting from the longer interview, and an increased level of cultural agreement.

References

Abu-Lughod, L. (1986) *Veiled Sentiments: Honor and Poetry in a Bedouin Society*, Berkeley: University of California Press.

Baumann, G. (1996) *Contesting Culture: Discourses of Identity in Multi-ethnic London*, Cambridge: Cambridge University Press.

Borgatti, S.P. (1992) ANTHROPAC 4.91, Columbia: Analytic Technologies.

Bowie, F. (1993) 'Wales from Within: Conflicting Interpretations of Welsh Identity', In S. Macdonald (ed.) *Inside European Identities*, Oxford: Berg.

Brow, J. (1996) *Demons and Development: The Struggle for Community in a Sri Lankan Village*, Tucson: University of Arizona Press.

Caulkins, D. (1992) 'The Unexpected Entrepreneurs: Small High Technology Firms and Regional Development in Wales and Northeast England', in F. Rothstein and M. Blim (eds) *Anthropology and the Global Factory: Studies in the New Industrialization of the Late Twentieth Century*, New York: Bergin and Garvey.

Caulkins, D. and Hyatt, S. (1999) 'Using Consensus Analysis to Measure Cultural Diversity in Organizations and Social Movements', *Field Methods* 11(1): 5–26.

Caulkins, D. and Weiner, E. (1999) 'Enterprise and Resistance in the Celtic Fringe: High Growth, Low Growth and No Growth Firms', in R. Byron and J. Hutson (eds) *Local Enterprise on the North Atlantic Margin: Selected Contributions to the Fourteenth International Seminar on Marginal Regions*, Aldershot: Ashgate.

Huntington, S. and Lawrence, E. (eds) (2000) *Culture Matters: How Values Shape Human Progress*, New York: Basic Books.

Ingelhart, R. (1998) *Human Values and Beliefs: A Cross-Cultural Sourcebook*, Ann Arbor: University of Michigan Press.

Menter a Busnes (1993) 'Characteristics of Welsh Speakers in Business', Unpublished report.

Menter a Busnes (1996) 'Success Story: A Report on the Work of *Menter a Busnes* 1995–96', Unpublished report.

Riesman, P. (1992) *First Find Your Child a Good Mother: The Construction of Self in Two African Communities*, New Brunswick NJ: Rutgers University Press.

Romney, A., Weller, S. and Batchelder, W. (1986) 'Culture as Consensus: A Theory of Culture and Informant Accuracy', *American Anthropologist* 88(2): 313–38.

Strauss, C. and Quinn, N. (1997) *A Cognitive Theory of Cultural Meaning*, Cambridge: Cambridge University Press.

Trosset, C. (1993) *Welshness Performed: Welsh Concepts of Person and Society*, Tucson: University of Arizona Press.

Williams, G. (1978) 'Social Ranking in a Welsh Community', in G. Williams (ed.) *Social and Cultural Change in Contemporary Wales*, London: Routledge & Kegan Paul.

Part VI
The Making (and Unmaking) of Community: Ethnicity, Religiosity, Locality

Introduction to Part VI
Nigel Rapport

The chapters in this section examine the nature of community: its making and unmaking through the use of different kinds of discourse which individuals strategically and contingently draw on in the course of their lives. Community is seen to be a matter of shared practices of representation.

This is true whether the substantive basis of community turns out to be ethnicity, religiosity or locality. The latter notions cannot be treated analytically as descriptions of social identities always or essentially there, or there unstrategically, unwittingly. The unmakings of community, the negotiated and contested criteria of its membership, the multiple and serial memberships, the possible invisibility of community to non-members, the contrariety of one's senses of belonging . . . all go to evidence the subtleties of this discursive usage. Socially and mentally people can be elsewhere than their communities at the same time of their lives as they cherish (or abhor) them. The reality of community existence, its contingencies and ambiguities, may be very different from the rhetoric of essentialism and chauvinism in which its spokespersons may indulge.

In Chapter Thirteen, 'Armenian and Other Diasporas: Trying to Reconcile the Irreconcilable', Vered Amit explores the social and symbolic construction of Armenian identity in London. Her essay has two main foci. First is the notion of ethnicity. Clearly there are moments and situations when a discourse of ethnicity is deployed in the constitution of identity and community across a sprawling urban milieu. However, it is also clear that this is no essential or lone or even overriding identity. Rather it is one of an armoury of strategies, from a tool-box of language-games, which 'Armenians' determine upon as resourceful *bricoleurs*. Hence, Amit's description of the organization of a 'part-time' ethnic community in 1980s' London in which intra-ethnic connections episodically become disconnections in the alternative social contexts of everyday, cross-ethnic relations.

Second, Amit's discussion is a revisiting of the concept of 'ethnicity' (which may be said to have held anthropological sway in the 1980s) in the light of more recent conceptualizations of identity and community which employ the concept of 'diaspora' in its place. How might the case of London Armenians be used to assess the analytical contribution provided by 'diaspora studies'? Intellectual fashion aside, Amit warns against essentializing descriptions and catch-all terms:

immigrants, refugees, exiles, tourists, intellectuals and guest-workers should not be treated analytically as mere fellow-travellers on a global stage. Global travellers, meanwhile, promenading diasporic credentials, may be far from cosmopolitan; far from celebrating spatial and temporal boundlessness and hybridity, their rhetoric of belonging may be based on all manner of ethnic primordialism and exclusivity. Anthropologists should themselves beware of celebrating these suspect and politically dangerous movements out of an ethos of 'cultural rights' or communitarianism.

In Chapter Fourteen, 'Both Independent and Interconnected Voices: Bakhtin among the Quakers', Peter Collins works toward a more subtle understanding of the place of religiosity in the formation and maintenance of social groups: how religiosity is creatively manipulated and reconstituted in particular contexts and how community is born as a result.

The anthropological study of religion has rightly prided itself in an emphasis on individual doings, not merely sayings: on the practice of ritual as distinct from dogma, on the manipulation of symbols, on the mundane work of managing finances, chairing committees and making the tea. Into this debate, in the context of research among Quakers ('The Religious Society of Friends') in a north English town, Collins would draw Mikhail Bakhtin's notion of the 'dialogic', a concept the Russian literary theorist employed to put across the inherent and tensive dualities of linguistic usage: something between self and other, between the individual and the group, between past and present, between presence and absence. Here is an attempt not merely to reverse polarities in paired concepts (practice versus thought, Little versus Great Traditions) but in fact to collapse distinctions. To understand Quakerism, then, is to gain purchase on a sense of 'doing (and undoing) the religious'. Quaker community is a triangular meeting of the canonical, the vernacular and the prototypical (or individual); these three elements talk to one another continuously, in different contexts, making The Religious Society of Friends one of a number of social groups in Britain to which individuals' habitual interactions give rise.

In Chapter Fifteen, 'The Body of the Village Community: Between Reverend Parkington in Wanet and Mr Beebe in *A Room with a View*', Nigel Rapport explores the making of community – the defining of boundaries, the asserting of criteria of distinctiveness, the measuring of belonging – in the village and dale of Wanet in north-west England. In the process he compares 'the discourse of village community' he finds in Wanet with the ways in which community is represented and understood in the novel *A Room with a View*, by the English writer E.M. Forster, which portrays the fictional village of 'Summer Street' in southern England.

In both Wanet and Summer Street, Rapport recounts, the Anglican minister can be seen to be known for his failure to cross a social divide between 'locals' and 'outsiders'; he and his church remain in a sense 'other'. This is the case, Rapport argues, because for Forster's characters as for his village informants, community is something substantiated and lived largely in terms of a reciprocal physicality. The ministers Reverend Parkington and Mr Beebe may both serve as witness to local physical exchanges, formal and informal (marriages, business exchanges, extra-marital affairs, pub fights), but they are never expected or permitted to partake of that physicality themselves.

This exercise in literary anthropology also elucidates the manner in which community is a matter of discourses of representation – in everyday gossip as in a novel – Rapport contends. This means that village communities geographically and temporally distant, as Wanet and Summer Street are, can come to be (and to be comprehended) in similar terms; also that under the aegis of different discourses, by individuals playing different language-games, those communities can similarly cease to be.

–13–

Armenian and Other Diasporas: Trying to Reconcile the Irreconcilable

Vered Amit

In his sketch of cosmopolitanism, Ulf Hannerz carefully distinguishes the footlooseness, 'willingness to engage with the Other', the idiosyncratic assemblage of cultural sources and personal autonomy associated with this perspective, from the orientations of other contemporary travellers (1996: 102–6). He notes that the exile, in contrast, has involvement with another culture forced on him or her; his or her competence in this culture may be more a matter of reluctant necessity than embraced opportunity. And the labour migrant is also not likely to be a cosmopolitan: striving to keep the cost of involvement with another culture as low as possible, he or she seeks to establish a 'surrogate home . . . with the help of compatriots, in whose circle one becomes encapsulated' (ibid.). These distinctions are of course relative ones, descriptions of orientation rather than lifestyle per se. No one can be entirely open to new cultural stimuli, and anything other than the briefest of sojourns in new locales is likely to require some level of engagement with the 'Other'. After all, the syncretism, hybridity and creolization which cultural theorists have often associated with contemporary mobility, however often over-exaggerated or fetishized, is not simply fanciful. Yet the distinctions Hannerz is attempting to draw between different orientations towards mobility and cultural engagement are nonetheless crucial ones that are all too often elided in a tendency to lump together refugees, immigrants, exiles, guestworkers, tourists and intellectuals as undifferentiated fellow travellers in a relentlessly mobile world.[1]

As Carole Fabricant (1998) notes, the movements of these different categories of voyagers involve very different kinds of resources, can invoke harshly different receptions and present a range of opportunities increasingly polarized between privileged wanderers and the masses of poorer migrants. As Ulf Hannerz himself notes, the cosmopolitan can *choose* to disengage from his or her culture of origin. While he or she may embrace an alien culture, he or she always knows where the exit is (Hannerz: 1996: 104), an option not equally available to all travellers. Fabricant argues that the struggle to make oneself at home in the world is still a relevant and progressive project in spite of the seemingly exhilarating bound-lessness of the 'cosmopolitan diasporic space' (Chow, cited in Fabricant 1998:27) embraced by postcolonial theory (ibid.: 26–9). I strongly concur with Fabricant's critique but I want to take a step further back and argue that if we accept Hannerz's definition of cosmopolitanism as a deliberate search for the 'alien' in an effort to assert personal autonomy vis-à-vis one's culture of origin, there is an even more fundamental contradiction in the attempt to read diaspora in terms of this orientation. In this chapter, I will use my research with the Armenian community in London to argue that in principle, if less often in social application, the effort to maintain diasporic spaces/communities is antithetically opposed to the postmodern celebration of hybridity, interstitiality and boundlessness. The construction of diasporas is fundamentally about the effort to assert and sustain very particular social boundaries across space and time, to 'make oneself at home in the world' through an avowal of membership in an ethnonational collectivity. The diasporic protagonist is hence more likely to subscribe to the ambivalence of the exile on whom new cultural engagements have been imposed than to the excitement of the cosmopolitan deliberately seeking new experiences and competences. Diasporas may be deterritorialized, but they are hardly boundless. The recent effort to associate diaspora with cosmopolitanism is thus an effort to reconcile deterritorialized but highly circumscribed – historically, symbolically and morally – conceptions of collective identity with a transcendent openness to cultural sampling and experimentation. It is, in short, an effort to reconcile the irreconcilable.

Diaspora as an Icon of Postmodernity

Amid the proliferating appearance of diaspora in a variety of scholarly literatures, two particular trends stand out. In one of these, diaspora appears tacked onto fairly conventional and localized accounts of immigrant populations. Accounts which might once have had 'ethnic' or 'immigrant' as identifying descriptors now rely on the euphemism of 'diaspora' without much in the way of justification or theorization. Tellingly, diaspora often appears more prominently in the titles of such pieces than in the texts they head (for example Fortier 1998; Yon 1995; Portes and Grosfoguel 1994). In these instances, one would have to wonder whether the term 'diaspora' is being drawn on less for a new theory of mobility and cultural hybridity than for the cachet of fashionability it bestows on otherwise well-trod terrain. Thus, it may be that we have not so much moved on from 'ethnicity' to new topics and theoretical interests, as Marcus Banks recently contended (1996), as renamed it. For someone like myself who in the 1980s studied a classic diasporic community through the paradigm of ethnicity, it seems more than a little ironic to see the former now being invoked to contemporanize the latter.

But there is also another genre of literature which has struggled to use diaspora and particularly the concept of 'diasporic space' to chart new theoretical openings. One of the most influential of these efforts has been Paul Gilroy's notion of the

'Black Atlantic' (1993). Gilroy employs the concept of a Black diaspora to assert a web of personal, historical and cultural connections that connects the Americas with Europe and in turn with Africa. Staking out the ground of anti-anti-essentialism, Gilroy seeks to chart a middle ground between the 'purified appeal of either Africentrism or the Eurocentrisms it struggles to answer' (1993: 190) without giving up on the notion of continuity or community. Instead, he proposes to historicize tradition, to see it as an ephemeral, 'magical' process of connectedness that binds Africa to Black diaspora cultures without ignoring the cultural flows, invention and fragmentation which undo any efforts to assert a linear narrative of cultural continuity. Critical of the tendency of Africentricity to efface intraracial variations, he instead celebrates hybridization, intermixture, the messiness and inspiration of interstitiality, the stories of love and loss which constitute the communities of sentiment and interpretation making up the Black Atlantic.

As James Clifford has noted, in Gilroy's presentation, diasporic subjects are 'distinct versions of modern, transnational, intercultural experience. Thus historicized, diaspora cannot become a master trope or "figure" for modern, complex, or positional identities, crosscut and displaced by race, sex, gender, class and culture' (Clifford 1994: 319). But such cautions notwithstanding, diaspora and particularly Gilroy's version of diaspora, has indeed become just such a trope because it manages to be so quintessentially postmodern without the political fatalism to which this particular intellectual orientation has so often succumbed. It poses diasporas as vigorous 'counterdiscourses to modernity', 'cultures of resistance' (ibid.) that are at once ethnically particularist and politically open. In the light of the 1990s which saw ethnicity and nationality all too often summoned as the basis for the harshest of brutality, it is easy to understand why Gilroy's vision of a 'response to racism that doesn't reify the concept of race', 'a series of answers to the power of ethnic absolutism that doesn't try to fix ethnicity absolutely but sees it instead as an infinite process of identity construction' (Gilroy 1993: 223) should be so appealing. But to assert the redemptive and transcendent aspect of diaspora, Gilroy had to strip it of social relations and turn its ideological bias on its head.

With all due respect to Avtar Brah's enthusiastic introduction of diaspora as a space which involves both those who move and those who stay put, natives and migrants (Brah 1996: 181), this is hardly a novel discovery. In 1969, Fredrik Barth had already recognized that ethnic differentiation is not an outcome of cultural isolation but of ongoing intergroup interaction, and much of the ensuing twenty-five years of ethnic studies has provided a copious stream of case studies to substantiate this observation. The key question this raises – both then and now – is what practices, narratives and rationales people use to assert their categorical distinctiveness in the midst of constant social and cultural engagement with the

'Other'. What is disappointing, but not really surprising (given its postmodern routing), about the current celebration of diaspora is that much of this literature, as in Brah's or Gilroy's expositions, displays very little curiosity about this social dimension of diaspora, i.e. how it actually works and is reproduced over time.[2] As a result, these scholars appear little concerned with the possibility that the processes they are celebrating as the progressive *raison d'être* of diaspora are more likely to be the subject of anxiety, denouncement or denial by its principal stakeholders. There is no intrinsic problem with an intellectual effort to imagine political and cultural possibilities not allowed for in current social relations, but when hopes of what might be slip into and shape interpretations of what is, the analytic and critical usefulness of the concept of diaspora is undermined and is more easily diverted towards the legitimation of some dubious political positions.

The degree to which expectations of progressive possibilities can shape readings of contemporary diasporic politics is highlighted in a 1998 article by Pnina Werbner. In it Werbner is concerned with a sphere of political debate among South Manchester Pakistanis. Restricted to Pakistani men, this sphere had remained closed and largely invisible to the wider public until the publication of Salman Rushdie's 'The Satanic Verses', when South Asian settlers in Britain spearheaded a global mobilization of Muslims against the author and his book. Werbner draws attention to the legacy of anti-Muslim prejudice which was spun off by this campaign. She notes the paradoxes of a movement that used threats of violence to enforce demands for respect. She observes the 'internecine fighting, mismanagement of communal institutions and constant appeals for state handouts and recognition which plagued communal affairs' and which resulted in a loss of local control by Manchester Pakistanis over key institutions (1998: 22). She is keenly aware of the 'male stranglehold on the diasporic public sphere'. Yet hers is ultimately a tale of the triumph of diasporic activism, of women newly empowered, of extremists rendered less powerful, of new forms of volunteerism and activism arising from the shards of a shattered alternative civil order. Amid a set of events and processes unflinch-ingly observed as redolent of polarization, violent polemic, exclusions and radical disagreements, diaspora still manages to rise transcendent, united through heterogeneity, 'a shared space of dialogue', a context for an activism in which 'passive victims can become the imaginative agents of their own destiny' (1998: 27–8)

Werbner's reading of diaspora as an interpretative community in which protoganists share the premises of their debate even as they take opposed positions in it is very familiar to me. I recognize it because as I illustrate below, my account of the London Armenian community more than a decade earlier shared this orientation (Amit Talai 1989, 1988; Talai 1986a, 1986b). Unfortunately the celebration of communal resilience which shaped my earlier research staked out an uncritical intellectual stance which this work shared with many of the studies produced during the heydey of ethnic studies in the 1970s and 1980s. This tendency is, if anything, even more acutely apparent in the current enthusiasm over the progressive potentialities of diaspora. A new generation of scholars appears to have dampened their own capacity for critical scepticism in a determination to render diaspora as an exemplar transnational space for critical insight and political alternatives (Tölölian 1991; Gilroy, 1993; Clifford, 1994). Looking back therefore, on the impetuses towards an earlier abrogation of critical doubt in ethnic studies may provide some useful cautions in respect to its successor diaspora paradigms.

Contextualizing the Armenian Study

In the late 1960s and 1970s, the efflorescence of ethnic studies was driven by a reinterpretation of the historicity of ethnicity. During the first half of the twentieth century, inspired by an earlier generation of European theorists from Durkheim to Tönnies, scholars such as the members of the Chicago School led by Robert Park, had tended to regard ethnic affiliation as a premodern anachronism and, as such, assumed that it would inevitably be overtaken by the forces of state formation, industrialization and urbanization (Park 1916, 1950; Wirth 1938). To the extent that they also associated modernity with rationality and instrumental calculation and premodernity with sentiment and emotion, ethnicity's premodern status also invested it with passionate and irrational loyalties.[3] By the early 1970s, a number of research developments had taken place which encouraged a rethinking of this stance. Anthropologists such as A.L. Epstein and Clyde Mitchell working in the Copperbelt cities of southern Africa or Abner Cohen in southern Nigeria and social scientists such as Nathan Glazer and Daniel Moynihan in New York City argued that ethnicity was not simply a lag from premodern periods but a response and adaptation to modern urban and state politics (Epstein 1958, 1978; Mitchell 1956, 1970; Cohen 1969, 1974; Glazer and Moynihan 1963, 1975). The collective ascriptions of premodern societies, they argued, were a very different matter from the urban ethnicities of a decolonizing Africa or of the jostle for position and resources in New York. Ethnicity was remade as modern and by inference rational and instrumental. If the passions and sentiments once identified with ethnicity had nonetheless not disappeared, now these were interpreted, in the work of Abner Cohen and Glazer and Moynihan in particular, as expressive handmaidens to the impetuses of collective interest, providing informal vehicles through which shared political and economic objectives could be furthered.

For anthropologists, this reinterpretation of ethnicity provided an especially useful analytical vehicle at a time when many of the collectivities and places they had traditionally studied were being incorporated into newly emerging states and greater interest was being evinced in more broadly contextualizing local ethnographies. Ethnicity in its new modern form provided a particularly convenient medium for responding to these developments. It allowed anthropologists to retain their micro focus while reformulating the status of their ethnographic subjects, now no longer 'small-scale societies' but ethnic groups mobilizing in response to their incorporation into modern state systems. A wide variety of groups were rapidly subsumed under the rubric of ethnicity from Karen hill farmers in Thailand (Keyes 1979) to Creole elites in Sierra Leone (Cohen 1981) to the residents of inner-city London suburbs (Wallman 1984). The tendency of anthropologists to study 'down' and to view themselves as protectors of their ethnographic subjects[4] converged neatly with the inclination of a larger range of social scientists to regard ethnic groups in Western countries, particularly in North America, as subordinate and disadvantaged minority groups competing for scarce resources.[5] It was therefore probably not surprising to find social scientists increasingly inclined not only to view the perpetuation of ethnicity as a rational response to modernity but to cloak this form of mobilization in heroic garb. Then, as now among scholars of diaspora, the expanding ambit of ethnicity was represented not (or at least not primarily) as a factor of scholarly re-presentation but as a 'new' phenomenon, a feature of the times (Glazer and Moynihan, 1975). As ethnicity became heroic and the study of it thoroughly modern, ethnic studies became more celebratory than critical. In 1978 John Higham complained about the lack of a critical perspective in American ethnic studies. In 1994, on the occasion of the twenty-fifth anniversary of the publication of his seminal edited volume *Ethnic Groups and Boundaries*, Fredrik Barth chastised anthropologists for regularly operating 'too narrowly as (self-appointed) advocates and apologists for ethnic groups in their grievances' (1994: 24). It was within this context that I carried out my doctoral study of Armenians in London in the early 1980s.

Numbering by the most generous of estimates only 10,000–12,000 persons scattered over many different districts of one of the largest conurbations in the world, the Armenians were not easy to find. When social scientists, however, set out to find ethnic groups, they usually succeed. I thus found a much smaller set of approximately 1500 people who were busily organizing a shifting set of voluntary associations which sponsored a small cultural centre, two churches (one rented from the Church of England, the other a tiny chapel donated by the wealthy Armenian Gulbenkian family), a Sunday school and a wide variety of less regular activities from lectures to movies to music recitals to teas or fund-raising dinner dances. In Britain, still largely first-generation immigrants, London Armenians originated from a number of countries, spoke two principal dialects of Armenian (Eastern and Western Armenian) and a wide variety of subsidiary languages, expressed opposing political affiliations and different rates and types of religious observance; it was thus often easier to identify what divided Armenians than united them as a community. These divisions were represented in alternations of apathy and passion as a proliferating range of associations were established to express varying contending perspectives of how the organized community should develop but often replacing organizations that had fallen moribund. Armenians alternately bemoaned the ongoing difficulties of recruiting volunteers to run these associations or audiences for these activities or complained about the unrelenting pressure to participate in them. 'If I attend one then I'll have to attend all of them so I don't go to any', explained one exasperated individual. One of the reasons for their focus on the activities of the voluntary associations was that the functions they sponsored constituted the only consistent social vehicle for Armenians to gather together. For much of the round of their activities in London, at school, at work or in their local neighbourhoods, Armenians interacted with non-Armenians. Theirs, I concluded, was a 'part-time ethnicity', packed into evenings and weekend spaces and competing with the desire of many Armenians to spend their leisure time in other ways and/or with other people. Particularly for Armenians born and raised in Britain, who had often built up a network of non-Armenian consociates, pressure to participate in the activities of the voluntary associations could be construed and resented as a litmus test of their ethnic loyalty, pressure to *be* Armenian by being *with* and *seen* to be with Armenians.

But this round of activities was largely invisible to non-Armenians. At the time of my fieldwork, which occurred before events such as the 1988 earthquake in Armenia, the conflict over Ngorno Karabagh or the breakup of the former Soviet Union, Armenians were still largely anonymous in London. There was little awareness among other Londoners that such an ethnic cohort existed and operated in their city, and often little sense of the attributes of this ethnic identity altogether. Armenians complained that when they identified themselves as Armenians, they were usually greeted with puzzled incomprehension: 'what is that?', they were asked, ' is that a religion, a country?' This anonymity could be troubling or exasperating to those claiming Armenian identity but it was also advantageous. At the very least, it meant that no opprobrium was attached to this identity and there were few barriers to the participation by Armenians in wider social or economic spheres. Thus I never heard Armenians describing themselves as targets of racist prejudice nor identifying their situation as comparable to that of other more stigmatized ethnic minorities in Britain. Anonymity furthered but was also enabled by the dispersal of Armenians, reinforcing the low profile they both sought and bemoaned.

Yet most of the Armenians I spoke to in London evaluated this state of affairs in negative terms. In comparison with Armenian communities elsewhere, the London community, I was told, was not a 'good one'. With so many divisions and disagreements, local associations, it was noted, couldn't even agree on the conditions necessary for establishing a community centre which could facilitate and house the dispersed events on the Armenian community calendar. The gap between the hundreds who regularly attended association activities and their own varying estimates of thousands of Armenians resident in Greater London was frequently trotted out as a clear indicator of the failure of the community to retain adherents and reproduce itself. Parents raising children complained that it was almost impossible to counter the engulfing British practices transmitted to their children through schools, friends, etc., and British-born Armenians were often pointed out as the least likely to attend association-sponsored gatherings or to achieve proficiency in the Armenian language. Assimilation, it was felt, lapped at the heels of even the most avid community activist.

In contrast, I interpreted these processes as a success story of ethnic commitment and perpetuation. The part-time nature of Armenian ethnicity, I argued, increased the self-consciousness with which they approached the expression and organization of collective identity. They couldn't treat it as a simple concomitant of residential or occupational clustering. They had to go outside their usual routines and invest effort and time in creating opportunities to be with Armenians. They had to reflect on, and syncretically reinvent as Armenian, elements such as language, food, dance, political affiliations of diverse origins, through which they could mark their identity and communicate it to others, especially to their children. The tendency for disagreements over these issues to be expressed through the establishment of new associations rather than through participation and negotiation within already established organizations, I argued, provided more opportunities for participation.

> What this associational proliferation does do, however, is to increase the numbers of Armenians actively involved in organizations and increase the number and kinds of activities on offer to Armenians in London. In a population so dispersed and heterogenous as the London Armenians, where a community is defined and manifested in terms of collective public gatherings, this enhances the very existence of the community rather than hastens its dissolution (Amit Talai 1989: 39).

Ethnic identity among the Armenians I encountered in London was indeed highly self-conscious and expressed through associational proliferation and confrontation rather than consolidation and consensus. But then, with me having set out to find Armenians in this city, and given their dispersal and anonymity, it is hardly surprising that those I found were more likely to be activists, and hence more likely to be self-conscious and organizationally engaged. Others with a different or no version of Armenianness were simply less visible. In short, the self-consciousness and engagement I found could have been at least partially a factor of my search for it. That I regarded this as a success story of ethnic reproduction probably said much more about my theoretical paradigm than about the prospects of an Armenian diasporic future as, in the wake of Middle East tensions and political upheavals, Armenians moved onward toward new settlements in Europe and North America.

The Armenian Diaspora Through the Looking Glass

In the early 1980s, the diasporic network of the London Armenians seemed important in understanding this particular case but certainly did not have the celebrated standing it has now been accorded. However, it seems that, in the shift from ethnicity to diaspora as master tropes of social diversity and migration, two unfortunate tendencies have been preserved: respectively an inclination toward ever more expansive definitions of the related concept and the interpretation of this status (i.e. first ethnic and then diasporic) in celebratory rather than critical terms. Thus in a trajectory reminiscent of the earlier reworking of ethnicity, diaspora has now been far extended from its classic Armenian or Jewish forerunners and identified as an emblem of the historical moment. If ethnicity was redefined as a feature of modernity, diaspora has become an icon of postmodernity.

Two concomitants of postmodernism's rejection of universal standards and metanarratives are relevant to our present concerns. First, it was associated with a concerted critique of science and rationality as a hegemonic language/system of power and social detachment (Scheper-Hughes 1995: 418; Abu-Lughod 1991, cited in D'Andrade 1995: 405). Sentiment and poetics, the perceived antitheses of science, were redeemed as newly authentic. Second, without a universal standard of evaluation, criticism from 'outside' was rendered not only invalid but potentially oppressive because it represented a struggle not over truth but over the power of contingent and specifically situated perspectives. Diaspora's redefinition as postmodern brought ethnicity back full circle, reinvested once again as a phenomenon of passion and poetry. Now, however, such sentiment is not treated as inferior to rational calculation but as more authentic.

Thus as Werbner has noted it is the experiential and aesthetic dimensions of diaspora which have received the greatest emphasis in this theoretical genre; the connectedness of scattered and differentiated individuals is 'magical' according to Gilroy. Magically connected, only tenuously subject to objective political scrutiny, the fragmentation and dispersal of diasporas becomes homologous with the fragmentation and interconnection of the contemporary world. But since diaspora has retained ethnicity's earlier identification with political marginalization or subordination it has become an emblem for not only the postmodern moment but a subaltern one. Thus it is possible to see why diaspora is both heralded as being so thoroughly of the moment and at the same time mooted as an 'alternative' public sphere (cf. Gilroy 1993; Brah 1996; Werbner 1998), 'nontotalizing globalization from below' (Clifford 1994: 325). And it is also possible to understand perhaps why both Werbner and Gilroy would insist on the politically open and redemptive character of diaspora even when they are respectively aware of the insular nature of the male-dominated South Manchester Pakistani 'public' sphere or the essentialism of Africentrism. This, however, is to attribute progressivism by ascription rather than commitment.

So how does this relate to the tiny pocket of the Armenian diaspora which I observed in London during the 1980s? The diasporic dimensions of Armenian ethnicity were acutely apparent in London during this period. Most of the Armenians resident there were still first-generation immigrants. They had emigrated from more than seven different countries, with the largest groupings hailing from Cyprus, Lebanon and Iran. The dispersal of Armenians throughout the Middle East as a consequence of the genocide of 1915 was reflected in the life histories of most of the Western Armenian-speakers whose parents or grandparents had been expelled from Eastern Turkey. The longest-settled residents had arrived from Cyprus, taking advantage of a temporary offer of full British passports to migrate to London either just before or after the independence of Cyprus. Since such a large proportion of the Armenian community in Cyprus was involved in this movement, quite a few of these former Cypriot Armenians had many members of their extended families with them in London. This was much less often the case for Armenian migrants from other parts of the Middle East who were travelling under less propitious conditions. In Iran, Armenians had formed a much larger minority population. Some had arrived several years before to pursue their studies and found their expected return stymied by the upheaval of the Iranian Revolution; others arrived singly or as nuclear family groups in the lead up to or in the immediate aftermath of these political events. They didn't have British passports and they sought residence in London at a time of general tightening of the immigration regulations. Most therefore experienced considerable difficulty in acquiring permission to remain permanently in Britain; they certainly had little possibility of bringing other members of their families to join them and they faced the likely prospect of moving onto further destinations, most likely in North America. In spite of the differences between these situations, most Armenians in London, of whatever origins, had experienced the transnational dispersal of significant family members. Mr. G, a Lebanese Armenian, had a brother still living in Beirut and another living in the USA, while his mother moved regularly between three continents visiting her sons in turn.

In the Middle East there had been extensive movements and contacts between Western Armenian-speaking communities in different countries, taking advantage of extensive personal networks as well as organizational connections. Many of the ethnic associations this diverse set of Armenians established in London were branches of transnational organizations with similar offshoots in many Armenian diaspora communities. In London, Armenians often established new branches of associations with which they had been familiar in their country of origin. The three Armenian political movements (the Ramgavar, Hnchaks and Dashnaks)[6] which had been established at the end of the nineteenth and beginning of the twentieth centuries were present through their affiliates in London as they had been similarly established, if somewhat unevenly, throughout the diaspora. While the status of the Armenian Caucasus republic in the Soviet Union had been a source of considerable tension among Armenians elsewhere during the height of the Cold War in the 1950s, in 1980s London there was a general pride in the existence and accomplishments of the Armenian Soviet Republic. Films, magazines and books were imported and scholars, artists and other notables visited the London community from Soviet Armenia. Groups of London Armenians were regularly sent on visits to the Republic. And there was similar regular input from other diaspora communities.

In spite of the extensive personal and organizational resources which had linked Armenians in dispersed diaspora communities before their arrival in London and which continued to connect them with Armenians elsewhere, they were acutely aware of the distinctions which had been nurtured by this dispersal. Armenians originating from communities established through the exile from Eastern Turkey spoke the Western Armenian dialect. On the other hand, Armenians from Iran who were able to trace their presence in that country over some 300 years spoke the Eastern Armenian dialect also spoken in the Armenian republic. While the majority of Armenians in London were at least nominally members of the Armenian Apostolic Church, a minority were Roman Catholic or Protestant. The Apostolic services, adapted from originally much longer monastic liturgy, had been variably abridged in different communities and could be affiliated with one of two different Apostolic sees. In London, Armenians had quickly incorporated the general secularization of their host country and few attended church with any regularity. Food, secondary languages and other practices had all been influenced by and varied in accord with the settlement of Armenians in different countries. The experience, length and future of settlement in London varied between Armenians arriving from different countries in different periods, with different statuses.

This internal differentiation was an explicit aspect of the descriptions provided to me by London Armenians and a key feature in the negative evaluation of the organized community. Divisiveness could be represented as an intrinsic aspect of ancient Armenian history, but more commonly the dispersal of Armenians was named as the source of internal divisions within the wider diaspora as a whole and within London specifically. In London, the most overt and common distinction was attributed to the differentiation between Eastern Armenian-speaking Iranian Armenians and Western Armenian-speakers in general or the Cypriots who particularly predominated in this latter set. Western Armenian-speakers complained that Iranian Armenians had adopted far too many Farsi words into their dialect making them difficult to understand. Iranian Armenians claimed that their version of Armenian was the more authentic of the two dialects spoken in London. More generally, Armenians with longer settlement in London, most commonly Cypriots, were viewed by more recent Iranian Armenians as being too Anglicized and Westernized, less authentically Armenian altogether. The internal political distinctions which occurred in London as they did in most diasporic communities were also linked to different organizational histories, with Western Armenian-speakers establishing affiliates identified with the Ramgavar party while Iranian Armenians established affiliates associated with the only Armenian political party which had held sway in Iran, the Dashnaks. More generally, association control and membership as well as informal friendship sets tended to fall along, and to be represented in terms of, Western and Eastern Armenian divisions. The process of settlement in London and in Western countries more widely was hardly expected to unify these divisions, since the increased rate of exogamous marriages, decreased proficiency in Armenian among British-born or -raised Armenians and limited participation in associational activities were seen as impetuses for further fragmentation and likely eventual assimilation.

Fragmentation, dispersal, transnational contact and hybridity, all features identified with diaspora formations, were certainly therefore denoted but more often denounced or worried over than celebrated by these Armenians in London. To transcend these differences, to assert a moral and affective national unity, Armenians reached back beyond these contemporary or recent practices to assert the continuity and antiquity of their identity as a people and of their connection to the 'lands' in Eastern Turkey. I was surprised to find no small number of Armenians interested in apparently esoteric archaeological and linguistic literature analysing the historical settlement of the Caucasus and Eastern Anatolia regions. It didn't take long before I realized that this interest in apparently ancient history was partly related to a concern to establish the primacy of Armenian claims to territories in these regions, which have also been settled by other peoples. As one Armenian respondent explained:

> Armenians tend to be worried about any suggestion that the Armenians were migrants. Because if they were migrants, the Turks were also migrants then they also have a right to be on the lands of Eastern Anatolia. (Amit Talai 1989: 127)

To assert the indigenous status of Armenians in Asia Minor, seemingly neutral archaeological or philological research was avidly scoured for evidence of a historical legacy that could buttress an existential charter of ultimate origins. Physical distance, dispersal and differentation became expiated by a reaffirmation of the roots of all Armenians, wherever their contemporary locations, in the ancient Armenian 'homeland'. Antiquity and continuity also became, in themselves, constitutive elements in defining the transcendent quality of Armenian ethnicity.

> Other ancient nations, like the Hittites and the Assyrians, the Medes and the Babylonians may have waxed and waned, declined into but a shadow of their former greatness, or entirely disappeared but the Armenians have 'survived the ravages of history to the

present day . . .' [began] the London-Armenian writer in his 'perspective' on Armenian history . . . But this concept of continuity refer[ed] not only to the people themselves but to their culture. 'Other nations like the Assyrians or the Kurds, there are a lot of them but they have lost their culture', explained Mr. VJ. (ibid.: 128)

Or it was argued that other also ancient nations had not experienced a genocide. So, the continuity and antiquity of culture and people was also a heroic endurance against all odds. A 'historical' narrative was thus invoked as a charter of transcend-ent and distinctive unity for a dispersed set of exiles who were acutely aware of the differences between them. At the same time this symbolic codex established a moral obligation for self-perpetuation, for resistance to assimilation, a commitment to carry on this legacy in the name of all who died, so tragically and violently, because they too were identified as Armenian.

Conclusion

The transcendent unity of the 'diasporic' divided Armenians was established through the proclamation and narrative reiteration of a primordial connection. Tellingly, even Iranian Armenians whose ancestors had not, for the most part, been involved in the massacres of 1915 claimed these events and the 'lands' on which they occurred as an intrinsic part of their heritage. These themes of exile, antiquity, homeland, tragedy and redemption are not unique to Armenians. Indeed, they have been adopted, more or less, as the virtual sine qua non of diaspora constitutive narratives (Clifford 1994; Gilroy 1993). Here I think it becomes important to distinguish between this use of diaspora as a charter of identity and the efforts of an increasing number of individuals to manage personal networks dispersed across region and state borders. The latter have variously and confusingly been referred to under the rubrics of transnationality or ethnoscape and even diaspora but, this conceptual muddle aside, the efforts of individuals to respond to the scattering of their significant alters need not in and of themselves necessarily involve either exclusivity or primordial claims of communality. However, primordialism and essentialism are not haphazard or occasional features of the effort at reproducing diasporas as ideological vehicles of identity. They are fundamental to this process. To be able to assert categorical claims of shared identity across the palpable and anxious differences of experience, geography, history and outlook, it becomes necessary to posit an essential, anterior and 'magical' connection. To borrow Gilroy's terms, it is roots and not routes which are, in the course of these efforts, redeemed as the salvation of diaspora. Africentricity was hence not an accidental diversion in the formation of the Black diaspora. In one version or another, some such narrative would have to be invoked to assert a rationale for the integrity and limits of 'black' connections spanning Africa, Europe and the United States across centuries. If primordialism and essentialism are key elements in the efforts to define the ideological rationale and boundaries of diaspora, it is difficult to see how anthropologists who have fought so hard against both can now embrace them as vehicles for subaltern political liberation.

To return to the issues with which this chapter started, the peripatetic lifestyles of exiles and cosmopolitans may be similar in important respects but they are likely to be animated by different motivations and perspectives. It may be tempting for analysts to deconstruct and reinterpret the articulation between practice, ideology and social relations constituting diasporic identities in terms redolent with more hopeful political possibilities. But in doing so, they could find themselves inadvertently legitimating some very suspect and even dangerous political movements.

Acknowledgements

I would like to thank Nigel Rapport for the opportunity to revisit my early research and rethink it in the light of contemporary debates. I would also like to thank him and Noel Dyck for their comments on this chapter. An abridged version of this chapter was presented at the Institute of Anthropology at Copenhagen University and I would like to thank the members of this department for their helpful comments and suggestions. However, final responsibility for the arguments presented in this paper rests with the author.

In order to protect the confidentiality of the persons who participated in my study of Armenians in London, I have used aliases in place of their real names.

Notes

1. For examples of this tendency see Arjun Appadurai 1990; James Clifford 1992. For a critique of this tendency see Carole Fabricant 1998.
2. This is a point noted by Pnina Werbner 1998.
3. See Anthony Cohen 1985 for a useful examination of this tendency directed in this case as a critique of the assumption by members of the 'Chicago School' that communities of any kind would not persist in urban, modern societies.
4. Note the 1971 version of the AAA statement on ethics (as amended through November 1986) which instructed anthropologists that their 'paramount responsibility is to those they study. When there is a conflict of interest, these individuals must come first. Anthropologists must do everything in their power

to protect the physical, social and psychological welfare and to honor the dignity and privacy of those studied' (pg. 1).

5. In a 1974 article, Ulf Hannerz noted the tendency in the United States to regard minorities as ethnic groups but the dominant white Anglo-Saxon Protestants as simply Americans.

6. See Panossian 1998 for an account of the formation of these parties and the differences between them.

References

American Anthropological Association (1986) 'Statement on Ethics: Principles of Professional Responsibility' Adopted by the Council of the American Anthropological Association May 1971 (As amended through November 1986). http://www.ameranthassn.org/stmts/ethstmnt.htm

Amit Talai, V. (1988) 'When Ethnic Identity is a Mixed Blessing: London Armenians', *Ethnos* 53(1–2): 50–62.

—— (1989) *Armenians in London: The Management of Social Boundaries*, Manchester: Manchester University Press.

Appadurai, A. (1990) 'Disjuncture and Difference in the Global Cultural Economy', in M. Featherstone (ed.) *Global Culture: Nationalism, Globalization and Modernity*, London: Sage.

Banks, M. (1996) *Ethnicity: Anthropological Constructions*, London and New York: Routledge.

Barth, F. (1969) 'Introduction', in F. Barth (ed.) *Ethnic Groups and Boundaries*, London: Allen and Unwin.

—— (1994) 'Enduring and Emerging Issues in the Analysis of Ethnicity', in H. Vermeulen and C. Grovers (eds.) *The Anthropology of Ethnicity: Beyond 'Ethnic Groups and Boundaries'*, Amsterdam: Het Spinhuis Publishers.

Brah, A. (1996) *Cartographies of Diaspora: Contesting Identities*, London and New York: Routledge.

Clifford, J. (1992) 'Traveling Cultures', in L. Grossberg, C. Nelson and P. Treichler (eds.) *Cultures Studies*, New York and London: Routledge.

—— (1994) 'Diasporas', *Cultural Anthropology* 9(3): 302–38.

Cohen, Abner (1969) *Custom and Politics in Urban Africa*, London: Routledge & Kegan Paul.

—— (1974) 'Introduction: The Lesson of Ethnicity', in A. Cohen (ed.) *Urban Ethnicity*, London: Tavistock.

—— (1981) *The Politics of Elite Culture: Explorations in the Dramaturgy of Power in a Modern African Society*, Berkeley: University of California Press.

Cohen, Anthony, P. (1985) *The Symbolic Construction of Community*, London: Tavistock.

D'Andrade, R. (1995) 'Objectivity and Militancy: A Debate. I. Moral Models in Anthropology', *Current Anthropology* 36(3): 399–408.

Epstein, A.L. (1958) *Politics in an Urban African Community*, Manchester: Published on behalf of the Rhodes-Livingstone Institute by Manchester University Press.

—— (1978) *Ethos and Identity: Three Studies in Ethnicity*, London: Tavistock.

Fabricant, C. (1998) 'Riding the Waves of (Post)Colonial Migrancy: Are We All Really in the Same Boat?', *Diaspora* 7(1): 25–52.

Fortier, A.-M. (1998) 'The Politics of "Italians Abroad": Nation, Diaspora and New Geographies of Identity', *Diaspora* 7(2): 197–224.

Gilroy, P. (1993) *The Black Atlantic: Modernity and Double Consciousness*, Cambridge, Mass.: Harvard University Press.

Glazer, N. and Moynihan, D. (1963) *Beyond the Melting Pot*, Cambridge, Mass.: MIT and Harvard University Press.

—— (1975) *Ethnicity: Theory and Experience*, Cambridge, Mass.: Harvard University Press.

Hannerz, U. (1974) 'Ethnicity and Opportunity in Urban America', in A. Cohen (ed.) *Urban Ethnicity*, London: Tavistock.

—— (1996) *Transnational Connections: Culture, People, Places*, London and New York: Routledge.

Higham, J. (1978) 'Introduction: The Forms of Ethnic Leadership', in J. Higham (ed.) *Ethnic Leadership in America*, Baltimore: John Hopkins University Press.

Keyes, C. (ed.) (1979) *Ethnic Adaptation and Identity: The Karen on the Thai Frontier with Burma*, Philadelphia: Institute for the Study of Human Issues.

Mitchell, J. C. (1956) *The Kalela Dance*, Rhodes-Livingstone Paper No. 27, Manchester: Manchester University Press.

—— (1970) 'Tribe and Social Change in South Central Africa: A Situational Approach', *Journal of Asian and African Studies* 5: 83–101.

Panossian, R. (1998) 'Between Ambivalence and Intrusion: Politics and Identity in Armenia-Diaspora Relations', *Diaspora* 7(2): 149–96.

Park, R. (1916) 'The City: Suggestions for the Investigation of Human Behaviour in the Urban Environment', *American Journal of Sociology* XX: 577–611.

—— (1950) *Race and Culture*, Glencoe, Ill.: Free Press.

Portes, A. and Grosfoguel, R. (1994) 'Caribbean Diasporas: Migration and Ethnic Communities', *The Annals of the American Academy of Political and Social Science* 533: 48–59.

Scheper-Hughes, N. (1995) 'Objectivity and Militancy: A Debate, 2. The Primacy of the Ethical: Propositions for a Militant Anthropology', *Current Anthropology* 36(2): 409–20.

Talai, V. (1986a) 'Mobilization and Diffuse Ethnic Organization: The London Armenian Community', *Urban Anthropology* 13(2–3): 197–217.

—— (1986b) 'Social Boundaries Within and Between Ethnic Groups: Armenians in London', *Man* 21: 251–270.

Tölölian, K. (1991) 'The Nation State and its Others: In Lieu of a Preface', *Diaspora* 1(1): 3–7.

Wallman, S. (1984) *Eight London Households*, London: Tavistock.

Werbner, P. (1998) 'Diasporic Political Imaginaries: a Sphere of Freedom or a Sphere of Illusions?', *Communal/Plural* 6 (1): 11–21.

Wirth, L. (1938) 'Urbanism as a Way of Life', *American Journal of Sociology* 44: 1–24.

Yon, D. (1995) 'Identity and Differences in the Caribbean Diaspora: Case Study from Metropolitan Toronto', in A. Ruprecht and C. Taiana (eds.) *The Reordering of Culture: Latin America, The Caribbean and Canada in the Hood*, Ottawa: Carleton University Press.

–14–

Both Independent and Interconnected Voices: Bakhtin among the Quakers

Peter Collins

'. . . all we seem to do is talk . . . ' (A Quaker after a particularly gruelling meeting for church affairs)

'I . . . hear voices in everything, and dialogic relations among them.' (Bakhtin 1986:169)

Introduction

There are two libraries in the Quaker meeting house in Dibdenshaw (a pseudonym), in the North of England. As I browse through and rearrange the small collection of books stored on shelves and tables near the entrance I find several that relate, in one form or another, to 'the Quaker story' (for instance Brayshaw 1982; Christian Faith and Practice 1960; Gorman 1981; Gillman 1988; Punshon 1984; Ormerod Greenwood 1975–78; Milligan 1968). Continuity figures large in Quaker discourse, and British Friends (a synonym for 'Quakers') have a strong sense of the historical trajectory of the group: the past is folded into the present. Quakerism is understood to have emerged in the mid-seventeenth century amid the social and political turmoil of the English Civil War. Despite concerted persecution from the outset, Quakerism, a creedless religion with a priesthood of all believers, was probably at its most influential during the 1660s. The movement survived the Commonwealth and Restoration and was relatively settled by 1700 (Braithwaite 1923). There followed a 'Quietist' phase characterized by 'an excessive deference to tradition' (Brayshaw 1982). Divisions within the Religious Society of Friends (Quakers) began to manifest themselves during the nineteenth century, but were dissipated by events culminating in 'the Manchester Conference' held in 1895. The contemporary Society of Friends is summed up pithily in the title of chapter six in Gillman (1988): 'Quakers Today: Respect for Diversity'. The library also contains back numbers of three Quaker periodicals (*The Friend, Quaker Monthly*, and *The Friends' Quarterly*). Each of these journals contain articles on Quakerism past, present and future, many of which confirm Gillman's point: here is a diverse group of people who somehow continue to combine to rally under the same banner.

Currently, there are approximately 17,000 Quakers in Britain grouped into 500 Quaker Meetings. In a Quaker context, the term 'meeting' describes both a thing and an event. 'A meeting' is a particular local congregation comprising a group of people who to a greater or lesser extent consider themselves as belonging to the Religious Society of Friends (Quakers). Each meeting is a voluntary group with particular attributes and aspirations constituting both religious congregation and most local unit for conducting 'meetings for church affairs' (business meetings). 'Meeting' also refers to the event known as meeting for worship which is held on Sunday mornings and which I shall describe in more detail below. Quaker meetings (as local congregations) vary considerably in size, some comprising two or three participants, others 100. Dibdenshaw meeting, the urban setting in which I carried out my research, might in these terms be considered medium-sized.

When I began my research at Dibdenshaw I struggled to find accounts which might be comparable with my own. Even though the study of religion has been central to the anthropological enterprise, anthropologists seem to have studied religion everywhere except in Britain. Morris (1987: 229–40) lists over a hundred anthropological monographs on religion 'for further reading' but includes none based on fieldwork in Britain. There are a number of informative overviews of religion in Britain (Thomas 1988; Bruce 1995; Davie 1994), though relatively few detailed published accounts of particular religious groups. And although accounts of religious groups in Britain have begun to accumulate, these have often been carried out by researchers whose main approach has not been ethnographic and whose interests are not primarily anthropological. Notable exceptions include Moore (1974), Clark (1982), Luhrmann (1989), Jenkins (1999) and Stringer (1999).

The reasons for this lack of interest are unclear, though the general tendency, already noted in the Introduction to this book, for anthropologists in the academy to send their postgraduates overseas to conduct fieldwork has been an important factor. In any case, there are at least two important consequences of this apparent disinterest in the anthropology of religion in Britain. First, there is still a dearth of good comparative material; second, the development of anthropological theory has benefited hardly at all from the study of religion in Britain. My own fieldwork and subsequent research seek to address these shortcomings.

I began fieldwork with what seemed to me to be a relatively innocuous question: what is a Quaker Meeting? It is a problem to which I have returned frequently because, as so often happens, an apparently straightforward question refuses to submit to a simple or unitary answer. To some extent, this complexity stems from my simultaneous involvement in Quakerism as both adept ('insider') and anthropologist ('outsider'). In this case the emic and etic standpoints are not easily separated. I first attended a Quaker Meeting in 1985 and became a member of the Society of Friends in 1986. Since then I have been an active participant in Quaker meetings in various parts of Britain. My own ethnographic research was carried out largely within Dibdenshaw Meeting in the north of England in 1991–1992, though I was also a participant in that Meeting before and after that period. I have participated in many different Quaker meetings and events and have read hundreds of books and pamphlets both by and about Quakers – as both anthropologist and Quaker. Cohen (1992: 229) asks 'how should we use the self ethnographically?' and usefully suggests that we should do so 'experientially'. I intended to make a virtue out of my situation as an 'insider'. This close involvement has had both its advantages and its disadvantages in relation to my own writing about Quakerism and religion more generally, though there is not space here to discuss this further (Collins 1996a, in press).

During the past few years I have responded to my initial question in a number of different ways and this chapter represents one more 'answer' – a continuation of the dialogue between my self as Quaker and as anthropologist. This particular reply derives from my growing interest in the ideas of Mikhail Bakhtin, from whose work I draw extensively below. Although Bakhtin has long been an inspiration to literary theorists, references to his work are rarely made by anthropologists. However, I agree with Vice (1997: 2) who asserts that, despite his strong association with the study of the novel and 'novelness', Bakhtin certainly offers us 'more than lit crit'.

Practice Precedes Belief

As both Quaker and anthropologist I began my research with a number of preconceptions, the most important of which in relation to my initial approach was to take for granted the essence of what it was I was studying. From the outset I had no doubt that I was researching a *religious* group. By way of preparation, then, I spent a great deal of time reading texts on the anthropology (and sociology, and psychology, and philosophy . . .) of *religion*. And didn't I myself see my commitment to Quakerism as a return to the *religious* life after shaking off the cobwebs of the Welsh Baptist tradition in which I was brought up? When I came to commence fieldwork, then, I looked at the world through lenses thoroughly coated with a thick film of *religion*.

Quakerism is typically nonconformist in its eschewal of outward signs, preferring to foreground the *Inner Light*. George Fox, generally taken to be the 'founding father', wrote in 1652,

> Therefore to *the light in you* I speak, that when the book of conscience is opened then shall you witness me and you all judged out of it. So God Almighty direct your minds who love honesty and sincerity, that you may receive mercy in the time of need. *Your teacher is within you* . . . (Nickalls 1952: 143, my italics)

And rather more recently, Gillman begins his introductory text with a chapter entitled 'The Foundation: God Within the Heart' and later says of the Quaker meeting house: 'There will be no religious symbolism: no statues, no crosses, no crucifix, no altar, no pulpit' (1988: 25). Quakers tend to present themselves (and are presented as such by others) as having a simple liturgy, in which ritual and symbolism are largely absent. Quakerism in this respect would seem to coincide with the practice of anthropology, then: each understands itself as dealing in hidden or at least partially occluded meanings. One newcomer to meeting told me that she was escaping an 'oppressive Catholic upbringing' and found the 'absence of stuffy ritual a breath of fresh air'. I reminded myself that meeting *was* in any case a religious enterprise and so there must be ritual! I would observe meeting more carefully and analyse more thoroughly. It was not long before I began concentrating on the most overtly religious aspects of the Quaker Meeting: meeting for worship – broadly speaking, the religious service held in silence at the meeting house on Sunday mornings. It was not difficult to discover ritual and symbolism here, and the minimalism of silent worship seemed to provide an opportunity to say something different. Van Gennep (1960) and Turner (1969) offered a useful framework for understanding what went on at Meeting for worship. My fieldnotes concurred with the masters' analysis. Meeting was a three-phase ritual. *Preliminal*: between 10 and 11 a.m. Friends arrived in dribs and drabs (noise, movement, informal talk . . .) gathered in groups and talked, often loudly; *liminal*: by 11 o'clock most people had settled down in the meeting room (silence, stillness, formal talk . . .) ; *postliminal*: at 12 o'clock worship ends, the clerk reads out notices and everyone repairs to another room for tea (noise, movement, informal talk . . .). And describing the process in fine grain was fun and a bit of a challenge – much could be described in terms of binary oppositions (Turner 1969; Leach 1976; Levi-Strauss 1976). My growing disillusionment with this approach stemmed from a hiatus separating my understanding of Quakerism as an anthropologist and my experience of meeting as a Quaker, of which more below.

I was further influenced by Geertz (1973). I have elsewhere (Collins 1996b) attempted an analysis of the symbolism of Quaker worship and here shall merely indicate the drift of my approach. Historically, Quakerism grew up opposing the State Church, becoming what Anglicanism was not. The current organization of Quaker worship might be seen largely as a result of that historical process. For instance, Quakers not only flag but foreground the absence of the host during worship, thus differentiating themselves from Anglicans who (mistakenly) retain this (unnecessary and distracting) 'outward sign'. To elucidate briefly: at the centre of the meeting for worship is a table which, although marked as a religious space (it has copies of the Bible and sometimes other overtly religious texts), is defined as a purely practical device: 'it's just something for us to put the collecting boxes on' or 'the clerk needs a table for her notebook during business meetings' or 'it's just there to focus our attention'. It is interesting that the presence of the table is taken for granted, although its meaning is not shared (Rapport 1993; Stromberg 1986; Wallace 1961). Most tellingly it does not support a crucifix or the items required for the celebration of the eucharist – it functions, symbolically as a 'not-altar', a more articulate reminder of the Quaker denial of 'outward signs' than a mere empty space. During the first year of my fieldwork, I soon found it relatively easy to carry out this form of 'Geertzian' anthropological analysis. Geertz had defined religion as: '*(1) a system of symbols which acts to (2) establish powerful, pervasive and long-lasting moods and motivations in men* [sic] *by (3) formulating conceptions of a general order of existence and (4) clothing these conceptions with such an aura of factuality that (5) the moods and motivations seem uniquely realistic*' (1973: 90, italics in the original). Having assimilated Geertz's influential definition of religion I applied it somewhat mechanistically to the Meeting. The problem again was that this approach did not coincide with the way I participated in meeting. It seemed somehow too cerebral. Meeting seemed to emerge out of events, in the interactions of individuals, in what they did and particularly in their talk. As Southwold (1983: Chapter 11) says in the context of Sinhalese Buddhism, 'practice precedes belief'. Beliefs are slippery, they are likely to be half-stated, provisional, symbolic, even metaphorical (Lewis 1980). This is particularly true of Quakers who eschew creeds. Practice is more easily fixed.

Quakerism is 'religion as practice' in at least two senses. First, the form of meeting for worship has largely become fixed. In an important sense, meeting for worship embodies Quakerism. Friends sit in meeting *as if* they are doing the same thing. The form of worship represents equality – the circular and non-hierarchical seating arrangement, the absence of ritual specialists such as priests or shamans and of 'outward forms' (the props generally found in Christian ritual), the opportunity given to anyone to minister. Whereas there is considerable diversity of belief, there is little diversity in the forms of meeting (Dandelion 1996: Chapter three). Second, discussion during business meetings, various committee meetings and other events tended to focus on actions to be taken: whether to plant up a 'wild garden' and exchange existing light bulbs for 'greener' long-life ones, whether to invite a Quaker theatre company to come and perform at the meeting house, which charities to support, whether to organize a peace vigil and so on. Beliefs were seldom aired, except perhaps during worship where (significantly) discussion about them was explicitly proscribed.

Looking back through my field notes I find that the most striking characteristic of the Quaker Meeting is the breadth and depth of dialogue I discovered there. Participation in Dibdenshaw meeting seemed to me to consist primarily of 'talking relationships' (Rapport 1993, 1997). One could argue interminably regarding the beliefs and practices of Quakers in relation to sin, prayer, redemption, good and evil, heaven and hell, ritual, worship, baptism, death – but whatever the Quaker or anthropologist might say that they do, it is incontrovertibly true that they talk – an irony given the emphasis on silence in worship. They talk a lot and on a very wide range of subjects though not very much about 'religion' or about 'the religious'. Having said that, the point is made considerably more complex by the commonly held Quaker belief that all of life is sacred and therefore that nothing said or done falls outside the religious life. Quaker theology aside, I found, rather as Watling (1999) found among Dutch protestants, that Quakers prefer not to talk about their beliefs or things overtly religious. It might be the case that Quakers, given the evident diversity of their beliefs, avoid religious subjects in conversation because they anticipate stirring up controversy (Dandelion 1996: 257).

To specify a day when I entered the field seems rather contrived, silly even. But to name the day when it first occurred to me that I was not observing or participating in *essentially religious* action marks an important stage in my becoming an anthropologist. Doing anthropology meant that I was becoming increasingly self-conscious of my practice of Quakerism. Whatever else it was, the Quaker Meeting was a discursive venture. I began to visualize the discursive meeting in terms of a triangular model.

Meeting Discourse: A Trinity

In considering these further aspects of meeting I began to develop a threefold delineation of Quakerism as encountered in the field. Quakers not only talk – they write, and emphasize the written text. It is among the texts in the two libraries at Dibdenshaw that we most easily locate examples of the first mode of Quaker discourse. First, then, we can identify a canonic discourse, best exemplified by the text entitled *Quaker Faith and Practice* (1995), the revised version of *Christian Faith and Practice (1960)*. In a nutshell, this is a collection of excerpts from Quaker writings, from journals, doctrinal books, speeches, minutes and a wide variety of other sources: it contains the voices of thousands. It is currently divided into 29 chapters, each dealing with broad topics such as 'Approaches to God', 'Quaker Marriage Procedure', 'Caring for one Another', 'Our Peace Testimony', 'Finance', and 'Social Responsibility'. In a sense this book, revised and compiled by a committee, defines Quakerism. It is this text that is often presented to individuals when they come into membership of the Society, and is found in every meeting house; it is regularly quoted during meeting for worship and in other contexts. Britain Yearly Meeting, the annual national business meeting, oversees its revision once every 25 years or so, and took over seven years revising the current edition. As Bakhtin points out (1986: 88–9), typically focusing on human relations:

> In each epoch, in each social circle, in each small world of family, friends, acquaintances, and comrades in which a human being grows and lives, there are always authoritative utterances that set the tone.

Quaker Faith and Practice constitutes just such a collection of 'authoritative utterances'. Other canonic texts might include the Journal of George Fox and the Epistles and Minutes of Yearly Meeting – both are excerpted widely *in Quaker Faith and Practice* – and 'classic' histories such as those by Braithwaite (1921, 1923) and Jones (1921). Apart from written text, the canon, however vaguely defined, also includes traditional phrases uttered in business meetings and the form of worship and it comes nearest to providing a Quaker ideology. In Anthony Cohen's terms, this is the flag that Quakers, in spite of their differences, can unify behind (Cohen 1985: 21).

A second sphere of discourse is the vernacular, 'village' Quakerism as it were. This is the manner in which Quakerism is expressed locally. While there is a considerable degree of uniformity across meetings and it is more than likely that, were an individual Friend to turn up at any local meeting on a Sunday morning he or she would fit in (and be fitted in) without too much discomfort, there are significant variations. The place of meeting may be more or less easy to find: some are centrally placed, others are not; some have clear signs, others do not. Although a visitor would eventually find a building devoid of Christian or any other religious symbols, meeting may take place in a community centre, a school hall or a member's house. He or she may be greeted at the door with a handshake and someone would probably engage him or her in conversation, during which she would more or less tactfully be asked whether she had attended a meeting before. Upon answering in the affirmative, the visitor would almost certainly be introduced to an ex-member of his or her local meeting, or to a relative or close Friend of such a member: an oft-heard phrase at such times is, 'The Society of Friends in Britain is a small world'. At 10.45 or maybe 11 a.m. he or she would be accompanied into the meeting room and would take his or her place in the hollow square or circle of chairs or benches. The visitor would glance around a group of men and women, mostly over 50 years of age, and perhaps a few children. The walls of the meeting room are plain and probably bare except for benches or chairs and a central table. If there are children they may sit with the adults for the first ten minutes, or come in towards the end, having spent much of meeting in a separate room. The room would become silent for an hour unless one or more Friends felt called to stand and speak. In some meetings vocal ministry is regular, while other meetings are largely silent. The content of ministry varies but tends to be anecdotal, autobiographical and tied to a Quaker text. After an hour, the visitor would find his or her neighbour offering to shake hands (a canonic gesture) before a Friend (probably the clerk of the meeting) would stand and read the notices – often relating to local events. The visitor might be asked to introduce him- or herself and would in any case be asked to stay for a cup of tea. Meeting for worship in Britain does not vary greatly from this rough sketch. On the other hand, no two meetings are the same either. As Morson and Emerson (1990: 24) remark, 'life is lived where tiny changes occur . . .' And each 'tiny change' serves to mark one local meeting off from another.

The 'new' Dibdenshaw meeting house happened to be situated right in the centre of town and included rooms which were let on a regular basis to outside groups. This has given rise to a complex structure involving a warden employed to live on the premises, a Finance and Premises Committee comprising six or more members meeting more or less monthly, and an abiding concern for the maintenance of the building and its grounds. The meeting, in attempting to maintain its useful and rather striking premises in a reasonable state of repair, sought to increase its lettings. While raising revenue, it also caused a number of problems which Friends needed to spend time and effort in order to overcome. Some Friends wondered whether the premises were actually more a hindrance than a help in living out the Quaker testimonies. The possibility of developing a 'wild garden' was considered at length until Finance and Premises Committee agreed that the warden and a group of volunteers might start work. There was much talk before, during and after the garden had been created. The wild garden was not universally approved because, especially at first, it looked unkempt. On the other hand it meshed with Quaker 'Green Concerns' – the idea was to plant only British species, and preferably ones which would attract wildlife of one form or another. The wild garden was directly under the windows of the room in which Friends met for tea after worship and thus stimulated much conversation. Furthermore, to have an opinion on the wild garden was to flag up one's identity as a Quaker who belonged to this *particular* meeting: the meaning of Quakerism is *contextual* (Bakhtin 1986: 159).

Participants in meeting differed according to class, gender, age, place of birth and nationality, ethnicity, their status as member or attender (one who participates in Quaker events but who is not a member of the Society), length of membership, degree of commitment, interests both within and outside of their involvement in Quakerism – some were heavily involved in the peace movement, others maintained only the slightest interest, others were concerned with prison reform, education, ensuring that the meeting house was maintained properly and so forth. Some were keen singers, others enthusiastic cyclists, some went walking, others spent their leisure time in the garden. Although the majority of participants were white-collar workers, there were teachers, doctors, nurses, administrators, secretaries, retired people, shopworkers, janitors, academics and students. These differences ensured that Friends with shared interests and concerns gathered regularly in twos and threes to continue conversations which had developed over the course of weeks, months and often years.

The point is that these particular characteristics gave rise to a local meeting that was different in terms of both structure and function from other meetings. Despite aspiring to live up to the canonic ideals broadly shared by all local meetings of the Society of Friends, this particular meeting chose a particular set of challenges, and constituted a unique expression of local Quakerism. I have wondered when reading influential and otherwise brilliant accounts in the anthropology of religion (Evans-Pritchard 1956; Middleton 1960; Lienhardt 1961), the extent to which local difference is unfortunately glossed over for the sake of generalizability, the particular sacrificed for the sake of the universal.

Prototypical Quakerism, as a sphere of discourse, depends on the auto/biography of the individual as they come to participate in Meeting, though canonic and vernacular narratives were assimilated and recreated by individuals in interaction. As Bakhtin says (1993: 45), we each participate in Being from 'our own unique place'. In an important sense, therefore, each manifestation of Quaker discourse is absolutely unique and 'repetition' can never be anything other than citation. One participant had a long-standing involvement in the peace movement and had worked as a volunteer in the office of one organization. She helped re-establish a peace group within the meeting, distributed posters and fliers, brought the dates of demonstrations, peace vigils and similar events to the notice of Friends, and introduced the sale of white poppies at the time of Armistice Day. She became interested in the Society of Friends largely because of its historic peace testimony. On the few occasions when she stood to speak during meeting for worship it was on the theme of peace and pacifism. Before she was aware of Quakerism she was interested in and attended Buddhist meetings and she was one of several Friends who liked to draw comparisons between Quakerism and Buddhism – particularly their emphasis on non-violent protest. We can see in this example the unity as well as the diversity of the three spheres of discourse. The peace testimony is a central pillar of canonic Quakerism; one way in which this manifested itself as practice in the context of this particular meeting was the Christmas peace vigil held in the town square. This public demonstration was one important means by which Friends in this place signalled their identity to others and to themselves. Individual Friends assimilated 'the peace discourse' and recreated it in a manner of their choosing. In the case of this particular participant in meeting, her sense of identity was dependent to an important degree on her orientation towards pacifism – Quakerism might be seen as one vehicle, one narrative thread, in the construction and reconstruction of that identity.

Further illumination is provided by Bakhtin who argues that the social world consists of centripetal (official) and centrifugal (unofficial) forces (See also Bateson 1958: 277–9). The centripetal most nearly represents the canonic in my model, while the centrifugal is most obviously like prototypical discourse. Vernacular discourse stands between the two and may be adopted or co-opted both by those conservatives who wish to sustain the traditional and by those radicals who strive to overturn the status quo. All this leads me to suggest the model shown in Figure 14.1.

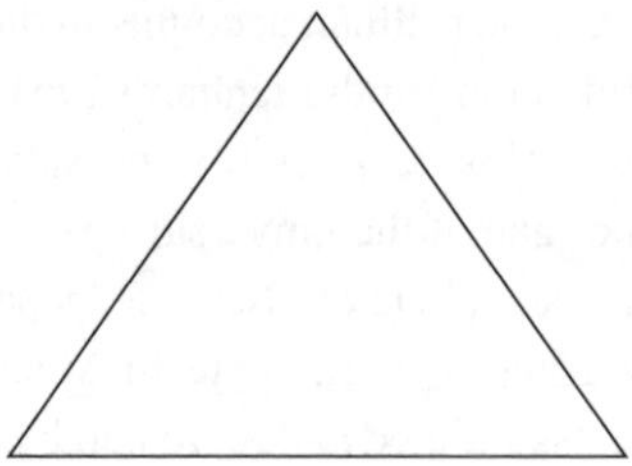

canonic Quakerism

vernacular Quakerism   prototypical Quakerism

Figure 14.1 A Preliminary Model of Quaker Discourse

The space enclosed by the triangle represents Quaker discourse. Text, defined broadly to mean communicative acts – pinning up a notice, wearing a hat during worship, a remark made over tea, the donation of a chair, not buying a white poppy, etc. – would be located somewhere within this space depending on its constitution. Dibdenshaw meeting house would lie towards the corner labelled 'vernacular Quakerism', though the building is also partially defined by canonic (Christian/ religious props and symbolism are largely absent) and individual Quakerism (furniture, pictures and books have been donated by individuals). *Quaker Faith and Practice* (the book) is primarily defined as canonic though is unlikely to be devoid of the vernacular and prototypical, and may be put to uses which are almost wholly one or the other. The contribution of an individual in a meeting (any meeting) is primarily prototypical discourse, though cannot wholly be so. The canonic and vernacular do not describe actual social or physical entities but rather moments in a dynamic process: an utterance, a poster, a chair or a building may at one time be an instantiation of canonic discourse while exemplifying vernacular discourse at another. The same text is, as I shall explain further below, never the same text twice: the model identifies processes rather than products.

Let us take just one example. There is a small watercolour on the wall near the entrance to Dibdenshaw meeting house. For over two years I simply took it for granted. One morning I got talking to a participant relatively new to the meeting and to Quakerism. In order to make a point he drew my attention to the picture and explained that its 'quiet calm' seemed to epitomize Quakerism. I mentioned this to a Friend of rather longer standing and he smiled and looked pensive. After some prompting he went on to explain that some years ago a visitor from overseas came to the meeting and arranged accommodation with a local Friend. He was grateful for the hospitality he received and donated to the meeting this picture he had painted. It should be clear that this particular 'text' participates in a different discourse on each occasion. However, as Bakhtin (1986: 91) warns:

the situation is considerably more complicated. Any concrete utterance is a link in the chain of speech communication of a particular sphere . . . Utterances are not indifferent to one another, and are not self-sufficient; they are aware of and mutually reflect one another.

Bakhtin points up the importance of narrative here, but narrative that is fundamentally co-authored. My own interest in the watercolour stemmed from participating in the conversations and debates concerning two other pictures depicting the person of Jesus in different (and equally contentious) ways, after which I paid far more attention to all the other pictures hanging in the meeting house. So long as we broaden 'utterance' to include all manner of responses then this is true of all the communicative exchanges which comprise Quaker discourse.

Why differentiate between the canonic, the vernacular and the prototypical? There are a number of reasons. First, these distinctions obviate the more mechanistic dualism individual/society, and allow for a more sophisticated and flexible analysis. Second, it helps avoid an all-too-common determinism in allotting to the individual a considerable degree of agency. This has a number of advantages: for instance we allow for the possibility, the probability even, that structures legitimated by ideology can be manipulated and thoroughly reconstituted by local groups and by individuals. Third, in adopting this approach one avoids the mistake, identified by Southwold and others, of privileging the canonic discourse to the extent of denying altogether the existence of the vernacular. Fourth, the approach is likely to encourage a more nuanced approach to religion as a dynamic social phenomenon in that here is at least a tentative means of identifying sources of change. And finally, the approach would seem useful as a means of pursuing comparative studies. The researcher might begin by asking to what extent does religion as practised in this place rely primarily on the canonic, the vernacular, the prototypical discourse? To what degree do the canonic and vernacular coincide? Which individuals, in constructing their own discourse, draw particularly on the canonic, which on the vernacular? Finally, the spheres of discourse mark out degrees of authority. All things being equal the canonic claim trumps the vernacular, and both outflank the prototypical. Things are seldom 'equal', of course, and so the picture is not half as simple as this. Individuals who want to change some aspect of meeting draw on either the canonic, the vernacular or both – naturally developing their own prototypical narratives in doing so.

Quakerism might also be described in terms of habitus (Bourdieu 1977), though as a model it has the disadvantage of seeming overly deterministic. Quakerism, constituted as it is by these modes of discourse, might more usefully be characterized as a *genre*, in the Bakhtinian sense.

Language is realized in the form of individual concrete utterances (oral and written) by participants in the various areas of human activity . . . Each separate utterance is individual, of course, but each sphere in which language is used develops its own *relatively stable types* of those utterances. These we call *speech genres*. (1986: 60)

The three modes of discourse I have identified combine to form an identifiable genre. Todorov (1984: 81) reminds us that 'the notion of genre is not the exclusive prerogative of literature; it is rooted in the everyday use of language'. I repeat here, Quakers do indeed spend a great deal of time talking to one another at meeting, but they communicate in a variety of other ways – through gesture and posture, dress, notices, use of furniture and other props, use of space and time, and so forth. Together these modes of communication produce an identifiable Quaker genre. Bakhtin (ibid.: 80), does rather more than Bourdieu to emphasize individual agency:

> Genres must be fully mastered in order to be manipulated freely . . . The better our command of genres, the more freely we employ them, the more fully and clearly we reveal our own individuality in them (where this is possible and necessary), the more flexibly and precisely we reflect the unrepeatable situation of communication – in a word, the more perfectly we implement our free speech plan.

This bears a striking resemblance to Bourdieu's use of the term 'feel for the game' in describing the proficiency of individuals in manipulating the rules established by the habitus (1990: 61).

From Talk to Narrative

At first, meeting seemed to be merely a hodgepodge of talk. After a year or so, however, I came to appreciate the way in which talk was patterned, or thematized – or storied. As Bell (1998: 53) concisely puts it, 'conversation . . . is not random'. Conversations at Meeting consisted primarily of the exchange of narratives. Friends introduced and then developed their stories, embroidering them week after week. Plot lines were anticipated, sometimes with enthusiasm, sometimes with a certain dread. In any case narrative has a undeniable *momentum*. Friends talked most regularly with those with whom they could share a narrative, whether it be Quaker theology, local history, music, gardening, schoolteaching, family, friends, green environmentalism, pacifism or whatever. Furthermore, 'every utterance is also related to previous utterances, thus creating intertextual (or dialogical) relations' (Todorov 1984: 48). I came to see this as the glue which held meeting together (cf. Gluckman 1963).

As I became more familiar with narrative theory this discovery seemed less surprising. Writers across a variety of disciplines have argued for some time that narrative is fundamental to being human – it serves, one might say, to define sociality. Cognitive psychologist Jerome Bruner argues persuasively that there are two way of knowing, 'the paradigmatic or logico-scientific' mode and narrative. For Bruner, telling stories is a means of constructing reality (1986: 11–12).

At meeting Friends co-construct narratives – of family, friends, Friends, gardening, literature, 'green issues', pacifism, vegetarianism, Quaker business, football, music. These narratives both consist of and contribute towards the spheres outlined above – the canonic, the local and the individual. I discovered that the same plots surface with considerable regularity. There is a distinct pleasure in discovering order in apparent chaos. I made a mistake, however, in overestimating the monologic character of these narratives. As is commonly the case in narrative analysis, one emphasizes the telling of a story *by* one person *to* another. Reading Bakhtin has encouraged me to think again about the narratives I collected (and participated in) at Meeting. More importantly though, the concept of dialogism provides a means, hitherto lacking, of articulating the three modes of discourse I have identified. But we need to beware: as Bernard-Donals (1994: 34) warns, 'The terms "dialogue" and "dialogism" are often confused or misunderstood'. He goes on (ibid.):

> Dialogue is not so much a discourse between two people (as in Saussure's notorious model of one interlocutor 'pitching' and another 'catching' meaning), as it is a metaphor for the welter of communication that exists in the social world generally. Rather than involving an exchange of meanings, there occurs an exchange of selves, since language is the medium with which subjects conceive of their world and their placement in it.

Although in using the terms 'discourse', 'talking relationship' and 'dialogic' I have focused attention on narratives expressed verbally, discourse has a rather wider remit, including gesture, written texts, furnishings, items hung on the walls and so on and so forth; narratives are most obviously developed through talk but are not restricted to that means of communication alone. Dialogic interaction may take place over the course of seconds – or years: there is always the possibility of response.

Conclusions: From Discourse (and Narrative) to Dialogism

My preference for the term 'dialogism' (rather than 'discourse' or 'narrative' for example) is easily explained. Before fully appreciating the importance of Bakhtin's ideas relating to the construction of our selves I argued in favour of the fundamentally co-authored nature of everyday narratives (Collins 1996a). Bakhtin endeavoured over the course of several decades to develop, though rather unsystematically (Dentith 1995: 88; Morson and Emerson 1990: 232) the concept of the dialogic to express and emphasize both the connectedness of what may appear to be individual (in his terms 'monologic') narratives. As I re-read texts on the nature of narrative I am increasingly struck by the non-dialogic basis of these accounts and see this as a major failing (cf. De Peuter 1998). Dialogism, furthermore, helps us understand the articulation of the modes of Quaker discourse identified above.

Although Bakhtin did not coin the term dialogism it goes some way toward identifying his primary concern: 'all Bakhtin's writings are animated and controlled by the principle of dialogue' (Holquist 1990:15). Dialogue consists of an utterance (or communicative act), a reply, and, critically, a relation between the two. For Bakhtin dialogism and sociality are two sides of the same coin. And while I agree with Taylor (1991: 314) when he states, 'Human beings are constituted in conversation', I repeat yet again that although I might seem to equate dialogue with talk, I envisage a much broader remit for the term, to include conversation by means of any system of communication: speech, gesture, dress, architecture, furnishings, art and so forth – any means by which individuals and groups can construct and even share meanings. All these sign systems are alive and well in the Quaker meeting: a sapling donated by Freda was planted by her small daughter Sally. Sally now has grown-up children who have talked about their drawings of the tree (a huge cherry immediately outside the meeting room window) with Friends in meeting. More than one Friend has drawn the attention of meeting to the tree during spring, when it is in blossom, deriving Quakerly lessons from it. Existence, according to Bakhtin, is not just an event, but an utterance: 'The event of existence has the nature of dialogue in this sense: "there is no word directed at no one"'. (Holquist 1990: 27). Dialogism is central to Bakhtin's epistemology, but what then does it amount to and how might it further illuminate our understanding of the Quaker Meeting?

In the first place, Bakhtin's work is both anti-Hegelian and anti-determinist. An appreciation of his work does not predispose one to accept religion as a thing, as an external force (whatever its origin) which structures the way an individual acts and interacts with others. Quakerism is emergent in the interaction of individuals. Secondly, to grasp dialogism is to appreciate the fundamental importance of otherness. Indeed, as Holquist remarks, 'in dialogism consciousness *is* otherness' (ibid.: 18, italics in the original). The self, for Bakhtin, can only be properly comprehended as dialogic, as a relation. Third, Holquist argues, Bakhtin draws on the theory of relativity in arguing that 'one body's motion has meaning only in relation to (or in dialogue with) another body. In relation to the Quaker meeting for worship, each Friend co-ordinates his or her sitting and posture or *hexis* (Bourdieu 1977: 93–4), and even his or her subtle movement and proxemic relations, with those of other participants. Even though all participants may not agree on the meaning of sitting in a circle during worship, they continue to form a circle. Finally, Smith (1988: 64) is prompted by her reading of Bakhtin to suggest that texts, whether canonic, vernacular or prototypical, are 'active'. They reverberate with voices and provoke response. And how apt it is, given Bakhtin's emphasis on the relationships that sustain sociality, that so much of Quaker talk revolves around the notion 'meeting'.

Dialogue's drive to meaning does not lead to a Hegelian unity; in the Quaker meeting as in Bakhtin, there is no one meaning being striven for: 'the world is a vast congeries of contested meanings, a heteroglossia so varied that no single term capable of unifying its diversifying energies is possible' (Holquist 1990: 24; cf. Rapport 1993). Furthermore, Bakhtin's meditations on the quotidien, according to Morson and Emerson (1990: 236–7), lead him to argue that our understanding of the world is necessarily open-ended:

> The dialogic sense of truth manifests unfinalizability by existing on the threshold of several interacting consciousnesses, a 'plurality' of 'unmerged voices'. Crucial here is the modifier *unmerged*. These voices cannot be contained within a single consciousness, as in monologism; rather their separateness is essential to dialogue.

And this must be equally true for the poet and the scientist, the anthropologist and the Quaker. Dialogue depends on difference and difference depends on the other. And as Bakhtin points out, the other is all around us.

Todorov compares Bakhtin's 'philosophical anthropology', especially the mutually dependent relationship of I and thou, with the work of Jacobi, Fichte, von Humboldt, Kierkegaard, Feuerbach, Buber, Sartre and G.H. Mead and says, 'As is common in these matters, it is not the idea that is new in Bakhtin, but the place that it occupies in his system of thought, and the consequences it leads to' (1984: 118). Although it may appear otherwise, I have not intended this chapter as a presentation of increasingly 'true' accounts of a Quaker meeting. However, it is the case that a Bakhtinian analysis appeals to both the anthropologist and the Quaker in me and the chapter is itself a part of a continuing and reflexive dialogue between anthropology and Quakerism. It does not represent a conclusion, and is far from being even my last word on the subject. To sustain conversation is to be human and the Quaker meeting facilitates this project. It seems reasonable to suggest that what we have said about the Quaker meeting will be meaningful in relation to other religious groups, both in Britain and in other places. At least, I hope so.

The last time I was in Dibdenshaw meeting house, it took me some time to find the canonic text I was looking for. A Friend had rearranged the books according to a different logic.

Acknowledgements

I am grateful to Simon Coleman and Nigel Rapport for their constructive comments on earlier drafts of this chapter.

References

Bakhtin, M.M. (1981) *The Dialogic Imagination* trans. C. Emerson and M. Holquist, Austin: University of Texas Press.
—— (1986) *Speech Genres and Other Later Essays* trans. V.W. McGee, Austin: University of Texas Press.
—— (1990) *Art and Answerability* trans. V. Liapunov, Austin: University of Texas Press.
—— (1993) *Toward a Philosophy of the Act* trans. V. Liapunov, Austin: University of Texas Press.
Bateson, G. (1958) *Naven*, Stanford: Stanford University Press.
Bell, M. (1998) 'Culture as Dialogue', in M. Bell and M. Gardiner (eds), *Bakhtin and the Human Sciences*, London: Sage.
Bender, C. (1998) 'Bakhtinian Perspectives on "Everyday Life" Sociology', in M. Bell and M. Gardiner (eds), *Bakhtin and the Human Sciences*, London: Sage.
Bernard-Donals, M. (1994) *Mikhail Bakhtin: Between Phenomenology and Marxism*, Cambridge: Cambridge University Press.
Bourdieu, P. (1977) *Outline of a Theory of Practice* trans. R. Nice, Cambridge: Cambridge University Press.
—— (1990) *In Other Words: Essays Towards a Reflexive Sociology*, Cambridge: Polity.
Braithwaite, W.C. (1921[1919]) *The Second Period of Quakerism*, London: Macmillan.
—— (1923[1912]) *The Beginnings of Quakerism*, London: Macmillan.
Brayshaw, A.N. (1982) *The Quakers: Their Story and Message*, York: Sessions.
Bruce, S. (1995) *Religion in Modern Britain*, Oxford: Oxford University Press.
Bruner, J. (1986) *Actual Minds, Possible Worlds*, Cambridge, Mass.: Harvard University Press.
—— (1990) *Acts of Meaning*, Cambridge, Mass.: Harvard University Press.
Christian Faith and Practice in the Experience of the Society and Friends. Volume One of the Book of Discipline of London Yearly Meeting Of the Society of Friends (1960) London: London Yearly Meeting.
Clark, D. (1982) *Between Pulpit and Pew, Folk Religion in a North Yorkshire Fishing Village*, Cambridge, Cambridge University Press.
Cohen, A.P. (1985) *The Symbolic Construction of Community*, London: Routledge.
—— (1992) 'Self-Conscious Anthropology', in J. Okely and H. Callaway (eds) *Anthropology and Autobiography*, London: Routledge.
Collins, P.J. (1996a) 'Narrative, Auto/biography and the Quaker Meeting', *Auto/Biography* 4(2/3): 27–38.

—— (1996b) '"Plaining": The Social and Cognitive Practice of Symbolisation in the Religious Society of Friends (Quakers)', *Journal of Contemporary Religion* 11: 277–88.

—— (1998) 'Quaker Worship: an Anthropological Perspective', *Worship* 72(6): 501–15.

—— (in press) 'Connecting Anthropology and Quakerism', in E. Arweck and M.D. Stringer (eds), *Theorising Faith*, Birmingham: Birmingham University Press.

Dandelion, P. (1996) *A Sociological Analysis of the Theology of Quakers*, Lampeter: Edwin Mellen Press.

Davie, G. (1994) *Religion in Britain since 1945: Believing Without Belonging*, Oxford: Blackwell.

Dentith, S. (1995) *Bakhtinian Thought: An Introductory Reader*, London: Routledge.

De Peuter, J. (1998) 'The Dialogics of Narrative Identity', in M. Bell and M. Gardiner (eds), *Bakhtin and the Human Sciences*, London: Sage.

Evans-Pritchard, E.E. (1956) *Nuer Religion*, Oxford: Oxford University Press.

Geertz, C. (1973) *The Interpretation of Cultures*, New York: Basic Books.

Gillman, H. (1988) *A Light that is Shining: An Introduction to the Quakers*, London: Quaker Home Service.

Gorman, G.H. (1981) *Introducing Quakers*, London: Quaker Home Service.

Gluckman, M. (1963) 'Gossip and Scandal', *Current Anthropology* 4(3): 307–16.

Holquist, M. (1990) *Dialogism: Bakhtin and His World*, London: Routledge.

Jenkins, T. (1999) *Religion in Everyday Life*, Oxford: Berghahn.

Jones, R. (1921) *The Later Periods of Quakers*, 2 vols, London: Macmillan.

Kent, T. (1991) 'Hermeneutics and Genre', in D. Hiley, J. Bohman and R. Shusterman (eds) *The Interpretive Turn: Philosophy, Science, Culture*, Ithaca and London: Cornell University Press.

Leach, E.R. (1976) *Culture and Communication*, Cambridge: Cambridge University Press.

Lévi-Strauss, C. (1976) *The Savage Mind*, London: Weidenfeld & Nicholson.

Lewis, G. (1980) *Day of Shining Red: An Essay on Understanding Ritual*, Cambridge: Cambridge University Press.

Lienhardt, R.G. (1961) *Divinity and Experience: the Religion of the Dinka*, Oxford: Oxford University Press.

Luhrmann, T.M. (1989) *Persuasions of the Witch's Craft*, Oxford: Basil Blackwell.

Middleton, J. (1960) *Lugbara Religion: Ritual and Authority Among an East African People*, Oxford: Oxford University Press.

Milligan, E. (1968) *The Past is Prologue*, London: Quaker Peace and Service.

Moore, R. (1974) *Pit-Men, Preachers and Politics, The Effects of Methodism in a Durham Mining Community*, Cambridge: Cambridge University Press.

Morris, B. (1987) *Anthropological Studies of Religion, An Introductory Text*, Cambridge: Cambridge University Press.

Morson, G.S. and C. Emerson (1990) *Mikhail Bakhtin: Creation of a Prosaics*, Stanford: Stanford University Press.

Nickalls, J.L. (ed.) (1952) *Journal of George Fox*, Cambridge, Cambridge University Press.

Ormerod Greenwood, J. (1975–78) *Quaker Encounters*, 3 Vols, York: Sessions.

Punshon, J. (1984) *Portrait in Grey: A Short History of the Quakers*, London: Quaker Home Service.

Quaker Faith and Practice: The Book of Christian Discipline of the Yearly Meeting of the Religious Society of Friends (Quakers) in Britain (1995), London: London Yearly Meeting.

Rapport, N. (1993) *Diverse World-Views in An English Village*, Edinburgh: Edinburgh University Press.

—— (1997) *Transcendent Individual*, London: Routledge.

Smith, D.E. (1998) 'Bakhtin and the Dialogic of Sociology: An Investigation', in M. Bell and M. Gardiner (eds), *Bakhtin and the Human Sciences*, London: Sage.

Southwold, M. (1983) *Buddhism in Life: The Anthropological Study of Religion and the Sinhalese Practice of Buddhism*, Manchester: Manchester University Press.

Stringer, M.D. (1999) *On the Perception of Worship: The Ethnography of Worship in Four Christian Congregations in Manchester*, Birmingham: Birmingham University Press.

Stromberg, P.G. (1986) *Symbols of Community: The Cultural System of a Swedish Church*, Tucson: University of Arizona Press.

Taylor, C. (1991) 'The Dialogical Self', in D. Hiley, J. Bohman and R. Shusterman (eds) *The Interpretive Turn: Philosophy, Science, Culture*, Ithaca and London: Cornell University Press.

Thomas, T. (ed.) (1988) *The British, Their Religious Beliefs and Practices 1800–1986*, London: Routledge.

Todorov, T. (1984) *Mikhail Bakhtin: the Dialogical Principle* trans. W. Godzich, Minneapolis: University of Minnesota Press.

Turner, V. (1969) *The Ritual Process*, London: Routledge & Kegan Paul.

Van Gennep, A. (1960[1908]) *Rites of Passage* trans. M. Vizedom and G. Caffee, London: Routledge & Kegan Paul.

Vice, S. (1997) *Introducing Bakhtin*, Manchester: University of Manchester Press.

Wallace, A.F.C. (1961) *Culture and Personality*, New York: Random House.

Watling, T. (1999) 'Negotiating Religious Pluralism: The Dialectical Development of Religious Identities in the Netherlands', Unpublished PhD dissertation, University of London.

–15–

The Body of the Village Community: Between Reverend Parkington in Wanet and Mr Beebe in *A Room with a View*
Nigel Rapport

[Man] is a sort of novelist of himself who conceives the fanciful figure of a personage with its unreal occupations and then, for the sake of converting it into reality, does all the things he does.

José Ortega y Gasset, *Man and People*

Introduction

Important correspondences exist between literary and anthropological enterprises, I would contend, such that reading the English novelist E.M. Forster furthers my interpretation of lives in the English village of Wanet (the site of my field research), while writing about Wanet furthers my appreciation of Forster; I can profitably zigzag between the voices of Forsterian characters and those of my informants in Wanet, and list significant overlaps in the ways they and their authors (Forster and I) symbolically construct the world. Such a literary-anthropological enterprise throws into sharp relief the possible and necessary blurring of genres of represent- ation in contemporary sociocultural accounting (cf. Rapport 1994).

In this chapter I present an example of these correspondences and overlaps in the form of an elucidation of the position of Revd John Parkington, the Anglican vicar in Wanet, a small rural English village and dale in the county of Cumbria, as set against the figure of Mr Arthur Beebe, the Anglican rector of the Surrey village of Summer Street, in E.M. Forster's novel *A Room with a View*. Between novel and ethnography the chapter traces one set of expressed ideas, running through people's talk in Wanet as they negotiate relations and engage in the continuing symbolic construction of their environments and selves just as it runs through Forster's story-line. These ideas concern the failure of the local minister of religion to partake in that reciprocity of physical relations which, in the eyes of a number of local inhabitants, is necessary for local belonging. for membership in the body of the community. Parkington and Beebe alike stand outwith the boundary of community and, indeed, are used by locals in Wanet as by Forster in order to identify where precisely that boundary lies and by what it is constituted.

The Church in Wanet

The Church has perhaps long been significantly and tactically 'other' to the Wanet farmer. Certainly for Mary Stirling, running a milk-round, a milking herd and a sheep flock on land she owns with husband Sam, farming means both having little time from her labours to go to church and pray, even on a Sunday, and also being bound to a workaday world whose tensions and frustrations cause her unavoidably to curse and swear, and thus unfit her for the innocence of church-going.

Equally, for Mary, the otherness of the Church has been exacerbated by the arrival in Wanet of a permanent 'offcomer' population and the alien urban way of life it has attempted to introduce. In Mary's judgement, the Church in Wanet has gone 'up the shit', manifesting itself primarily in pomp, and a weekly competition over who can parade the best fur coat; whereas religion should not properly bother about such matters at all. Furthermore, the Wanet church now traffics in hypocrisy. For while Mary refrains from attending and would distinguish between the purity, the ethereality, of the Church on one side and the corner-cutting pragmatics of the world of business survival on another, others do not. Hence, Wanet churchgoers look down their noses at the rest. They call themselves religious but they are more grasping, selfish and hateful than so-called non-religious people, indulging in foul tempers and 'f'-ing and blinding at all and sundry. When it comes to their neighbours, indeed, churchgoers behave in a more weird and cock-eyed fashion, and are less 'straight' than anyone else. They think evil and do evil; it was a neighbouring churchgoer who stole Mary's hay. Even becoming church sidesmen does not stop them cheating at the local markets so as to get a better deal on their stock, it seems, and 'screw' everyone else in the process. Finally, the present church administration has the effrontery to request outright that Wanet women organize fund-raising coffee-mornings – as if local people had not always stood by their church over the past centuries, and ensured its survival, in their own subtle ways! In short, for Mary the arrival of the offcomers has made the otherness of the Church into something blatant, aggressive, even threatening. For if she does not now expressly support the coffee-mornings, and if she does not go about her Sunday farmwork quietly and unobtrusively, then far from respecting her hard work and her belief in it, far from appreciating her farm schedule and its demands, the churchgoers are likely to boycott her milk-round and threaten her business survival.

Having introduced Mary and begun to elaborate upon her views, let me at this point explain something about the wider context of Wanet as a place. Wanet is a dale of some 650 people situated in a very scenic part of Cumbria, north-west

England (Rapport 1993). Traditionally, Wanet's economy centred around pastoral hill-farming with a full accompaniment of artisans, traders and servicemen. This was not a peasant economy, however, for the community was wholly involved in a cash nexus: individual farmers and their farm-labourers producing cash crops (wool and milk, primarily) for a commodity market which included ready sales of land and labour. But the economy was based on large numbers of people labouring on the land. Nowadays, farming remains the single most frequent occupation but it is mechanized farming, on a larger scale, catering for far fewer family units and fewer paid labourers. Nor has Wanet's comparative remoteness and distance from urban centres of population historically entailed its isolation from industrialism or urbanism. In recent years, indeed, Wanet has seen an influx of residential newcomers from the city, buying up property in the dale, raising prices and making housing scarce. Some of this purchasing is for holiday homes, but most is for houses for retirement, or else houses in which to escape the urban rat-race – while still following one's profession as artist, architect, teacher, or even still commuting to the computer job in the city. Of the 650 residents of the dale, then, some 190 are now relative newcomers – or 'offcomers', come from off-aways.

Of Wanet's buildings, the two Anglican churches are among the dale's oldest, with St Nicholas's (dating back to Norman times) probably *the* oldest. In sociological terms too, the churches are closely interwoven with the overt structures of local life. Thus, since statutes of Henry VI in the fifteenth century, the right of patronage to the living of the Anglican minister in Wanet (his selection and funding) has been shared with the bishop of the diocese by a committee of 24 local landowners known as sidesmen, or synodsmen, or statesmen. The Wanet Parochial Church Committee is also empowered to disburse rental income from church-owned lands to local charitable causes (such as the Badminton and Youth Clubs, the Choral Society, the Reading Room Association) and, now that the workhouse is defunct, to house local needy on church-owned properties with inexpensive leases. Meanwhile, church services are closely tied to the agricultural calendar as well as bearing witness to local rites of passage throughout the year. Finally, the church also provides the location for the dale's institutional business, from the storage of population registers in the vestry, to the monthly parish council meeting in the church hall.

However, Mary is not alone in finding the Church 'other'. Thus, there is a frequent distancing, if not depreciation, in local gossip of church-sponsored activities as 'high-brow', as Richard puts it; the choral and dramatic events involving the church and its predominant social circle are nowadays 'too high-powered for the likes of a village', Barbara claims. Meanwhile, 'the first *local* buildings', Arthur emphasizes to the tourist, 'date from around the 1300s' – whatever may be the purely physical claims of the Norman church; while as a test of my own genuineness and trustworthiness on my arrival in Wanet to undertake anthropological fieldwork – a 'mystery man' and possible spy or terrorist – Des suggests I be set the task of 'dynamiting the vicarage'.

Of special significance is that other local voices share Mary's bitterness that the Church and its supporters no longer play fair: do not reciprocate with behavourial proprieties befitting, matching, her own. Thus, for instance, on having her own services enlisted for the coffee-morning fund-raising drive, Hattie complains that the Church receives enough help already and what would be nice would be the organization of a Wanet Diners' Club to assist in the upkeep of her restaurant business: she would help the Church if the Church helped her! Similarly, Harry, irate at having his darts game in the local pub interrupted by the arrival of a group of carol-singers, admits he would sooner 'tell them to bugger-off than give them a penny! They're parasites who never come to the Eagle to drink the rest of the year so why bother with them now?'. Instead of seeking outside contributions, they should keep 'their Communion and their religious frenzy' to themselves.

What is striking in such spoken accounts is the linkage made between the otherness of the Church and its failure to reciprocate economically in local business relations. At the core of these expressions of discontent with the Church, of separation, indeed alienation, from the way its affairs are locally handled, is its seeming refusal to play a reciprocal part in (at least have a reciprocal respect for) the harsh world of village survival. And talk of reciprocity, I want to suggest, is a crucial way of marking boundaries of local sociality.

Reciprocity

Reciprocity has also long been a crucial part of the social-scientific toolbox of sociality. It is reciprocity which is essential for social cohesion, asserted Simmel; stable interpersonal relations and a stable social system depend on a reciprocity of gratification, Parsons averred; economic transaction between two parties entails continuing reciprocal action and reaction from both sides, Sahlins attested; 'homo reciprocus', Becker concluded.

For a definition of reciprocity we may turn to a classic article of Alvin Gouldner's: 'a mutually contingent exchange of benefits between two or more units', whereby units can refer to either individuals or groups (1977: 31). Here is 'a basic particle of socialization', 'a prescription both for initiating and maintaining stable social interaction'. Here is a norm ('Do as you would be done by'), vague and indeterminate enough for all manner of strategic and *ad hoc* use: an all-purpose moral cement flexible enough to serve as the basis of social relations and also to fill the cracks between them (1977: 35–9).

In a particularly pertinent section of his article, Gouldner considers the distinctions between reciprocity and complementarity: while complementarity describes a situation where one party's rights are another's obligations and vice versa, reciprocity implies that each party has comparable rights in and duties to the other: here is a symmetry which complementary relations lack (1977: 34). Yet, returning to Wanet, it is precisely this symmetry of relations which statements by the likes of Mary, Harry and Hattie claim to be missing between locals on the one side and the Anglican vicar, the Church and its set of energetic, often recently arrived, supporters on the other. Here is a discourse on reciprocity which Cyril Hethering, in summary fashion, rehearsed for me:

> You seem to like Wanet, Nigel, and I've enjoyed your company. You look like you'll be here for good: people either love it here or hate it, and you seem to love it. You're not as daft as you look! . . . Maybe this is a stupid speech and I'm not saying it the right way, but I think you and I share a philosophy of life. I mean some people come here and understand nothing of our way of life but you've kept your eyes open: you know, you've been privileged in being allowed to see some aspects of village life . . . Like, something I really admire in village life is that there's always someone to help you out, even do your work for you if necessary. Like, recently I was ill and without asking me or expecting pay, someone stepped in and did my work for me! Traditionally, you know, everyone was like this. You walked down the street, you knew everyone and you would help them all, without thinking about what you were getting out of it. And my recipe of life has always been to give and to help others. I'm not religious and I'd help someone of any religion – Protestant, Jewish, whatever – as a fellow human being; religious differences are no big problem, see. Because most folks are good; you get a few bad buggers but most are good, and from them you'll get a return, sometime and in some form, even if at first you don't recognize it as such . . . But, you know, in the last ten years it's changed. Because there's been population moving in intent on grabbing all they can for themselves but not keen on working for the benefit of the village and putting nowt back. They're simply here for their own profit not for helping the village as a whole or the dale of Wanet; but they're the important things. These folks are content to exploit the ancient name of the dale and all its features but they're just using it to line their own pockets, see lad? They just grab what they can for themselves without a real feeling for the village or the dale. All this happened in the last ten years, see, and they certainly haven't helped the village . . . Now you know I'm an honest man and I speak my mind and this is just what I feel.

When Mary wants to point the finger at a single figure responsible, at an epitome of the rottenness of the situation, her criticism invariably alights on the Anglican vicar, Revd John Parkington; he serves to emblemize for her the present Church. Moreover, he is an offcomer, Mary complains, who does not understand how local people behave, the Wanet way of doing things. Indeed, he himself 'does nothing', and he is 'weak as water', to boot.

It is true that Revd John Parkington and his family are recent arrivals in Wanet. A Cambridge University graduate, he resided at a number of parishes around the country, most recently in a southern seaside town, before reaching Wanet. He has a number of adult children, a son about to sit his Oxbridge entrance exam and two more daughters in secondary schools. While attempting friendliness, it is Revd Parkington's wife, who grew up in the Berkshire countryside, and his children, who have lately grown up in Wanet (and supported secular associations such as the Badminton Club, besides the sacred duties required of them – playing the church organ, ringing the church bells), who have succeeded more in negotiating local relations. But with the taint of his association, all remain rather secluded in the Anglican vicarage, a family apart from the local community.

The vicarage is one of the largest private houses in Wanet. An imposing Victorian stone edifice, it stands in its own grounds near the centre of the village (when a stray cow gets beyond the garden walls, indeed, the vicar complains vehemently of the hoofmarks in the lawn). However, now that domestic servants cannot be afforded and heating costs are prohibitive too, the vicarage has become unviable and parish council plans are currently afoot to build a new, smaller vicarage. It was the need to secure further funds for this project which eventuated in the rota of coffee-mornings among the Wanet women to which Mary and Hattie took such exception: as if the church was shorter of money than local farmers; as if the vicar's family was too posh simply to split the existing vicarage into two and sublet one half.

But the division between the vicar and Church and the community of locals goes deeper than this, I suggest. The otherness of the Church precedes the arrival of the present incumbent, goes beyond the influx of offcomers, and overshadows differences between the practicalities of a workaday world and the niceties of ideal, ethereal morality. Church and community in Wanet can never be conjoined, I argue, because community belonging, as it is constructed in the words of Mary and Cyril *et al.*, is based on a notion of reciprocity which is in essence physical: it is in terms of reciprocal physical (earthy, bodily, fleshy) doings that belonging in Wanet is seen as deriving. At least for some inhabitants, sometimes, Wanet represents a community of the flesh, and it is by way of certain reciprocal physicalities, both proper (business exchanges, marriages, pub recreations) and improper (business loans, extra-marital affairs, pub fights), and their gossipy appreciation, that community belonging comes to be measured, substantiated and witnessed. Furthermore, this is something to which Revd Parkington and his Church are never to be admitted. In fact, they can be used as the very emblems of non-belonging: introduced into inference and interaction as very evidence of the boundary, and the separateness and alienness of all those who stand outside it.

The Church in *A Room with a View*

Before proceeding further with Wanet, however, let me juxtapose against my description of Revd John Parkington and his Church that of Forster's Mr Arthur Beebe, the rector of Summer Street in the novel *A Room With a View* (1983[1908]).

For Forster's detailed observation and analysis of the manners and mores of an English society in which he was also a participant means that the 'social novelist' is able here to suggest important insights to the social anthropologist. Not only will this elucidate the situation under scrutiny in Wanet but may also suggest a way of viewing some of Mr Beebe's behaviour in the novel over which Forster's editor Oliver Stallybrass describes readers as cavilling ever since its publication in 1908.

A Room With a View concerns itself with the meeting and marriage of two young English people of different upbringing, world-view and class, Lucy Honeychurch and George Emerson. George, a railway clerk and motherless, has been brought up by his free-thinking father as a socialist and with the habit of always saying exactly what he means, of speaking the truth as he sees it. As Mr Beebe describes him, George seems a nice creature, if pessimistic and immature; goodly not good, with brains and his father's mannerisms, without the manners and tact to keep his opinions to himself. He reads Nietzsche and Schopenhauer but has not yet learned to talk in society – even if the chances are that he will work off his crudities in time. Lucy, on the other hand, fatherless but brought up by a mother and aunt in a well-appointed country house and the bosom of provincial society, is socially well adept. Again, as described by Mr Beebe, she is a pretty young lady but a quiet uneventful childhood has left her critical discernment undeveloped; she 'loves everything' and from pictures to clothes sense misses life's true beauties. What saves Lucy in Mr Beebe's eyes is the wonderful way she plays the piano – Beethoven especially. Musicians, he knows, are more complex than other artists, more puzzling, because they know less of themselves and their wants; but if, as is reasonable, the watertight compartments within Lucy break down so that her life and her music mingle, then she and her consociates will be in for a very exciting time.

On the face of it, then, George and Lucy seem an unlikely pair. But then as the above accounts show, the development of their characters and their relations is closely scrutinized not to say supervised by Mr Beebe, the book's sometime participant-observer, with 'pet theories', as well as Anglican vicar. George and Lucy first met in Italy, while staying at the same pension in Florence, run by the cockney Signora Bertolini. Part One of the book takes place here, in and around Florentine piazzas and hill-sides, before the drama turns to Lucy's house, Windy Corner, and the village of Summer Street in Surrey. In Florence, it soon becomes clear that Lucy and George are not the only social mismatch with which Forster is concerned. Most glaring, initially, is the abyss dividing the radical secular Emersons, father and son, from the remainder of polite English society both on vacation in the pension and in expatriate residence in Florentine villas. But then divisions are also signalled between the critical appreciation of those domiciled in Florence and those just passing through; and between the temperament of the

English as a whole and that of the Italians. When the action switches to England, divisions continue to multiply: between the fashionable society of London and that of the provinces, between feminine sensibilities and masculine, between the possessors of leisure and of an occupation, between the blindness of youth and the blindfolds of maturity, and so on. What is especially significant here is that Mr Beebe attempts to straddle them all; indeed it is his awareness of them, his reflection upon them which causes ours. Right the way through the novel, Mr Beebe acts as the conduit of almost all successful social interaction and relationship. It is only at the novel's end that his social skills and understanding are seen to leave him, in the scene with which, Stallybrass reports, readers are dissatisfied; but we shall consider that a little later. For the moment it would be fair to describe Mr Beebe as omniscient in his mediation and observation. The confidence of his tones really serve *in loco auctoriensis*, were it not for the winning way in which Forster has him 'discover' the other characters and make considerations of the plot alongside the reader.

For example, it is not long after meeting Lucy Honeychurch and her chaperoning aunt, Charlotte Bartlett, and 'gazing rather thoughtfully' upon them that Mr Beebe retires to his room 'to write up his philosophic diary'; an entry, we later learn, which takes the form of sketches in which Lucy is a kite whose string, held by Miss Bartlett, eventually snaps. That is, Mr Beebe serves *in loco lectoriensis* too, abstracting from meetings and incidents and reaching sociologic and artistic generalizations which Forster offers for our meta-consciousness of his novel, initially at least; indeed it is the 'heroic' consciousness of Mr Beebe and our identification with him which makes Forster's final 'betrayal' of him all the more shocking. But allow me to introduce him and his mission a little more first.

Mr Beebe is a 'stout but attractive' figure, bald, with a pair of russet whiskers, a man whose 'social resources' Forster describes as 'endless'. Lucy describes him as 'nice' and indeed so prone to laugh and see good in everyone that 'no one would take him for a clergyman'. What Beebe has at his disposal is a great felicity of phrase. This he uses to put his fellows at ease in one another's company. He also acts as go-between, advises on liaisons, guarantees their propriety, acts as a 'neutral' in factional dispute, and 'gently' tries to improve sociality.

Mr Beebe's life-speciality, it seems, is dealing with maiden ladies with which his profession is said to provide him ample opportunities. It is their nervous social exchange, their verbal fetishes, that he has most chance to study, becoming knitted, as a rector is wont, 'in a web of petty secrets, and confidences, and warnings'. Nevertheless, 'for rather profound reasons', Mr Beebe, we hear, 'was somewhat chilly in his attitude to the opposite sex', his frequent association with old maids turning upon his knowing how to deal with their gossiping, and preferring to indulge himself in this competence rather than risk becoming enthralled by the vacuous prettiness of their younger social counterparts. Beebe himself, it should be said at this point, remains unmarried although he does entertain visits from his ageing mother and his brother's thirteen-year-old daughter; his own conclusion is that ideally he is 'better detached'.

Mr Beebe's habit of consciously separating his professional responsibilities and competency from his more philosophic predilections, his fluency in the society of maiden ladies, for example, as opposed to his disregard for the circumspection of their attitudes, is highly significant for my purposes here, not to mention Forster's in the novel. It is expressed most fully and significantly in regard to his behaviour towards George and Lucy.

When, at the outset, I described Mr Beebe as supervising relations between George and Lucy, this was not strictly true. The end result of his ministrations was, indeed, their union but this was not his intention – as cleric, at least. Instead this end result came from a confusion of Mr Beebe's professional and philosophic energies; so let me continue my exposition of Forster's narrative. Mr Beebe is described as having infinite tolerance for the young – that is, for those who have not yet 'come out' into society; he expects their antics to be ungracious, but he has no inclination to snub them. For what Beebe sees in the young is the potential for an individual to shape his or her life before slipping into a mould and having society – or as they might tend to phrase it, Fate – shape it for them. Beebe knows himself and his fellow adults to be leading lives of mere 'suburban' range: 'poor little Cockney lives', he calls them, bolstered up by all manner of 'weapons of propriety'. In a word, they are lives of manners. But there are other lives to lead. The Italians they meet on holiday, the 'things Italian' which Beebe and his fellows seek out, evidence a life of very different balance where manners give way to feeling and romance; the Italians draw the contrast between the mannered and the romantic, the professional and the philosophic, the socially good and evil, far more out into the open and the everyday.

What excites Beebe here, or rather engages his philosophic side, is Lucy Honeychurch's potential for leading a life which rises above suburban English quietude – as revealed by her playing of Beethoven. Her music can make her 'heroic', he says: that word we have seen Beebe associate with Italian society; she may be about to set out upon a life of heroic gestures and passions – whether these come to be dubbed good or bad. In fact, in Lucy's presence Beebe finds he can no longer act the parson 'without apology'. This admission is crucial. For here is Beebe embarrassed by the limitations of his English groundedness, by his religious profession, by the way in his own life that his propriety has held down his own philosophic desire. And here is Beebe imagining a severing of the knot between his two halves: on the one hand the professional parson adept in English society, on the other the philosophic diarist appreciative of the truthful relationship between Italian society and romance; surely here is Beebe not just willing a kite-like Lucy to rise but imagining flying free with her, unfettered by all but the wholly encompassing air.

Mr Beebe's moment of perhaps greatest joy in the novel comes when Lucy breaks off an engagement with the urbane and effete, pretentious and cerebral character, Cecil Vyse (whom she also met in Italy). However, Beebe's moment of greatest despair, for certain, is on realizing that Lucy loves George Emerson and will soon marry him. Just returned from Evensong, a 'long black column' in his vestments, and hearing the news, Mr Beebe goes very quiet 'and his white face with its ruddy whiskers, seemed suddenly inhuman'. "'I am more grieved than I can possibly express", he says, "It is lamentable, lamentable – incredible"' (1983: 225). It is this 'unexpected transformation' into someone unfeeling and inhuman which Stallybrass recounts readers cavilling over. In his editorial introduction (to the Penguin edition), he explains how critics have attributed it to Forster's 'invincible anticlericalism', if not his homosexuality: that Mr Beebe, a vicarious sensibility for Forster's own in many instances in the novel, had been in love with George Emerson himself. My reading, however, would suggest a different explanation. It is true that, in the climactic scene, Beebe exclaims with pique how George 'no longer interests him', but the real fount of his emotionality and the deep focus of his attention is revealed in the latter part of his outburst: 'Marry George, Miss Honeychurch. He will do admirably' (1983: 225). It is Lucy who has captivated, challenged, stimulated, Beebe all along and whom Beebe has now lost: the person she has turned to as spouse is really secondary; and he would dismiss him, whosoever.

Lucy and George return as a couple to Florence, but Mr Beebe as a character in the novel never recovers. We hear how he never forgives Lucy and George, never regains interest in them, never stops influencing others at home against them. So what is it precisely he has lost to cause such a hiatus in his sensitivity? It is not that he wanted Lucy for himself in a physical sense – he is too practised a bachelor for that and realizes he is 'better detached'. Nevertheless, he desperately wanted permanent access to Lucy as a medium, a mediatory device. The great irony of the novel is that it is the clergyman, the seeming arch social mediator who comes to realize that Lucy, the unconscious, non-social musician (and not he) is the crucial intermediary. And what she offers Beebe, philosophically speaking, is that holism where body and mind, flesh and high society, romance and propriety, passion and prose, can be imagined coming together as one. Mr Beebe, like Forster himself, is encompassed and encumbered by spinsterly women, from his ageing mother to Lucy's widowed mother and maiden aunt, to the majority of his rectorial congregation and acquaintance; all are nervily engaged with the intricacies of conventional English exchange. Also, Mr Beebe is old and fixed in his ways, and he is celibate. But if Lucy were to remain celibate too, as Beebe realizes he greatly desires her to be, then he could both retain his unalterable position in English society and overcome it too. With her as the very reverse of the women by whom he is surrounded – comparable to them in her spinsterhood, yes, compatible with him in her celibacy, yes, but still the opposite in her physical capacity to immerse herself in the currents of the air like a kite – then he could get hold of her string and be carried aloft as well. Now, however, through her marital engagement, his opportunity to hold that string and be transported is lost.

Before leaving Forster's novel and returning to Wanet, let me spell out the main point I would draw from it. Here is an Anglican cleric unable to move into a world of completeness of his parishioners, where the flesh and critical facilities combine, so long as he is intent on keeping his professional competencies intact. As rector to the village of Summer Street, he must remain tied to a round of spinsterish encounters, cut off from communion with the physical and deprived of an appreciation of the natural holistic view on the world it would provide. Here is Forster seeming to identify and comment upon a discourse which corresponds to one I would show use of in Wanet.

The Physicality of Community Belonging

When Cyril was asked by the elderly religious (Methodist) spinster, Margaret Wick, why he did not go to chapel, he told me one evening in the pub, he replied that he did not believe:

> Or not enough to go to chapel, anyway, and take up time that I could be out watching nature's world. See, lad, my chapel is nature's world. Now, if you watch my eyes, you see they never stop. They follow every movement. So when I'm driving down the dale in my taxi I see all around me at the same time. Behind me too: I see every movement and I'm always after new ones. I know all the tracks, see. And they're all related, you know lad. So if you see one sign then you know the others must also be there somewhere. Nature is a whole, lad.

It is this whole which Cyril is intent on observing, then: worshipping, indeed. And, despite the reticence of his farming neighbours (despite their embarrassment with, and avoidance of, the stereotypes with which they knew townies and other offcomers used to ridicule them, such as the earthiness of farmers and the animalism of their farmyards), Cyril's sentiments were often echoed. To cite just one more voice then, Mary would show her appreciation of nature, its fleshy completeness, in this fashion:

> Nowt beats nature, Nigel: being out on the farm. Being up in the hills with the animals is the best life in all weathers. Because you're busy with a different job everyday. Because you have responsibility for so much life. And because the animals change everyday, especially when it comes up to calving and lambing, each with their different name and character.

And Mary would extend this celebration to her human dealings as well. If farming animals gives you a feel of the fullness of life, its complexity and change, then similarly, 'a family should give you all you need to feel in life: it should make you happy and sad, proud and yes, even annoyed sometimes too'. In her family, as in nature, there is a wholeness of life and futurity in which she, like Cyril, is intent upon immersing herself. Furthermore, Mary's reasoning (the 'becauses' in the above quotation) is significant for what and whom it excludes; she is contemptuous of those who seem intent on missing out on life and nature completely – the offcomers – and simply fixating on history and death. Mary dislikes history. She can only watch half a television programme on 'all that stuff about rocks and bones and things' before becoming bored; she is not in the least interested. But sometimes that is all these offcomers seem able to be interested in. Death may be natural but offcomers seem to fill their lives with it: 'they drag what is past into present', and so succeed in thinking away their futures. And that's beyond her: she will 'never understand offcomers' different way of life'.

Mary's emphasis on offcomers and their fetish for history might have been made to some extent for my benefit, since I was presenting my interests in Wanet as primarily in local history. But it evidences, nevertheless, a more regular line of her thought: 'I'm not even interested in new dresses. I'm more interested in more realistic things like farming and animals. I love living and breathing things – animals and nature.' And, for example, when lambing time comes around and she helps the birthings and sortings out of lambs and mothers, she repeats:

No: dead lambs don't bother me, Nigel. Its the live ones I'm interested in, and finding them mums. Just like you shouldn't bring a dead person into the future. What's past is gone, and if you keep thinking about the dead, and try and think them into the future, like, you just get ill. Death shouldn't interest you.

From Mary and from Cyril, then, we hear of an appreciation of life in Wanet as a life in nature – observing, busily responding, tracking and helping. Life in Wanet – animal and human, farm and family, natural and workaday – should be seen as one; it is visual, gustatory, gestatory, emotional, in a word, physical. This is a life imbued with the knowledge of being part of a larger ongoing organic whole, and with an awareness of, an attunement to, those physical signs which evidence the growth and change of this whole as it moves from present to future. Indeed, the fleshy presence, the present, of life is so overwhelming, so encompassing, that those who can miss it, who see only their separate part of the whole or else fetishize what is fixed, past and dead, must themselves be a separate breed. They do not belong here in Wanet and should be shunned. While those who share the knowledge and the way of life celebrate their appreciation and their fellow belonging in appropriately fleshy interaction with each other – working, marrying, boozing together.

Let me elaborate on this latter point of community interaction by describing a scene in the pub one night in December towards the start of my own immersion as an anthropological fieldworker in Wanet. I select it because on reading through my fieldnotes I find that this scene and its aftermath signalled dramatic changes in tone and attitude towards me by my Wanet neighbours. I should say that at this early stage of my fieldwork it was in the pubs that I saw most people; and also how different routine pubbing was for me from the more ascetic regimen I had practised before the field: I was not an experienced boozer. But now I was becoming someone else. Hence, I was renting a local cottage and driving to the record office in a nearby town during the day in search of historical data; while in the evening (when not occasionally helping out my landlady by waiting on table in the small restaurant she ran) I was repairing to the local pubs in the hope of getting myself rapidly and acceptably known . . .

It is 10.25 p.m. and approaching the end of a quiet Friday evening in the Eagle. When I had walked in at 8 o'clock, Dave had called out, 'Hey, here's Leighton Philips' (the Welsh professional darts champion), in honour of the fact that I was from Cardiff, was bearded, and at a recent darts competition in the pub had gained some notoriety by a lucky defeat of one of the local darts champions. People had laughed with Dave. 'No, Rolf Harris, more like' (the Australian singer, and equally foreign, therefore, but short too), Dave's brother Des had retorted, to more laughs. Des had then bought me a beer while I had lent out my darts to Wendy, so that she could play Philip, before I had retreated to a quiet corner to play dominoes with old-timers Arthur and Jane, and Molly.

Now, having put the dominoes 'to bed', Arthur asks if I have enjoyed the evening; he likes just sitting quiet and he certainly needed a sit-down after standing working all day. But then I had better get drinking because I still have one-and-a-half pints to finish. I'm 'backwatering', Molly agrees. Now, do I know what that means round here, she asks. It means not keeping up with the local drinking rate: not a good thing to be accused of. Suddenly, there are laughs from the main body of the pub where Richard, beer glass in hand, is hopping around doing a comic dance and singing a little ditty. Soon his place is taken by Dave, singing a Scottish folk song in a loud voice that gets the womenfolk laughing and cringing; and it is not long before Des joins in too, competing with his brother over who sings better and knows more of the Scottish dialect. Wandering over, I join in too, and then Dave demands a Welsh song from me. So I start off 'Land of my Fathers' and soon run out of words, but Des joins me in 'la-la'-ing the tune. Then he tries 'Men of Harlech' and I suggest Blake's 'Jerusalem' which Des swops over to and Gary starts up too, before Dave drowns us out with a different version of 'Jerusalem' and Martin chimes in with 'God, you lot must be all Jews! Go away.' We stop, laughing, while Gary exaggeratedly strokes his nose and tells Martin to 'Piss Off'. Having stopped singing I notice that on the floor beside us, Wendy, Mary and Sue, giggling loudly, are showing off how they can do gymnastic crabs. This is then followed by Lance and Harry attempting handstands. Then Steven, the landlord, who used to teach gym in a Penrith school before he came to Wanet as a publican, marches round from behind the bar and shows us all not only how to balance properly in a handstand but that he can walk on his hands too. There are congratulations for Steven as he rights himself, Harry studying his hands to see the trick is not in their unusual size. Then I ask Steven if he can raise himself into a handstand from a headstand and, pleased that he cannot, show him that I can. Steven is impressed, and explains to the audience the difficulty of what I am attempting. So next, Dave dives down and does some press-ups, followed by Des asking Steven what you call those things they do on the 'Superstars' programme on TV, before showing us a few squat-thrusts. I ask Dave if he can do fist press-ups and show him a couple before deciding some one-arm press-ups might be even more impressive. As I start on these, I hear Sue calling Wendy over to watch and then her counting them out. After struggling to 14, Steven suggests to me that's enough because I'm beginning to look silly. So I get up in time to see Sue, Wendy, and Mary on the floor again doing more crabs, this time joined by Jenny too, as Linda fixes a flash cube to her camera and takes their picture. Steven is not finished yet, however, and he attempts to crawl under the row of arched female backs; but they all collapse on him in a hysterical heap.

Just then, Will, Wendy's husband and the Eagle darts team captain, walks over from the other side of the pub and demonstrates how he can raise himself up from a deep crouching position with his legs folded under him, and he challenges me to do the same. Then he poohpoohs my efforts before walking back to his seat. But no one is really interested any longer and the gymnastic activities come to an end; people return to the bar and their drinks. Philip then engages me in a deep discussion about weight-lifting, and about how broad his shoulders are, and how Will, inexplicably, is keeping him out of the Eagle darts team. But there is still a general atmosphere of bonhomie in the pub and I feel in the thick of it.

At last it is time to go, and Philip and I head for the back door. There we say goodnight to Wendy, Will's wife, who asks if we are both going to the village dance on Saturday night in support of Wanet Badminton Club. Wendy, I know from my landlady's restaurant, where she works as a waitress, as well as from the Badminton Club which I have joined. I say I am looking forward to a dance with Wendy, as Philip mimics the sound of a square-dance compere and leads Wendy round a do-si-do. Just then, Will butts in and asks me if I'll be back here in the Eagle on Saturday night, playing darts. I tell him, 'No, I'll be at the barn dance with him, surely, and Wendy.' 'Right! That's all I wanted to know. Thanks!' he cries, slams down his whisky on the bar, and storms furiously away. When I realize he's serious, I'm stunned. 'What did I say?' I complain. 'What's the matter, Will?' Philip joins in, but Will just warns him to stay out of this because 'he wasn't talking to him and it's none of his business.' But Philip won't keep out: 'Oh Fuck Off, Will', he says next, 'And stuff your darts! Don't expect me to play for the Eagle.' Will cannot believe what he's hearing (it takes me aback too), and he shouts, 'Are you telling me, here, to Fuck Off?!' Philip repeats that he is and storms out the back door. Will is now in two minds about whether to get back to me or chase after Philip, but finally decides on the latter and exits too, shouting and pushing away the restraining hands of his wife and others who have gathered, like Dave and Richard. I am speechless. Others in the pub are pretending not to be involved in the scene, and Sue, washing up glasses behind the bar – it's nearly 1 a.m. by now – suggests I slip out quietly by the front door and avoid the rumpus. Steven unlocks the door for me and agrees, 'Just avoid the noisy scene, Nigel, and don't worry.'

Notwithstanding, having reconstructed all the incidents which could link me and Wendy in Will's eyes and to which my naivety and ethnographic eagerness had blinded me, by the following morning I was all set to be drubbed out of the village. The outcome, however, was quite opposite. When I next entered the pub, people had never been as friendly: smirks, nods and nudges-in-the-ribs all round. Linda gave me copies of some of her photos. Lance inquired after my stiffness from doing the press-ups. Des suggested we set up a regular Eagle Male-Voice Choir, and gave me all the details about the end of the fight and then repeated them before a larger, mostly female audience: how he and Steven had finally separated Philip and Will, but Philip wouldn't stop ragging him, with 'Balls to you, mate!', which then set Will off chasing him again. And finally Molly toasted me as her successful dominoes partner against the old champions Arthur and Jane, and reminded me what a good night it had been – apart from the end:

> But I just keep right away from that sort of behaviour, Nigel, avoid it all together. Terribly bad behaviour that was, and only Will would indulge in it. But don't worry, local people know that Will is like that and none of it's gonna come back on you. Local people expect it from Will, even if from no one else. So don't worry. Everyone knows it was nothing and I was telling someone else how idiotic Will had been because you'd been playing dominoes all evening with me, hadn't you, while Wendy had been playing darts. Wendy's going to the dance with Jenny and not with Will, and so all the fuss. But that's okay for two girls to go together. Still, it might be a good thing on your part to apologize.

It was confusing. Here was everyone seemingly friendlier than ever, and I was even encouraged to stay and dance when the jukebox was switched on at the end of the evening, and people swopped partners for some dancing, cuddling and kissing. And yet, to some extent Molly was confirming my worst fears about Will's suspicions and suggesting I apologize!

Nevertheless, the events marked a turning-point in my relations in Wanet and henceforward I was to be welcomed into local interaction in a way I never had been previously. The singing, the press-ups, even the accusation of infidelity and near-fight had been a local success. Indeed, it fuelled further jokey gossip: if I wasn't having an affair with Wendy, then maybe Philip, my darts partner, was! The confusions of the night were translated into, even ramified by, intricacies of gossip: gossip extended the night's physicality.

Stepping away from the scene and its aftermath, I would say that in gossip a community can be seen to paint a self-portrait: the gossip of a community is an inherent part of its identity, a confirmation indeed of its very existence, in which all members portray and simultaneously are portrayed. What most characterizes this portrait is its continuousness, its democratic completeness and, above all, its range. Here is a conflation of situational and historical events from far and near; here is a conflation of the proper and improper, ideal and condemnable. All is included so as to testify to the wholeness, the completeness and the togetherness of local life. We have heard Mary and Cyril describe life in Wanet in this way, the complex and diverse physical whole which a natural local life represents, and I suggest that there is a physical wholeness which characterizes both the above scene and its recounting in local gossip. Gossipers declare their presence at or, at worst, knowledge of events which attest both to the actuality of present physical states of affairs and to their potential to be or become physically other. Steven walked on his hands: Linda has it on film; Philip ragged Will: Des gives repeated accounts of how he restrained them; Will is irate, because his wife goes to a dance without him: maybe she has been courted by Nigel or Philip, maybe she will flirt with someone else we know.

Here is reciprocation of information both on actual events and relations and on their possible futures. And that is not all. For these gossipers not only share information on each other, they also share their bodies: gossiping together is a physical activity – a secondary elaboration on a previous physical engagement; at least, a vicarious engagement if the former event was missed. And gossip extends and ramifies past physicalities into the future; events are kept embodied, their consequences multiplied and an appreciation of their intricacies fostered. Furthermore, it is here that exclusions are made. Outsiders may spy on the present and record the past. Outsiders may know of events and overhear gossip. They may even guess at the future. But outsiders do not partake of the doing. And it is this logic, I want to suggest, which accounts for an exclusion from Wanet not so much of offcomers per se as of the Anglican vicar and his offcomer Church: vicar and Church are permanently excluded from belonging to a local community which is bounded by reciprocal engagement in, and gossip of, a varied, complex and physical local life. Managing a farm, bringing up a family, having sex, inside marriage and out – these may be the most obvious avenues of such engagement, but doing crabs and press-ups, playing darts and dominoes, drinking and dancing, sharing gossip – these entail reciprocal physicality too. To all of this, the Anglican church and its officiant may bear witness but they do not take part. Revd John Parkington knows of Mary and Cyril, Dave and Des, Molly and Wendy: he keeps birth, marriage and death registers on them in the church vestry; he fixes their past – or, rather, the formally recognizable remnants that the actual events leave behind; he formally thanks their local councils and committees for their annual efforts; he speaks for their continuity; he sermonizes them in church on their formal, moral futures and guesses at their immoral potentialities. But he never *does* with them. With him there is never any physical exchange, vicarious or other. Nor will there ever be: he is always 'Mr Parkington', physically apart in his big secluded house with his family; he is always out of place on those occasions when ongoing local relations are being physically shaped.

A Diversity of Reciprocal Physicalities

I have spoken broadly of the reciprocal physicality of local community belonging – doing, watching and gossiping together in Wanet – and somewhat blithely of the logic of the vicar's exclusion. Let me be a bit more precise by drawing the different aspects of this physicality together, for the picture which emerges is of relations of reciprocal physicality (of Gouldnerian symmetry) of a number of kinds, giving rise to a number of wholes of interrelatedness, which are then themselves symmetrically interrelated.

Thus, there are the reciprocal physicalities of *nature*, amounting to a whole world of interrelated tracks and a circle of life and death without beginning or end. One can see this wholeness represented in a living pond, and one can see it represented in a working farm – farmers and animals together on the hills through all seasons and weathers. Then again, there are the reciprocal physicalities of a world of *business*, each business financially dependent on help and cooperation from the others, each physically interlinked in a valley of contiguous houses and land. Moreover, all are firmly anchored to the day-to-day practicalities and tensions of labouring and budgeting for survival; each business knows the circumstances of the others and will stand in as substitute labour if necessary. And again, there are the reciprocal physicalities of the world of the *pub*, people drinking, singing, dancing together, playing darts and dominoes and comparing physical feats. Each of these recreational activities is coordinated in terms of the presence of individual participants and framed by the pub's bounded physical space.

Moreover, the complexity of reciprocal relations that characterizes each of these worlds does not eventuate in any fixity or stasis. Thus, animals – with individual characters – go through an array of physical changes together within one herd, while human beings within one family experience together the whole range of different emotions. For both, there is no radical break between present togetherness and future, simply a beautiful continuousness. Meanwhile, businesses of different natures undergo an array of fortunes but always pay one another their dues, at some time and in some form. All have a sense of the range of the valley whole of which they are part. Meanwhile, individual inhabitants, with an array of interests and skills, move around within a range of different pub activities, but all are coordinated to a sharedness of pub time and place.

In sum, here are a number of worlds of interrelatedness, each a complex, symmetrical whole and each characterized by a certain physical sharing which is ongoing. And finally, these various worlds are themselves complexly and symmetrically interrelated; so that not only are the characteristics of natural life mirrored by those in the family, in business, in gossip, in the pub, as we have seen, but a knowledge, an understanding, a sharing of one translates into that of the others. The farms and families one is busy with are at the same time the businesses one works with and also the pub regulars one relaxes with. Dale life, as community, manifests itself in a particular oneness of people, animals, activities, relationships and space; and as Mary can fatefully conclude: 'They say we don't know all we'll have to answer for in the end. And we all have more than we ever think!' The Wanet circle always completes itself.

From this community, the separateness of Church and vicar is striking. Indeed, Church and vicar can appear the very embodiments of separateness – it constituting their very nature. For as life in Wanet is represented by interrelated spheres of physical engagement, so church and vicar may be represented by an isolation, a separating-out: the ethereal as distinct from the workaday, the innocent separated from the pragmatic, purity isolated from physicality. The ethos of Church and the vicar is inexorable compartmentalization: Sunday set apart from working days, Church buildings from secular ones, what is preached from what is done, religious and supposedly moral people from others, the dead from the living, the past from the future. And this treating the world as if composed of singularities, in separate compartments, inevitably leads in local discourse to sterility, ugliness and social decay. Thus it is that the vicar, 'weak as water', can only stand on the sidelines as life in Wanet is lived. His capacity, and that of offcomers like him, is limited to espying, and then recording, what has transpired – and expired. 'He's always an outsider', Lance concludes.

With the arrival of more offcomer (stranger) residents in Wanet the situation has become slightly more complicated. For now, for the first time, there is a need to erect boundaries to members' local networks of activities and gossip within the dale itself. Hence, the exclusion of Revd Parkington, as we heard in the criticism of Cyril and Mary, now has to be extended to include his offcomer cronies too. However, the point has not altered. Revd Parkington and his Church and its supporters may remove dead parings but they do not partake of the community's living body.

A Common Discourse

In closing, let me elaborate upon what I feel I am *not* describing for Wanet and so distinguish this thesis from others. I am not describing that oft-claimed division between peasant and clergy, the latter being part of a set of people (including nobility, intellectuals and cosmopolitans) set apart in the countryside by reason of occupation, ideas, language and dress (cf. Shanin 1972: 182). Wanet is no peasant community, as I have said, and Revd Parkington's exclusion cannot be construed as an inevitable cultural isolation from inferiors in wealth, self-assurance, modernity, even mobility.

Equally, I am not describing the effect of a transition from *Gemeinschaft* to *Gesellschaft*, from community relations to ones of contract or class. This is not to say that where once the local clergyman integrated the parish – entering into, criticizing, and passing judgement on all its houses – the growth of class-consciousness, industrialism and urbanism has lessened, as is widely claimed, the respect this confederate of the upper social echelons is deemed due (cf. Littlejohn 1963: 49–50, 68–70). Inhabitants of Wanet frequently admit to class ambitions just as they do to the need for a respectable village church; they are proud of local traditions just as they are eager for urban comforts, whereas the overt exclusion of Revd Parkington continues aside from such considerations.

Lastly, I am not describing a traditional differentiation between religiosity and the pleasures of the flesh, between the domains of the sacred and the profane; it is not that, as sometimes suggested, supporters of Church and pub form discrete social and aesthetic camps, and that a general secularizing of society has led to a privileging of the physical over the metaphysical and a heightening of the legitimacy and overtness of physical pleasuring (cf. Mewett 1982: 117–121). Many Wanet inhabitants pass between Church and pub settings with ease, and churchwardens and sidesmen are represented among the pub's most steadfast regulars, while others enter a sacred chapel whenever they immerse themselves in the physicality of nature. Whereas for others, it is their physical 'excesses' – having an 'irresponsible' number of children, suffering the 'improprieties' of major surgery or disease – which debar them from informal interaction and gossip. But the exclusion of Revd Parkington carries on regardless.

My description of the vicar and his Church is distinct from the above theses because it is not something I would claim always to characterize interaction in Wanet, nor to be true for all its inhabitants. Here is one form of expression which, I have argued, makes for the constitution and identification of a bounded community. But community as a symbolic construct is not necessarily always constituted by the same criteria, or with the same members, or boundaries, or consequences, even in the ideation of the same individuals. Indeed, there is no need for individuals to consider themselves as members of communities at all. Hence, in following the one set of ideas, one form of expression, in this chapter, I do not say that those who speak in this way *always* do so (always shunning the vicar, say, or necessarily speaking of him at all when considering community in Wanet). Mary Stirling, for example, can talk like this and still be polite when Revd Parkington comes to her farm to buy milk; she can talk like this and still be proud to go to church and hear her son read the Sunday morning lesson, smartly dressed in his Army uniform, when home on leave. Margaret Wick, meanwhile, need never talk like this, and be unable to consider Wanet as a community without ministers of religion such as its Methodist lay preachers and Anglican vicar. The discourse of reciprocal physicality which I identify is not about all possible physicality in Wanet nor about physicality per se; here is a shared way of conversing together in Wanet, a common discourse, by which a certain structure was given to local life, a situational order imposed.

The situationality of discourse does not, of course, belie its significance; here, I can say, is a particular form of life which Mary, Cyril and others inhabit for the expression of significant moments of their being. Nevertheless, there is no essential singularity or typicality to Wanet (no overarching 'social structure') which might also be identified. Rather, it is of a diversity of such interactional routines or discourses – an aggregation of 'limitless discursive perspectives', as David Parkin puts it (1987: 66) – of which social life can be said to consist.

If my reading of E.M. Forster is a feasible one, then here too is a discourse which might be described as possessing a certain provenance and longevity: a form of life as available and pertinent to Forster conjuring up characters and their social relations in Summer Street in 1908 as to me in Wanet in 1980. The discursive form partakes of the formulaic or stereotypical: with an inertia such that it lives on in different English sociocultural milieux, and an ambiguity such that any number of individuals may come together under its aegis (cf. Rapport 1995). The form is a convenient home for the expression of a great and changing diversity of meanings, moods and motivations: a means to realize the individual world-views of novelist, farmer, villager and anthropologist alike.

References

Forster, E.M. (1983) *A Room With a View*, Harmondsworth: Penguin.

Gouldner, A. (1977) 'The Norm of Reciprocity: a Preliminary Statement', in S. Schmidt, J. Scott, C. Lande and L. Guasti (eds) *Friends, Followers and Factions*, Berkeley: University of California Press.

Littlejohn, J. (1963) *The Sociology of a Cheviot Parish*, London: Routledge & Kegan Paul.

Mewett, P. (1982) 'Associational Categories and the Social Location of Relationships in a Lewis Crofting Community', in A.P. Cohen (ed.) *Belonging*, Manchester: Manchester University Press.

Ortega y Gasset, J. (1957) *Man and People*, New York: Norton.

Parkin, D. (1987) 'Comparison as a search for continuity', in L. Holy (ed.) *Comparative Anthropology*, Oxford: Blackwell.

Rapport, N.J. (1993) *Diverse World-Views in an English Village*, Edinburgh: Edinburgh University Press.

—— (1994) *The Prose and the Passion: Anthropology, Literature and the Writing of E.M. Forster*, Manchester: Manchester University Press.

—— (1995) 'Migrant Selves and Stereotypes: Personal Context in a Postmodern World', in S. Pile and N. Thrift (eds) *Mapping the Subject*, London: Routledge.

Shanin, T. (1972) *The Awkward Class*, Oxford: Oxford University Press.

Part VII
Epilogue

The 'Best of British' – with More to Come . . .
Anthony P. Cohen

Looking over the contents list of this book, I feel prematurely patriarchal. I have known nine of the authors since they were graduate students, and a tenth as an undergraduate. They have all made substantial and distinctive contributions to the anthropology of Britain, and have all seen opportunities to develop and enhance the topics characteristic of their fields by pursuing them in Britain. While I might not go quite as far as Nigel Rapport does in his claims for the potentiality of work on Britain, I have long thought that it does offer possibilities of depth of enquiry and understanding, and of prolonged and repeated immersion in the field, which is denied for practical and logistical reasons to all but a very select few anthropologists at British institutions who do fieldwork far from their academic homes. Critics may reasonably ask if anthropologists of Britain have always made good use of these possibilities and the unsurprising answer would be that some have not done so. Over the last thirty years of the twentieth century Britain had its share of indifferent anthropological work, not least because practitioners may not have realized how difficult it is to conduct research in a context where you cannot claim any licence for incompetence, and in which the people you study hold you minutely accountable for all aspects of your conduct, and later may also be your readership. I am quite certain that, with increasing experience, the standard of work being done on Britain strengthened and improved enormously in the last two of those three decades; and I know that the authors who have contributed to this book have indeed done much to enhance the field, and that their work does represent some of the 'best of British'.

The proposition that anthropological research on Western industrialized societies could contribute to the very core of the discipline has been close to my heart throughout my academic career since I undertook my Doctoral fieldwork in Newfoundland in 1968. But so far as work on Britain was concerned, the proposition had little demonstrable or accepted substance until the early 1980s. A crucial milestone was passed when Marilyn Strathern's work on Elmdon began to appear (Strathern 1981). She offered a brilliant and seminal analysis of kinship as a cultural form and medium (rather than as structure and social architecture); and in doing so, engaged directly with the ways in which anthropologists understood kinship and used it as a tool of social analysis, rather than as its object. Her influence continues to resonate in the anthropology of Britain, not least through the work her colleagues and collaborators are doing on contemporary issues of relatedness. But we should not overlook the significance of the fact that although her approach was entirely original, notwithstanding the influence of David Schneider's earlier and less successful work on American kinship, her topic came out of anthropology's top drawer. Kinship was the discipline all neophyte anthropologists had to master before they were judged worthy of the name. Perhaps it is a measure of the way the discipline has grown and changed that a number of the authors in this volume have developed work on topics that anthropologists working in non-Western societies had simply not attempted, either because it was too difficult to do in another and esoteric language, or because it was simply not regarded as appropriate to or accessible by anthropological study. Rapport's own work may be the paradigmatic case. He has gone further than any other anthropologist in juxtaposing the individual to society in order to examine the nature of their relationship and our assumptions about it. It is still too soon to be certain where his work will lead – in this volume he holds out the challenging and counter-intuitive prospect of a real rapprochement between anthropology and psychology – but it seems highly likely that his resolute insistence that the individual and individual creativity must stand at the centre of cultural interpretation and analysis will also influence the agenda of anthropology in a most significant way.

However, this is to address only one question, albeit the one which the editor foregrounds: what have anthropologists of Britain done for anthropology? There is another question which should be posed, and arguably it is more important: what have anthropologists of Britain done for Britain? The answer does not have to be found just in the formulation and application of practical policy – although there is plenty of evidence that it is increasingly useful in this regard. But we also need to be concerned with the ways (if any) in which anthropological research and writing on Britain has enhanced our understanding of British societies and cultures. What, for example, have been its distinctive and essential themes? Has it generated a cumulative body of knowledge and/or a characteristic set of concerns? What value has it added to the work of other humane sciences on Britain (and, thereby, on comparator societies)?

Before the anthropology of Britain achieved the athleticism apparent in this book, it went through two periods of limbering-up exercises, during both of which it focused on rural, often remote societies. The first phase, prefaced by the classic work of Arensberg and Kimball, occurred in the late 1950s and 1960s (for example Frankenberg 1957; Messenger 1969; Littlejohn 1963; Emmett 1964) and coincided with the much-maligned and excessively criticized sociological genre of the 'community study'; the second gathered pace during the 1970s (Harris 1972; Leyton 1975; Fox 1978), and lasted throughout the 1980s (Strathern 1981; Byron 1986; Cohen 1982, 1986, 1987; Okely 1983) and developed what became and have remained some of the distinctive themes of turn-of-the-century British ethnography: the concerns with identity and boundary symbolism. These two phases had in common their predominantly, if not exclusively, rural focus. It was mostly classic single-site fieldwork, picking up locally-generated ethnographic issues which were then theorized anthropologically. It is too crude to characterize this work as the recreation of bush anthropology, but its practitioners certainly had a very marked consciousness of the comparative ethnographic record and of the anthropological literature as its academic context. Speaking purely for myself, I was very conscious, perhaps over-conscious, of the need to establish the legitimacy of what I was doing as 'proper' anthropology.

Overlapping with the second phase, but gathering momentum and expanding dramatically during the 1990s, came the real maturation of anthropological studies of Britain. In this coming-of-age, practitioners took their craft to very different kinds of setting – urban milieux such as old-age homes, work places and schools; to occupational groups; to distinctive cultures of the life cycle; to ethnic and other minority groups – to study topics which grew out of post-structuralist social science. This really is the point at which anthropologists of Britain began to pursue problems characteristic of, if not exclusive to, postmodern globalizing Western society. Work on kinship was extended to problematize the nature of relatedness in the context of new reproductive technologies and of adoption. Studies of ethnicity began to focus on variable and negotiable ethnic identity, and on dispersed identity groups; Rapport developed first a literary ethnography focusing on the narrative in everyday conversation, and then explored ways of harnessing literature both as an ethno-graphic resource and as a model of anthropological thought and representation. We gained studies – of the kind represented in this volume – of national variations on global art forms; of the social and cultural expression of deindustrialization; and of the means through which, and the reasons why, people reconstruct or recapture the past which they have so suddenly and rapidly shed, as they would a once-encumbering but now fondly remembered cocoon.

The anthropology of Britain came of age when it ceased to be defensive, or was sufficiently self-confident not to feel the need for self-justification. We began to catch up rather belatedly with our colleagues in Europe, especially those in France and Norway who had long since charted the course – over the second half of the twentieth century, the *Centre d'ethnologie française* produced a remarkable body of sophisticated work on France – and more or less contemporaneously with our peers in North America. And anthropology itself changed coincidentally and even, perhaps, partly as a consequence. The subject matter of contemporary research in social and cultural anthropology now has an extraordinary range. Long, long gone is the stultifying dominance of the conventional monographic topics of religion, politics, economics and kinship, even though they may still provide the elementary grammar of the discipline. Now we study the internet and other institutions and processes of globalization; we study national and supra-national politics; finance houses as well as long houses; industry, as well as ritual; the media, the scientific laboratory, the aid industry and AIDS. It has become apparent, and is no longer seriously challenged from within the subject, that anthropology is capable of application to the study of any aspect of social and cultural process. But what is its value? What do we add to what can be known by other means? Once again, how does the anthropology of Britain enhance our understanding of Britain.

This book is a sampler, not a survey. It gives a taste of the range of topics to which anthropology is now applied in the study of Britain, although the required brevity of the chapters does not always allow the distinctive competence of the anthropological approach to be made fully explicit. We tend to make rather grand claims for the rigour of our method, to distinguish ourselves from sociologists. We make much of our reference to culture as the organizing device and elementary matter of society which thereby links its various aspects, to distinguish ourselves from the other humanities and social science disciplines which confine themselves to more specialized areas of social organization. Our subject no longer needs to be as defensive or as precious as it was twenty or thirty years ago: its territory is secure. We can view it a little more modestly than we did previously: as being different, rather than as necessarily superior. Much though its subject matter and its research sites may have changed, anthropology's central concern has continued to be with 'otherness': not to fetishize it, nor even to distance it from the proximate and the familiar, nor to use it to reify cultures. Otherness is not exclusively a problem which inheres in the boundaries between cultures and social groups: it is also a problem of mind. This statement may need more unpacking than there is really space for here, but to state the issue baldly: our experience of the frequency of misunderstanding and miscommunication among people who believe they know each other well should alert us to the extreme difficulty of interpreting correctly other people's meanings and intentions. This experience does not invalidate the apparently preposterous claim that it is possible to achieve an understanding of another culture; but it should alert us to what it is that is that we claim to understand. If our personal experience is anything of a guide, we should regard cultures as supposedly shared bodies of ideas, values, symbols and communicative systems within which people commonly misunderstand each other. In Britain, as in other predominantly urban and economically advanced societies, the ostensible similarities among people and social forms may mask, but does not diminish, the reality of difference and of 'otherness' among them. The distinctive competence of anthropology is to disclose and penetrate that otherness, and to identify the problems of method and complexities of interpretation in doing so. It does not matter whether the otherness discriminates individuals or communities, the understanding of it is always problematic. Its disclosure, fine-grained description and interpretation definitely enriches our understanding of the larger society.

By putting otherness at the centre of our concern, we can qualify the tendency in the other social sciences to generalization. It is obviously not the case that we have a gratuitous interest in particularity, but no one should have any interest at all in the generalization which is insubstantial or excessively simple in the context of individuals' experience. Highly sophisticated quantitative techniques demonstrably produce richly insightful accounts and analyses of social issues. The distinctive contribution which anthropologists can make to these kinds of data is to qualify them in terms of the social experience of individuals and groups, persons who compose fields of a size amenable to ethnographic study. It is perhaps worth emphasizing that people live most of their lives in circumstances of particularity – family, friendship, work and collegial relationships – which themselves qualify those of generality, such as class, gender, ethnicity, nationality and so forth. The peculiar competence of anthropology is to substantiate, inform and signal reservations about larger-scale statements; and that is and should continue to be its role among the humane sciences.

Why, then, does it not have a higher profile in the formulation and discussion of social and public policy in Britain? The question is cultural, as well as academic, and applies to other social sciences as well. One element of the answer to this complex question must be that as practitioners and writers, we have not worked with sufficient determination or skill to make our work accessible. Reconciling accessibility with the need to avoid the distortions of simplification is difficult, but possible. Other than in fairly specialized areas, such as development and other explicitly policy-related studies, we may not have made adequate efforts in this regard, principally because we have been more interested in talking to each other than to interlocutors and audiences beyond our own colleagues. Even now, having gone through nearly twenty years of disciplinary introspection about the role of the anthropologist as fieldworker and author, many anthropologists still seem deliberately to succumb to the worst excesses of professional language. Polysyllabism rules. Anthropologists, like angels, dance on the heads of pins, notwithstanding the fact that the dance may have become postmodern, post-structural, post-colonial, post-feminist, post-everything, and it may risk becoming posthumous if it does not attend adequately to the failings of its own expression.

This does not require that we must weigh our work on the specious scales of 'relevance'. It does mean, I think, that we have to try more deliberately to engage with the other humane sciences in addressing and enlightening problems of mutual interest. The kinds of issue reported in this book are precisely the ground on which a more collaborative social science can meet. Secondly, we have to think about our work with the clarity needed to enable us to write about it clearly. Interpretative social science is pointless if it is impenetrably complex. It would be a contradiction in terms to suggest that in great creative art, the difficulty of technique should dominate the aesthetic. Yet so much academic writing seems to be devoted to persuading the reader how terribly difficult and clever it all is.

Not all of the fault lies with the anthropologist. I mentioned earlier that we had lagged far behind our French and Norwegian colleagues in studying our own societies, and this may itself indicate national differences of political culture and of the politics of culture. Until very recently, the UK was an unusually centralized state. Not only were the institutions of political and economic power excessively concentrated in London, but an unusually developed and dominant national press was also located there; broadcasting policy and practice was (and still is) dictated from there; London and the so-called 'home counties' provided the norms of speech and attitude; everywhere else was 'the provinces'. More recently, the 'provinces' became the 'regions'. London spoke 'English'; people everywhere else spoke in accents. It is difficult to think of a comparable country in the West in which the core has been so concentrated, and the periphery so extensive; and in which the mentalities of centre and periphery have been so replicated and ramified throughout the society. The cultural diversity of British society went unremarked other than as gross caricature, because powerful London was simply unaware of it. They knew the natives were a bit odd, a bit different and, like natives elsewhere, could be explained as a bit backward. I generalize and exaggerate, of course, but not excessively. Culture apart from high literature, ceremonial and the dominant icons of Britishness just was not valued. Where for the French *patrimoine* was people, for the British it ('heritage') was buildings and landscape. It was only recently that 'culture' was given a seat in the UK government's cabinet; it was really only during the 1960s, with large-scale commonwealth immigration and with the popular cultural revolution in music, fashion and speech, that the cultural hegemony of London and the south-east was broken, insofar as it has been broken. Even now 'culture' (in the anthropological sense) is understated and underappreciated, while the weekend press is full to tedious overflowing with 'lifestyle'. If culture has any standing in the rest of the UK, it is as an instrument of resistance against the dominance of the English; and, in England, against the dominance of the south-east. So when anthropologists harp on about 'culture', they are unlikely to be understood by those who occupy the centres of power in Britain. 'Culture' isn't logical; it doesn't respond to political imperatives; it isn't expressed in the bottom line. There is a hostility to culture among the powerful if it is different from their own. Like information, to which they are also pretty hostile, it complicates their biases.

But it would be idle and pointless to blame them for this apparent failing. People who hold power, in governments or in organizations, are bound to simplify the issues and variables, or else they would be quite unable to take decisions. Complexity may be intellectually satisfying, but it does not assist decision-making. Anthropologists cannot do much to alter this, other than continuously to strive to demonstrate the importance of their work by showing how it can enhance understanding and qualify knowledge, and to ensure that their own failures of expression and presentation do not impede this effort.

There is enormous pressure on the academic social sciences in Britain to collaborate with each other, both for reasons of economy and because the nature of contemporary society requires multidisciplinary approaches. Most 'real world' social sciences (which obviously excludes economics) have responded to this in some way. Recent experience suggests that such collaboration is possible, without risking the hybridization of disciplines or the dilution of their integrity. This seems to be where the immediate future lies. The contributors to this book are flagging the way ahead.

References

Byron, R.F. (1986) *Sea Change: a Shetland Society, 1970–79*, St John's: ISER.

Cohen, A.P. (ed.) (1982) *Belonging: Identity and Social Organisation in British Rural Cultures*, Manchester: Manchester University Press.

—— (ed.) (1986) *Symbolising Boundaries: Identity and Diversity in British Cultures*, Manchester: Manchester University Press.

—— (1987) *Whalsay: Symbol, Segment and Boundary in a Shetland Island Community*, Manchester: Manchester University Press.

Emmett, I. (1964) *A North Wales Village*, London: Routledge & Kegan Paul.

Fox, R. (1978) *The Tory Islanders: a People of the Celtic Fringe*, Cambridge: Cambridge University Press.

Frankenberg, R. (1957) *Village on the Border*, London: Cohen & West.

Harris, R. (1972) *Prejudice and Tolerance in Ulster: A Study of Neighbours and Strangers in a Border Community*, Manchester: Manchester University Press.

Leyton, E. (1975) *The One Blood: Kinship and Class in an Irish Village*, St John's: ISER.

Littlejohn, J. (1963) *Westrigg: The Sociology of a Cheviot Parish*, London: Routledge & Kegan Paul.

Messenger, J.C. (1969) *Inis Beag: Isle of Ireland*, New York: Holt, Rinehart.

Okely, J. (1983) *The Traveller-Gypsies*, Cambridge: Cambridge University Press.

Strathern, M. (1981) *Kinship at the Core: an Anthropology of Elmdon, a Village in North-west Essex, in the 1960s*, Cambridge: Cambridge University Press.

Index

Abu-Lughod, L. 239, 271
Adam, B. 100
aesthetics, 15–16, 28–9, 68–9, 71, 74, 79–80,
    194, 207, 254, 271, 317, 327
  defined, 67–8
age, 141, 144, 147, 149, 156–60, 169–70, 218,
    220–1, 229, 243, 246–9, 288
  childbirth, 163, 170–1, 175n11, 217, 314
  children and childhood, 15–16, 43–4, 117,
    127–9, 132, 136–7, 141, 143–60, 168–71,
    214, 216–18, 232, 242–3, 270, 287, 307,
    317
  the elderly, 107–118, 209–13, 216–20, 243,
    308, 325
agency, 11, 75, 103, 108, 131–2, 141, 143,
    146–8, 217, 266, 291–2
  see also determinism
  see also will
Ahmed, A. 226
Alberti, K. 226–7
alcohol and drink, 110, 112, 145, 312, 314–15
Alderson, P. 147
Amit, V. 15, 63n2, 259, 266, 270, 274–5
Anderson, B. 136
Andreasen, N. 128–9
Annas, G. 225
anthropology
  as science, 8–9, 13–15, 17
  'at home', 4, 6–8, 17, 18n2, 18n3, 18n5, 69,
    149, 163, 182–3, 211, 215, 220–1, 223,
    282
  existential, 10, 13–14
  literary turn, 6, 14, 164, 325
  post-cultural, 9–10, 13, 15
Anwar, M. 6
Appadurai, A. 92, 276n1
Archard, D. 147
Ardener, S. 18n1
Arensberg, C. 4, 324
Armstrong, D. 145
Armstrong, G. 216, 218
Armstrong, R. 67
art, 28–9, 67, 70, 79, 111, 137, 164, 188, 240,
    325, 327

artefact, 77, 88–9, 95–6, 99–102, 107, 135, 137
  defined, 136
  see also culture (material)
  see also technique
Asad, T. 135
Ashley, K. 7
Auge, M. 10, 14, 18n2, 194
authenticity, 187, 193–5, 271, 273

Baily, J. 80n3
Bakhtin, M. 260, 281, 283, 286, 288–95
Banes, S. 75
Banks, M. 80n2, 264
Banton, M. 4, 6
Barnard, R. 164
Barr, J. 165
barter, 93
Barth, F. 15, 265, 268
Batchelder, W. 244
Bateson, G. 11, 13, 289
Baudrillard, J. 193–4
Baumann, G. 18n1, 253
Becker, H. 302
belief, 37–8, 40, 79, 109, 121, 123, 167,
    175n12, 226, 230, 285–6
Bell, M. 292
Bellah, R. 38
belonging, 15–17, 28, 37, 60–1, 78, 87,
    97–100, 117, 148, 188, 221, 259–60,
    282, 288, 304, 310, 314–15
Berger, J. 3, 13
Berger, P. 38
Bernard-Donals, M. 293
Bernstein, B. 16
Bilig, M. 38, 44
Birke, L. 165
Birnbaum, N. 32, 44
Black, D. 128–9
Blacking, J. 75
Blaikie, A. 104n3
Blatchford, P. 151
Bloch, M. 4, 7, 223
Blumler, J. 35, 38
Bocock, R. 38

body, 29, 68–9, 74–5, 79, 81n7, 110, 116, 122,
    127–37, 186–7, 212, 214, 217–18, 221,
    261, 294, 299, 314, 316
    and mind, 10–13, 16, 19n8, 69, 75, 121,
    124–5, 136, 143, 166, 192–5, 205, 308,
    326
    metabolic energy, 3, 11–13
    physicality, 299, 304–318
    see also health
    see also performance
Borgatti, S. 244
Botros, S. 231
Bourdieu, P. 81n7, 145, 148, 185, 291–2, 294
Bowie, F. 241, 253
Bowman, M. 35
Brah, A. 265–6, 271
Braithwaite, W. 281, 287
Brayshaw, A. 281
Britan, G. 224
British Empire, 37, 51, 55, 56, 58, 67, 72,
    81n6, 328
Brow, J. 239
Brown, C. 15, 206
Bruce, S. 282
Bruner, J. 292–3
Buckley, A. 31
Bulmer, M. 108
bureaucracy, 206, 223–4, 235–6
Byron, R. 4, 324

Cannadine, D. 52, 64n14
capitalism, 102, 174n4
Carr, E. 57
Carrier, J. 89
Carrithers, M. 164
categorization, 16–17, 39, 143–4, 147–50,
    154–5, 159–60, 164, 166, 187, 193, 206,
    217–21, 228, 232, 236, 242, 244, 251–4,
    263,265, 275
    see also essentialism
    see also labelling
Caulkins, D. 15, 206–7, 241, 244, 250, 252
centre–periphery relations, 328
ceremony and ceremonial, 27–8, 31, 35, 38, 49,
    51–8, 62, 64n14, 328
Chambers, R. 175n7
Chandler, J. 35
charity, 111
Charsley, S. 18n1

children and childhood, *see* age
Christensen, P. 150–1, 153, 160n2, 160n4
citizenship, 91, 142, 147–8, 166
city, *see* urbanism
Claeson, B. 173
Clark, D. 282
Clark, L. 38
Clark, S. 107–8
Clarke, M. 81n11
class 10, 17, 18n5, 70, 107, 116, 144, 207, 218,
    241, 265, 317, 327
    in Britain, 34, 68, 81n4, 88, 104, 107, 121,
    149–50, 157, 240, 246–8, 250, 254, 288,
    304–5
Clifford, J. 104n3, 265, 271, 275, 276n1
Cohen, Abner, 18n1, 62, 267–8
Cohen, Anthony, 4–6, 18n6, 49, 61, 78, 97,
    104n3, 108, 215, 221, 276n3, 283, 287, 324
Cohen, R. 224
Cohn, B. 64n14
Cole, M. 136
Coleman, S. 35, 36
Collins, P. 15, 260, 283–4, 293
colonialism, 28, 51, 55–8, 64n14
    see also post-colonialism
Comaroff, Jean, 61
Comaroff, John, 61
commodity, 87, 89–90, 92–4, 96, 100, 102–3,
    301
    see also barter
common sense 8, 142
communalism and communitarianism, 87,
    112–13, 260
communication, *see* language
community 8, 60–2, 64n13, 70, 78, 99, 108,
    112, 144, 155, 160n1, 172, 189, 207,
    215–21, 225, 240–6, 249–50, 253–4,
    259–61, 264–75, 276n3, 287, 299–301,
    304, 311, 314–18, 324, 326
comparison 9, 14, 103, 160, 291
computing, 122, 141–2, 152, 205, 207, 216,
    301
    see also technology
connotation and denotation 7, 101
consciousness, 7–8, 10–11, 14, 74, 88, 127,
    130, 136, 183, 185, 215, 221, 294–5
    altered states 122, 124, 127, 131–2, 135
consumption, 87, 94, 96–7, 99, 100, 148, 173
    see also shopping

context 10, 13–14, 141, 143, 148, 151, 158, 167–8, 172, 182, 190–1, 205, 215–16, 220, 223, 230, 236, 259–60, 282, 286, 288–9, 300, 323, 325
see also situation
conversation, 38, 74, 107, 115, 117, 122, 155, 159, 168–9, 172–3, 215, 286–95, 318, 325
cosmopolitanism, 70, 115, 165, 174n7, 260, 263–4, 276, 317
creativity, 9, 12, 111, 137, 165–6, 173, 324, 327
see also imagination
creolization, 263
crime, 206, 220, 232–5
Crisp, C. 81n11
Crocker, C. 126
Crompton, R. 108
Csikszentmihalyi, M. 69
culture 7, 10, 12, 14, 18n6, 59, 62, 70, 79, 80n2, 91, 97, 99, 103, 116, 132–7, 141–3, 149, 159–60, 164–7, 174n1, 174n7, 181–2, 186, 191–4, 198, 206–7, 217, 220, 224, 239, 244–54, 255n1, 263–5, 275, 323–8
British, 32, 72, 79
capital, 27, 70, 77, 87, 173
compression, 59, 103, *see also* creolization
Manx, 59–61
material, 97, 102–3, 143, 192
popular, 124
subculture, 16, 81n4, 121, 244–7
Welsh, 239–42
youth, 81n4
see also value
Cunnison, S. 4, 5, 6

dance, 28–9, 49, 51, 54, 57, 62, 67–81, 242, 246, 268, 270, 313–15
ballet, 28–9, 67–81
see also poetry
Dandelion, P. 285–6
D'Andrade, R. 164, 271
Davie, G. 282
Dawson, A. 15, 70, 88, 108, 112–14, 116–18, 119n2
death, 110, 113–14, 118, 128, 170–2, 211–21, 228, 242–3, 285, 310, 314–16
democracy, 27–8, 31, 33, 45, 142
Denby, E. 72
Dennis, N. 3, 108

Dentith, S. 293
De Peuter, J. 294
determinism 7–10, 13–14, 291, 294
de Valois, N. 73
Devereux, G. 7, 9, 61
devolution, 37, 45
dialogics, 260, 283, 285, 292–5
diaspora, 259–60, 263–76
discourse 7, 10, 15, 17, 27–9, 37, 43, 60, 79, 94, 97, 112–13, 141, 146–7, 230, 235, 241, 259–61, 281, 286, 289–94, 303, 309, 316, 318
dominant or hegemonic, 39, 134, 207, 233, 239, 253, 271
official or canonic, 45, 141, 144, 163, 206, 286–95
Donnan, H. 3, 224
Douglas, J. 10
Douglas M. 31
Draper, J. 217–18
dress and clothing, 67–8, 74–9, 81n12, 127, 186–7, 294, 310, 328
Dunk, T. 108
Durant, J. 175n12
Durkheim, E. 38, 267

Eade, J. 37, 38
economy, 90, 143, 164, 172–3, 174n6, 191, 215, 218, 251, 267, 288, 300–2, 315–16, 325–9
Ashington, 108–9
global, 58–60, 63n2
Manx, 50, 58–60, 63n2, 64n12
see also entrepreneurism
see also production
Edelman, G. 11
education, 70, 166, 173, 242, 247–9, 288
Edwards, J. 6, 15, 104n1, 141, 176n15
Eliade, M. 122
Elsner, J. 35, 36
Emerson, C. 287, 293, 295
Emmett, I. 324
emotion, 11, 37, 125, 129, 132, 137, 141, 158, 173, 207, 216, 239–43, 249–50, 254, 267, 307–10, 315
see also senses
entrepreneurism, 241, 243, 250–1, 254, 300, 302–4
essentialism, 17, 68, 141, 181, 193, 259, 265, 271, 275–6, 318

Index

ethnicity, 6, 10, 15–16, 18n5, 29, 61, 70–1, 79,
    80n3, 81n4, 88, 107, 109, 117, 143, 149,
    206–7, 239–41, 245–54, 259–60, 264–76,
    277n5, 288, 325, 327
    see also race
environment, 11–12, 14, 134, 136, 145, 149,
    174n7, 195, 209, 211, 213, 215, 292, 299
Epstein, A. 267
Erikson, E. 135
European Union, 45, 51, 224–5
Evans-Pritchard, E. 215, 289
everyday life, 87–90, 92, 96, 100–3, 112,
    141–50, 154, 156, 159–60, 164, 184, 195,
    205–6, 210–11, 220, 226, 231, 240–2, 259,
    292–3, 309, 325
exchange, 87, 89–93, 101, 104n2, 110, 205,
    216, 291–3, 306, 315
experience, 7–15, 36–41, 44, 55, 60, 67, 69,
    75, 78, 81n4, 87–8, 98, 100, 103, 117,
    121–31, 134–7, 142–5, 150–6, 159–60,
    170–1, 174n5, 176n16, 181, 185–90, 193–7,
    205, 210, 214, 217, 220–1, 235, 239–42,
    247, 253–4, 264, 271–5, 283–4, 326–7

Fabricant, C. 263–4, 276n1
family, 32, 61, 88, 116–18, 141, 144, 146,
    149–53, 156–9, 168, 215–16, 220–1, 242–3,
    247–8, 254, 272, 286, 292–3, 304, 310,
    314–17
Featherstone, M. 218–19
feminism, 75, 135, 142, 181–90, 198n1,
    199n13, 327
fetishization, 87, 89, 102–3
Fever, W. 111
fieldwork, 6–7, 15, 33, 68–9, 81n5, 91, 121–2,
    130, 135, 149, 205, 209–10, 215, 220–3,
    236, 241, 269, 282, 285, 299, 302, 310, 323,
    325
    see also method
Finnegan, R. 18n1
Firth, R. 6, 17n1
football, 4, 88, 115–17, 151, 157, 293
form and meaning 7–15, 18n5, 18n7, 27–8, 37,
    40–2, 45, 49, 51, 61–2, 80n2, 87, 91, 101–2,
    134, 145, 160, 181–4, 189, 192, 194, 205,
    214, 223, 239, 284–8, 293–5, 318, 323, 326
Forster, E.M. 71–2, 260–1, 299, 304–9, 318
Fortier, A.-M. 264
Foster, S. 81n10

Foucault, M. 74
Fox, R. 324
Frankenberg, R. 4, 5, 6, 18n2, 324
friendship, 34–5, 41, 81n4, 150, 217, 270, 286,
    292–3, 304, 313, 327
Friends, Religious Society of, *see* religion
Fulford, K. 226
Fuller, C. 226
Fuller, S. 165
function 10, 67, 288

Geertz, C. 17, 160, 164, 284–5
Gellner, E. 14
gender, 10, 18n5, 88, 107–9, 112–17, 119n2,
    132, 141–4, 149, 156, 163, 169–70, 181–98,
    207, 217, 220, 229, 241, 246–9, 254, 265–6,
    271, 288, 300, 304–7, 313, 327
general and particular, 7, 10, 14, 18n6, 149,
    154, 158, 163, 230, 289, 327–8
    see also stereotype
Giddens, A. 103, 145, 148, 150, 215
gift, 34, 35, 40, 41, 42, 43, 87, 89–90, 92–4,
    112
    see also commodity
Gilbert, C. 226
Gillman, H. 281, 284
Gilroy, P. 264–7, 271, 275
Ginsburg, F. 163
Gittens, D. 147
Glazer, N. 267–8
globalism, 16, 67, 99, 141, 144, 147, 165, 182,
    191–2, 215, 260, 266, 271, 325
    see also cosmopolitanism
    see also economy
Gluckman, M. 6, 62, 292
Godard, V. 5
Goffman, E. 4, 39, 42, 43, 44
Goldberg, L. 130
Goleman, D. 124
Goody, J. 136
Gorman, G. 281
gossip, 54, 62, 261, 301, 304, 306, 313–17
    see also conversation
Gouldner, A. 302, 315
Grace, E. 173, 176n20
Gray, J. 18n1
Green, J. 167
Green, M. 175n7
Green, S. 15, 142, 182

Greene, G. 9
Greenwood, 281
Grillo, R. 224
Grodin, M. 225
Grosfoguel, R. 264

habitus, 10, 29, 145, 148, 205, 291
Hacking, I. 132
Hall, J. 32
Hallam, E. 214
Hamilton, W. 32, 44
Hammond, P. 38
Handelman, D. 58, 62, 64n14
Handler, R. 97
Hannerz, U. 80, 263–4, 277n5
Haraway, D. 164–5, 193
Harner, M. 133
Harre, R. 16
Harries, U. 226
Harris, C. 18n1
Harris, R. 324
Harrison, T. 18n2
Harvey, D. 103, 190, 193
Haseler, S. 32, 33
Hastrup, K. 70, 211
Hayden, I. 39
health, 15, 116, 118, 149–50, 213, 215, 219,
    221, 227, 229, 232–6, 317
  disability, 145
Hegel, G. 295–6
hegemony 7, 11, 174n7, 207, 239, 248, 254, 328
  see also discourse
Hendrick, H. 146
Hendry, J. 117
Henley, P. 33, 34
heritage, 37, 50, 60, 87, 89, 102, 112, 115, 328
Hervik, P. 211
Herzfeld, M. 107, 191, 224
Hides, S. 97
hierarchy and stratification, 27, 31, 39, 45, 149,
    155, 181, 192–3, 196, 210–11, 240–2,
    249, 254, 285, 317
  see also democracy
Higham, J. 268
Hirsch, E.D. 12
Hirsch, Eric, 104n4
history, 8–15, 19n7, 27, 37, 51, 55–62, 72, 77,
    89–93, 96, 109, 118, 130, 159, 165, 183,

186, 194, 230, 264–5, 274–5, 281, 284,
    287, 292, 301, 310–11, 314
  see also tradition
Hitchens, 32, 39, 44
Hobart, M. 175n7
Hobsbawm, E. 57, 58
Hockey, J. 15, 156, 205–6, 211–13
Holquist, M. 294–5
home, 27, 36, 60, 68–70, 99, 145–6, 149–50,
    154–60, 212–13, 215–16, 263
Hook, R. 9
Hoover, 38
Hoskins, J. 90, 93–4, 96–7, 100
human nature 13, 14
Huntington, S. 239
Hutchins, E. 136
Hyatt, S. 244

identity 9–12, 15–16, 27–8, 31, 36–9, 43, 58,
    60–1, 70, 78, 88, 90, 97–103, 107–8, 112,
    116, 127–30, 136, 143–50, 159, 186–8,
    194–5, 207, 210, 225, 233–5, 239–40,
    245–6, 251–3, 259, 265–9, 275–6, 289,
    314, 325
  British, 37, 40, 45
  identity politics 17, 141, 143, 146, 148, 190,
    192
  see also authenticity
  see also self
imagination, 13, 19n7, 19n8, 28, 36, 125–7,
    131–2, 160, 190–1, 205, 215–16, 219, 266
  see also irony
individual, 7–14, 17, 38, 60–2, 78, 87–8, 97,
    104n3, 107–8, 118, 124–5, 127–8, 133–7,
    141–4, 159–60, 205–7, 217–20, 231, 233,
    235, 239–40, 248, 254, 259–61, 275,
    285–6, 289–94, 307, 317–18, 324, 326–7
  see also personalization
  see also psyche
industrialism and post-industrialism, 37, 90–1,
    96, 98, 108, 116–18, 142, 174n4, 219,
    267, 302, 317, 323, 325–6
  mining, 3, 88, 108–14, 116, 118
Inglehardt, R. 239
Ingold, T. 60, 164
institution, 7, 10, 12, 27, 32, 37, 39, 87–8, 92,
    100, 123, 135, 141, 148, 156–7, 167, 184,
    196, 206, 215, 224, 235, 266, 301, 325, 328

interaction 7, 13, 15, 18n5, 19n7, 27, 43, 62,
136, 141–2, 147, 167, 172, 184, 194,
205–6, 210–11, 214–20, 223, 235, 245,
254, 260, 265, 269, 285, 293–4, 302, 304,
306, 310–13, 317–18
see also conversation
see also dialogics
interpretation 8, 11, 13, 17, 19n7, 28, 31–2, 39,
42–5, 49, 61, 74, 88, 121, 126, 134, 141,
226, 230, 241–2, 246, 265–6, 271, 299,
324, 326
see also experience
interview, *see* methodology
Ions, E. 10
irony 8, 74, 78, 117, 308

Jackson, A. 6, 211, 220
James, Adrian, 144, 155
James, Allison, 15, 141, 144–5, 147–8, 150–1,
153, 155, 156, 160n4
James, W. 124, 131, 135
Jenkins, R. 3
Jenkins, T. 282
Jenks, C. 144, 147, 153, 160n2
Jensen, G. 132
Johnson, J. 10
Jones, R. 287
Jordan, B. 163

Kay, L. 164
Keller, E. 165, 174n2
Kennedy, I. 228
Kenney, M. 31
Kermode, D. 63n4
Keyes, C. 268
Kimball, S. 4, 324
Kingerly, W. 77
kingship, *see* monarchy and kingship
kinship, 104n3, 142, 168, 172, 176n16, 182,
323–5
Kinvig, R. 53
Kisselgoff, A. 73
knowledge 163, 165–6, 172–3, 174–5n7, 205,
224–5, 230–1, 235, 244, 248, 253–4, 293,
310, 314, 316, 324, 328
Kopytoff, I. 92
Kosslyn, S. 125
Kuznar, L. 164

labelling, 16, 17, 235
La Fontaine, J. 18n1, 134
language, 6–7, 12, 16, 74–5, 108, 112, 116–17,
134, 143, 187, 211, 223–4, 229, 231, 241,
260, 290–3, 324, 326
Armenian, 268, 270, 271, 273–4
genre, 291–2, 299, 324
language-game, 16–17, 145, 205–6, 259, 261
Manx, 49–50, 60, 64n15
talking-relationship, 285–6, 292–3, 299
Welsh, 241–2, 245–7, 250–4
see also connotation and denotation
Latour, B. 164
Lave, J. 164, 166
law, 109, 115, 144, 147, 150, 155, 160n3, 191,
206, 225–7, 231–5
Manx, 50–1, 53, 64n10
Lawrence, E. 239
Leach, E. 14, 19n8, 174n3, 226, 284
leisure, 15, 87–8, 107–118, 207, 215, 218, 269,
288, 306, 311–15
clubs, 110–112, 118, 301, 304, 312
Levi, P. 19n7
Levi-Strauss, C. 284
Levy-Bruhl, L. 166
Lewis, G. 166, 285
Lewis, S. 15, 28
Leyton, E. 4, 324
Lienhardt, G. 289
life-course, 9, 19n7, 205, 214
life-project, 148, 159, 187–8, 254, 263
life-world, 9, 13–14, 220
liminality, 284
literature, 15, 260–1, 283, 299–318, 325, 328
see also poetry
Littlejohn, J. 6, 18n1, 317, 324
Llobera, J. 5
locality, 17, 87–8, 91, 97–102, 108–12,
115–18, 134, 141–2, 147–8, 151, 154,
157–60, 169, 190, 195–6, 205, 207, 215,
220, 224, 226, 230, 242, 250–1, 259, 264,
267, 269, 288–93, 299, 302, 310, 314–18
locals and incomers, 49, 59–61, 63n2, 68,
80n4, 104n3, 109, 116–18, 175n7, 212,
242, 245, 250–1, 260–1, 263, 265, 268,
271–4, 284, 299–304, 309–10, 313–14,
316, 328
Lock, S. 224

Lofland, J. 219
Loudon, J. 6, 17n1
Lowenthal, D. 89
Loyola, I. 125
Lubar, S. 77
Luhrmann, T. 15, 88, 282
Lux, A. 227

Macdonald, D. 19n7
Macdonald, S. 15, 87, 90, 97
McFarlane, G. 3, 224
McGuire, M. 38
Mach Z. 80n3
Mackrell, J. 72
MacPherson, C. 97
magic, 27, 88, 92, 121–7, 131, 133–4, 165,
    265, 271, 275
Malinowski, B. 93, 165–6, 215
Maquet, J. 79
marriage, 32, 212, 214–15, 274, 304, 306,
    308–10, 314
Marsh, P. 16
Marx, E. 18n4
Marx, K. 96, 102
mass media, 32–3, 81n4, 107, 115, 142, 144,
    167, 191, 219–20, 232, 326, 328
Mass Observation, 3, 18n2
Matthews, C. 124
Matthews, J. 124
Mauss, M. 40, 43, 89–90, 92
meaning, *see* form and meaning
medicine, 15, 145, 163, 168, 172, 206, 217–18,
    223–35
    see also health
    see also psychiatry
Meisner, N. 71
memory, 128–32, 136, 205, 212–13, 216, 219
    memorabilia and mementoes, 34–5, 95, 102
Merck, M. 39
Messenger, J. 4, 324
methodology, 14–15, 205, 209–10, 215, 241,
    326–7
    emic and etic, 282
    ethics committees, 223–36
    ethnomethodology, 7, 14, 205
    interview, 205, 209–21, 241–5, 248, 255n1
    statistics, 241, 244–52
    see also comparison
    see also general and particular

Mewett, P. 317
Middleton, J. 289
Mielke, F. 225
migrants, *see* locals and incomers
Miller, D. 18n1, 94, 101
Milligan, E. 281
mimesis, 135, 214
Mises, L. von, 10
Mitchell, C. 267
Mitscherlich, M. 225
modernity, 87–8, 99, 142–4, 187, 192, 194,
    219, 230, 265, 267–8, 271, 276n3, 317
monarchy and kingship, 33, 37–40, 43–4,
    50–1, 95
    see also royalty and royalists
Moore, R. 282
Morgan, W. 108
Morin, V. 94, 96, 100
Morphy, H. 67, 74, 79, 80n2
Morrah, D. 38
Morris, B. 282
Morson, G. 287, 293, 295
Moynihan, D. 267–8
museum, 77, 87, 89–104
myth, 27

Nader, L. 165, 174n4, 176n19
Nairn, T. 32
Narayan, K. 18n4, 70
narrative and story, 7, 12, 73, 87–8, 91, 94–7,
    118, 125, 127, 130–1, 134, 144, 148, 150,
    154–5, 206, 220–1, 265, 271, 275, 289,
    291–3, 307, 325
nation-state and nationalism, 10, 15, 27–29,
    38–40, 44–5, 49, 58, 61, 67, 68–74,
    79–80, 81n9, 87, 91, 99, 116, 143, 227,
    254, 264–5, 274–5, 286, 288, 325–8
    Manx, 56, 57, 58, 59, 62
    Welsh, 247, 249–50
National Health Service, 223, 227–9
nature, 164, 174n6, 192–3, 309–10, 314–17
Neale, B. 156
network, 34–5, 108, 118, 142, 181–5, 188–92,
    196–8, 246, 252, 269, 271–2, 275, 316
Neville, G. 4
Newby, H. 40
Nickalls, J. 283
Nietzsche, F. 14, 305
Norris, 216, 218

occupation, 87–8, 207, 215, 218, 243, 247, 270, 301, 306, 325
Okely, J. 5, 164, 224, 324
Ormerod, J. 281
Ortega y Gasset, J. 299
Overing, J. 15

Paine, R. 59
Panossian, R. 277n6
Park, R. 267
Parker, C. 226
Parkin, D. 318
Parman, S. 4
Parsons, T. 302
Paxman, J. 80
Peace, A. 3
Penhale, 213
performance, 27–8, 49, 59–62, 69, 74, 78–9, 87, 111, 115, 131, 136, 186, 207, 212, 239–43, 250, 254, 285
personalization, 12, 14, 62, 94, 104n3, 159, 219, 221, 248, 264, 275, 289, 326
personhood, 87, 90, 97, 135, 166, 183, 189, 191–4, 198, 206, 239–41, 254
see also role
Pietz, W. 102
pilgrimage, 27, 35–8, 69, 87, 89
play, 88, 131, 137, 145, 148, 151–7
poetry, 88, 111–14, 119n3, 271, 295
policy, 143, 146, 155, 159, 160n3, 224, 232, 243, 324, 327–8
see also state
Portes, A. 264
postcolonialism, 80, 81n6, 267, 327
see also subaltern
postmodernism, 107, 181, 186, 189–94, 198, 215, 264–6, 271, 325, 327
power, 10, 13, 15, 79, 110, 112, 114, 117, 122, 125, 127, 129, 135, 141, 147, 149, 151–5, 157–9, 160n4, 173, 174n2, 174n6, 230, 236, 243, 254, 265, 271, 328
production, 87, 94, 97–8, 101, 113
see also consumption
Proesler, M. 98
Prout, A. 144, 147–8
psyche, 8–9, 13, 17, 87–8, 136–7
see also human nature
psychiatry, 223–4, 234–5
dissociation, 88, 127–37

see also trauma
Punshon, J. 281
Putnam, F. 130

Quayle, B. 5
Quinn, N. 253
Qvortrup, J. 149

Rabinow, P. 8, 164, 192–3
race, 17, 68, 70, 81n4, 117, 141, 144, 166, 185–7, 265, 269, 275
Rapp, R. 163
Rapport, N. 7, 13–15, 62, 68–70, 80, 164, 215, 221, 260–1, 285, 295, 299, 301, 318, 323–5
rationality, 15, 88, 102, 121, 142, 164–5, 234, 267–8, 271
see also common sense
reciprocity, 302–4, 314, 318
see also sociality
recreation, *see* leisure
Rees, A. 3
refugee, 109, 118–19n1, 260, 263
see also diaspora
Reily, S. 80n3
religion, 15, 38, 44, 88, 122–7, 131–7, 165, 195, 242, 246–8, 259–61, 268–9, 273, 277n5, 282–95, 299–318, 325
civil, 27, 38, 39, 45
defined, 285
Quakerism, 281–95
vernacular, 35, 37, 45, 260, 287, 289–91, 294
see also sacred
see also pilgrimage
Richards, A. 6, 223
Richards, M. 167, 175n12
Riesman, P. 239
rights, 143, 147, 157, 225, 231, 233, 235, 260
see also democracy
ritual, 27–8, 38, 44, 52, 61–2, 88, 110, 121–2, 124–5, 127, 132, 134–6, 206, 260, 284–5, 301, 326
see also ceremony and ceremonial
see also sacrifice
Robin, J. 6, 223
role, 240
Romney, A. 244
Rose, H. 165

Roseneil, S. 143
Ross, A. 174n1
Rosser, E. 16
Rowbottom, A. 15, 27, 28, 33, 34
royalty and royalists, 27–8, 31–45, 110, 220
Rushdie, S. 266

sacred, 35–6, 38, 92, 101, 165, 217, 226, 286,
    300, 304, 316–17
sacrifice, 27, 240
Sahlins, M. 302
Sallnow, M. 37, 38
Samuel, R. 102
Sartre, J.-P. 12, 295
Saumerez-Smith, C. 104
Saussure, F. de 293
Sawday, J. 218
Scheper-Hughes, N. 4, 271
Schneider, D. 324
Schopenhauer, A. 8
Schreiner, O. 9
Schuetz, A. 7
science, 15, 107, 121, 141–2, 163–76, 193,
    225, 228–30, 271, 293, 295, 326
  genetics, 167, 172–3, 174n2, 175n10,
    175n11, 175n12, 175n13, 192
  public understanding of, 166–7, 172–3,
    175n8, 175n9, 175n11, 175n12
  see also rationality
Scott, C. 174n5
self, 10, 87, 94, 110, 117, 123, 128–32, 135,
    137, 141–4, 148, 150, 159, 192, 219, 240,
    254, 260, 283, 293–4, 299
senses, 11, 69, 125, 127–8, 211, 214, 259
Sereny, G. 233
sex and sexuality, 15, 113–14, 116, 129, 134,
    141–2, 144, 181–90, 215–16, 314
  homosexuality, 181–98, 308
Seymour, J, 143
shamanism, 121, 133–5, 285
Shanin, T. 317
Sharma, U. 18n1
Shils, E. 35
shopping, 94, 151
Shore, C. 5, 224
Simmel, G. 9–10, 302
Simpson, B. 18n1, 214–16
situation 10–11, 14, 19n7, 163, 175n11, 271,
    314, 318

Slouka, M. 195
Smart, C. 156
Smith, D. 294
Snow, C.P. 174n1
social structure 10, 144, 147, 192, 223, 235,
    246, 251, 288, 291, 294, 301, 318, 323
  structuration, 145, 318
sociality, 181–5, 191, 196, 292, 295, 302, 306
socialization, 144–7, 150, 154, 157, 160, 302
  see also age
society, 10, 12, 18n6, 28, 33, 38–9, 62, 74, 89,
    100, 107–8, 136, 148, 163–4, 173, 181,
    187, 215, 219, 231, 236, 245, 268, 276n3,
    291, 307, 317, 324, 326
  British and Western, 68, 70–1, 87, 146, 150,
    156, 206, 218, 223–4, 232, 235, 305–7,
    323–5, 328–9
  Manx, 49, 60, 62
  microsociety, 16
Solly, M. 64n11
Southwold, M. 285, 291
Stacey, M. 167
Stafford, C. 149
Stainton-Rogers, R. 146
Stainton-Rogers, W. 146
Stallybrass, P. 102
state, 62, 64n14, 143, 266–8, 275, 284, 328
Stephens, S. 143
stereotype, 29, 68, 73, 94, 100, 111, 134,
    145–6, 164, 191, 309, 318
Stewart, K. 167
Stock, B. 136
Stokes, M. 80n3
Strathern, M. 6, 18n1, 91, 164, 176n15, 188,
    198, 323–4
Strauss, C. 253
Strawson, G. 14
Street, B. 136
Stringer, M. 282
Stromberg, P. 285
subaltern, 271, 276
Suryani, L. 132
symbol, 13, 15, 18n5, 58–9, 62, 79, 81n11,
    87–8, 90, 100–1, 109–10, 114, 116, 128,
    137, 149, 217, 260, 264, 275, 284–7, 290,
    299, 317, 325–6
  animal symbolism, 109–10, 116, 135,
    309–10, 315
symbolic classification, *see* categorization

taboo, 110, 114
Taylor, C. 99, 294
technique, 69, 88, 122, 124–7, 132–3, 241, 244, 327
technology, 87–8, 98, 134, 136, 174n2, 176n19, 190–8, 216–19, 250–1
    information and communication, 142, 181–4, 188–98, 218, 220, 325
    new reproductive, 6, 141–2, 167–9, 172, 175n13, 176n14, 176n15, 176n16, 176n20, 192, 228, 325
    social, 136–7
text, *see* writing
Thomas, N. 79, 80n2
Thomas, T. 282
Thompson, D. 33
Thompson, K. 38
time, 88, 92, 94–6, 100, 102–3, 124, 126, 131, 149–58, 189, 194, 211, 213–21, 231, 260, 264, 266, 270, 288, 292, 310, 314–16, 325
Todorov, T. 292, 295
Tololian, K. 267
tourism, 50, 54, 55, 63, 99, 260, 263, 301
    see also travel
tradition, 37–9, 49, 52, 54, 57, 59–60, 62, 81n6, 107, 111, 123, 144, 148, 265, 281, 289, 301, 303, 317
    see also heritage
transnationalism, 27, 29, 67–70, 72–5, 78–9, 91, 97, 264–7, 272, 274–5, 305, 325
    see also cosmopolitanism
trauma, 87–8, 122, 127–33, 136
travel, 34–5, 70, 117, 127–8, 260, 263, 272
Traweek, S. 164
Trosset, C. 4, 15, 206–7, 239–42, 246, 252
Tulley, J. 227
Turner, B. 38
Turner, V. 7, 61, 284

urbanism, 68, 70, 91, 108–9, 117, 142, 149–50, 160, 184, 196–7, 218–19, 243, 259, 267–70, 276n3, 300–1, 307, 317, 325–6
Urry, J. 89, 215

value, 15, 42, 61, 143, 206–7, 223–4, 236, 239–54, 326
Van Gennep, A. 284
Vice, S. 283
violence, 13, 19n7, 183, 234, 266, 275, 289, 304, 313

visuality, 68, 75, 80n2, 121, 124–7, 130–3, 185–8, 219, 286, 310
Vollman, J. 224

Wade, A. 156
Walby, S. 108
Wallace, A. 11, 285
Wallman, S. 18n1, 268
Walter T. 33, 35
Watling, T. 286
Watson, C.W. 117, 220
Weber, M. 100
Weiner, A. 90, 93, 95, 100–1
Weiner, E. 250
Weller, S. 244
Werbner, P. 6, 18n1, 266, 271, 276n2
Wheatcroft, G. 19n7
Wight, D. 108
will, 7–8, 13, 19n7
Williams, G. 246
Williams, W. 3
Williamson, J. 44
Wilmott, P. 3
Wilson, A. 33
Wilson, E. 31, 32, 44
Winau, R. 224
Winnicott, D. 137
Wirth, L. 267
witchcraft, 88, 121–2, 133–4
    see also shamanism
Wolcott, H. 164
Woodhead, L. 42, 43
Woolf, V. 128
work, 15, 88–9, 107–8, 114, 117, 167, 216, 218, 269, 288, 300, 303–4, 310, 316, 325, 327
    see also occupation
world-view, 9, 13, 143, 305, 318
    see also life-world
Wright, P. 102
Wright, S. 18n1, 224
writing, 15, 111, 117, 136, 141, 164, 221, 229, 231, 286–7, 290, 293–4, 327
Wulff, H. 15, 28, 68, 70, 80, 81n7, 81n9

Yon, D. 264
Young, A. 132Young, M. 3, 35

Ziegler, P. 35